Cases on Small Business Economics and Development During Economic Crises

Simon Stephens
Letterkenny Institute of Technology, Ireland

A volume in the Advances in Business Strategy and Competitive Advantage (ABSCA) Book Series

IGI Global
PUBLISHER of TIMELY KNOWLEDGE

Published in the United States of America by
IGI Global
Business Science Reference (an imprint of IGI Global)
701 E. Chocolate Avenue
Hershey PA, USA 17033
Tel: 717-533-8845
Fax: 717-533-8661
E-mail: cust@igi-global.com
Web site: http://www.igi-global.com

Library of Congress Cataloging-in-Publication Data

Names: Stephens, Simon, 1980- editor.
Title: Cases on small business economics and development during economic crises / Simon Stephens, editor.
Description: Hershey, PA : Business Science Reference, [2022] | Includes bibliographical references and index. | Summary: "This book will help readers better understand the impacts that a crisis episode has on a small business, entrepreneurs, and the SME sector by drawing on evidence (quantitative, qualitative and mixed methods) based on experiences and practices in multiple jurisdictions and offering novel insights, practical ideas. theoretical frameworks and policy recommendations"-- Provided by publisher.
Identifiers: LCCN 2021026755 (print) | LCCN 2021026756 (ebook) | ISBN 9781799876571 (hardcover) | ISBN 9781799876588 (paperback) | ISBN 9781799876595 (ebook)
Subjects: LCSH: Small business--India--Management. | Financial crises--India. | Human capital--India.
Classification: LCC HD2346.I4 C37 2022 (print) | LCC HD2346.I4 (ebook) | DDC 332.7/420954--dc23
LC record available at https://lccn.loc.gov/2021026755
LC ebook record available at https://lccn.loc.gov/2021026756

This book is published in the IGI Global book series Advances in Business Strategy and Competitive Advantage (ABSCA) (ISSN: 2327-3429; eISSN: 2327-3437)

British Cataloguing in Publication Data
A Cataloguing in Publication record for this book is available from the British Library.

For electronic access to this publication, please contact: eresources@igi-global.com.

Advances in Business Strategy and Competitive Advantage (ABSCA) Book Series

Patricia Ordóñez de Pablos
Universidad de Oviedo, Spain

ISSN:2327-3429
EISSN:2327-3437

Mission

Business entities are constantly seeking new ways through which to gain advantage over their competitors and strengthen their position within the business environment. With competition at an all-time high due to technological advancements allowing for competition on a global scale, firms continue to seek new ways through which to improve and strengthen their business processes, procedures, and profitability.

The **Advances in Business Strategy and Competitive Advantage (ABSCA) Book Series** is a timely series responding to the high demand for state-of-the-art research on how business strategies are created, implemented and re-designed to meet the demands of globalized competitive markets. With a focus on local and global challenges, business opportunities and the needs of society, the **ABSCA** encourages scientific discourse on doing business and managing information technologies for the creation of sustainable competitive advantage.

Coverage

- Outsourcing
- Balanced Scorecard
- Economies of Scale
- Differentiation Strategy
- Entrepreneurship & Innovation
- Foreign Investment Decision Process
- International Business Strategy
- Value Creation
- Tacit Knowledge
- Ethics and Business Strategy

IGI Global is currently accepting manuscripts for publication within this series. To submit a proposal for a volume in this series, please contact our Acquisition Editors at Acquisitions@igi-global.com or visit: http://www.igi-global.com/publish/.

The Advances in Business Strategy and Competitive Advantage (ABSCA) Book Series (ISSN 2327-3429) is published by IGI Global, 701 E. Chocolate Avenue, Hershey, PA 17033-1240, USA, www.igi-global.com. This series is composed of titles available for purchase individually; each title is edited to be contextually exclusive from any other title within the series. For pricing and ordering information please visit http://www.igi-global.com/book-series/advances-business-strategy-competitive-advantage/73672. Postmaster: Send all address changes to above address.

Titles in this Series

For a list of additional titles in this series, please visit: www.igi-global.com/book-series

ICT as Innovator Between Tourism and Culture
Célia M. Q. Ramos (University of Algarve, Portugal) Silvia Quinteiro (University of Algarve, Portugal) and Alexandra R. Gonçalves (University of Algarve, Portugal)
Business Science Reference • © 2022 • 330pp • H/C (ISBN: 9781799881650) • US $215.00

Impact of Disruptive Technologies on the Sharing Economy
Ford Lumban Gaol (Bina Nusantara University, Jakarta, Indonesia) Natalia Filimonova (Vladimir State University, Russia) and Chandan Acharya (College of Staten Island, City University of New York, USA)
Business Science Reference • © 2021 • 269pp • H/C (ISBN: 9781799803614) • US $245.00

Global Corporate Social Responsibility Initiatives for Reluctant Businesses
Syed Abdul Rehman Khan (School of Management and Engineering, Xuzhou University of Technology, Xuzhou, China & Department of Business Administration, ILMA University, Karachi, Pakistan & Beijing Key Laboratory of Urban Spatial Engineering, Beijing, China) Zhang Yu (Chang'an University, China) Mirela Panait (Petroleum-Gas University of Ploiesti, Romania & Institute of National Economy, Bucharest, Romania) Laeeq Razzak Janjua (Poznan University of Economics and Business, Poland) and Adeel Shah (Institute of Business Management, Pakistan)
Business Science Reference • © 2021 • 280pp • H/C (ISBN: 9781799839880) • US $195.00

Impacts and Implications for the Sports Industry in the Post-COVID-19 Era
Armand Faganel (University of Primorska, Slovenia) Igor Rižnar (University of Primorska, Slovenia) and Arne Baruca (Texas A&M University, USA)
Business Science Reference • © 2021 • 304pp • H/C (ISBN: 9781799867807) • US $215.00

Computational Thinking for Problem Solving and Managerial Mindset Training
Luisa Dall'Acqua (University of Bologna, Italy & LS TCO, Italy)
Business Science Reference • © 2021 • 293pp • H/C (ISBN: 9781799871262) • US $225.00

Bioentrepreneurship and Transferring Technology Into Product Development
Swati Agarwal (Banasthali University, India) Sonu Kumari (Banasthali University, India) and Suphiya Khan (Banasthali University, India)
Business Science Reference • © 2021 • 335pp • H/C (ISBN: 9781799874119) • US $245.00

Handbook of Research on Strategies and Interventions to Mitigate COVID-19 Impact on SMEs
Neeta Baporikar (Namibia University of Science and Technology, Namibia & University of Pune, India)
Business Science Reference • © 2021 • 628pp • H/C (ISBN: 9781799874362) • US $365.00

IGI Global
PUBLISHER of TIMELY KNOWLEDGE

701 East Chocolate Avenue, Hershey, PA 17033, USA
Tel: 717-533-8845 x100 • Fax: 717-533-8661
E-Mail: cust@igi-global.com • www.igi-global.com

Table of Contents

Detailed Table of Contents

This is a descriptive study that aims to estimate the impact of three economic crises (i.e., the 1997/98 Asian financial crisis, the 2008/09 global financial crisis, and the COVID-19 pandemic crisis) on small businesses in Indonesia and to explore their crisis mitigation measures (CMMs). It adopted an exploratory methodology with comprehensively reviewing the available literature (e.g., policy documents, research papers, and reports) on the subject being studied. The data collection technique applied was literature study. It shows that different types of crises have different transmission channels through which such crises affected small businesses. CMMs adopted by affected small businesses also vary by different types of crises and hence different business risks. To the best of author's knowledge, this is the first study that examines transmission channels through which such crises affected small businesses in Indonesia.

The COVID-19 pandemic has created devastating consequences for all businesses globally, including the small businesses in Bangladesh. The small business sector in Bangladesh is a key driver of its economic growth and has been hit particularly hard by the pandemic due to its pre-existing vulnerabilities and lower resilience to crisis. This chapter investigates the impact of COVID-19 on small-scale businesses, their subsequent response measures, and learning experiences that have created a route to resilience. A qualitative investigation on six small-scale enterprises across manufacturing and service areas was included in the study. The cases covered fashion and clothing and organic food and beverage businesses. The findings of the study suggest that the impacts of the pandemic are primarily financial, operational and supply chain, and logistical in nature. The policymakers need to take urgent measures to ensure the sustainability of this sector amid the ongoing pandemic.

Businesses and individuals have experienced multiple crises that have led to major financial and developmental impacts for entrepreneurs and small and medium sized enterprises (SMEs). Researchers believe that entrepreneurs should be innovative through means of resilience skills, risk management, and identifying new opportunities. This chapter aims to investigate entrepreneurial resilience during crisis episodes, investigating the development of resilience and how it helps a business survive a crisis episode while considering the likelihood that entrepreneurial resilience and risk management are linked, how it is linked, and if it can be improved and utilised for success. An anonymous survey was conducted to investigate how entrepreneurs have been impacted by the pandemic, their attitudes surrounding risk assessments, and how their adaptations and innovations impacted the development and survival of their business. The conclusion discusses research findings and suggestions to support the survival of entrepreneurs and SMEs during crisis episodes.

Indian economy post-COVID 19 pandemic may witness a massive reengineering of all its economic activities. Some will cherish the change, while others will perish over time. The post-pandemic scenario will have a drastic impact across industries and sectors regardless of their scale or size. The magnitude of impact on SMEs and entrepreneurship is unfathomable considering the prevailing intensity of the crisis. SMEs should come up with plausible innovation and talented human force to sustain in the market. The enterprises should develop and nourish 'talent culture' and should focus on 'talent', which remains the most neglected component in Indian SMEs until today. Hence, adopting an exploratory approach with a systematic literature review, the chapter focuses on positioning the importance of talent management and its components in the SME framework to manage the post-pandemic crisis. In the process, the chapter deliberates on the key strategies for rearing SMEs through proper management of critical talent and human resources.

Underpinning this chapter on vulnerability and resilience theoretical views, the authors examine the survival strategy of small businesses (SBs) facing triple crises. They adopted a descriptive survey research design as the most appropriate strategy while relying on the primary data collected through structured questionnaires. In the absence of a sample frame for the target population, a sample size of 400 managers of SBs was selected purposively based on objective eligibility criteria. Out of the sample, 257 managers of SBs returned their completed questionnaires. The findings support largely the resilient view and also affirmed the vulnerability view because the four entrepreneurial marketing (EM) dimensions, namely entrepreneurial orientation, market orientation, innovation orientation, and customer orientation, have mixed impacts on the financial and non-financial performance of SBs facing triple crises. The study recommends that vulnerable SBs, when faced with economic crises, should be resilient and leverage the four EM dimensions for business continuity.

Resilient entrepreneurial strategy is a concept of great importance as it captures how entrepreneurs can ensure business sustainability in the face of harsh economic conditions of a market. In the wake of the economic crisis induced by the COVID-19 pandemic, it is not surprising to observe that scholars and practitioners are shifting their attention towards entrepreneurial resilience especially in the context of SMEs. With this in mind, this chapter focuses on the resilient entrepreneurial strategies adopted by Zimbabwean SMEs during the COVID-19 pandemic. The study established five strategies, namely strategic alliance, product differentiation, cost containment, innovation, and product differentiation. It is, therefore, recommended that SMEs should harness online technology and constantly re-evaluate entrepreneurial strategies in order to augment their agility to shocks emanating from the business environment.

This chapter aims to analyze the market of fertilizers in México during the pandemic crisis. This analysis of the fertilizer market in Mexico points out that the consumption of fertilizers has undergone a change in the structure in favor of consumers with the highest concentration and diversification. The method used is the analytical-descriptive and the critical reflexive based on the quantitative data obtained from secondary sources. This situation has contributed to a drop in the consumption of fertilizers because the farmer's real income has fallen during the pandemic crisis. To take advantage of the opportunities arising from the crisis, it analyzes the functioning of an integral model of entrepreneurship in green innovation business (GIB) that is currently emerging and in the process of internationalization. This chapter analyzes a particular company that specializes in ecological biomineral organic fertilizer, where no chemical product is used to produce the composition; everything that is marketed is made up of a base of organic minerals and other organic compounds.

The world has been struck by multiple crises that crippled the socio-economy of nations in the past. The impact of these crises was so significant that they initiated numerous policy changes worldwide. The radical crises in this context refer to the Spanish flu, the Asian financial crisis, the global financial crisis, and the current COVID-19 pandemic. Due to their small capital structure with limited resources and fragile nature, SMEs were severely impacted by these crises. Many SMEs were forced to close down their business operations. Somehow, the remaining SMEs managed to persist and survive through the crises. Moving forward, SMEs can better prepare for future crises by understanding and learning from the predicaments of these past crises. Consequently, SMEs must also be adaptive to new business environments and responding promptly to crises by realigning their strategies to achieve business sustainability in the long term.

Keywords: family business; internationalization; SMEs; family SMEs; international expansion; family ownership

The COVID-19 pandemic has had a devastating and immediate effect on all economies, impacting in the lifestyles and livelihoods of people around the world. There are strong concerns about how the crisis will affect SMEs that represent over 90% of all firms worldwide. In emerging countries, SMEs already operate in challenging contexts characterized by institutional voids and scarce resource environments where entrepreneurs need to continuously develop strategies to survive. The purpose of this study is to examine the role of resources in a single case of a Brazilian SME and its strategies to survive the impact of the COVID-19 crisis. The study applies the resource-based view (RBV) to understand how the type and nature of resources influence the activities pursued by this SME and relate the crisis with their usual challenges. Findings highlight the important role of different key resources in the survival, growth, and sustainability of SMEs, along with the need of institutional conditions to support and foster entrepreneurship.

Preface

The aim of this book is to develop an understanding of the impact that the COVID-19 crisis has on entrepreneurs. Drawing on the work of academics from a diverse range of countries we are able to present an International perspective. This is an important contribution because, the literature has struggled to fully comprehend how entrepreneurial activity is impacted by crisis episodes, especially when they are global in nature (Doern et al., 2019; Ratten, 2020, Hegarty *et al.*, 2020).

Foss (2000) proposes that given the omnipresence of entrepreneurship in the global business environment, it is crucial that we understand how the COVID-19 crisis impacts the small business community. Unfortunately, as we publish this book it is clear that the business community, specifically, entrepreneurs, have during 2020-21 operated in a volatile business environment and face significant uncertainty again in 2022. Spillan and Hough (2003) warn that not only can a crisis adversely impact business owners and entrepreneurs, it can destroy the business entity and wreak havoc on suppliers, customers, partners, competitors, families and the community in which the business is based.

The World Health Organisation (WHO) declared COVID-19 a pandemic on March 11th, 2020 (Liguori and Winkler 2020). As a result, the routines of society changed and there was a significant decrease in economic activity (Ratten 2020). In response to the COVID-19 crisis, government and support agencies have focused on the short-term impacts on entrepreneurs (Brown *et al.*, 2020). Although the COVID-19 crisis emerged relatively recently there is an emergent, albeit small body of research on the impact that COVID-19 has had on entrepreneurs (Kuckertz *et al.*, 2020; Liguori and Pittz, 2020; Nummela et al., 2020; Stephens *et al.*, 2021).

Despite the best efforts of government and health agencies the COVID-19 restrictions continue. Appropriate support systems are complex to design and deliver. The situation is fluid and so designing, financing and implementing appropriate interventions is a significant challenge. The evidence presented in this book provide a snapshot of the experiences of entrepreneurs, in different countries who faced the consequences of the COVID-19 pandemic. The findings from the individual chapters provide a valuable insight for policy makers who wish to aid business recovery and help identify the supports that are required. The length of the pandemic will inevitable determine the ultimate impact on businesses and entrepreneurs. It will also determine the scale and scope of government interventions. Entrepreneurs who have been impacted by COVID-19 need supports for their business, and for themselves.

BOOK COVERAGE

Chapter 1: Development of Small Businesses During Economic Crises – Evidence From Indonesia

In this chapter the author begins by explaining that economic crises are not new and that overtime an economy and its small businesses will experience many crisis periods. Specifically, the author explains that Indonesia experienced two economic crises before, namely the Asian financial crisis that hit several countries in Southeast and East Asia in 1997–1998 and the global financial crisis in 2008–2009. The author continues by proposing that the COVID-19 crisis can be considered as a domestic supply and demand crisis due to declined consumption and production as a direct consequence of policies on social/physical distance. The author adopts a exploratory methodology, and comprehensively reviews the available literature, including policy documents, research papers, and reports. In Table 3 the author provides and excellent overview of the impacts on small business reported in the literature. In their discussion the author explains that different types of crises have different transmission channels through which the crises affect small businesses and pose different business risks. They conclude that the COVID 19 crisis can be considered as a combination of market demand and market supply (production) crises, as a result of the anti-COVID 19 impact policy.

Chapter 2: Impact, Reaction, and Learning From the COVID-19 Crisis – Evidence From Bangladesh

In this chapter the authors begin by explain that small businesses have been hit particularly hard by the crisis due to their greater vulnerability to exogenous shocks. Next, the authors provide an excellent overview of small business in Bangladesh, explaining that In Bangladesh, small businesses create 11 percent of all non-farm jobs and 26.9 percent of total employment, involved in agriculture, fishing, manufacturing, service, wholesale, retail, and trade-based sectors, thereby bridging the urban-rural income gap. The authors reflect that the small businesses, due to their dependence on global supply chains, were directly disrupted by the pandemic. The crisis has established a necessity for small businesses to redesign their operations and adapt resilience measures. The authors adopt a qualitative research approach using the multiple case study method. They present six fascinating case studies which provide valuable insights into the impact of the crisis on small business. The authors conclude that understanding the pandemic's impact is essential to develop policy measures to help small-scale firms navigate the crisis.

Chapter 3: Entrepreneurial and SME Resilience During Crisis Episodes – Evidence From Ireland

In this chapter the author begins by proposing that a small business is either fighting a crisis or preparing to fight for an upcoming crisis. They continue by explaining that entrepreneurs need to act innovatively and dynamically during a crisis episode and that this is best achieved by a rigorous approach to risk management. The author provides an engaging discussion of entrepreneurial resilience and the merits of risk management. They then provide the results from a short survey. The data provides valuable insights into the approach to risk management adopted by small business owners in Ireland.

Chapter 4: Post-Pandemic Restorative Talent Management Strategy for SMEs – Evidence From India

In this chapter the authors propose that, talent management plays a vital role in the resilient process of SMEs and entrepreneurship. The authors explain that along with understanding the need to hire, develop, and retain talented people, organizations are aware that they must manage talent as a critical resource to achieve the best possible results. The authors provide a comprehensive overview of talent management, as it relates to small business, with an emphasis on crisis episodes. They then provide a six-step framework for the successful implementation of talent management.

Chapter 5: Small Business Survival of Crisis – Evidence From Yola, North-East Nigeria

In this chapter the authors examine the survival strategy of small businesses facing triple crises. They present data from a survey with a sample size of 257 managers. Their findings support largely the resilient view, and also affirmed the vulnerability view because the four entrepreneurial marketing dimensions, namely: entrepreneurial orientation, market orientation, innovation orientation, and customer orientation have mixed impacts on the financial and non-financial performance. The conclude by recommending that when faced with economic crises small business owners should be resilient, and leverage the four EM dimensions for business continuity.

Chapter 6: Resilient Entrepreneurial Strategies Adopted by SMEs During Economic Crises – Evidence From Zimbabwe

In this chapter the authors explain that the pursuit of entrepreneurship by individuals is by no means an easy task due to multiple obstacles and unforeseen impediments such the recent COVID-19 crisis. The authors propose that entrepreneurs should continuously keep tabs on global changes and changing contingencies in order to come up with resilient strategies and then align their goals. The chapter provides an excellent and engaging overview of the evolving small business community in Africa. They then present fascinating data from 10 SME owner-managers in Gweru who were directly affected by the economic crisis amid the COVID-19 pandemic outbreak period. This chapter extends the scarce literature on entrepreneurial resilience. The authors conclude that the most common strategies adopted by SMEs particularly in the retail sector include strategic alliances, innovation, product reengineering, differentiation, and cost leadership strategies.

Chapter 7: The Market of Fertilizers in Mexico During the Pandemic Crisis – The Case of a Comprehensive Entrepreneurship Model for Organic Fertilizer Businesses

In this chapter, the author presents an interesting case study based on the market for fertilizers in México. This analysis points out that the consumption of fertilizers has undergone a change in the structure in favor of consumers with the highest concentration and diversification. The COVID-19 crisis has resulted in a drop in the consumption of fertilizers because the farmer's real income has fallen during the pandemic crisis.

Chapter 8: Advancing SME Sustainability – Rising Above Atrocities of Crisis

In this chapter the authors begin with a review of multiple crises that have crippled the socio-economy of nations in the past. They then explain that due to their small capital structure with limited resources and fragile nature, SMEs were severely impacted by these crises. The authors reflect that the experience can provide valuable lessons to the present SMEs, offering them some clear hints in developing relevant measures to counter future crises. Understanding and learning from past crises is a practical approach for SMEs in enhancing business foundation and sharpening resilience. The authors conclude by explaining that SMEs must be receptive to innovate their business models and operating procedures to be successful in the new normal.

Chapter 9: Struggling for Survival – Internationalization Drivers in Family SMEs

In this chapter the authors focus on family owned and run SMEs. They argue that these enterprises have unique characteristics and face significant resource constraints, thus providing an interesting case study. They provide evidence from a systematic literature review with theoretical and empirical articles in the last 15 years. The outcome is a valuable theoretical basis from which to assess the elements that may lead these firms, not only, to their long-term survival but their success and prosperity in international markets.

Chapter 10: The Impact of COVID-19 – A Major Crisis or Just Another One?

In this chapter the author explains that the COVID-19 pandemic has had a devastating impact on the lifestyles, and livelihoods of people around the world. He then explains that in emerging countries, SMEs already operate in challenging contexts characterized by institutional voids and scarce resource environments where entrepreneurs need to continuously develop strategies to survive. What follows is a case of a Brazilian SME and its strategies to survive the impact of the COVID-19 crisis. The study applies the resource-based view (RBV). The findings highlight the important role of different key resources in the survival, growth and sustainability of SMEs.

Chapter 11: Suggestions for SMEs as They Emerge From Crisis Periods

In this chapter the author explains that the existing financial problems of SMEs deepen even more in times of crisis, affecting businesses negatively and leading them to failure. In the crisis conditions, the strategies that SMEs have implemented in order to maintain their balance in their economic activities and to be successful are of critical importance. The author, following their review of the literature recommends a regular financial check-up should include production and sales strategies.

Simon Stephens
Letterkenny Institute of Technology, Ireland

REFERENCES

Brown, R., Rocha, A., & Cowling, M. (2020). Financing entrepreneurship in times of crisis: Exploring the impact of COVID-19 on the market for entrepreneurial finance in the United Kingdom. *International Small Business Journal Researching Entrepreneurship, 38*(5), 380–390. doi:10.1177/0266242620937464

Doern, R., Williams, N., & Vorley, T. (2019). Special issue on entrepreneurship and crises: Business as usual? An introduction and review of the literature. *Entrepreneurship and Regional Development, 31*(5–6), 400–412. doi:10.1080/08985626.2018.1541590

Foss, N. J. (2020). Behavioral strategy and the COVID-19 disruption. *Journal of Management, 48*(6), 1322–1329. doi:10.1177/0149206320945015

Hegarty, C., Stephens, S., Gallagher, P., & Cunningham, I. (2020). Entrepreneurs and business failure: Taking a second chance. *International Review of Entrepreneurship, 18*(4), 561–582.

Kuckertz, A., Brändle, L., Gaudig, A., Hinderer, S., Morales Reyes, C. A., Prochotta, A., Steinbrink, K. M., & Berger, E. S. C. (2020). Startups in times of crisis – A rapid response to the COVID-19 pandemic. *Journal of Business Venturing Insights, 13*, e00169. doi:10.1016/j.jbvi.2020.e00169

Liguori, E., & Winkler, C. (2020). From offline to online: Challenges and opportunities for entrepreneurship education following the COVID-19 pandemic. *Entrepreneurship Education and Pedagogy, 3*(4), 346–351. doi:10.1177/2515127420916738

Nummela, N., Paavilainen-Mäntymäki, E., Harikkala-Laihinen, R., & Raitis, J. (2020). When all doors close: Implications of COVID-19 for cosmopolitan entrepreneurs. *International Small Business Journal, 38*(8), 711–717. doi:10.1177/0266242620954127

Ratten, V. (2020). Coronavirus (Covid-19) and entrepreneurship: cultural, lifestyle and societal changes. *Journal of Entrepreneurship in Emerging Economies*. doi:10.1108/JEEE-06-2020-0163

Spillan, J., & Hough, M. (2003). Crisis planning in small businesses: Importance, impetus and indifference. *European Management Journal, 21*(2), 398–407. doi:10.1016/S0263-2373(03)00046-X

Stephens, S., Cunningham, I., & Kabir, Y. (2021). *Female entrepreneurs in a time of crisis: evidence from Ireland*. Gender and Entrepreneurship. doi:10.1108/IJGE-09-2020-0135

Chapter 1
Development of Small Businesses During Economic Crises:
Evidence From Indonesia

tulus tambunan
Center for Industry, SME and Business Competition Studies, Universitas Trisakti, Indonesia

EXECUTIVE SUMMARY

This is a descriptive study that aims to estimate the impact of three economic crises (i.e., the 1997/98 Asian financial crisis, the 2008/09 global financial crisis, and the COVID-19 pandemic crisis) on small businesses in Indonesia and to explore their crisis mitigation measures (CMMs). It adopted an exploratory methodology with comprehensively reviewing the available literature (e.g., policy documents, research papers, and reports) on the subject being studied. The data collection technique applied was literature study. It shows that different types of crises have different transmission channels through which such crises affected small businesses. CMMs adopted by affected small businesses also vary by different types of crises and hence different business risks. To the best of author's knowledge, this is the first study that examines transmission channels through which such crises affected small businesses in Indonesia.

INTRODUCTION

The outbreak of coronavirus disease (COVID-19) has had a devastating effect on the Indonesian economy, as on the world economy as well, due to declined consumption and production as a direct consequence of policies on social/physical distance, work and schools from home, and the necessity for companies in non-strategic sectors to stop their activities. Suryahadi et al. (2020) estimated that COVID-19 would reduce Indonesia's economic growth to between 1% and 4%. Whereas the Financial System Stability Committee (KSSK) predicted that the spread of COVID-19 would hit the Indonesian economy in 2020 to reach around 2.3% to - 0.4%.

DOI: 10.4018/978-1-7998-7657-1.ch001

But this is not the first time that Indonesia faces an economic crisis. The country had experienced two economic crises before, namely the Asian financial crisis that hit several countries in Southeast and East Asia in 1997–1998 and the global financial crisis in 2008–2009. The first crisis was triggered by a sudden capital flight from Indonesia which led the Indonesian rupiah (IDR) to depreciate significantly against the US dollar. The depreciation was soon followed by a national banking crisis and ended up as a national economic crisis. Through the rupiah depreciation and higher interest rate (as the monetary authority's direct response in that time in order to stop capital flight), the crisis hit first middle-and high-income groups such as employees in the financial/banking sector and large-scale industries which heavily dependent on credits from bank or other financial institutions and imports. After several months, domestic inflation started to increase, and this accompanied with the increase in unemployment due to many laid off employees in crisis-affected firms which resulted in a significant increase in poverty in 1998.

The second crisis, which was seen by many as the most serious world financial crisis since the great depression in the 1930s, has impacted many countries through various channels, i.e. exports, investment (including foreign direct investment/FDI), and remittances. However, for Indonesia the most important channel was export. Many exporting firms experienced a decline in their orders from abroad. Retrenchments mounted in many of these firms, while working time fell along with increased downward pressure on wages. Also many employees in these firms were laid off and many of them migrated back to rural areas and shifted to informal and vulnerable employment.

In both crises, many companies in Indonesia were impacted, especially the 1997/98 crisis. The impact of this crisis was so severe that the country's economy slumped into a deep recession. Its gross domestic product (GDP) experienced a negative growth rate at 13 per cent. Many small businesses, represented by micro, small and medium enterprises (MSMEs), were also suffered seriously (although not in all sectors), because they were encumbered by many problems especially financing. (Mustafa and Mansor, 1999; Abdullah, 2002; Griffith-Jones and Ocampo, 2009; Tambunan, 1998, 2010a,b, 2011; Tambunan and Busneti, 2016).

With respect to the initial causes and main transmission channels through which the crises affected local small businesses, these two crises are indeed different than the COVID-19 pandemic crisis in 2020/2021. As explained before, the initial cause of the 1997/98 crisis was capital flight that led to the depreciation of the rupiah. Many local small businesses were impacted through the following transmission channels: i) domestic demand declined, (ii) no credit was available, (iii) imported raw materials and other inputs that became very expensive, and (iv) many local small businesses as suppliers of multinational companies experienced low orders or order cancellations (Mustafa and Mansor, 1999; Abdullah, 2002).

While the initial cause of the second crisis was the decline in world demand which also affected many Indonesian small businesses, particularly in the export sector as well as those acted as subcontractors to large-sized exporting companies in labour-intensive manufacturing (e.g., textile, garment, footwear, seafood processing, and electronic) and small businesses producing items for tourism (Griffith-Jones and Ocampo, 2009; Khor & Sebastian, 2009; Nguanbanchong, 2009; Hartono, 2011).

In contrast to the two crises, the COVID-19 pandemic crisis in Indonesia was generally considered as domestic supply and demand crisis due to declined market demand as a direct consequence of government policy on social/physical distance, work and study from home and regulations requiring all companies in non-strategic and non-basic needs sectors to stop their activities temporary. As in many other countries, this policy has affected domestic economic activities in many sectors. Many small, medium and large companies in some sectors especially tourism, transportation, construction, non-food manufacturing industries, trade and services were negatively affected (e.g. Rahman, 2020; Santoso, 2020; Tambunan, 2020; Hermansah, 2020).

Based on the problem identified, this study has the following two questions:

1. How was the impact of the COVID-19 crisis on small businesses and through what channels, and what are the differences between this crisis and the other two crises before?
2. Second, what were the main business risks of the affected small businesses and what were their widely adopted crisis mitigation measures (CMMs)?

This study aimed to:

1. Examine the impacts of the COVID-19, the 1997/98 and the 2008/09 crises on small businesses;
2. To examine theoretically the transmission channels through which the crises affected small businesses; and
3. To explore the CMMs most widely adopted by the affected small businesses.

LITERATURE REVIEW

The Impact on Small Businesses

Economic crisis can be defined as the wild fluctuations, outside the acceptable limits of change, in the prices or supplies of commodities. Economic crisis is usually seen as a situation in which the economy of a country experiences a sudden downturn in its aggregate output or gross domestic product (GDP). There are many early triggers of an economic crisis, for instance, due to the sudden weakening of the exchange rate of a currency (commonly called the currency crisis) or a sudden collapse of the financial sector in a country (called the financial or banking crisis), or as happening now caused by the COVID-19.

There is already a lot of literature about the 1997/98 Asian financial crisis and the 2008/09 global financial crisis. Most of the literature examined the impact of the crises on social-macroeconomic variables such as economic growth, export growth, imports, foreign loans, employment/unemployment, poverty, migrant workers, child labor, farmer household income, education, and health (e.g., Bello, 1999; Hartono, 2011; Pearson and Sweetman, 2011; Priyambada et al., 2005; Shin and Kim, 2015; Tambunan, 1998, 2010a,b, 2011; Tambunan and Busneti, 2016; UNICEF, 2009; World Bank, 2009). Literature on the impact of the COVID-19 on the economy has also been increasing (e.g. ADB, 2020; Chesbrough, 2020; Kim et al., 2020; ILO. 2020a,b,c,d; Shakil et al. 2020; Suryahadi et al., 2020; UNCTAD, 2020a,b; and UNDP, 2020a,b).

In Indonesia, the Asian financial crisis began with the depreciation of the IDR against the USD by more than 200% between 1997 and 1998. As a result, many domestic companies that relied heavily on foreign loans and imports of processed raw materials, semi-finished products, components, machinery, production equipment, and other inputs were forced to stop their activities. The impact of this crisis was so severe that the country's economy slumped into a deep recession with an overall negative growth of about 13%. Whereas the 2008/09 global financial crisis was generally regarded as an international trade or export crisis as global demand for exports from many countries including Indonesia declined significantly (Griffith-Jones and Ocampo, 2009; Khor & Sebastian, 2009; Hartono; 2011). The impact of this crisis, however, was not as severe as the first crisis, and Indonesia managed to maintain positive growth rates in 2008 and 2009.

The current COVID-19 crisis is generally considered as domestic supply and demand crisis due to declined consumption and production as a direct consequence of policies on social/physical distance, work and study from home, and closure requirements for all companies in non-strategic sectors. Suryahadi et al. (2020) estimated that COVID-19 would reduce Indonesia's economic growth to between 1% and 4%. Even, it was estimated that the Indonesian economy will experience a recession of minus 5.4% (OECD Eurostat).

With respect to small businesses, it is often stated in the literature that one comparative advantage of small businesses, in particular micro and small enterprises (MSEs), relative to larger enterprises is their flexibility and capacity to move from one product to another when market demand changes, and they can expand easily when the economy grows, and to contract easily in case of economic crisis (Tambunan, 2019). Berry et al. (2001) argued that small businesses are very important in industries or economies that face rapid market or economic condition changes, such as a sharp macro-economic downturn because they work as a shock absorber in the business cycle. In Sandee et al. (2000), it is stated that small businesses can be expected to perform better under volatile macro-economic conditions than big companies that produce more standardized products, where the reorganization of the assembly line takes time.

However, some authors argued that small businesses, as with their larger counterparts, can also be severely affected by an economic crisis. Rashid and Ratten (2021), for instance, argued that small businesses globally are always vulnerable to changes in the external environment. The external environmental conditions are both positive and negative vibrations among members of the entrepreneurial ecosystem. The entrepreneurial ecosystem is not only limited to the support and facilitation of tangible resources and networks but also provides other necessary supports.

The seriousness of the impact of an economic crisis on local small businesses depends, among other factors, on the type of crisis and its main transmission channels through which the crisis affects them. Experiences in many countries in Southeast Asia showed that credit, import and domestic demand were the most important transmission channels through which the 1997/98 Asian financial crisis affected local small businesses. For instance, in Thailand, some findings from, among others, Chantrasawang (1999), Berry et al. (2001), Bakiewicz (2004), and Régnier (2005) showed that many Thai small businesses were forced to discontinue their production activities mainly because credit from banks was not available, interest rate was extremely high, and domestic demand for their products dropped significantly. The same was true in Malaysia where many small businesses were affected because of (i) domestic demand declined, (ii) no credit was available while they relied heavily on loans from banks and other formal financial institutions, (iii) they were highly dependent on imported raw materials and other inputs that became very expensive, and (iv) many small businesses were key suppliers to multinational corporations that were also affected by the crisis that led to low orders or order cancellations (Mustafa and Mansor, 1999; Abdullah, 2002). In the Philippines, many local small businesses in certain industries such as the auto parts and electronic goods industries had to stop production as domestic demand for new cars and electronic goods declined significantly during the crisis (Tecson, 1999; Berry and Rodriguez, 2001).

With respect to the 2008/09 global financial crisis, it revealed from many developing countries that the most important transmission channel was the decline in world demand which also affected export-oriented small companies as well as small companies acted as subcontractors to large-sized exporting companies in labour-intensive manufacturing (e.g., textile, garment, footwear, seafood processing, and electronic) and small companies producing items for tourism (Griffith-Jones and Ocampo, 2009; Khor and Sebastian, 2009; Nguanbanchong, 2009; Hartono, 2011).

Another important transmission channel was the banking sector which caused the loss of international confidence in the local banking system and thus the letter of credit could not be issued, and no domestic bank and trade credits were available (Humphrey, 2009). ADB (2009) also reported that the shrinking of trade finance due to the 2008/2009 crisis was one of the major transmission channels. However, based on evidence in Central Asia during the crisis, Pasadilla (2010) conjectured that big firms were going to be harder hit by the shrinking of trade finance than small firms because of the former's heavier reliance on foreign bank borrowing and global capital markets. The possible adverse impact on small businesses would include weakness in demand, both domestic and foreign, which could affect their sales and profits, and thus their capacity to raise financing which these enterprises relied upon heavily.

Claessenss et al. (2011) examined the impact of the crisis on firm performance and the role of different transmission channels on a sample of 42 advanced emerging economies. Using accounting data for 7,722 non-financial firms, they investigated the role of three particular channels: the financial channel, the demand channel and the export channel. Their findings indicate that export and demand channels were the most important in transmitting the crisis. With respect to country specifics, the results point to trade linkages as the prime propagator of shocks, while financial linkages were found to play a considerably weaker role.

Chakraborty (2012) analysed the channels through which the 2008/09 crisis affected export-oriented firms in India by using income statement and balance sheet indicators for around 5,000 manufacturing firms. The findings showed that the worse export performance of Indian firms was mostly explained by the negative demand shock from India's major trading partners, with the impact being higher from US than the EU. On the other hand, domestic financial conditions, accompanied by loose monetary policy, acted as a supporting factor to export-oriented firms.

By using the firm-level data provided by the Central Register of the Republic of Macedonia (CRM), Jovanovikj and Georgievska (2015) investigated the impact of the crisis on the country's economy by evaluating the relative importance of three transmission channels, i.e. the domestic demand channel, the export channel and the financial channel. The results suggest that firms that produced and sold domestically had relatively weaker performance. The trade channel appeared important only for exporting companies, whereas the financial channel did not play a significant role during the crisis.

With respect to the COVID-19, OECD in its updated report on small businesses policy response to the crisis (2020a,b) explains that the COVID-19 crisis affected small businesses through both the supply and demand sides. On the supply side, small businesses faced a shortage of labour, as workers were unwell or needed to look after children while schools were closed and movements of people were restricted. Measures to contain the disease by lockdowns and quarantines has led to further and more severe drops in capacity utilisation. As supply chains were also interrupted by the crisis, many small businesses experienced shortages of parts, intermediate goods or processed raw materials. On the demand side, small businesses also suffered from a cash shortage due to a dramatic decline in demand and revenue. All these effects were compounded because workers were laid off and firms were not able to pay salaries. More generally, small businesses were likely to be more vulnerable to 'social distancing' than their larger counterparts. The impact of the virus could have potential spill-overs into financial markets which would make small businesses suffer even more. These various impacts affected both small and large businesses. However, according to the report, the effect on small businesses was especially severe, particularly because of higher levels of vulnerability and lower resilience related to their size.

Shafi et al. (2020) collected data from 184 Pakistani small businesses by administering an online questionnaire, and the data was analyzed through descriptive statistics. It reveals that most of the participating enterprises have been severely affected by the significant drop in demand and they were facing several issues such as financial problem, supply chain disruption, decrease in demand, reduction in sales and profit, among others. Further, more than two-thirds of participating enterprises reported that they could not survive if the lockdown lasts more than two months.

Results of an ILO SCORE Programme survey indicate that small businesses were struggling to survive the effects of COVID-19 (ILO, 2020). Of the 1,000 small businesses surveyed from eight countries across four continents, 70% have had to shut down operations. Half (50%) have temporarily closed their business by following direct instructions from the authorities, while the other 50% have closed temporarily due to a reduction in orders, cases of staff COVID-19 infection, or more sadly, permanently. More than 75% of small businesses were experiencing or expecting a reduction in revenues through 2020. In some cases, the reductions in revenues were very high. One-third (33%) of businesses anticipated losing more than half of their revenues. 75% of companies were suffering from reduced demand and one-third (33%) were experiencing a more than 50% drop in customer orders. Nearly 9 out of 10 businesses were experiencing a shortage in cash flow.

Crisis Mitigating Measures (CMMs)

The ILO survey shows that small businesses were responding to the economic fall-out from COVID-19 in several ways (ILO, 2020b,c,d). Half of the businesses surveyed have reduced their production of goods and services to match demand reductions and constraints on their production. Over one-third (38%) of the sampled businesses negotiated wage modifications with their workers or revised payment terms with their banks and suppliers. Less frequently, some businesses in the sample tried to diversify their sales channels or products to try to reduce the effects of the crisis on their business.

Shafi et al. (2020) from their research in Pakistan also provides evidence on CMMs adopted by affected small businesses. The enterprises surveyed have chosen a different variety of strategies to curb the crisis. Particularly, 31% of the sampled enterprises have shut down the business completely, while 19% have partially closed their businesses, whereas 18% planned to apply for a loan. Moreover, 12% of investigated businesses continued to operate their business. Only 4% expressed that they were planning to change the business line to address the COVID-19 challenge. Additionally, 2% struggled to work remotely. Working remotely as much as possible was one of the best ways to stay safe and minimize the exposure to get infected. Nevertheless, not all businesses in the sample, especially micro and small enterprises in the rural or backward regions have the required resources to adopt such a strategy.

In Indonesia, from many sources of information, it reveals two main forms of CMM carried out by many affected small businesses in various sectors during the COVID-19 pandemic crisis, namely changing the business line and changing the way of marketing from offline to online or from waiting at the store to the home delivered via a telephone call, sms or wa (e.g. Afifiyah, 2020; Ciremaitoday, 2020; KB, 2020).

Research Method

This is a qualitative research with descriptive approach. It is not to examine statistically significance of the correlations between variables, but to find answers to the research questions mentioned before. It adopted an exploratory methodology with comprehensively reviewing the available literature, including policy documents, research papers, and reports on the issue being studied and analyzing secondary data. Having traced the successful development and implementation of qualitative methods in other social sciences, Dana and Dana (2005) have demonstrated that the use of this qualitative approach with more qualitative than quantitative data is a useful strategy, and it is applicable to research in small business and entrepreneurship as well (p.79).

The secondary data used in this research was collected from the National Bureau of Statistics (BPS) and the Ministry of Cooperative and Small Medium Enterprises, which provide annual data on total number of MSMEs and their profile in Indonesia.

The structure of the analysis consists of three sections: (i) the impact of the 1997/98 Asian financial crisis; (ii) the impact of the 2008/09 global financial crisis; and (iii) the impact of the 2020 COVID-19 pandemic crisis.

RESULTS AND DISCUSSION

The Impact of the 1997/98 Asian Financial Crisis

The 1997/1998 Asian financial crisis gripped most of Southeast Asia, including Indonesia. By mid. 1998 the Indonesian economy slumped into a deep recession with minus 13% of gross domestic product (GDP) growth along with the increase in unemployment and poverty as many employees were laid off in affected (mainly big) companies (Bello, 1999; Tambunan, 2010a,b, 2011).

Evidently, the impact of the 1997/1998 crisis or, more specifically, the depreciation of the IDR against the USD by more than 200% per August 1998 on local small businesses occurred through both demand- and supply-sides. The supply-side (SS) effects occurred through the market for factors of production and other inputs. The demand-side (DS) effects happened through the market for finished and semi-finished goods, and components The SS effects of the depreciation of the IDR have had both positive and negative effects. The negative effects came from two sources. First, the financial market: the significant increase in interest rate due to tight national liquidity as a direct monetary policy response to the depreciation of the IDR combined with the collapse of domestic banks due to their financial losses in their transactions with foreign banks and increased non-performing loans. As a result, many local small and large businesses faced financial difficulties because bank credits were no longer available or too expensive. Second, the inputs market: all import prices in local prices of processed raw materials, components and other inputs increased, and this hit severely local MSMEs that relied heavily on import for their inputs (Tambunan, 2019).

The positive SS effect was through the labour market. Many companies went bankrupt due to the weakening of the IDR, and so many people became unemployed. In a country like Indonesia where there is no unemployment benefit, those without formal jobs were forced to seek jobs in the informal sector that is dominated by micro and small enterprises or to run their own small businesses.

With respect to the DS effects, there are four main sources of demand for small businesses' products: (a) individuals/households, (b) business communities (companies), (c) national governments (e.g., departments), and (d) exports. The first source is domestic final demand, whereas the second and third comprise domestic demand for semi-finished or intermediate goods or components. The last source represents both final and intermediate demand from abroad.

With respect to the first source of demand, whether the DS effect will be negative or positive, theoretically, it depends on the relationship between the type of goods/services purchased from small businesses and the buyers' income level. If the purchased goods are inferior (or noninferior), which have a negative (positive) income elasticity of demand, then when consumer income declines, the DS effect will be positive (negative) for small businesses. Conversely, if consumer income increases. the DS effect will be negative (positive). To examine this effect empirically is however a difficult task because there is no data on consumed goods produced by small businesses. With respect to the second and third sources of demand, the stability of demand for small businesses' products during the crisis will depend strongly on the performance or ability to survive the crisis of large companies that used to purchase goods or services from small businesses (subcontracting arrangements) prior to the crisis. In this case, theoretically, the DS effect on small businesses is negative when large companies reduce their purchases due to the crisis. But the deprecation of IDR can have a substitution effect that generates market demand opportunities for small businesses: many large businesses that used to buy inputs from abroad before the depreciation of the IDR now with more expensive USD may have to buy cheaper inputs produced by small businesses in local markets. Also, local consumers may have to change their consumption behaviour from the usual purchase of imported goods to domestic goods produced by local small businesses at much cheaper prices.

Finally, with respect to export, the DS effect can also be positive or negative (or even no effect at all). Theoretically, the depreciation of the IDR will increase the price competitiveness in the international market of Indonesian exporting companies, *ceteris paribus*, other price determinants are constants. But Indonesia relies heavily on import of many goods, including processed raw materials, machinery, equipment, and other industrial goods. So, if exporting small businesses use many imported inputs to produce their export goods, the depreciation of the IDR can even reduce their exports.

Thus, the net effect of the IDR depreciation on local small businesses during the Asian financial crisis could be positive or negative, depending on whether the total positive 'substitution effect (SE)', 'export effect (EE)', and 'labour market effect (LME)' were stronger or weaker than the total negative 'import effect (IE)' and 'financial market effect (FME)'. As can be seen in Figure 1, secondary data provided by the Ministry of Cooperatives and Small and Medium shows obviously that the number of small businesses declined from nearly 39.8 million units in 1997 to 36.8 million in 1998. So, this may suggest that the total positive SE, EE, and LME were weaker than the IE and FME.

In 1999, the number of small businesses began to increase again and continued even during the 2008/2009 crisis. This may indicate that the first crisis was more severe than the second one for small businesses. To support this view, Figure 2 illustrates the percentages of change in real GDP and the number of small businesses in Indonesia during those two crises. As can be seen, the change pattern of the two variables is the same, and in 1998, both percentages of change were both negative, whereas in the second crisis, both variables continued to grow positively.

Quite a number of studies were carried out based on field surveys and direct observations of small businesses in various industries during the crisis period (Table 1). Whereas studies after 1999 were mostly based on secondary data analysis. In general, the results of these studies support the general notion that the 1997/98 crisis had a negative impact on small businesses. However, Jellinek and Rustanto (1999) pointed out interesting facts. They found that the crisis has also created greater domestic market opportunities for many small businesses in some industries because many individuals or households affected by the crisis changed their consumption behaviour from the usual purchase of imported goods to domestic goods at much cheaper prices. This shift in public consumption behaviour has resulted in higher demand for local small businesses.

Figure 1. Total number of small businesses in Indonesia (units)
Source: Indonesian State Ministry of Cooperative and SME (www.depkop.go.id).

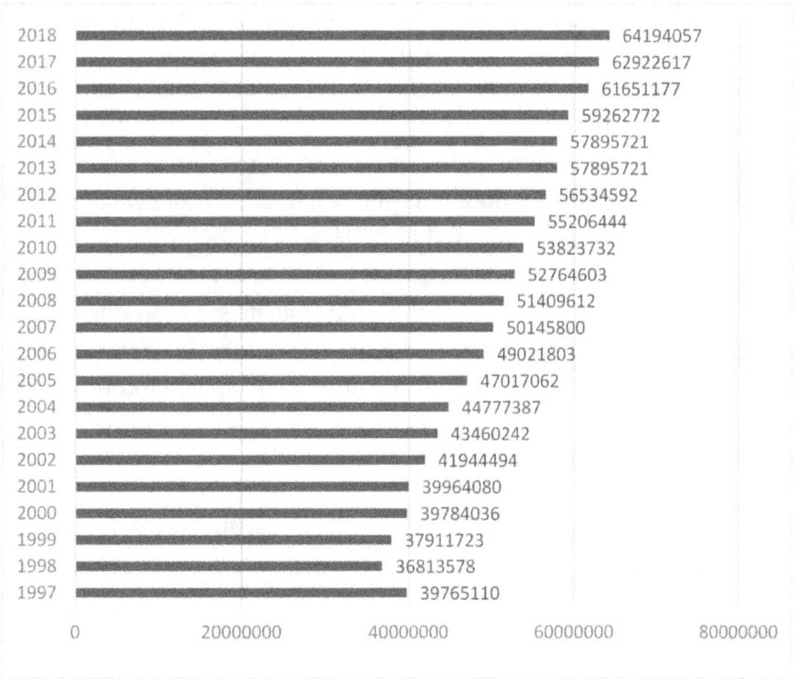

Figure 2. Percentage Changes of Real GDP and Total Number of Small Businesses in Indonesia
Source: Indonesian Ministry of Cooperative and SME (www.depkop.go.id).

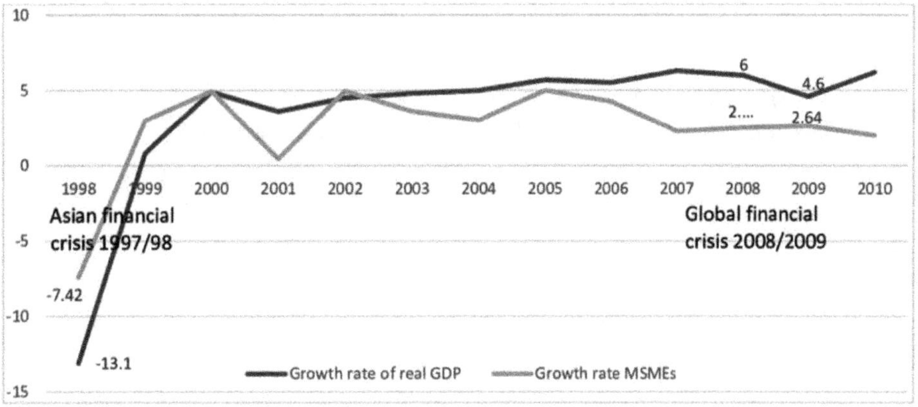

The Impact of the 2008/09 Global Financial Crisis

The 2008/2009 crisis was generally regarded as an international trade or a world demand crisis as the export market was the main important DS channel through which the crisis had caused exports of many developing countries in Southeast Asia to decline significantly (Griffith-Jones & Ocampo, 2009; Khor & Sebastian, 2009; Hartono; 2011). Indonesian exports were also affected (Figure 3). The most severely affected export-oriented industries in Indonesia were textile and clothing, footwears and other leather foods, and wood- and/or rattan-based furniture. These industries have traditionally been dominated by small businesses. The production of these goods is closely linked to regional and global value chains through trade and production systems associated with multinational companies and/or markets in countries such as Japan, the Unites States, and the major Eurozone countries (e.g., Germany, France, and United Kingdom) (Tambunan, 2019).

However, compared to the 1997/98 crisis, Indonesia was much better in dealing with the 2008/09 crisis. As proved in Table 2 (also shown before in Figure 2), in 2009 Indonesia managed to keep a positive growth rate, although at lower rate compared to 2008 or years before.

The 2008/2009 crisis had affected small businesses in Indonesia through two main transmission channels: (a) declined world demand for Indonesian small businesses' products which led exports of these enterprises to decline, and (b) declined foreign tourists resulting in decreased demands in the local market for small businesses goods and services especially handicrafts. motorbike rentals, travel agencies, and accommodations.

Table 1. Studies on the Impact of the 1997/98 Crisis on Small Businesses in Indonesia

Author	Methodology	Industry/sector	Main Transmission channels
Tambunan (1998), Dierman et al.(1998), Jellinek and Rustanto (1999), Musa (1998), Wiradi (1998), AKATIGA and the Asia Foundation (1999), Sandee et al, (2000), Berry et al. (2001), Hill (1999, 2001a,b), Sato (2000), Wie (2000), and Wengel and Rodriguez (2006),	-Field surveys -Direct observations -Secondary data analyses	e.g. footwear, furniture, batik (Indonesian traditional cloth), bricks, tofu, cigarette (*kretek*), and metal industry, agriculture	-expensive imported raw materials -no credit available -low domestic demand

Figure 3. Export growth rates of Indonesian manufactured goods (%)
Source: CIEC Data Company Ltd (Indonesia | Ekspor | Indikator Ekonomi (ceicdata.com)

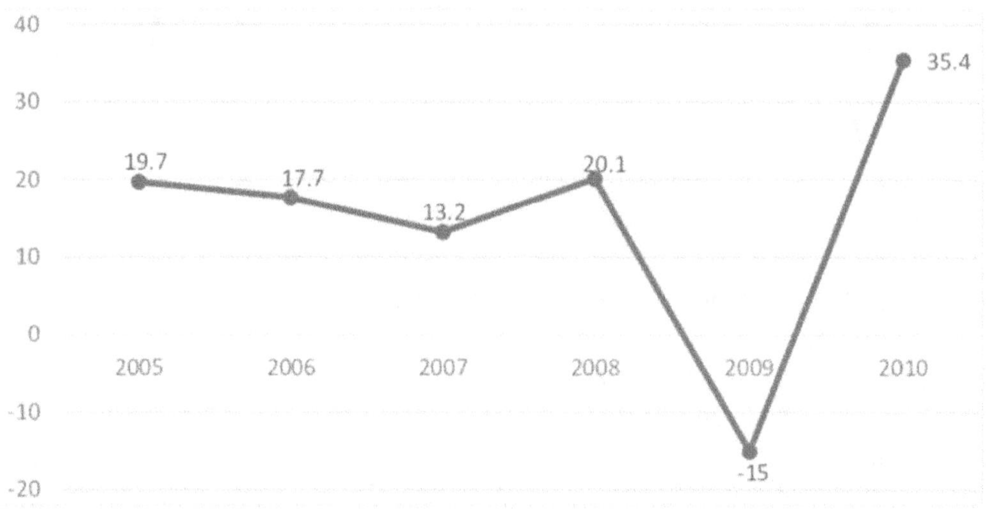

Table 2. Growth rates of real GDP in Southeast Asian countries, 2006-2010 (%)

	2006	2007	2008	2009	2010
Brunei Darussalam	4.4	0.2	−1.9	−1.8	2.6
Cambodia	10.8	10.2	6.7	0.1	5.9
Indonesia	5.5	6.3	6.0	4.6	6.1
Lao PDR	8.6	5.9	7.8	7.6	7.9
Malaysia	5.8	6.5	4.8	−1.6	7.2
Myanmar	13.1	12.0	10.3	10.6	10.4
Philippines	5.2	6.6	4.2	1.1	7.6
Singapore	8.7	8.8	1.5	−0.8	14.5
Thailand	5.1	5.0	2.5	−2.3	7.8
Vietnam	8.2	8.5	6.3	5.3	6.8

Source: ADB (2002)

Figure 1 (or Figure 2) may give the impression that small businesses were not severely affected by the 2008/09 crisis as the total number of small businesses in that particular period showed an increase, not declined as happened in 1998. This is not saying, however, that not even one firm had been negatively affected. There must be many small businesses experienced decline in their sales. For example, it was documented that many small businesses in the textile and garment industry in Bandung and Cimahi, West Java province, were affected. About 150 small businesses were threatened with bankruptcy due to rising prices of imported raw materials, which caused production costs to rise by about 20%, whereas on the demand side, they faced less orders especially from foreign buyers (SMERU, 2009).

In wood- and rattan-based furniture many export-oriented small businesses were also disrupted by the crisis. The industry was one of Indonesia's major export goods that was heavily affected by the crisis. This industry has traditionally been among the major industries of small businesses. As foreign demand for Indonesian furniture decreased due to the crisis, the industry had to lay off nearly 35,000 workers in early 2009. In the first and second quarters of 2009, compared with the first and second quarters of 2008, the value of Indonesian furniture exports fell by, respectively, 35% and 30%. Exports of timber also fell by 28% in the first quarter of 2009 compared with the same quarter of 2008, 23.2% drop in export volume of wooden furniture, doors, and window sills (Tambunan, 2019).

Many other studies from other countries have similar findings. For instance, Claessenss et al. (2011) have examined the impact of the 2008/09 crisis on more than 7 thousand firms in many advanced emerging economies. They found that most affected firms were involved in export activities and during that crisis their export demand dropped significantly. Similarly, from his sample of 5000 manufacturing firms in India, Chakraborty (2012) found that during the 2008/09 crisis the worse export performance of Indian firms was mostly caused by the negative demand shock from India's major trading partners, with the impact being higher from US than the EU.

The Impact of the 2020 COVID-19 Pandemic Crisis

From a lot of news in mass media during the whole year of 2020 it reveals that the economic crisis caused by the COVID-19 pandemic has severely affected many firms in Indonesia through four main channels

(Figure 4). The first channel was the result of the " anti-COVID 19 impact" policy which consisted of three main elements: (i) social/physical distancing' (ii) learn and work from home; and (iii) the temporary suspension of business activities in non-strategic sectors. The second element obviously has caused the number of buyers in the local market to decrease dramatically (↓). Thus, this policy element has affected business activities on the demand-side ('demand effect'). Whereas the third element of the policy has affected business activities on the supply-side ('supply effect'). These demand-side and supply-side effects did not happen only in companies supplying finished products but also in those supplying processed raw materials, components, spare parts, auxiliary goods, semi-finished goods and other inputs.

Figure 4. The Main Economic Transmission Channels of the Impact of the COVID-19 Pandemic on Domestic firms

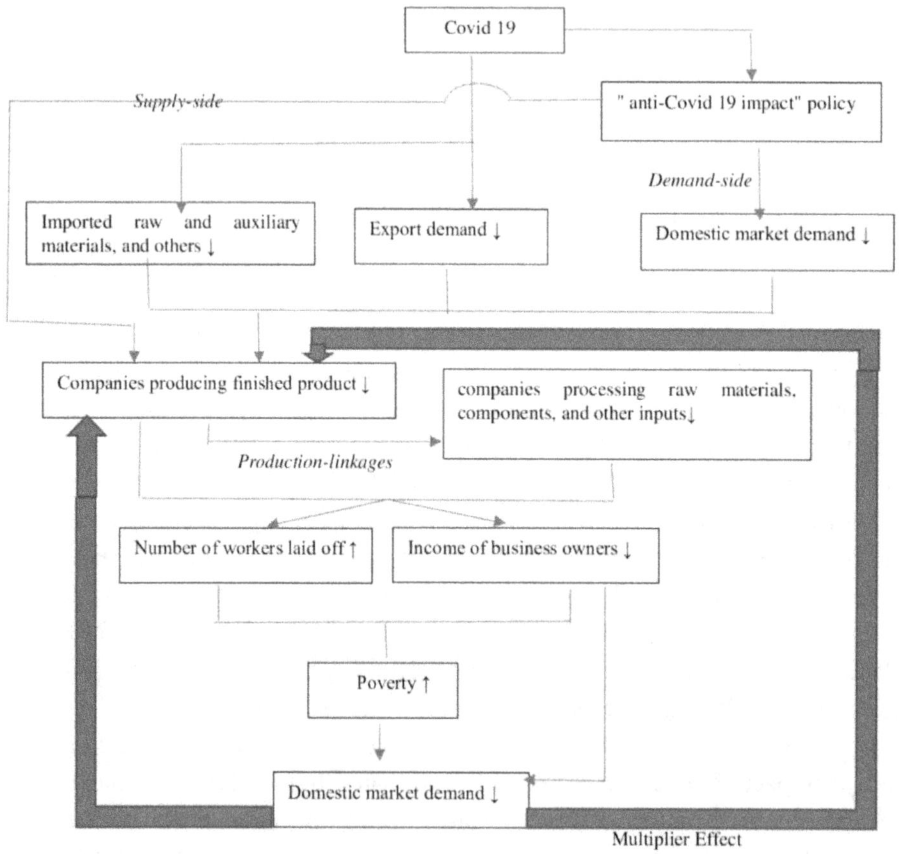

The second channel was the decrease in world demand, especially from China, for Indonesian products which caused Indonesia's exports to decline (ADB, 2020). The third channel was the decline in imports of processed raw materials and auxiliary materials, especially from China, which forced many companies, including MSMEs, in Indonesia which were highly dependent on import from China to reduce/stop their production (Kompas, 2020a, b). The fourth channel was the increase in the number of poor people as many employees have been laid off, or their wages were cut, which further led local market demand to decline that hit many domestic companies.

Since the end of the Asian financial crisis 1997-98, which caused Indonesia's economy to growth negatively, Indonesia's economy continued to grow positively until early 2020 when the COVID-19 pandemic broke out (Figure 5). Data from the National Statistics Bureau (BPS) shows that as a direct consequence of the " anti-COVID 19 impact" policy, the country's economy by the end of 2020 experienced a growth contraction of 2.07 percent. Business sectors that experienced the deepest growth contraction included transportation and warehousing with 15.04 percent; provision of accommodation and food and drink amounted to 10.22 percent; company services by 5.44 percent; other services by 4.10 percent; and large trade and retail; car and motorcycle repair by 3.72 percent. However, some other sectors in that period were still experiencing positive growth rates, including health services and social activities 11.60 percent; information and communication 10.58 percent; procurement water, waste management, waste and recycling by 4.94 percent; real estate of 2.32 percent; and agriculture, forestry and fisheries 1.75 percent.

Figure 5. Annual Growth of Indonesian Real GDP, 2000-2021 (%)
Source: BPS (https://www.bps.go.id/)

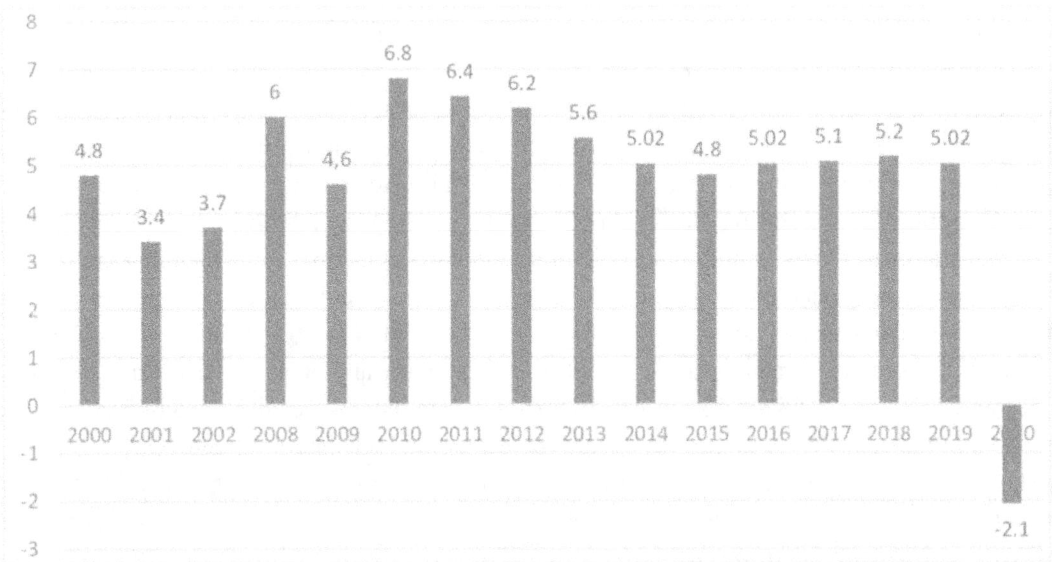

The sector hardest hit was the tourism sector. Judging based on those who entered through all international airports in the country, the number of foreign tourists visited Indonesia in January 2021 dropped significantly by 99.79 percent compared to the number of those visited in January 2020. All international airports in Indonesia experienced a decline, even at most airports the decline reached 100 percent. Meanwhile, the main international airport in Indonesia, Soekarno-Hatta, experienced a decrease at 99.34 percent. Figure 6 shows number of foreign tourists visited Indonesia per month for the period January 2020-January 2021.

Figure 6. Number of Visiting Foreign tourists in Indonesia during the Period January 2020 - January 2021 (thousand visitors)
Source: BPS (https://www.bps.go.id/)

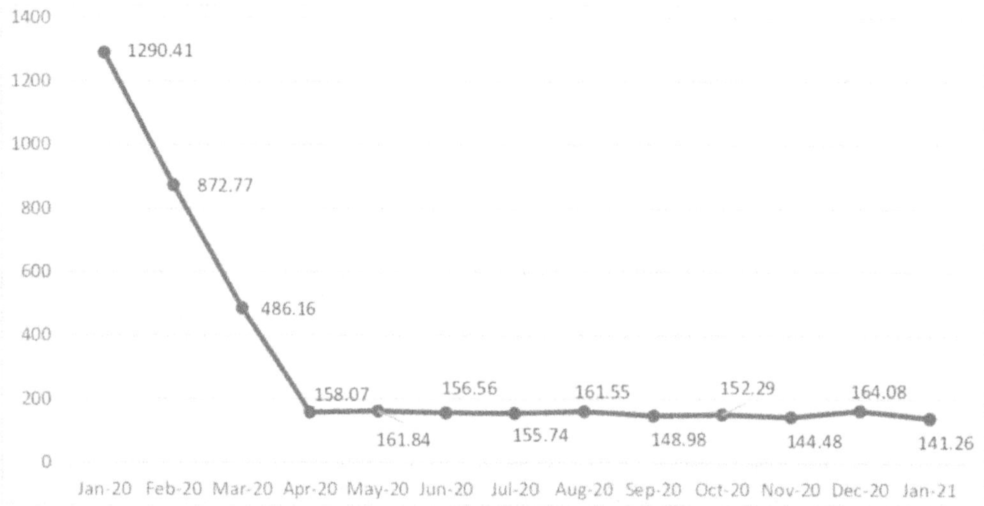

As illustrated in Figure 7, the negative impact of COVID-19 on the tourism sector in turn has a negative impact on many small businesses, both directly and indirectly, through several transmission channels. The direct impact was through the reduction of small business activities in the tourism sector, such as restaurants, cafes, travel agencies, local transportation, small shops, rentals, cheap accommodation/hotels, and various kinds of entertainment. Meanwhile, the indirect impact was a decrease in orders received by small-sized suppliers (e.g. catering, provision of food and beverages, cleaning services, repair services, rental of musical instruments, rental of sport equipment, laundry) from companies that are directly related to tourism as mentioned previously. In addition, the decrease in the number of tourists in Indonesia during 2020 both from abroad and domestically (due to the "anti-COVID-19 impact" regulations) has an impact on the volume of transportation activities both at home and on national airlines serving international routes such as Garuda and Lion Air. In turn, this decline also resulted in a reduction in orders for suppliers in the country, many of which were from the small businesses category.

The large number of companies that closed or reduced their activities during the COVID-19 pandemic automatically resulted in an increase in unemployment. According to official data from the government, the open unemployment rate in August 2020 was 7.07 percent of total labor force, an increase of 1.84 percentage points compared with August 2019. The population who worked as many as 128.45 million people, decreased as many as 0.31 million people from August 2019. The sector that experienced the largest decrease in employment during that period was in the manufacturing industry at 1.30 percent.

Since March 2020 news from various sources about the impact of COVID-19 on small business in many parts of the country began to emerge. Table 3 summarizes them for the period March and April 2020.

Figure 7. The Impact of Covid-19 on Small Businesses through Its Effects on Tourism

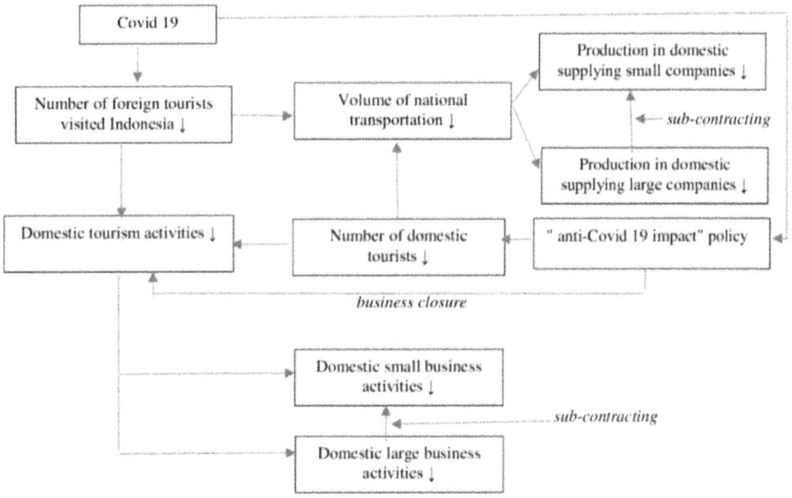

Table 3. Some Evidence on the Impact of COVID-19 on Small Businesses

Source	Impact
Rahman (2020), Santoso (2020), Tambunan (2020)	163,713 small businesses have been seriously affected. As many as 56% due to a decrease in sales, 22% difficulty in capital, 15% difficulty in the distribution of products and 4% difficulty finding raw materials
Hermansah (2020)	Based on a survey of small businesses in some sectors, 96% claimed to have been negatively impacted. As many as 75% experienced a significant decrease in sales; 51% believe that it is very likely that their business will only last one month to the next three months
Anwar (2020)	Of the 14,238 small businesses in Serang City, 10,238 were affected. Only 4,000 businesses have survived this epidemic
Kompas (2020c)	The decrease in demand for small businesses' products is expected to decrease by around 60% to 80%. This decrease was caused by a decrease in the number of buyers visiting shops
Sundari (2020)	Many small businesses in the Cimahi City have experienced a decline in sales of up to 80%. Even a large number of small businesses are forced to lay off their employees. Especially those that their businesses rely heavily on daily production activities are severely affected. Also export-oriented small businesses are also affected
Nurzaman (2020)	A case study: Ms. Tarli Sutarli is the manager of the Bueuk stamp coffee plant located in Golempang Hamlet, Ciliang Village, Parigi District, Pangandaran Regency. According to her, at normal times her turnover can reach 7 to 12 million IDR per month. Recently, hit by the corona pandemic crisis, she has almost closed her business because her turnover has dropped dramatically from day to day
Burhan (2020).	Small businesses revenues in the culinary, fashion retail and beauty services sectors fell during the corona pandemic. The culinary sector experienced a decline in daily income of up to 37%, the fashion retail by 35%, and beauty services by 43% percent. Also food orders at restaurants decreased very significantly by up to 60%. The negative impact of the pandemic was felt most significantly by small businesses that still ran their businesses offline
Kompas (2020d, e)	By April 2020, there were 212,394 laid off workers and 1,205,191 workers who were sent home but still paid (not full) from 74430 companies. From the informal sector, the number of workers affected and losing their jobs reached 282,000 people from 34453 enterprises, mostly from the micro and small enterprise category

Types of Business Risk and CMMs

It can be argued that when a company faces an unexpected fall in market demand for its products, especially if the decline is not expected as a short-term phenomenon, the company will take some adjustment measures to reduce the pressure on its profit. Similarly, if the price of a raw material goes up significantly due to an interference in its supply or a disruption in its distribution or because of national currency depreciation (in the case of imported raw material), companies that depend much on such raw material will take some adjustment measures to cope with it. Crisis mitigating measures (CMMs) can be in various forms such as fewer production volumes, less working days or hours per day, laid-off workers, substitution of raw materials, and change the way of marketing, depending on the type of crisis, the type of business risks, the apparent impact of crisis, and, perhaps more importantly, the owner's own expectation about the prospect of the current condition he or she is facing.

Experiences with the three crises show that different types of crises with different transmission channels pose different types of business risks, such as production risk, credit risk, or market risk. Therefore, different types of business risks require different alternative forms of CMMs.

1997/98: National Currency Crisis

Based on its initial trigger, the type of the1997/98 Asian financial crisis is a currency crisis. During this crisis, the types of business risk that many domestic companies faced, especially those which were heavily dependent on imported raw materials and other inputs are given in Table 4. For these types of business risk, Table 4 also suggests appropriate forms of CMMs.

Table 4. The 1997/98 Crisis: Types of Business Risk and Suggested Appropriate CMMs

Type of Crisis	Transmission channels	Type of Business Risk	Suggested appropriate forms of CMMs
Currency crisis)	-import -credit - export -domestic supply chain	1) Production risk: -high production costs due to high prices of imported raw materials 2) Credit risk: - high loan interest rate 3) Market risk: -less or no demand from LEs (stop subcontracting linkages)	-substitution of raw material -efficiency in using raw materials -Reducing number of workers/labor costs. -Reducing other non-labor and non-raw material cost4 -looking for alternative sources of funding -finding alternative sources for subcontracting arrangements at home and abroad

Although there are quite a number of studies on the impact of the 1998 crisis on small businesses (see again Table 1), most have not paid particular attention to CMMs. To the author's knowledge, there was only one research conducted by Dierman et al. in 1998 who tried to look at CMMs adopted by affected small producers in the furniture and batik industries in various locations in the Central Java province. They found that replaced imported raw materials with local raw materials were the most adopted CMMs. The weakening of the IDR was supposed, at least theoretically, to increase their price competitiveness. However, because many of the supporting materials they used were imported, the IDR depreciation did not have a significant positive impact for them.

2008/09: World Demand Crisis

Based on its initial trigger, the type of crisis with respect to the 2008/09 global financial crisis is a world demand or export crisis. In this type of crisis, the types of its business risk that domestic companies will face, especially exporting companies and those in the tourism sector given in Table 5. Given these types of business risk, Table 5 also suggests appropriate CMMs for this kind of crisis.

Table 5. The 2008/09 Crisis: Types of Business Risk and Suggested Appropriate CMMs

Type of Crisis	Transmission channels	Type of Business Risk	Suggested appropriate CMMs
World demand crisis)	-foreign tourists -export	Market risk: - less export demand - less domestic demand related to less foreign tourists visiting Indonesia	-Exploration of domestic market -Finding new markets (export market diversification) -Reducing production cost e.g. lay off some workers or reducing working time Cutting back on production

To take a closer look at the impact of the 2008/2009 crisis on Indonesian small businesses and their adopted CMMs, Tambunan (2019) conducted field surveys on small businesses in the furniture industry in three cities in Java island, i.e. Cirebon, Jepara, and Solo, over the period July–August 2009 adopted. These are the three main furniture production centres in Indonesia. Respondents (business owners) were interviewed using a structured questionnaire. Their selection was done as follows. First, small businesses affected by the crisis were identified based on information provided by the local offices of the Indonesian Furniture Producers Association (ASMINDO) in the three cities. Then, 37 out of them were randomly selected for the sample survey: 10 units in Jepara, 10 units in Cirebon, and 17 units in Solo. They exported their products directly or indirectly through trading or larger-sized exporting companies. In addition, unstructured interviews were also conducted with some relevant local government officials and other key stakeholders including the chairmen of regional ASMINDO in the three cities. It was found that all respondents experienced a decline in their export, although the percentage decline varied between respondents.

Table 6 presents the adopted CMMs by the respondents. As can be seen, the most adopted measures were seeking out new customers/markets and halting new recruitment. There were some producers in the sample who did not take a special measure to overcome the impact of the crisis, because, as they said, they expected that the crisis would not last forever. The survey also found that three respondents have closed their business. But as they explained during the survey, their decision to stop production was only temporary, and in the meantime, they did other things such as opening a small stall selling cigarettes, sweets, and other simple basic goods or working as a day labourer in the construction sector or as a supplier of certain materials for other furniture producers that were still operating in that time. They did such temporary activities while waiting for the market situation to be normal again, so they can restart their furniture business.

Although the initial trigger was the outbreak of the outbreak of coronavirus disease (COVID-19), it has created domestic market demand and production crisis. During this crisis, domestic companies including small businesses faced risks from both sides, i.e. demand-side caused by less movement of people and supply-or production-side because of government regulations that require companies to stop their operations. Table 7 also suggests appropriate CMMs for this kind of crisis.

Table 6. CMMs taken by the respondents to cope with the impact of the 2008/09 crisis (% of total sampled enterprises; N = 37)

Adopted Type of CMM	Distribution (%)
Seeking out new customers/markets	89.2
Halting new recruitment	81.1
Reducing non-labour cost	70.3
Cancelling/delaying facilities upgrading	62.2
Cutting back on production	51.4
Reducing labour cost	45.9
Closing down	8.1
Reducing working time	5.4
No special measures	2.7
Reducing total workers	2.7

Source: Tambunan (2019)

2020: Domestic Market Demand and Production Crises

Table 7. The 2020 Crisis: Types of Business Risk and Suggested Appropriate CMMs

Type of Crisis	Transmission channels	Type of Business Risk	Suggested appropriate CMMs
Production and market demand crisis	- import -export -domestic demand	1) Market risk: - less domestic demand 2) Production risk: - stop production (due to 'anti-Covid 19 impact' policy)	-Change business line - Change the way of marketing - Reducing production cost e.g. lay off some workers or reducing working time -Cutting back on production

From the findings of a number of studies, observations, papers presented in virtual seminars and interviews by newspaper reporters with a number of owners of small businesses (e.g. Afifiyah, 2020; Ciremaitoday, 2020; KB, 2020; Kompas, 2020c; Setyowati, 2020), it reveals four most adopted CMMs: i) changed their business line to other businesses which were not really affected by the crisis or had a chance to survive or even to growth; (ii) switched to the business of making masks and other personal protective equipment that were most sought after during the COVID-19 pandemic; iii) changed their way of marketing from offline to online or e-commerce by using existing trading platforms, and iv) changed their marketing method from just waiting for the buyer to visit the store to home delivery based on orders via telephone, SMS, or Whatsapp.

More recent evidence provided by Tambunan (2020) who conducted a survey on 137 MSMEs during May-September 2020 in various cities and sectors in Indonesia. They were from the food and beverage businesses including restaurants, food processing, and catering. Some other respondents were small shops or mini markets, clothing industries, café and coffee shops, photocopy services. haircut and washing services, transportation services, craft industries, music studio, creative content production workshops, groceries, printing, and laundry. Before COVID-19, most of them marketed their products in a conventional way (offline).

It revealed from the survey that several respondents chose more than one form of CMMs. Most of them experienced a decrease in turnover or an increase in production costs large enough to force them to take some adjustment steps. Table 8 shows the number of respondents according to the chosen form of CMMs. As can be seen, the most popular forms of CMM were reducing production volume and changing conventional or offline marketing systems to online marketing systems or e-commerce. With respect to the latter, this was indeed highly recommended by the Indonesian government that all MSMEs should switch to an online marketing system so that their sales can remain smooth or at least not fall too much in this COVID-19 period.

Table 8. CMMs taken by the respondents to cope with the impact of the 2020 crisis (% of total sampled enterprises; N = 137)

Adopted Type of CMM	Distribution %
No special designed strategy	0,81
Other measures	2,85
Offer directly to individual consumers	7,72
Go online	26,83
Change the raw materials	8,13
Debt restructuring	1,63
Change the type of business	2,44
Reduce production	29,27
Cut wages	8,94
Lay off workers	11,38

Source: Tambunan (2020)

CONCLUSION

As almost all other countries in the world, Indonesia has also been hit severely by the COVID-19 pandemic. It is not the first time Indonesia has faced an economic crisis. The country had experienced two major economic crises before, namely the 1997/1998 Asian financial crisis and the 2008/2009 global financial crisis. This study aimed to examine empirically the impacts of these three crises on small businesses and to explore the most adopted CMMs by the affected small businesses.

This study has shown that different types of crises have different transmission channels through which the crises affect small businesses and pose different business risks, and therefore require different CMMs. An economic crisis may not affect all small businesses in all sectors, but it depends on the type of the crisis and the transmission channels. For instance, the COVID 19 pandemic crisis can be considered as a combination of market demand and market supply (production) crises, as a result of 'the anti-COVID 19 impact policy'. From the market demand side, only small businesses that make finished products (good and service) and are completely dependent on offline marketing have been hardly hit as people are staying at home. Whereas from the market supply side, generally, only large companies with large numbers of workers such as textile and apparel companies, companies which become a gathering place for many people such as cafes and restaurants, entertainment venues, cinemas, hotels, and malls that must close the business during the pandemic period. Meanwhile, micro-businesses that only use less than 5 workers such as small car repair shops, small car washes, small shops, or business units without workers such as craftsmen, small traders, and food stalls remain open.

With respect to the policy implication of this study, if the government wants to assist crisis-affected small businesses, this study has two policy implications. First, to make a stimulus package program effective, small businesses most affected should be identified first. And for that, the government needs to know in advance the type of the crisis, and its main transmission channels and its related types of business risks. Second, the form of stimulus must be in line with the CMMs adopted by the targeted small businesses. In other words, a stimulus program must be complementary to the adopted CMMs. Thus, different CMMs taken by affected small businesses in response to different business risks need supports from the government with different policy approaches and different stimulus packages.

RESEARCH LIMITATION

This study has some limitations. The identification of transmission channels through which the crises affected small businesses was based more on presumptive theories than comprehensive evidence in the field. The problem was that the sampled small businesses were too few and only in certain locations and sectors.

REFERENCES

Abdullah, M. A. (2002). An overview of the macroeconomic contribution of small and medium enterprises in Malaysia. In C. Harvie & B.-C. Lee (Eds.), *The role of SMEs in national economies in East Asia*. Edward Elgar.

ADB. (2009). *Key indicators for Asia and the Pacific 2009*. Asian Development Bank.

ADB. (2020). *The Economic Impact of the COVID-19 Outbreak on Developing Asia. ADB Briefs, No.128, 6 March*. Asian Development Bank.

Afifiyah, S. (2020). *Jenis Usaha yang Justru Melejit Saat Wabah Covid-19*. Available online: https://www.tagar.id/jenis-usaha-yang-justru-melejit-saat-wabah-covid19

AKATIGA and the Asia Foundation. (1999). The impact of economic crisis on Indonesian small and medium enterprises. Study prepared for the United States Agency for International Development, Jakarta.

Anwar, K. (2020). *10.238 UMKM di Kota Serang Terdampak Wabah COVID-19*. Available online: https://banten.idntimes.com/business/economy/khaerul-anwar-2/10238-umkm-di-kota-serang-terdampak-wabah-covid

Bakiewicz, A. (2004). Small and medium enterprises in Thailand. Following the leader. *Asia & Pacific Studies*, *2*, 131–151.

Bello, W. (1999). The Asian financial crisis: Causes, dynamics, prospects. *Journal of the Asia Pacific Economy*, *4*(1), 33–55.

Berry, A., & Rodriguez, E. (2001). *Dynamics of small and medium enterprises in a slow-growth economy: The Philippines in the 1990s* (Stock No. 37181). The International Bank for Reconstruction and Development/The World Bank.

Berry, A., Rodriguez, E., & Sandee, H. (2001). Small and medium enterprise dynamics in Indonesia. *Bulletin of Indonesian Economic Studies*, *37*(3), 363–384.

Burhan, F. A. (2020). *Bisnis Anjlok akibat Pandemi Corona, UMKM Bisa Ubah Strategi Usaha*. Available online: https://katadata.co.id/berita/2020/04/15/bisnis-anjlok-akibat-pandemi-corona-umkm-bisa-ubah-strategi-usaha

Chakraborty, P. (2012). *The Great Trade Collapse and Indian Firms* (Unpublished PhD dissertation). Graduate Institute of International and Development Studies.

Chantrasawang, N. (1999). *Current issues of SMEs in Thailand: Its linkages with FDI and the impact of the financial crisis.* Paper presented at the International Conference on Small and Medium Enterprises At New Crossroads: Challenges and Prospects, Penang, Malaysia.

Chesbrough, H. (2020). To recover faster from Covid-19, open up: Managerial implications from an open innovation perspective. *Industrial Marketing Management*, *88*, 410–413. j.indmarman.2020.04.010 doi:10.1016/

Ciremaitoday. (2020). *Kisah Perajin Batik Perempuan di Cirebon, Bangkit Ditengah Pandemi COVID-19.* Available online: https://kumparan.com/ciremaitoday/kisah-perajin-batik-perempuan-di-cirebon-bangkit-ditengah pandemi-covid-19-1tGcuTSTNoV/full

Claessens, S., Tong, H., & Shang-Jin, W. (2011). *From the Financial Crisis to the Real economy: Using Firm-level Data to Identify Transmission Channels*. NBER Working Paper No.17360. Washington, DC: National Bureau of Economic Research.

Dana, L. P., & Dana, T. E. (2005). Expanding the scope of methodologies used in entrepreneurship research. *International Journal of Entrepreneurship and Small Business*, *2*(1), 79–88.

Dierman, van, P., Tambunan, T., Tambunan, M., & Wie, T. K. (1998). *The IMF 50-point program: Evaluating the likely impact on SMEs.* Draft report for the Asia Foundation.

Griffith-Jones, S., & Ocampo, J. A. (2009). *The financial crisis and its impacts on developing countries.* Working Paper No. 53. Brasilia: International Policy Center for Inclusive Growth.

Hartono, D. (2011). Assessing policy effectiveness during the crisis: The case of Indonesia. Geneva: International Labour Organization (International Institute for Labour Studies).

Hermansah. (2020). *Simak strategi bertahan bagi UKM hadapi krisis akibat Covid-19 Pastikan bisnis Anda tetap berjalan dan mampu bertahan pada saat kondisi pandemi saat ini*. Available online: https://www.alinea.id/bisnis/strategi-bertahan-bagi-ukm-hadapi-krisis-akibat-covid-19-b1ZLs9tpp

Hill, H. (1999). Indonesia in crisis. Unpublished draft postscript for the second edition of The Indonesian Economy since 1966. Cambridge University Press.

Hill, H. (2001a). Small and medium enterprises. *Indonesia Asian Survey*, *41*(2), 248–270.

Hill, H. (2001b). Small and medium enterprises in Indonesia: Old policy challenges for a new administration. *Asian Survey*, *41*(2), 248–270.

Humphrey, J. (2009). *Are exporters in Africa facing reduced availability of trade finance* (Unpublished research Paper). Institute of Development Studies.

ILO. (2020a). *COVID-19 and the world of work: Impact and policy responses. ILO Monitor* (1st ed.). International Labour Organization.

ILO. (2020b). *COVID-19 and the world of work: Updated estimates and analysis. ILO Monitor* (2nd ed.). International Labour Organization.

ILO. (2020c). *COVID-19: Protecting workers in the workplace.* Geneva: International Labour Organization. Available online: https://www.ilo.org/global/about-the-ilo/newsroom/news/WCMS_738742/lang–en/index.htm

ILO. (2020d). MSME Day 2020: the COVID -19 pandemic and its impact on small business. Geneva: International Labor Office. Available online: file:///D:/FILE%20FEB%202018/FILE%2001%20FEB%202018/DIKTI/BKD/

Jellinek, L., & Rustanto, B. (1999). Survival strategies of the Javanese during the economic crisis. Consultancy Report to the World Bank.

Jovanovikj, B., & Georgievska, L. (2015). Transmission Channels of the Global Economic Crisis: Micro Evidence for Macedonia. *Journal of Contemporary Economic and Business Issues*, *2*(1), 5–20.

KB. (2020). *Daftar Usaha yang Bisa Jadi Pilihan di Tengah Pandemi Virus Corona*. KumparanBISNIS. Available online: https://kumparan.com/kumparanbisnis/daftar-usaha-yang-bisa-jadi-pilihan-di-tengah-pandemi-virus-corona-1tDiIgDLASf/full.

Khor, N., & Sebastian, I. (2009). *Exports and the global crisis: Still alive, though not quite kicking yet.* ADB Economics Working Paper Series No. 190. Manila: Asian Development Bank.

Kim, J., Kim, J., Lee, S. K., & Tang, L. (2020). Effects of epidemic disease outbreaks on financial performance of restaurants: Event study method approach. *Journal of Hospitality and Tourism Management*, *43*, 32–41.

Kompas. (2020a). *Industri Terimbas*. Jakarta: Kompas Newspaper.

Kompas. (2020b). *Industri Terpukul Covid-19*. Jakarta: Kompas Newspaper.

Kompas. (2020c). *Peluang Memanfaatkan Lonjakan Pengunjung Laman E-dagang*. Jakarta: Kompas Newspaper.

Kompas. (2020d). *Jumlah Korban PHK Terus Bertambah*. Jakarta: Kompas Newspaper.

Kompas. (2020e). *Stabilitas Sosial Dijaga*. Jakarta: Kompas Newspaper.

Musa, A. (1998). A study on access to credit for small and medium enterprises (SMEs) in Indonesia before and during the economic crisis (1997–1998). Study prepared for the Asia Foundation and the United States Agency for International Development.

Mustafa, R., & Mansor, S. A. (1999). *Malaysia's financial crisis and contraction of human resource: Policies and lessons for SMIs*. Paper presented at the APEC Human Resource Management Symposium on SMEs, Kaoshiung.

Nguanbanchong, A. (2009). *Feminized recession impact of global economic crisis on women in Southeast Asia*. Paper presented at the seminar on Gender and the Economic Crisis: Impact and Responses, Oxford, UK.

Nurzaman. (2020). *Dampak Wabah Covid-19 UMKM (Usaha Micro Kecil Menengah) Banyak Gulung Tikar*. Available online: https://kicaunews.com/2020/04/07/dampak-wabah-covid-19-umkm-usaha-micro-kecil-menengah-banyak-gulung-tikar/

OECD. (2020a). *Coronavirus (COVID-19): SME Policy Responses*. Organisation for Economic Co-operation and Development.

OECD. (2020b). *Evaluating the initial impact of COVID-19 containment measures on economic activity*. OECD Policy Responses to Coronavirus (Covid-19). Available online: https://www.oecd.org/coronavirus/policy responses/evaluating-the-initial-impact-of-covid-19-containment- measures-on-economic-activity/

Pasadilla, G. O. (2010). *Financial Crisis, Trade Finance, and SMEs: Case of Central Asia*. ADBI Working Paper Series, No. 187. January. Tokyo: ADB Institute.

Pearson, R., & Sweetman, C. (Eds.). (2011). *Gender and the Economic Crisis*. OXAM.

Priyambada, Suryahadi, & Sumarto. (2005). *What Happened to Child Labor in Indonesia during the Economic Crisis: The Trade-off between School and Work*. Jakarta: SMERU Research Institute.

Rahman, R. (2020). 37,000 SMEs hit by COVID-19 crisis as government prepares aid. *The Jakarta Post*. Available online: https://www.thejakartapost.com/news/2020/04/16/37000-smes-hit-by-covid-19-crisis-as-governmentprepares-aid.html

Rashid, S., & Ratten, V. (2021). Entrepreneurial ecosystems during COVID-19: The survival of small businesses using dynamic capabilities. *World Journal of Entrepreneurship, Management and Sustainable Development, 17*(1).

Régnier, P. (2005). The East Asian financial crisis in Thailand: Distress and resilience of local SMEs. In C. Harvie & B.-C. Lee (Eds.), *Sustaining growth and performance in East Asia*. Edward Elgar.

Sandee, H., Andadari, R. K., & Sulandjari, S. (2000). Small firm development during good times and bad: The Jepara furniture industry. In C. Manning & P. Dierman (Eds.), *Indonesia in transition: Social aspects of reformasi and crisis*. Indonesia Assessment Series. Research School of Pacific and Asian Studies. Australian National University Canberra and Institute of Southeast Asian Studies.

Santoso, Y. I. (2020). *Menghitung dampak Covid19 terhadap dunia usaha hingga UMKM*. Available online: https://nasional.kontan.co.id/news/menghitungdampak-covid-19-terhadap-dunia-usahahinggaumkm?page=all

Sato, Y. (2000). How did the crisis affect small and medium-sized enterprises? From a field study of the metal working industry in Java. *The Developing Economies*, *38*(4), 572–595.

Setyowati, D. (2020). *Siasat Empat UMKM Bertahan di Tengah Pandemi Corona*. Available online: https:// katadata.co.id/berita/2020/04/20/siasat-empat-umkm-bertahan-di-tengah-pandemi-corona

Shafi, M., Liu, J., & Ren, W. (2020). Impact of COVID-19 pandemic on micro, small, and medium-sized Enterprises operating in Pakistan. *Research in Globalization*, *2*, 1-14. Available online: https://www.science direct.com/science/ article/pii/S2590051X20300071?via%3Dihub

Shakil, M. H., Munim, Z. H., Tasnia, M., & Sarowar, S. (2020). COVID-19 and the environment: A critical review and research agenda. *Science of the Total Environment*, 745. doi:https://doi.org/ 10.1016/ j.scitotenv.2020.141022

Shin & Kim. (2015). Liquidity and credit risk before and after the global financial crisis: Evidence from the Korean corporate bond market. *Pacific-Basin Finance Journal*, *33*, 38-61.

SMERU. (2009). *Monitoring the socioeconomic impact of the 2008/2009 global financial crisis in Indonesia. Media Monitoring No.04/FS/2009. November*. SMERU Research Institute.

Sundari, L. S. (2020). *Dampak Pandemi Covid-19, Omzet UMKM di Kota Cimahi Turun 80 Persen*. Available online: https://www.galamedianews.com/?arsip=254042&judul=dampak-pandemi-covid-19-omzet-umkm-di-kota-cimahi-turun-80-persen

Suryahadi, A., Al Izzati, R., & Suryadarma, D. (2020). *The Impact of COVID-19 Outbreak on Poverty: An Estimation for Indonesia*. SMERU Working Paper. Jakarta: SMERU Research Institute.

Tambunan, T. (1998). *Impact of East Asia currency crisis and economic development on Indonesia's SMEs and priorities for adjustment*. Paper prepared for the SME Resourcing Conference, ASEAN Chamber of Commerce And Industry, Jakarta.

Tambunan, T. (2010a). The Indonesian experience with two big economic crises. *Modern Economy*, *1*, 156–167.

Tambunan, T. (2010b). *Global Economic Crisis and ASEAN Economy. Theory and Empirical Findings*. Lambert Academic Publishing.

Tambunan, T. (2011). The impact of the 2008-2009 global economic crisis on a developing country's economy: Studies from Indonesia. *Journal of Business and Economics*, 2(3), 175–197.

Tambunan, T. (2019). The impact of the economic crisis on micro, small, and medium enterprises and their crisis mitigation measures in Southeast Asia with reference to Indonesia. *Asia & the Pacific Policy Studies*, *6*(1), 1–21.

Tambunan, T. (2020). *Dampak dari Covid-19 Terhadap UMKM*. Focus Group Discussion. Sigmaphi.

Tambunan, T., & Busneti, I. (2016). The Indonesian experience with two big financial crisis and their impacts on micro, small and medium enterprises. *Asian Research Journal of Business Management*, *3*(4), 83–100.

Tecson, G. (1999). Present status and prospects of supporting industries in the Philippines. In *Present status and prospects of supporting industries in ASEAN (I): Philippines—Indonesia*. Institute of Developing Economies. Japan External Trade Organization.

UNCTAD. (2020a). *The Covid-19 shock to developing countries: Towards a "whatever it takes" programme for the two-thirds of the world's population being left behind*. Geneva: *United Nations Conference on Trade and Development*.

UNCTAD. (2020b). *Investment trends monitor: Impact of the coronavirus outbreak on global FDI*. Geneva: *United Nations Conference on Trade and Development*.

UNDP. (2020a). *Assessment report on impact of COVID-19 pandemic on Chinese enterprises*. United Nations Development Programme.

UNDP. (2020b). *COVID-19: Looming crisis in developing countries threatens to devastate economies and ramp up inequality*. United Nations Development Programme.

UNICEF. (2009). *A Matter of Magnitude. The Impact of the Economic Crisis on Women and Children in South Asia*. Kathmandu: United Nations Children's Fund. Regional Office South Asia. Available online: https://www.unicef.org/infobycountry/files/amatterofmagnitude.pdf

Wengel, ter J., & Rodriguez, E. (2006). SME export performance in Indonesia after the crisis. *Small Business Economics*, *26*, 25– 37.

Wie, T. K. (2000). The impact of the economic crisis on Indonesia's manufacturing sector. *The Developing Economies*, *38*(4), 420–453.

Wiradi, G. (1998). *Rural Java in a time of crisis: With special reference to Curug village, Cirebon, West Java*. Paper presented at The Economic Crisis and Social Security in Indonesia, Berg-en-Dal, The Netherlands.

World Bank. (2009). *The Financial Crisis: Charting a Global Recovery*. Available online: https://www.worldbank.org/en/news/feature/2009/06/22/the-financial-crisis-charting-a-global-recovery

ADDITIONAL READING

Alves, J. C., Lok, T. C., Luo, Y., & Hao, W. (2020). Crisis Management for Small Business during the COVID-19 Outbreak: Survival, Resilience and Renewal Strategies of Firms in Macau. Research Article. Available online: doi:10.21203/rs.3.rs-34541/v1

Brown, R. (2020). The Impact of Covid-19 on Scottish Small and Medium-Sized Enterprises (SMEs): Prognosis and Policy Prescription. Economic Commentary. June. University of St Andrews. Available online: https://www.researchgate.net/publication/342448155_The_Impact_of_Covid-19_on_Scottish_Small_and_Medium-_Sized_Enterprises_SMEs_Prognosis_and_Policy_Prescription

Leprince-Rinquet, D. (2020). Pivot, not panic: How startups are coping with the coronavirus crisis. ZDNeT. Available online: https://www.zdnet.com/article/pivot-not-panic-how-startups-are-coping-with-the-corona virus-crisis/

Lu, X., Zhang, L., and Du, H. (2020). SARS-CoV-2 Infection in Children. *The New England Journal of Medicine*, 382, 1663-1665. . doi:10.1056/NEJMc2005073

Manning, H. H. (2020). A she-cession? Women hit hardest during COVID-19 downturn. The Hill. Available online: https://thehill.com/opinion/civil-rights/500220-a-she-cession-women-hit-hardestduring-covid-19-downturn

OECD. (2020). Women at the core of the fight against COVID-19 crisis. Available online; https://www.oecd.org/coronavirus/policy-responses/women-atthe-core-of-the-fight-against-covid-19-crisis-553a8269/

KEY TERMS AND DEFINITIONS

Economic Crisis: The wild fluctuations, outside the acceptable limits of change, in the prices or supplies of commodities. Economic crisis is usually seen as a situation in which the economy of a country experiences a sudden downturn in its aggregate output or real gross domestic product (GDP). The result of the economic crisis is a decline in real income per capita and an increase in unemployment and poverty.

Pandemic: An epidemic of an infectious disease that has spread across a large region or worldwide, affecting a substantial number of people. A widespread endemic disease with a stable number of infected people is not a pandemic.

Small business: A privately owned corporation, partnership, or sole proprietorship that has fewer employees and less annual revenue than a corporation or regular-sized business. Small business is usually represented by micro-and small-sized enterprises (MSEs). In Indonesia, MSEs are enterprises without employees (called self-employment) and with 1 to 19 workers.

Transmission Channel of an Economic Crisis: A path over which an economic crisis has affected macroeconomic and social variables such as production volume, real income per capita, prices, export, import, employment, income distribution, and poverty. electrical signals can pass; "a channel is typically what you rent from a telephone company" channel. transmission - communication by means of transmitted signals.

Chapter 2
Impact, Reaction, and Learning From Overcoming the COVID-19 Crisis:
Cases From Small-Scale Businesses in Bangladesh

Saptarshi Dhar
https://orcid.org/0000-0003-0435-1855
Jahangirnagar University, Bangladesh

Tahira Farzana
Jahangirnagar University, Bangladesh

Sabiha Saju Ibne Abedin
Jahangirnagar University, Bangladesh

EXECUTIVE SUMMARY

The COVID-19 pandemic has created devastating consequences for all businesses globally, including the small businesses in Bangladesh. The small business sector in Bangladesh is a key driver of its economic growth and has been hit particularly hard by the pandemic due to its pre-existing vulnerabilities and lower resilience to crisis. This chapter investigates the impact of COVID-19 on small-scale businesses, their subsequent response measures, and learning experiences that have created a route to resilience. A qualitative investigation on six small-scale enterprises across manufacturing and service areas was included in the study. The cases covered fashion and clothing and organic food and beverage businesses. The findings of the study suggest that the impacts of the pandemic are primarily financial, operational and supply chain, and logistical in nature. The policymakers need to take urgent measures to ensure the sustainability of this sector amid the ongoing pandemic.

DOI: 10.4018/978-1-7998-7657-1.ch002

INTRODUCTION

The Sars-COV-2 virus outbreak and subsequent COVID-19 pandemic have created a substantial social, financial, and economic crisis for societies and nations worldwide. Business enterprises have suffered terrible damages in terms of demand loss (Alves et al., 2020; Shafi et al., 2020), disruptions in supply chain and logistics (Lu et al., 2020), order cancellations (Juergensen et al., 2020), among others. In the business landscape, small businesses have been hit particularly hard by the crisis due to their greater vulnerability to exogenous shocks (Bartik et al., 2020; Thorgren & Williams, 2020).

Small businesses act as drivers of economic growth, poverty reduction, and financial empowerment for many countries worldwide, including Bangladesh. In Bangladesh, small businesses create 11 percent of all non-farm jobs and 26.9 percent of total employment (Bangladesh Bureau of Statistics, 2015). These businesses are located all over the country and are involved in agriculture, fishing, manufacturing, service, wholesale, retail, and trade-based sectors, thereby bridging the urban-rural income gap. Small businesses are indispensable drivers of growth in developing economies and are incurring significant losses following the Covid-19 pandemic (Bartik et al., 2020). From natural disasters and diseases to economic recessions, small businesses have experienced a severe trajectory across the world (Obrenovic et al., 2020). Although some businesses have shown resilience in adapting to the 'new normal' operating environments, almost all the industries faced lockdowns for months, significant reductions in consumption, and closure of the businesses (Gregurec et al., 2021). Small businesses across the agriculture, manufacturing, service, wholesale, retail, trade, and tourism sectors have been severely damaged by the preventive health measures imposed by local and national authorities (Kukanja et al., 2020). Financial and economic problems include scarcity of additional raw materials, product hygiene guarantee and environmental sanitation, financial instability, economic insecurity, job loss, and wage reduction (Irawan, 2020). Several reasons play a role in answering why small enterprises are more vulnerable to the crisis. First, small businesses are overexposed in sectors that were directly hit, such as tourism, retail, trade, and transportation. Second, as compared to the large companies, small businesses tend to have less cash in reserve and thus are more affected by human resource and capital underutilization. Third, small businesses are often more dependent on global and national supply chains, which were directly disrupted by the pandemic (Beglaryan & Shakhmuradyan, 2020). The crisis has established a necessity for small businesses to refurbish their operations and adapt resilience measures. The most effective strategy approaches adopted by small businesses as response measures include introducing work from home arrangements, paying higher salaries to employees working during the lockdown, shortening supply chains, shifting production, digitalizing and establishing online resource platforms, applying for government stimulus, and adhering to the latest guidance for businesses (Alves et al., 2020; Păunescu & Mátyus, 2020; Priyono et al., 2020). Other survival mechanisms include digital marketing, moving to smaller office space or shared space to save rent, staff number reduction, alternative day work arrangement, temporary pay cuts, reducing expenses on research and development, and hazard pay for frontline staff (Aladejebi, 2020; Thorgren & Williams, 2020). Widarti et al. (2020) state that small business owners must develop entrepreneurial knowledge, abilities, and strategic agility to improve business performance during times of crisis.

In Bangladesh, the current COVID-19 crisis and subsequent lockdown and social distancing measures put tremendous financial and economic pressures on these businesses. First, lockdown and mobility restriction measures disrupted the supply and logistics chain, creating disruptions in raw material procurement and product distribution. Second, mandatory business shutdown halted production activities while fixed costs such as salary, rent, and utilities accrued, creating liquidity issues. Third, social distancing measures and overall fear led to a decrease in revenue, especially for retail and service businesses such as restaurants and travel agencies. Additionally, small businesses experienced challenges in the form of temporary and permanent closure of business, layoffs, wage reductions, and loan defaults (Kader & Pattanayak, 2021). In terms of business characteristics, fashion and clothing, retail, wholesale and urban-based businesses had the worst impact, whereas agriculture, fishing, and rural-based small firms were the least affected (Kader & Pattanayak, 2021). As a response, small businesses primarily focused on optimizing costs through halting all marketing, rent, distribution, operation, and salary expenses (Light-Castle Analytics Wing, 2020). Although digital adoption is proven to be a viable means of response to the crisis (Guo et al., 2020), the lack of digital connectivity and skills makes digitalization challenging for small businesses in Bangladesh.

Therefore, this chapter demands an overall situational analysis of the small business landscape in Bangladesh in the context of the COVID-19 crisis. To explore the impact, response actions, and lessons learned by the small business entrepreneurs in Bangladesh to combat the effects of the pandemic, first, this chapter focuses on exploring two key issues: the COVID-19 pandemic situation in Bangladesh, followed by an exploration of small-scale business definitions and an overview of the small-scale business sector in Bangladesh. Second, the chapter investigates the constraints, and challenges of small businesses worldwide, followed by the challenges of COVID-19 on these firms at a global level. Third, cases from manufacturing and service-based small-scale businesses in Bangladesh are explored to identify the impact, response measures, and strategies developed and adopted by the small business entrepreneurs who sustained their businesses through the outbreak. Sector-specific effects and survival measures are explored to identify commonalities across manufacturing and service-based small businesses. Additionally, this section discusses the small business entrepreneurs' learning experiences and how the learnings shape their future business plans, followed by the conclusion, recommendations, and future direction for research.

METHODOLOGY

This chapter follows a combination of exploratory and descriptive study, emphasizing the exploratory side to explore the impact, subsequent reactions, and learning experiences of entrepreneurs engaged in the manufacturing and service-based small businesses in Bangladesh during COVID-19. The research design follows a qualitative research approach using the multiple case study method (Eisenhardt, 1989; Eisenhardt & Graebner, 2007). The case study method is considered one of the most effective methodologies when investigating a current phenomenon across multiple disciplines (Yin, 2017). It also explores a specific situation with a deeper understanding (Wellner & Pierce-Friedman, 2019). The cases were selected following theoretical sampling technique (Glaser & Strauss, 2017) and businesses that fulfilled the following criteria: a) operating as a small scale enterprise as per Bangladesh Bank definition, b) operating in either manufacturing or service industry, and c) operating for at least three years. Individual cases were constructed with the aid of narrative instrumental design. Interview instruments included semi-structured in-depth interview protocols. Interviews were conducted from February – March 2021 and administered online with the entrepreneurs engaged in manufacturing and service-oriented small businesses. The names of the respondents and the respective businesses have been changed to maintain the anonymity of the participants (Table 1).

Table 1. Summary of Case Participants

Case	Rainbow	Healthy Choice	Handloom House	Bhalo Jinish	Protidin	Green Mart
Main Products	Handcrafted fashion and clothing	Homemade organic food and beverage	Handloom fashion and clothing	Organic food and beverage	Organic food and beverage	Organic food and beverage
Target Market	National	Local	National	Local	Local	Local
Founded	2016	2015	2015	2019	2017	2016
Industry	Manufacturing	Manufacturing	Manufacturing	Service	Service	Service
Sales Channel	F-commerce	F-commerce	F-commerce, retail and wholesale	F-commerce and retail	E-commerce	E-commerce and retail
Respondent	Owner-manager	Owner-manager	Owner-manager	Owner-manager	Owner-manager	Owner-manager

COVID-19 PANDEMIC SITUATION IN BANGLADESH

Bangladesh is a densely populated lower-middle income developing country in South Asia that faced a significant health and economic crisis due to the emergence and spread of the coronavirus pandemic. The 1st case of COVID-19 in Bangladesh was reported on March 8, 2020. To limit the spread and infection, the Government of Bangladesh (GOB) declared a 10 day "general holiday" for all public and private institutions from March 26, 2020, to April 4, 2020 (The Daily Star, 2020). During this period, transportation and mobility restrictions were put in place except for emergency services. All businesses were shut down, barring essential services such as pharmacies and groceries. After the initial 10-day period, lockdown and social distancing measures were extended till May 30, 2020. Concurrently, local demands declined due to the outbreak and subsequent lockdown measures, and businesses reduced their production and operation to minimize loss, specifically the manufacturing concerns (Siddiquee & Faruk, 2020). Small enterprises were temporarily closed during the period of the lockdown and operated at partial capacity after restrictions were gradually lifted. An IFC survey found that businesses involved in fashion and clothing were hit hardest; most firms lost their sales, employees lost jobs, and a cash flow crisis was imminent (Kader & Pattanayak, 2021). However, the survey also found that small businesses fared better in adopting digital platforms than micro and medium enterprises.

The country adopted policies following WHO guidelines to limit rapid community transmission. The policies implemented include face masks, social distancing, mobility restrictions, and the use of hygiene products. On October 25, 2020, GOB imposed a "No mask no service" policy for all public organizations to tackle the pandemic's second wave. Additionally, a mandatory face mask rule was enacted for all offices, malls, courts, government establishments, and social gatherings (Dhaka Tribune, 2020). However, though the government adopted policies to help build awareness and limit the spread, a significant portion of the population have either poor knowledge or are misinformed about the transmission, symptoms, and incubation time of the coronavirus (Farhana & Mannan, 2020). Since the lifting of lockdown measures, promoting social distancing has been the primary strategy to control virus spread. While all business and other activities resumed normal activities, ensuring social distancing among a population so densely located became the principal challenge. In addition to the socio-cultural factors (travel during religious holidays and gatherings at weddings and cultural festivals), the socio-economic milieu of the country posed further complexities in ensuring that social distancing protocols are adhered to.

Macroeconomic variables of the country showed negative growth as a consequence of the pandemic (Table 2). The World Bank (2021) states that Bangladesh experienced a sharp growth in GDP that was as high as 8.2 percent in FY 2019, where manufacturing and service sectors contributed to 4.1 percent and 3.4 percent to GDP, respectively. The fallout of the pandemic decelerated a sharp fall in GDP, falling to an estimated 2.4 percent in FY 2020. The contribution of manufacturing and service sectors fell sharply to 0.4 percent and 1.7 percent in FY 2020, respectively. However, a rebound is expected in FY 2021 for Bangladesh (The World Bank, 2020). The outbreak and the subsequent healthcare burden coupled with the loss of employment accelerated the unemployment levels in FY 2020. According to ILO estimates, unemployment as a percentage of the total labor force rose to 5.3 percent in FY 2020 from 4.22 percent in FY 2019 (ILO, 2021).

Table 2. Macroeconomic Indicators

	FY 2014	FY 2015	FY 2016	FY 2017	FY 2018	FY 2019	FY 2020e
GDP Growth	6.1	6.6	7.1	7.3	7.9	8.2	2.4
Unemployment	4.39	4.38	4.35	4.37	4.29	4.22	5.3

Source: (The World Bank, 2021); e=estimated

In terms of poverty, unemployment, and loss of livelihood caused poverty to increase in FY 2020. 24.5 million new poor now constitute a part of the total population as of March 2021 (Dhaka Tribune, 2021), with the poverty rate increasing from 20 percent in 2019 to 42 percent by the end of 2020 (Raihan, 2021).

As of April 12, 2021, a total of 691,957 COVID-19 cases have been confirmed by RT-PCR, GeneXpert, and Rapid Antigen tests and 9,822 related deaths (DGHS Press Release, 2021). WHO places Bangladesh among the top 33 countries in COVID-19 cases accounting for 0.49 percent of all cases worldwide (World Health Organization, 2021).

On February 7, 2021, Bangladesh started its inoculation drive with the AstraZeneca-Oxford vaccine in Dhaka and the rest of the country. According to Our World in Data, as of April 11, 2021, the country has vaccinated (1st dose) at least 5.82 million people, ahead of Sweden, Singapore, and South Korea (Our World in Data, 2021).

DEFINITION OF SMALL BUSINESS

Typically, small businesses around the world are engaged in a wide variety of industries, such as agriculture, fisheries, animal husbandry, forestry, manufacturing, wholesale, retail, construction, hospitality, transportation and warehousing, software and IT, real estate, mining, and quarrying, oil, and gas extraction, utility services, information services, finance and insurance, professional and technical services, education, health care, and social assistance, arts and entertainment, and food. There is no uniform definition or classification for small businesses around the world for a sector with such variety in industry and business focus (Table 3). Instead, the classifications vary from country to country in terms of criteria such as industry, number of employees, turnover, size of business, and assets and investments (Dangayach & Deshmukh, 2005).

Table 3. Summary of Small Business Criteria for Different Countries

Country	Small Business Classification Criteria
USA	• Business Size: $1 million to $41.5 million • Employees: 100-1500
UK	• Turnover: < £6.5 million • Balance Sheet Total: < £3.26 million • Employees: < 50 employees
EU	• Turnover: £ 8.2 Million • Balance Sheet Total: £ 8.2 Million • Employees: <50
Australia	• Employees: 5-19
France	• Turnover: < EUR 50 Million • Employees: 10-249
Canada	• Employees: 1-99
China	• Employees: 5 or more • Operating Income: > 50 million RMB
Indonesia	• Net assets: IDR 50 million - IDR 500 million • Annual revenue: IDR 300 million - IDR 2.5 billion • Employees: 5-19
Malaysia	• Employees: > 5 to < 75 • Sales Turnover: > RM300,000 to < RM15 million
India	• Investment in Plant and Machinery or Equipment: < Rs.10 crore • Annual Turnover: < Rs. 50 crores

Source: (Australian Bureau of Statistics, 2020; Government of Canada, 2020; Insee, 2019; Ministry of Micro, Small and Medium Enterprises, 2020; OECD, 2016, 2018; SME Corporation Malaysia, 2020; UCL, 2021; U.S. Small Business Administration, 2019)

SMALL SCALE BUSINESSES IN BANGLADESH: AN OVERVIEW

Small businesses are an indispensable part of the economic growth of an emerging economy such as Bangladesh. The small business sector contributes 20.25 percent of GDP growth (Khalil, 2020). This sector is highly labor-intensive and contributes to eradicating poverty, promoting gender equality and women empowerment through employment generation (Bangladesh Bank, 2010). According to the 2013 economic census, there are a total of 859,318 small enterprises in Bangladesh, accounting for 11 percent of total business enterprises (Bangladesh Bureau of Statistics, 2015). Among the small enterprises, 61.80 percent are involved in trading and related businesses, followed by 29.32 percent involved in service-based activities. Only 3.59 percent of small businesses belong to manufacturing ones. Additionally, 26.9 percent of all employment is generated by these businesses. It should also be noted that the majority of small enterprises are informal (95.5 percent), meaning these are not registered under any government authority (The World Bank Group, 2019).

Small businesses have been working as a backbone of Bangladesh's economy by generating employment for its population. Despite its contribution, there was no uniform definition of micro, small and medium enterprises (MSMEs) in Bangladesh until 2016. Since 2003, there have been many definitions and classifications for MSMEs that are contradictory to each other and have a different basis for classification. For example, in the 2003 economic census, full-time employment was adopted as the singular basis for classification (Table 4). In contrast, in the 2010 industrial policy, the Ministry of Industry used fixed assets (other than land and buildings) and the number of employees as its basis (Table 5). In 2011, Bangladesh Bank followed a similar definition to that of the industrial policy; however, it changed the parameters to service, business, and industrial concern from service and manufacturing concern used in the industrial policy previously (Table 6). Later, some consistency in the definition and classification was achieved when the 2013 economic census followed the definition of the 2010 industrial policy. Finally, in 2016, the industrial policy adopted a revised definition and classification for MSMEs (Table 7) that was later adapted by Bangladesh Bank accordingly (Table 6). This definition is now considered a unified definition for MSMEs at all levels.

Table 4. Definition under 2003 Economic Census

Type of Firm	Number of Employees
Small	10-49

Source: (Economic Census, 2003)

Table 5. Definition under Bangladesh Industrial Policy, 2010

Type of Enterprise		Total Fixed Assets (Excluding Land and Factory Buildings)	Total Number of Employees
Small	Service	BDT 500,000 to 10 million	10-25
	Manufacturing	BDT 5 to 100 million	25-99

Source: (Doing Business 2018, International Finance Corporation)

Table 6. Definition under Bangladesh Bank, 2011

Type of Enterprise		Sector Fixed Asset (other than Land and Buildings)	Employed Manpower
Small	Service	BDT 50,000 – 5,000,000	25
	Business	BDT 50,000 – 5,000,0000	25
	Industrial	BDT 50,000 – 15,000,000	50

Source: (Bangladesh Bank, 2011)

Table 7. Unified Definition Adopted under the Bangladesh Industrial Policy, 2016

Type of Industry		Amount of Investment in Tk (Replacement Cost and Value of Fixed Assets, excluding Land and Factory Buildings)	Number of Employed Workers
Small	Manufacturing	BDT 7.5 to 150 million	31-120
	Service	BDT 1 to 20 million	16-50

Source: (National Industrial Policy, Government of Bangladesh, 2016)

Several government agencies are responsible for formulating policies, strategies and development activities, and supervision for small enterprises in the country. These are Ministry of Industry, SME Foundation, Bangladesh Small and Cottage Industries Corporation (BSCIC), Bangladesh Industrial Technical Assistant Centre, Ministry of Commerce, Business Promotion Council, Palli Karma Sahayak Foundation (PKSF), Bangladesh Council of Scientific and Industrial Research, and Bangladesh Bank.

SMALL SCALE BUSINESSES AROUND THE WORLD: AN OVERVIEW

Challenges and Constraints of Small Businesses

Small businesses cover a broad spectrum of industries and play a significant role in developed and developing economies. Regardless, small business entrepreneurs still struggle to build an enterprise, hire the right people, develop a customer base, and move forward with the business with proper entrepreneurial knowledge and skills (Psaltopoulos et al., 2005).

While rural and urban businesses differ in terms of diversity of characteristics, attitudes, and backgrounds, rural entrepreneurs tend to face more obstacles than their urban counterparts (Psaltopoulos et al., 2005). Rural small businesses tend to have less access to advice and support from the business web and do not benefit from the knowledge spillovers followed by the unavailability of financing options, thereby placing these entrepreneurs at a distinct disadvantage to raise capital and attract equity investment (Lamb & Sherman, 2010). The cash management challenges faced by small business owners across the world include lack of cash budgeting and bank accounts, poor cash management practices, cash flow difficulties, constraints in obtaining loans, bad debts, inventory control challenges, debtors' payments, creditors' payments, and more (Miglo, 2020; Mungal & Garbharran, 2014). It is a widespread phenomenon among the small businesses where they have minimal access to outside equity, most of which takes the form of difficulties in acquiring equity or the reluctance on the managers' part to raise equity when debt is available; access to organized equity markets leading to higher trading costs and flotation costs (Alauddin & Chowdhury, 2015; Bosri, 2016; Pettit & Singer, 1985). Small businesses often fall short on assets that make it hard for businesses to find a no-collateral business loan (Berger & Udell, 1998).

Along with financial drawbacks, small business entrepreneurs face work-related psychological stress, resulting in high costs for businesses and the economy (Andalib, 2020; Fernet et al., 2016). Traditionally, while large enterprises can minimize cost and achieve economies of scale through mass production and attain location economies via international production, small businesses miss out on such opportunities (Callaway, 2004). According to a study conducted on the South African small business sector, the constraints faced by the small businesses include legal and regulatory problems, access to markets, affordable finance and business premises, acquisition of skills and managerial expertise, quality of business infrastructure, access to technology and tax burden (Andrei et al., 2021; Zhu et al., 2011). The study suggests that the challenges are especially tough for women entrepreneurs and those living in rural areas (Tengeh, 2013). Existing literature (Table 8) focuses on the financing challenges of the small businesses where they cannot access the capital market or make an IPO or take bank loans like the giant firms. With all these challenges at hand, studies also show that financing opportunities in the form of venture capitals, excellent entrepreneur-investor relationships, and accessibility to crowdfunding platforms have been proven to support small businesses overcome obstacles (Herciu, 2017).

Table 8. Summary of Challenges for Small Businesses

Challenges Identified in Small Business Literature	References
Access to Finance	(Bosri, 2016); (Pettit & Singer, 1985); (Alauddin & Chowdhury, 2015)
Cash Management	(Mungal & Garbharran, 2014)
Collateral-based Loans	(Berger & Udell, 1998); (Mungal & Garbharran, 2014)
Inadequate Scale Advantage	(Bosri, 2016); (Callaway, 2004)
Inadequate Funds	(Alauddin & Chowdhury, 2015)
Access to Institutional Credits and Bad Debts	(Miglo, 2020); (Rahman et al., 2018)
Capital and Equity Investment	(Herciu, 2017); (Lamb & Sherman, 2010); (Miglo, 2020)
Cash Flow/Liquidity constraints	(Mungal & Garbharran, 2014)
Modes of Payment Preference and Payment System Security	(Meng et al., 2021); (Rahman et al., 2018)
Work-related Psychological Stress	(Andalib, 2020); (Fernet et al., 2016); (Schreibauer et al., 2020)
Access to Markets	(Andrei et al., 2021); (Deakins & Freel, 1998); (Herciu, 2017); (Tengeh, 2013); (Zhu et al., 2011)
Unaffordable Finance and Business Premises	
Inadequate Skills and Managerial Expertise	
Tax Burden	
Quality of Business Infrastructure	
Access to Information and Technology	(Meng et al., 2021); (Rahman et al., 2018)
Access to Advice and Support	(Deakins & Freel, 1998); (Lamb & Sherman, 2010); (Psaltopoulos et al., 2005)
Lack of Entrepreneurial Knowledge	
Managerial Inexperience	(Andalib, 2020); (Andalib & Halim, 2019); (Gomezelj Omerzel & Antončič, 2008); (Islam & Miajee, 2018)
Lack of Innovation Performance	
Increased Production Costs	
Employee Rights	

Source: Authors' compilation from the literature

A vibrant small business sector works as a vital driving force in the development of an emerging economy such as Bangladesh. It is estimated that the small business industry employs 70-80 percent of the non-agricultural workforce in the country (Asian Development Bank, 2012). Small businesses include restaurants, cottage, retail, manufacturing, dairy, knitting, agriculture, fishing, construction, transport, storage and communication, real estate, renting, education, health, social work, and food (Chowdhury et al., 2013). Similar to the global small business scenario, the primary constraint faced by the small businesses in Bangladesh is access to finance that gives rise to many other challenges such as insufficient funds, high cost and limited source of financing, collateral requirement, technological barriers, infrastructural difficulties, lack of entrepreneurial knowledge, lack of cash resources and access to information (Deakins & Freel, 1998; Islam & Miajee, 2018). Other than financial challenges, the growth of small businesses are deterred by the unfavorable business environment, regulatory and legal issues, local and global competition from established companies, managerial inexperience, lack of innovation performance, and increased production costs (Andalib, 2020; Andalib & Halim, 2019; Deakins & Freel, 1998; Gomezelj et al., 2008).

The journey of small businesses in Bangladesh and their growth has not been straightforward; the adoption of technology and open innovation plays a vital role in this regard. Small businesses may utilize open innovation by adopting new technology and collaborating with numerous horizontal research and development collaborators that provide a wide range of potential innovation outcomes (Meng et al., 2021). The scarcity of institutional credit access acts as one of the most significant constraints to small business growth in Bangladesh. Due to their small size and lack of technical proficiency, businesses fail to possess enough assets to offer acceptable collateral to the lending agencies. But in recent years, a significant boom in online businesses has been noticed where the internet-based or click and order business model has replaced the traditional brick and mortar one (Rahman et al., 2018). Traditional small businesses are providing services online, and this has been driven by the ICT infrastructure development, online payment systems, and the internet penetration rate in Bangladesh. This transition is not without challenges either; modes of payment preference and payment system security are the most common challenges for businesses and customers (Meng et al., 2021; Rahman et al., 2018).

Challenges of Small Scale Businesses amid the COVID-19 Crisis

COVID-19 pandemic has created a devastating impact on businesses of all sizes and across all sectors, including small businesses. Small firms were already vulnerable to various internal and external factors and survived on thin margins (Kader & Pattanayak, 2021) in pre-pandemic periods. The pandemic-driven government measures such as lockdown, social distancing, quarantine, isolation, work from home, closure of workplaces, mobility restrictions created severe distress for small firms leading to business closures, demand reduction, job loss, and cash flow crisis. A report from US Census Bureau showed that 78 percent of small businesses are experiencing adverse shocks after one year of the outbreak (Marroquin, 2021). Furthermore, a survey by Small Business Majority (2021) found that the pandemic's adverse effects are disproportionate, meaning the setbacks are significantly worse for small businesses owned by women and people of color. For example, a report by ITC finds that COVID-19 strongly affected 64 percent of female-owned businesses compared to 52 percent male-owned businesses (ITC, 2020). In the United Kingdom, 7 percent of small and medium enterprises have either permanently shut down or are on the verge of collapsing (Opinium Research, 2020). Small firms are facing distress in generating sales and paying operational expenses due to the supply and demand shock caused by the pandemic – rendering the firms financially vulnerable (European Investment Bank, 2020). To survive and overcome the financial uncertainty and insolvency, small businesses are forced to seek government aid in the form of incentives, tax relief, stimulus packages, and subsidies (Cook & Barrett, 2020).

Literature on the effects of COVID-19 on small businesses indicate that the impact of the pandemic has been predominantly negative for small firms (Table 9): a scarcity of raw materials (Irawan, 2020; Priyono et al., 2020), restrictions on business hours (Priyono et al., 2020), cancellation of orders (Juergensen et al., 2020; Priyono et al., 2020), liquidity shortage (Bartik et al., 2020; Juergensen et al., 2020; Lu et al., 2020; Priyono et al., 2020), supply chain and logistics disruption (Kuckertz et al., 2020; Priyono et al., 2020; Shafi et al., 2020), high production cost (Lutfi et al., 2020), labor shortage (Dai et al., 2020), job termination (Bartik et al., 2020; Thorgren & Williams, 2020) and breach of contract (Dai et al., 2020). To stay afloat, business owners changed business models, reduced wages and compensation, introduced new products, reformed HR policy, invested in technology and digitization, adopted health and safety protocols, reduced costs, and sought government aid (Alves et al., 2020). In contrast, others laid employees off, cut employee hours and temporarily closed business, and sold off business permanently, among other drastic measures.

Table 9. Summary of COVID-19 related challenges to small scale businesses

COVID-19 Related Challenges Identified in Literature	References
Minimize expenditure and operational costs	(Dai et al., 2020); (Vig & Agarwal, 2021)
Change in customer behavior and consumption	(Thukral, 2021); (Vig & Agarwal, 2021)
Maintaining social distancing at the workplace	(Vig & Agarwal, 2021)
Maintaining hygiene and sanitization	(Vig & Agarwal, 2021)
Reduced consumer spending/Drop in demand	(Dai et al., 2020); (Shafi et al., 2020); (Thukral, 2021)
Disruption in supply and logistics chain	(Dai et al., 2020); (Kuckertz et al., 2020); (Priyono et al., 2020); (Shafi et al., 2020); (Thukral, 2021)
Adoption of technology	(Akpan et al., 2020)
Shortage of raw materials	(Dai et al., 2020); (Irawan, 2020); (Priyono et al., 2020)
Restricted business hours	(Priyono et al., 2020)
Cancellation of orders	(Juergensen et al., 2020); (Priyono et al., 2020)
Shortage of liquidity/working capital	(Bartik et al., 2020); (Dai et al., 2020); (Juergensen et al., 2020); (Lu et al., 2020); (Priyono et al., 2020)
High cost of production	(Lutfi et al., 2020)
Employment termination	(Bartik et al., 2020); (Thorgren & Williams, 2020)

Source: Authors' compilation from the literature

IMPACT, RESPONSE AND LEARNING EXPERIENCE FROM COVID-19: CASE STUDIES

This section presents cases that have been developed based on the semi-structured in-depth interviews conducted with the entrepreneurs of manufacturing and service-based small-scale businesses in Bangladesh. These businesses are located across the country, both in and out of the capital city, Dhaka, and operate largely through online platforms. The online shopping space in Bangladesh is primarily dominated by f-commerce and e-commerce businesses involved in the grocery, food, and fashion segment (Islam, 2020). During the initial months of the pandemic, the e-commerce and f-commerce sector lost \$78.64 million in revenues (Islam, 2020; Sahoo et al., 2020). Expansion of mobile financial services, innovation, and diversification in online grocery and food businesses, however, led to a rapid recovery where online sales increased by 70-80 percent during July to September 2020, generating \$708.46 million revenue (Hasan, 2020; The Daily Star, 2020). While online grocers and food businesses thrived during the pandemic, small-scale online fashion and clothing businesses faced a massive disaster. The lockdown period coincided with several cultural and religious festivals in the country; all the investments made by the businesses in anticipation of festival sales generated almost no return (Islam, 2020).

The cases presented here describe the impact of the COVID-19 pandemic and subsequent government measures on small businesses and how they responded to the restrictions. Learning experiences from the owners have also been discussed.

Cases From Manufacturing Small Scale Businesses in Bangladesh

The cases described here include small businesses in the following areas: fashion and clothing and food and beverage. The summary of findings from the cases is presented in Table 10.

Case 1: Rainbow

Rainbow is an online fashion and clothing business offering handcrafted traditional Bengali clothing and home decoration pieces. Mollika started the business via Facebook in 2016, capitalizing on her designing and handicraft skills. The primary production hub is located in a rural area outside of Dhaka named Bogura. Deliveries are made all over the country through logistics partners.

After experiencing numerous ups and downs throughout the years, the business picked up a substantial spike in sales at the beginning of 2020. The revenue surge coincided with the outbreak of the COVID-19 pandemic and the enforcement of lockdown measures in Bangladesh. During the months of lockdown and the subsequent easing of it, Rainbow made sales of BDT 100,000 in about nine months in 2020.

Mollika attributes her success where many other fashion and clothing businesses struggled to a Facebook-based online community of female micro and small business owners. She became associated with the community in early 2020 and received business skill training arranged by the community leaders in addition to patronage and encouragement from fellow members.

Despite the success, COVID-19 did bring a multitude of problems to the business. First, lockdown and mobility restrictions made the sourcing of materials very difficult. Second, product delivery all over the country was suspended, creating challenges in distribution. Third, the sales opportunities during cultural and religious festivals (Bengali new year and Eid Ul Fitr) were missed as these coincided with the lockdown period.

In response, once measures were eased, Rainbow focused on a) designing new products, b) introducing new product lines (wedding collection), and c) offering exclusive collection at premium prices, d) expanding customer base to the Bengali communities living outside of Bangladesh.

Case 2: Healthy Choice

Healthy Choice is an f-commerce based online homemade organic food and beverage business operating within Dhaka metropolitan area. It offers seventy food and beverage items across three product categories: daily necessities, frozen items, and baby food. In the necessity category, product offerings include spices, butter, bread, cakes, buns, smoothie mixers, pickles, honey, tea, etc. Frozen items are cheeseballs, parathas, local traditional snacks, and baby food include cereals and custards. Healthy Choice promotes the concept of healthy and nutritious homemade food and beverage as its business positioning. It is primarily catered towards urban working families who prefer to purchase food online.

COVID-19 outbreak brought a positive impact on the business of online food and beverage producers in Bangladesh. Lockdown measures, business closures, mobility restrictions, and widespread fear of infection encouraged people to order food products online more than ever before. Healthy Choice experienced three times higher sales during the months of lockdown (March-May). The owner, Ulfat, stated that she hired additional delivery staff to assist with the increased order volume in addition to her usual logistics provider. According to her, she did not experience much difficulty running her operations during the crisis as food services were considered an essential business by the authorities. However, she experienced supply chain disruptions during the period, which led to an increase in the source materials' prices. Ulfat states she did not increase the price of products although production costs became high, leading to low profits. To help customers with cash shortages, she sold products on credit to promote customer loyalty.

After lockdown and mobility restrictions were lifted, Healthy Choice lost the high sales momentum. Ulfat lost the new customers she had gained, and the sales decrease continued till the end of 2020; however, it picked up again in the 1st quarter of 2021.

During the pandemic, Healthy Choice introduced two new categories of food products: frozen ready-to-cook snacks and spiced tea that were initially planned to be launched at the beginning of 2020. Ulfat states that the reasoning behind introducing new products was to bring back the lost customers she had gained during the lockdown period. She also offered promotional discounts and free delivery campaigns to boost sales during the sales slump.

Ulfat states that she learned two critical lessons from battling the pandemic: first, gaining and maintaining customer loyalty is crucial for survival, and second, positive word of mouth helps in bringing new customers.

Case 3: Handloom House

Established in 2015 by Lutfur, Handloom House is a fashion and clothing business that offers Bangladeshi traditional handloom weaved products. Its offerings primarily include handcrafted handloom-based fashion clothing for men and women. The clientele comprises B2B and B2C groups through f-commerce, wholesale and retail channels. Lutfur owns a factory in his hometown where weavers are hired to produce the handcrafted handloom products. Handloom House's primary sales channel is through a Facebook page, and it is working on developing a dedicated website to expand the customer base. Additionally, it also sells through its factory outlet located in the outskirts of Dhaka, in Tangail.

The impact of COVID-19 on Handloom House has been primarily negative. Lutfur states that the business was completely shut down from March to August 2020, and it was a common scenario for 90 percent of the handloom businesses. According to Lutfur, the reason for such an extended closure was lockdown measures and no demand for the handloom products. Additionally, the closure period coincided with cultural and religious festivals (1st day of Spring, Independence Day, Bengali New Year, and Eid Ul Fitr), during which significant sales opportunities were missed. Other impacts of the crisis included liquidity shortage, unsold products on the shelf, and forced leaves given to employees and weavers.

Handloom House resumed operations in September 2020 after almost six months of closure. However, after reopening, sales had declined to 60 percent compared to that of previous years. To pay employees, weavers, and other expenses, Lutfur took personal loans from family members and managed the working capital crisis from his reserve funds. Additionally, Lutfur released his unsold inventory offering discounts and promotional campaigns, sometimes even at prices lower than the production cost, thereby incurring losses.

In 2021, Handloom House is observing a slightly higher sales growth than that of 2020. However, the cost of production has increased, as prices of raw materials have increased manifold. Lutfur states that the reason handloom businesses suffered so terribly compared to other businesses could be attributed to the lack of business association for handloom producers and inadequate representation at local and national platforms.

According to Lufur, substantial policy support is needed to create digital and marketing knowledge among the small-sized handloom weavers and producers to save the handloom industry and its workers. He states that the weaver community in Bangladesh is going through a crisis for survival, as inadequate market knowledge and market manipulation by intermediaries threaten the community. Additionally, the Bengali community is constantly growing in and out of Bangladesh, so there is a massive market opportunity for handloom products nationally and globally. Policy support in terms of soft and collateral-free loans, training programs focusing on teaching export mechanisms, digital adoption, and marketing and branding will aid to make this business community survive through crisis environments.

Table 10. Summary of Impact, Response, and Learning Experience from COVID-19 for Manufacturing Small Businesses

Case	Impact	Response Action	Learning Experience
Case 1: Rainbow	• Supply chain disruption • Logistics disruption • Loss of Sales Opportunity	• New product categories • Geographic expansion	• Continuous research and development help to avoid product imitation
Case 2: Healthy Choice	• Sales increase during lockdown period • Sales decline after lockdown period • Supply chain disruption • Increase in production cost	• Hiring additional personnel for product delivery • Credit sales to customers • New product categories • Promotional discounts and free delivery campaigns	• Gaining and maintaining customer loyalty is crucial for survival • Positive word of mouth helps in bringing new customers
Case 3: Handloom House	• Operations closure from March-August, 2020 • Loss of sales opportunity • Sales decline after reopening in August 2020 • Revenue Loss • Liquidity crisis • Unsold inventory • Increase in production cost	• Utilizing personal loans and reserve funds to solve the liquidity crisis • Discounts and promotional offers	• Business associations provide support during crisis periods

Source: Authors' own

Cases From Service Small Scale Businesses in Bangladesh

The cases presented in this section include businesses primarily engaged in the organic food and beverage area operating through e-commerce and f-commerce platforms. Data from the cases show that the organic food and beverage service businesses had a mixed impact from COVID-19 and adopted responses similar to each other to combat the adverse effects (Table 11).

Case 4: BHALO JINISH

Bhalo Jinish started its journey to provide organic fruits and vegetables to its customers. Plabon realized there is a great demand for organic food and beverage among people, which motivated him to start Bhalo Jinish in 2019. He sources organic fruits and vegetables from 32 different regions in Bangladesh and sells through two channels: a Facebook page and a small-sized brick-and-mortar store.

The impact of COVID-19 on Bhalo Jinish has been mixed. Initially, the outbreak and resulting lockdown worked as a boon for the business, and its sales grew almost four times compared to that of other periods. As people could not move outside to buy their daily food and beverage demands, they shifted to online purchases. Plabon realized the massive demand from customers, thereby extended the product line by adding essential household items that further boosted sales.

On the negative side, sourcing products from different regions of the country faced disruption as transportation facilities were limited during the lockdown period. As a response, Plabon sourced products from alternate sources to meet increasing customer demand. On the other hand, making the delivery to customer doorsteps also posed some challenges as some areas in Dhaka were under quarantine, and access was prohibited. On the bright side, the local authorities tagged his physical outlet as an "essential" business and allowed it to run, although only for a few hours each day.

After the lockdown restrictions lifted, the initial sales boost experienced during the lockdown lost momentum as customers started going out and buying from convenience stores, large chain superstores, and local vendors. Additionally, potential investors dropped out from the committed investments causing a massive liquidity crisis for Plabon. He managed the situation from his reserve funds.

Plabon states that he has had three significant learning experiences from surviving through the COVID-19 pandemic. First, any small business must plan for the supply of cash flow at the onset of a crisis. Second, for a business to sustain in the long term and gain customer loyalty, meeting customers' satisfaction is crucial. Third, he states that building supplier relationships helps small companies to navigate through crisis periods.

Case 5: Protidin

With the ideology of building a healthy Bangladesh, Protidin started as an e-commerce food and beverage store in 2017. It sells grocery products across different categories, including vegetables, fruits, fish, meat, spices, tea, coffee, etc., directly sourced from producers across 44 regions in Bangladesh. Protidin is a partnership business owned by Didar, Akash, and Samia.

COVID-19 has had a mixed impact on the business of Protidin. From March to June of 2020, Protidin experienced significant growth in revenue and customer numbers. This surge, however, was coupled with a considerable number of challenges brought about by the lockdown enforcement. First, Protidin faced a significant disruption in its supply chain network. The business's primary sourcing hub lies in the country's northern and southern regions, which were inaccessible due to transportation restrictions. Second, the supply chain disruption led to Protidin operating only at a 60 percent capacity than usual with a minimized product portfolio. Third, logistics problems arose as areas under quarantine became inaccessible. Fourth, some customers canceled and returned product deliveries for fear of infections. Fifth, Protidin started facing fierce competition from new micro and small-scale start-ups from May-June onwards. As a result, those who had initially become Protidin's repeat purchasers switched to the competition. Additionally, once the lockdown period was over, people started going out to chain superstores instead of making ordering online, resulting in a loss of sales and customers in the later months of 2020. And fifth, all the issues mentioned above resulted in a severe liquidity shortage for the business.

As a response to these problems, Protidin adopted several measures to counter the adverse impacts. First, each delivery personnel was assigned personal protective gear and safety kit to ensure protection during travel and delivery for the personnel and customers. Second, Protidin leveraged its membership of the "E-commerce Association of Bangladesh," a representative platform for e-commerce businesses in the country. Through its membership, Protidin received permission from respective local authorities to make deliveries in quarantined neighborhoods. Third, Protidin froze all hiring activities even though to minimize personnel expenses, even though the workforce was limited to meet the rising customer demand. One of the owners, Didar, states that the reasoning for doing so was to be cost-effective by introducing overtime work. He says that employees who continued working from the office were paid risk allowances in addition to overtime payments. Fourth, Protidin received loans from the SME stimulus package announced by the GOB to meet the cash shortage.

Didar states that being a member of the "E-commerce Association of Bangladesh" helped the business immensely in terms of getting access to quarantined areas and access to loans from the stimulus package. He states that a strong association can be conducive to creating a supportive environment for small businesses during crisis periods.

Case 6: Green Mart

Manik and Simi started Green Mart in 2016 intending to offer organic food and beverage products to customers. Green Mart operates through an e-commerce page and a retail store that also serves as an experience center. The purpose of the experience center is to allow prospective customers to taste the food before purchase. The products of Green Mart include organic vegetables, rice, fish, rare herbs, fruits, spices, mustard oil, butter, tea, juices, etc.

The impact of COVID-19 on Green Mart has been primarily negative. First, the physical outlet and experience center remained closed from March to July 2020 because of the pandemic and lockdown. During this period, the owners ran operations through the e-commerce site only and offered home deliveries. Second, Green Mart experienced significant disruption in its supply chain in the form of sourcing delays and lack of access to suppliers. Third, issues with the supply chain resulted in the failure to meet the customer demands and ensure product delivery on time. Fourth, the owners faced fierce competition in the e-commerce landscape from the numerous home-grown businesses that popped up during lockdown. Fifth, fierce competition coupled with the inability to meet demands led to a loss in customer numbers to rival e-commerce businesses. Sixth, all the issues mentioned above ultimately led to a working capital crisis, where Green Mart experienced negative cash flow. Moreover, although the physical outlet was closed off, the owners had to make full payments on rent and utility in addition to employee expenses.

In response to the impacts, Manik and Simi opened up their physical outlet and experience center in August 2020. Additionally, they introduced a new product category in the form of ready-to-cook fish items to attract lost customers. The business hired a logistics company to ensure timely delivery and increase overall efficiency and cost-effectiveness. They are also planning to expand the business outside of Dhaka to increase service coverage.

According to Simi, her learning from the crisis is that for small businesses, the profit margin can be maximized if the cost of sourcing, production, and packaging can be minimized.

CONCLUSION AND RECOMMENDATION

Small-scale business entrepreneurs in Bangladesh are experiencing a turbulent situation from the COVID-19 pandemic that affects these businesses' existence and growth prospects. Considering that the COVID-19 pandemic is still an ongoing phenomenon, small-scale businesses face an uncertain future.

Table 11. Summary of Impact, Response, and Learning Experience from COVID-19 for Service Small Businesses

Case	Impact	Response Action	Learning Experience
Case 4: Bhalo Jinish	• Increase in sales during lockdown period • Decline in sales after lockdown period • Supply chain disruption • Logistics disruption • Loss of customer to competitors • Loss of investors • Liquidity crisis	• Alternate sources of materials • Product diversification • Reserve funds to meet liquidity crisis	• Plan in advance for cash flow supply • Maintain customer satisfaction • Build relationship with suppliers
Case 5: Protidin	• Increase in sales during lockdown period • Decline in sales after lockdown period • Loss of customer to competitors • Supply chain disruption • Logistics disruption • Hiring Freeze/Shortage of workforce to meet rising demand • Product returns by customers over virus infection • Liquidity crisis	• Protective gear and equipment to personnel • Availed stimulus package • Overtime work • Risk allowance to employees	• Business association membership provides leverage during crisis periods
Case 6: Green Mart	• Retail outlet closed from March-June • Supply chain disruption • Logistics disruption • Loss of customer to competitors • Liquidity crisis	• Product diversification	• Profit margin can be maximized if costs of sourcing, production, and packaging are minimized through alternate sources

Source: Authors' own

This chapter provides first-hand information about the impact of COVID-19 on small-scale businesses and their related responses and learning experiences from surviving through the crisis. Evidence from the cases covered indicates that COVID-19 has heavily impacted Bangladeshi small-scale enterprises with largely adverse effects on the fashion and clothing firms. Variation in demand levels and supply chain and logistics disruptions emerged as the most critical impact for manufacturing and service firms.

To control the virus's rapid spread, GOB imposed lockdown policies from March to May of 2020, thereby halting business activities. The study's findings may provide clues for what happens to small businesses amid crises in other countries, particularly for developing ones.

Understanding the pandemic's impact is essential to develop policy measures to help small-scale firms navigate the crisis. Both manufacturing and service-focused small-scale businesses experienced predominantly adverse outcomes arising from the COVID-19 pandemic. For manufacturing businesses the outcomes are lost sales opportunities (Case 1 and 3), disruptions in supply chain and logistics (Case 1, 2, and 3), unsold inventory (Case 3), and thus, ultimately leading to a crisis of liquidity (Case 3) and increase in production costs (Case 2 and 3). Business owners responded by adopting measures to increase sales, such as promotional discounts and free deliveries, adding new product categories, and selling on credit to customers. Concurrently, liquidity crises were managed through personal reserve funds and loans.

For service-focused businesses included in the study, the impact of COVID-19 was primarily mixed in nature. During the general holiday, implemented towards the end of March and the subsequent lockdown extended to the end of May, demand levels increased for food and beverage businesses. After the measures were gradually lifted at the end of May, demand for online deliveries started declining as people were free to shop for food and beverages from physical marketplaces. Additionally, many new online services popped up during this time, which posed direct competition to the studied cases. Other impacts include supply chain and logistics disruptions (Case 4, 5, and 6), loss of customers due to service failure and steep competition (Case 4, 5, and 6), loss of investment (Case 4), product returns (Case 5), thereby leading to liquidity crisis (Case 4, 5 and 6). Owners undertook response actions in the form of finding alternate sourcing (Case 4), product diversification (Case 4 and 6), introducing overtime (Case 5), adopting safety protocols and paying risk allowance to employees (Case 5), solving liquidity crisis through loans from GOB stimulus package (Case 5) and reserve funds (Case 4).

The COVID-19 outbreak imparted some critical lessons for small-scale entrepreneurs. For instance, for a small business to survive in a dynamic environment, several factors must be taken into consideration. First, continuous research and development in design and innovation are needed to thwart possible product imitations (Case 4). Second, customer loyalty promotes repeat purchases, and positive word of mouth generates new customers (Case 5). Third, business association memberships provide support and leverage during crises and adverse periods (Case 3 and 5). Fourth, planning for cash flow and building relationships with suppliers (Case 4) aid in preventing unexpected financial and operational setbacks. And fifth, profit margins can be maximized if sourcing, production, and packaging costs can be minimized through alternate sourcing (Case 6).

Based on the findings, several recommendations can be suggested for policymakers and small business owners to ease small businesses' adversities. For policymakers, it is essential that the stimulus package loans come with low-interest rates and extended repayment periods and are approved only after performing due diligence to avoid misplacement of funds. Policymakers can also add concessions or entirely suspend the rent payments on commercial properties, given that many small businesses do not own the outlets, shops, and factories they run. Thus, property owners can be advised to offer concessions or suspend rents for periods of lockdown. Additionally, the GOB can provide subsidies on business related utility charges, such as electricity, water, gas, etc., till small businesses recover from the crisis.

Small businesses suffered from a shortage of working capital, given that their cost of operations exceeded revenue. Therefore, it is recommended that, first, small businesses focus on online sales and digital adoption to increase revenue. In addition to f-commerce, they need to expand to other sales channels such as e-commerce platforms and build online infrastructures so that operations can continue and sales can be made during future lockdowns and restrictive measures. Second, small businesses need to focus on building a resilient supply chain and logistics network. They need to find the weak spots in the supply chain and take immediate responsive actions to minimize the weaknesses and strengthen the resiliency. Third, build positive relationships with stakeholders, i.e., customers, employees, and business associations, to create a network that can cooperate during crises and uncertain periods.

FUTURE RESEARCH DIRECTION

The study provides critical theoretical and practical insights on the impact of COVID-19 on small-scale businesses; however, some limitations remain that offer direction for future research. The study's field research is limited to a small number of entrepreneurs, thereby not adequately representative of the respective industries and restricts generalization of the findings. Thus, future research could involve investigating a larger sample and adopting a longitudinal study to better explore the effects of the pandemic on small-scale businesses.

REFERENCES

Akpan, I. J., Udoh, E. A. P., & Adebisi, B. (2020). Small business awareness and adoption of state-of-the-art technologies in emerging and developing markets, and lessons from the COVID-19 pandemic. *Journal of Small Business and Entrepreneurship*, 1–18. Advance online publication. doi:10.1080/08276331.2020.1820185

Aladejebi, O. (2020). Managing small businesses in Nigeria during covid-19 crisis: Impact and survival strategies. *IOSR Journal of Business and Management, 22*(8), 24-34.

Alauddin, M., & Chowdhury, M. M. (2015). Small and medium enterprise in Bangladesh-Prospects and Challenges. *Global Journal of Management and Business Research. C Finance, 15*(7), 1–10.

Alves, J. C., Lok, T. C., Luo, Y., & Hao, W. (2020). Crisis challenges of small firms in Macao during the COVID-19 pandemic. *Frontiers of Business Research in China, 14*(1), 1–23. doi:10.118611782-020-00094-2

Amankwah-Amoah, J., Khan, Z., & Wood, G. (2020). COVID-19 and business failures: the paradoxes of experience, scale and scope for theory and practice. *European Management Journal.*

Andalib, T. (2020). A conceptual model to resolve frustration of employees in the SMEs of Bangladesh. *Indian Journal of Science and Technology, 13*(09), 1015–1026. doi:10.17485/ijst/2020/v013i09/147200

Andalib, T., & Halim, H. (2019). Convergence of Conceptual Innovation Model to Reduce Challenges Faced by the Small and Medium Sized Enterprises' (SMEs) in Bangladesh. *Journal of Open Innovation, 5*(3), 63. doi:10.3390/joitmc5030063

Andrei, J., Chivu, L., Gheorghe, I., Grubor, A., Sedlarski, T., Sima, V., Subić, J., & Vasic, M. (2021). Small and medium-sized enterprises, business demography and european socio-economic model: Does the paradigm really converge*? Journal of Risk and Financial Management, 14*(2), 64. doi:10.3390/jrfm14020064

Asian Development Bank. (2012). *The Informal Sector and Informal Employment in Bangladesh.* Asian Development Bank and Bangladesh Bureau of Statistics. https://www.adb.org/sites/default/files/publication/30084/informal-sector-informal-employment-bangladesh.pdf

Australian Bureau of Statistics. (2020). *Australian Industry.* https://www.abs.gov.au/statistics/industry/industry-overview/australian-industry/2018-19

Bangladesh Bank. (2010). *SME Credit Policies & Programs.* https://bb.org.bd/sme/smepolicye.pdf

Bangladesh Bureau of Statistics. (2015). Economic Census 2013. Statistics and Informatics Division, Ministry of Planning. Dhaka: Government of the People's Republic of Bangladesh.

Bartik, A. W., Bertrand, M., Cullen, Z., Glaeser, E. L., Luca, M., & Stanton, C. (2020). The impact of COVID-19 on small business outcomes and expectations. *Proceedings of the National Academy of Sciences of the United States of America, 117*(30), 17656–17666. doi:10.1073/pnas.2006991117 PMID:32651281

Beglaryan, M., & Shakhmuradyan, G. (2020). The impact of COVID-19 on small and medium-sized enterprises in Armenia: Evidence from a labor force survey. *Small Business International Review*, *4*(2), e298. doi:10.26784bir.v4i2.298

Berger, A., & Udell, G. (1998). The economics of small business finance: The roles of private equity and debt markets in the financial growth cycle. *Journal of Banking & Finance*, *22*(6-8), 613–673. doi:10.1016/S0378-4266(98)00038-7

Bosri, R. (2016). SME financing practices in Bangladesh: Scenario and challenges evaluation. *World Journal of Social Sciences*, *6*(2), 39–50.

Callaway, S. (2004). Elements of infrastructure: Factors driving international entrepreneurship. *New England Journal of Entrepreneurship*, *7*(1), 27–37. doi:10.1108/NEJE-07-01-2004-B004

Chowdhury, M., Alam, Z., & Arif, M. (2013). Success factors of entrepreneurs of small and medium sized enterprises: Evidence from Bangladesh. *Business and Economic Review*, *3*(2), 38. doi:10.5296/ber.v3i2.4127

Cook, L., & Barrett, C. (2020). *How Covid-19 is escalating problem debt*. https://www.ft.com/content/4062105a-afaf-4b28-bde6-ba71d5767ec0

Dai, R., Feng, H., Hu, J., Jin, Q., Li, H., Wang, R., Wang, R., Xu, L., & Zhang, X. (2020). The Impact of COVID-19 on Small and Medium-sized enterprises: Evidence from two-wave phone surveys in China. *Center for Global Development*. https://www.cgdev.org/publication/impact-covid-19-small-and-medium-sized-enterprises-evidence-two-wave-phone-surveys-china%0ACenter

Dangayach, G., & Deshmukh, S. (2005). Advanced manufacturing technology implementation. *Journal of Manufacturing Technology Management*, *16*(5), 483–496. doi:10.1108/17410380510600473

Deakins, D., & Freel, M. (1998). Entrepreneurial learning and the growth process in SMEs. *The Learning Organization*, *5*(3), 144–155. doi:10.1108/09696479810223428

DGHS Press Release. (2021, April 12). *COVID-19 Press Bulletin*. https://corona.gov.bd/

Dhaka Tribune. (2020, October 31). *No mask, no service*. https://www.dhakatribune.com/bangladesh/government-affairs/2020/10/31/no-mask-no-entry

Dhaka Tribune. (2021). *Survey: New poor in Bangladesh stands at 24.5 million*. Author.

Eisenhardt, K. M. (1989). Building Theories from Case Study Research. *Academy of Management Review*, *14*(4), 532–550. doi:10.5465/amr.1989.4308385

Eisenhardt, K. M., & Graebner, M. E. (2007). Theory Building from Cases: Opportunities and Challenges. *Academy of Management Journal*, *50*(1), 25–32. doi:10.5465/amj.2007.24160888

European Investment Bank. (2020). *Does this change everything? Small business gets sick*. https://www.eib.org/en/stories/smes-coronavirus

Farhana, K. M., & Mannan, K. A. (2020). Knowledge and perception towards Novel Coronavirus (COVID 19) in Bangladesh. *International Research Journal of Business and Social Science*, *6*(2), 76–87. doi:10.2139srn.3578477

Fernet, C., Torrès, O., Austin, S., & St-Pierre, J. (2016). The psychological costs of owning and managing an SME: Linking job stressors, occupational loneliness, entrepreneurial orientation, and burnout. *Burnout Research, 3*(2), 45–53. doi:10.1016/j.burn.2016.03.002

Glasser, B. G., & Strauss, A. L. (2017). *The discovery of grounded theory: Strategies for qualitative research*. Routledge. doi:10.4324/9780203793206

Gomezelj Omerzel, D., & Antončič, B. (2008). Critical entrepreneur knowledge dimensions for the SME performance. *Industrial Management & Data Systems, 108*(9), 1182–1199. doi:10.1108/02635570810914883

Government of Canada. (2020). *Key Small Business Statistics – 2020.* http://www.ic.gc.ca/eic/site/061.nsf/eng/h_03126.html#definition

Gregurec, I., Tomičić Furjan, M., & Tomičić-Pupek, K. (2021). The impact of COVID-19 on sustainable business models in SMEs. *Sustainability, 13*(3), 1098. doi:10.3390u13031098

Guo, H., Yang, Z., Huang, R., & Guo, A. (2020). The digitalization and public crisis responses of small and medium enterprises: Implications from a COVID-19 survey. *Frontiers of Business Research in China, 14*(1), 1–25. doi:10.118611782-020-00087-1

Hasan, A. (2020, August 23). *The growth of e-commerce during the pandemic in Bangladesh.* New Age.

Herciu, M. (2017). Financing small businesses: From venture capital to crowdfunding. *Studies in Business and Economics, 12*(2), 63–69. doi:10.1515be-2017-0022

Insee. (2019). *Small and medium enterprises / SME.* https://www.insee.fr/en/metadonnees/definition/c1962

Irawan, A. (2020). Challenges and opportunities for small and medium enterprises in Eastern Indonesia in facing the COVID-19 pandemic and the new normal Era. *TIJAB, 4*(2), 79. doi:10.20473/tijab.V4.I2.2020.79-89

Islam, K., & Miajee, M. R. K. (2018). Small and Medium Enterprises (SMEs) financing in Bangladesh: A review of literature. *International Journal of Small and Medium Enterprises, 1*(1), 11–15. doi:10.46281/ijsmes.v1i1.62

Islam, M. Z. (2020, April 28). *Online grocers fail to seize the day during biggest opening yet.* The Daily Star.

ITC. (2020). *COVID-19: The great lockdown and its impact on small business.* International Trade Centre.

Juergensen, J., Guimón, J., & Narula, R. (2020). European SMEs amidst the COVID-19 crisis: Assessing impact and policy responses. *Economia e Politica Industriale, 47*(3), 499–510. doi:10.100740812-020-00169-4

Kader, A. W., & Pattanayak, M. (2021). *Business Pulse Survey: Impact of COVID-19 on MSMEs in Bangladesh (English).* https://documents.worldbank.org/curated/en/172841613718788462/Business-Pulse-Survey-Impact-of-COVID-19-on-MSMEs-in-Bangladesh

Khalil, T. (2020, August 11). The impact of COVID-19 on small businesses. *The Daily Star.* https://www.thedailystar.net/lifestyle/news/the-impact-covid-19-small-businesses-1942713

Kuckertz, A., Brändle, L., Gaudig, A., Hinderer, S., Morales Reyes, C. A., Prochotta, A., Steinbrink, K. M., & Berger, E. S. C. (2020). Startups in times of crisis – A rapid response to the COVID-19 pandemic. *Journal of Business Venturing Insights*, *13*(April), e00169. Advance online publication. doi:10.1016/j.jbvi.2020.e00169

Kukanja, M., Planinc, T., & Sikošek, M. (2020). Crisis management practices in tourism SMEs during the Covid-19 pandemic. *Organizacija*, *53*(4), 346–361. doi:10.2478/orga-2020-0023

Lamb, W., & Sherman, H. (2010). Developing high-growth businesses in rural areas: A study of four US States. *New England Journal of Entrepreneurship*, *13*(2), 9–19. doi:10.1108/NEJE-13-02-2010-B001

LightCastle Analytics Wing. (2020, April 25). *COVID-19: Impact on Bangladesh's SME Landscape*. https://covid-19-impact-on-bangladeshs-sme-landscape.html

Lu, Y., Wu, J., Peng, J., & Lu, L. (2020). The perceived impact of the Covid-19 epidemic: Evidence from a sample of 4807 SMEs in Sichuan Province, China. *Environmental Hazards*, *19*(4), 323–340. doi:10.1080/17477891.2020.1763902

Lutfi, M., Buntuang, P. C. D., & Kornelius, Y. (2020). The impact of social distancing policy on small and medium-sized enterprises (SMEs) in Indonesia. *Problems and Perspectives in Management*, *18*(3), 492–503. doi:10.21511/ppm.18(3).2020.40

Marroquin, M. (2021, March 22). *COVID-19 continues to hurt NY's small businesses. New data show how many are hurting*. https://www.lohud.com/story/money/business/2021/03/22/covid-new-york-small-business-report-pandemic-impact-revenue/4769606001/

Meng, L., Qamruzzaman, M., & Adow, A. (2021). Technological adaption and open innovation in SMEs: A strategic assessment for women-owned SMEs sustainability in Bangladesh. *Sustainability*, *13*(5), 2942. doi:10.3390u13052942

Miglo, A. (2020). Financing of entrepreneurial firms in Canada: Some patterns. *Administrative Sciences*, *10*(3), 50. doi:10.3390/admsci10030050

Ministry of Micro, Small and Medium Enterprises. (2020). *What's MSME*. https://msme.gov.in/know-about-msme

Mungal, A., & Garbharran, H. (2014). Cash management challenges of small businesses in a developing community. *Mediterranean Journal of Social Sciences*, *5*(27 P1), 11. doi:10.5901/mjss.2014.v5n27p11

Obrenovic, B., Du, J., Godinic, D., Tsoy, D., Khan, M., & Jakhongirov, I. (2020). Sustaining Enterprise Operations and Productivity during the COVID-19 Pandemic: "Enterprise Effectiveness and Sustainability Model. *Sustainability*, *12*(15), 5981. doi:10.3390u12155981

OECD. (2016). *Financing SMEs and Entrepreneurs 2016: An OECD Scoreboard*. OECDnPublishing. . doi:10.1787/fin_sme_ent-2016-en

OECD. (2018), SME and Entrepreneurship Policy in Indonesia 2018. OECD Studies on SMEs and Entrepreneurship, OECD Publishing. doi:10.1787/9789264306264-en

Opinium Research. (2020). *Impact of coronavirus on UK SMEs*. Opinium Research.

Our World in Data. (2021, April 12). *Coronavirus (COVID-19) Vaccinations*. https://ourworldindata.org/grapher/cumulative-covid-vaccinations?tab=chart&time=latest

Păunescu, C., & Mátyus, E. (2020). Resilience measures to dealing with the COVID-19 pandemic: Evidence from Romanian micro and small enterprises. *Management & Marketing. Challenges for the Knowledge Society*, *15*(s1), 439–457. doi:10.2478/mmcks-2020-0026

Pettit, R., & Singer, R. (1985). Small business finance: A research agenda. *Financial Management*, *14*(3), 47. doi:10.2307/3665059

Priyono, A., Moin, A., Aini, V. N., & Putri, O. (2020). Identifying digital transformation paths in the business model of SMEs during the COVID-19 pandemic. *Journal of Open Innovation*, *6*(4), 104. doi:10.3390/joitmc6040104

Psaltopoulos, D., Stathopoulou, S., & Skuras, D. (2005). The location of markets, perceived entrepreneurial risk, and start-up capital of micro rural Firms. *Small Business Economics*, *25*(2), 147–158. doi:10.100711187-003-6456-6

Rahman, M., Islam, M., Esha, B., Sultana, N., & Chakravorty, S. (2018). Consumer buying behavior towards online shopping: An empirical study on Dhaka city, Bangladesh. *Cogent Business & Management*, *5*(1), 1514940. doi:10.1080/23311975.2018.1514940

Raihan, S. (2021). *Strategies to tackle pandemic induced poverty in Bangladesh*. The Daily Star.

Sahoo, S., Hossain, M. N. A., & Hassan, K. S. (2020). *A boon for online commerce: How COVID-19 is transforming the industry in Bangladesh*. Next Billion. https://nextbillion.net/online-commerce-covid19-industry-bangladesh/

Schreibauer, E. C., Hippler, M., Burgess, S., Rieger, M. A., & Rind, E. (2020). Work-related psychosocial stress in small and medium-sized enterprises: An integrative review. *International Journal of Environmental Research and Public Health*, *17*(20), 7446. doi:10.3390/ijerph17207446 PMID:33066111

Shafi, M., Liu, J., & Ren, W. (2020). Impact of COVID-19 pandemic on micro, small, and medium-sized enterprises operating in Pakistan. *Research in Globalization*, *2*, 100018. doi:10.1016/j.resglo.2020.100018

Siddiquee, M. S. H., & Faruk, A. (2020). *COVID-19's Impact on Bangladesh Economy*. https://bigd.bracu.ac.bd/wp-content/uploads/2021/01/Working-Paper_COVID-19s-Impact-on-Bangladesh-Economy.pdf

Small Business Majority. (2021). *Scientific Opinion Poll*. Small Business Majority. https://smallbusinessmajority.org/sites/default/files/research-reports/COVID-19-national-small-business-poll.pdf

SME Corporation Malaysia. (2020). *Guideline for SME definition*. https://smecorp.gov.my/images/garispanduan/2020/Guideline_SME_Definition_updated_Sept_2020.pdf

Tengeh, R. (2013). Advancing the case for the support and promotion of African immigrant- owned businesses in South Africa. *Mediterranean Journal of Social Sciences*, *4*(2), 347. doi:10.5901/mjss.2013.v4n2p347

The Daily Star. (2020, March 23). *Coronavirus outbreak: Govt orders closure of public, private offices from March 26 to April 4*. https://www.thedailystar.net/coronavirus-deadly-new-threat/news/govt-offices-closed-march-26-april-4-cabinet-secretary-1884730

The Daily Star. (2020, October 20). *Shopup raises $22.5 million Series A financing round*. https://www.thedailystar.net/online/news/shopup-raises-225-million-series-financing-round-1981209

The World Bank. (2020). *Beaten or broken? Informality and COVID-19*. The World Bank.

The World Bank. (2021). *Bangladesh Development Update*. doi:10.1596/26642

The World Bank. (2021). *ILOSTAT database: Unemployment, total (% of total labor force) (modeled ILO estimate) – Bangladesh*. https://data.worldbank.org/indicator/SL.UEM.TOTL.ZS?end=2020&locations=BD&start=1991&view=chart

The World Bank Group. (2019). *Financing Solutions For Micro, Small And Medium Enterprises In Bangladesh*. https://documents1.worldbank.org/curated/en/995331545025954781/Financing-Solutions-for-Micro-Small-and-Medium-Enterprises-in-Bangladesh.pdf

Thorgren, S., & Williams, T. A. (2020). Staying alive during an unfolding crisis: How SMEs ward off impending disaster. *Journal of Business Venturing Insights*, *14*(November), e00187. doi:10.1016/j.jbvi.2020.e00187

Thukral, E. (2021). COVID-19: Small and medium enterprises challenges and responses with creativity, innovation, and entrepreneurship. *Strategic Change*, *30*(2), 153–158. doi:10.1002/jsc.2399

UCL. (2021). *Small & Medium Size Enterprises (SMEs)*. https://www.ucl.ac.uk/procurement/suppliers/smes

US Small Business Administration. (2019). *Small business size standards*. https://www.sba.gov/document/support--table-size-standards

Vig, S., & Agarwal, R. N. (2021). Repercussions of COVID-19 on small restaurant entrepreneurs: The Indian context. *Strategic Change*, *30*(2), 145–152. doi:10.1002/jsc.2398

Wellner, L., & Pierce-Friedman, K. (2019). The Types of Case Studies in Research and Career-Based Endeavors. In Case Study Methodology in Higher Education (pp. 83-108). IGI Global. doi:10.4018/978-1-5225-9429-1.ch005

Widarti, W., Desfitrina, D., & Zulfadhli, Z. (2020). Business process life cycle affects company financial performance: Micro, small, and medium business enterprises during the Covid-19 period. *International Journal of Economics and Financial Issues*, *10*(5), 211–219. doi:10.32479/ijefi.10516

World Health Organization. (2021). *Bangladesh COVID-19 Morbidity and Mortality Weekly Update (MMWU)*. https://www.who.int/bangladesh/emergencies/coronavirus-disease-(covid-19)-update/

Yin, R. K. (2017). *Case study research: Design and methods*. Sage Publications.

Zhu, Y., Wittmann, X., & Peng, M. (2011). Institution-based barriers to innovation in SMEs in China. *Asia Pacific Journal of Management*, *29*(4), 1131–1142. doi:10.100710490-011-9263-7

KEY TERMS AND DEFINITIONS

Coronavirus Pandemic: A global pandemic caused by the SARS-COV-2 virus that first emerged in December 2019.

COVID-19 Crisis: Health, economic, financial, and social crisis caused by the global coronavirus pandemic.

Lockdown: An emergency ban on human movement within a specific geographic area, usually triggered by a serious threat.

Logistics: A subset of the supply chain responsible for planning and executing transportation and storage of goods from one point to another.

Manufacturing: The process of producing goods or items manually or via automation that is sold to customers after completion.

Service: The process of creating intangible value or outcomes from seller to customers without the ownership of any physical or tangible goods.

Small-Scale Business: A privately owned enterprise with limited start-up capital, a small number of employees, low revenue, and profit margin compared to regular scale business.

Supply Chain: A network of entities involving individuals, organizations, activities, processes, information, and technology involved in sourcing, production, and transporting goods from supplier to end user.

Chapter 3
Entrepreneurial and SME Resilience During Crisis Episodes:
Are Risk Management and Entrepreneurial Resilience Linked?

Andrea Sandra Brear
Ulster University, Ireland

EXECUTIVE SUMMARY

Businesses and individuals have experienced multiple crises that have led to major financial and developmental impacts for entrepreneurs and small and medium sized enterprises (SMEs). Researchers believe that entrepreneurs should be innovative through means of resilience skills, risk management, and identifying new opportunities. This chapter aims to investigate entrepreneurial resilience during crisis episodes, investigating the development of resilience and how it helps a business survive a crisis episode while considering the likelihood that entrepreneurial resilience and risk management are linked, how it is linked, and if it can be improved and utilised for success. An anonymous survey was conducted to investigate how entrepreneurs have been impacted by the pandemic, their attitudes surrounding risk assessments, and how their adaptations and innovations impacted the development and survival of their business. The conclusion discusses research findings and suggestions to support the survival of entrepreneurs and SMEs during crisis episodes.

INTRODUCTION/BACKGROUND

Previous crises within the last century have highlighted that businesses should either be fighting a crisis or preparing to fight for an upcoming crisis. Throughout history, it has become apparent that many businesses forget about crises that have previously occurred and therefore do not prepare for the next upcoming one (Ribera, 2020). Within the last decade there has been SARS, Ebola, Zika, MERS and

DOI: 10.4018/978-1-7998-7657-1.ch003

HIV/AIDS pandemics, which suggests that pandemics are not rare, however pandemics are usually confined to geographic areas or particular groups, decreasing the impact on a global level (Phillips-Wren et al., 2020). With that said, the crisis episode that is the COVID-19 pandemic has snowballed, creating devastating impacts on businesses across the world (Caliguiri et al., 2020). Disasters and crisis episodes are abrupt and often cause devastating results such as death, destruction and economic uncertainty for individuals and businesses. Disasters take place unexpectedly throughout the world whether they are natural disasters or a result of man-made developments in which governments and other leadership bodies are responsible for finding ways to cope and guide the nation/country that is experiencing the disaster (Olson & Wu, 2020).

Entrepreneurship is thought to be one of the main elements that lead to the development of local economies as entrepreneurial ventures create jobs, social inclusion and an increase in productivity. Due to this, European policy makers have placed an emphasis on fostering entrepreneurship in deprived societies and communities in an attempt to encourage employment and productivity in young citizens (Kleinhans et al., 2017). Entrepreneurs are considered to be one of the main drivers for economic progress within a country as they create wealth in the society that they open and operate their business in (Peng & Shekshnia, 2001).

Some researchers believe that an entrepreneur should act innovatively and dynamically during a crisis episode (Ratten, 2020) and research has highlighted that the entrepreneur achieves these actions through the identification of opportunities, risk management, innovation, proactivity and resilience skills (Branicki et al., 2018; Portuguez Castro et al., 2020). Previous research has suggested that innovation is the main tool for entrepreneurs (Drucker, 1994) and that entrepreneurship and innovation are intrinsically correlated as innovation is not necessary for starting a new business and conversely an individual could be considered an innovator whether or not they have created a new business. There have been suggestions that the entrepreneurial ventures that involve innovation create the highest level of value (Lima, 2021) and innovative businesses grow at a faster pace as they introduce new methods of products, open new markets and they are involved in the introduction of new goods and organisations within multiple industries.

There is a paradox that suggests that while entrepreneurs are more likely to take risks, they do not have a higher risk propensity. Along with this, entrepreneurs do not think that they should be considered risk takers (Palich & Bagby, 1995) as they are desensitised to the risks that they come up against and therefore do not think that the decisions they make are risky and they accept any risks that they may possibility come up against as they do not think that they will happen (Busenitz, 1999). Additionally, entrepreneurs tend to act quickly on their business venture, exploiting brief windows of opportunity (Hambrick & Crozier, 1985), therefore making a risk analysis too time consuming and almost impossible to evaluate (Gilmore & Kazanjian, 1989; Shapira, 1995). Although many entrepreneurs consider creating a risk management plan too time consuming, even if they made time to create a risk management plan the likelihood that the risk management plan would have considered a crisis episode is very small. Eduardsen, (2021) discusses how the traditional risk management plan does not consider risks where the likelihood of the risk occurring is low, thus still leaving entrepreneurs and SMEs vulnerable to many crisis episodes.

This chapter is going to evaluate whether or not risk management can be considered a contributing factor to the success of an entrepreneur being resilient in the same way that innovation is often considered a factor in entrepreneurial resilience.

GOVERNMENT RESPONSES TO COVID-19

Governments responded to the announcement that COVID-19 was a global pandemic by implementing policies and restrictions in an attempt to contain the disease. These policies and restrictions included lockdown measures, restrictions on exports and imports and travel limits paired with the closure of borders; together all of these restrictions have impacted the demand and supply of goods and services (Baldwin & Tomiura, 2020).The Organisation for Economic Co-operation and Development (OECD) published a report in 2020 that highlighted that the policies created during the lockdowns due to COVID-19 have impacted small and medium-sized enterprises (SMEs) in relation to the maintenance of staff and attempting to avoid bankruptcy due to cash-flow implications as a result of a reduction in the amount of sales and/or services entrepreneurs and SMEs have been able to provide. The COVID-19 pandemic has resulted in global economic uncertainty (IMF, 2020) due to a near-standstill of the economy. Border closures and social distancing has impacted sales, resulting in SMEs not having the liquidity to enable their business to be able to meet payroll and overhead bills (OECD, 2020; World Bank, 2020) thus resulting in rising levels of unemployment and business failure. The impacts that job losses and business failures have on an economy and society are devastating and are a contributing factor to financial downturns and recessions. The World Bank (2020) stated that "the pandemic is expected to plunge most countries into recession... with per capita income contracting in the largest fraction of countries globally since 1870" thus creating uncertainty for stability for both employees and entrepreneurs.

Uncertainty is defined as an inability to predict the outcome of a business environment due to a lack of information or the inability to differentiate relevant and irrelevant information. Levels of uncertainty tend to increase during crisis episodes, therefore impacting entrepreneurs and individuals that fund their business ventures. Uncertainty is considered to be an integral aspect when ascertaining how an entrepreneur is affected by a crisis episode, such as what has been experienced with COVID-19 (Brown & Rocha, 2020). Wenzel et al. (2020) stated that uncertainty increases with crisis episodes such as terrorist attacks, global financial crises, Brexit, the Gulf Wars and COVID-19.

COVID-19 has resulted in a high level of financial uncertainty not only for entrepreneurs and SMEs but also for investors. Investors carry out considerable monitoring and control procedures due to the uncertainties around finance for start-ups and SMEs that are trying to grow (Brown & Rocha, 2020). A large part of investors' work consists of close relational interactions that tend to be face-to-face with the businesses that they invest in (De Clercq & Sapienza, 2006). Personal networks are used to obtain deals in investment along with supervising the investee firm in an act of investors staying 'close to their money' (Shane & Cable, 2002; Cumming & Dai, 2010; Colombo et al., 2019; Brown & Rocha, 2020). Given the inherent nature of entrepreneurial finance and how investors interact with their investees, it is expected that sources of equity finance would be impacted by economic crises such as what has resulted during the COVID-19 pandemic. The impacts on investment during COVID-19 has been labelled as 'financial distancing' (Howell et al., 2020). Financial distancing and uncertainty for investors will impact start-up companies and those that were trying to improve their business as they were already struggling if they were relying on investors due to their inability to obtain investment elsewhere.

LITERATURE REVIEW

Entrepreneurial Resilience

The word resilience has been described as an overarching construct that consists of multiple factors and is considered as a characteristic for individuals that have the ability to overcome setbacks that are connected to their career aspirations, business and life. Zautra et al., (2010) suggested that resilience is the descriptive word for an individual that is able to recover quickly and easily from setbacks that they may come against while Bernard and Barbosa (2016) described entrepreneurial resilience as a form of emotional and cognitive ability that is useful for the entrepreneur, especially when bouncing back after failures that are linked to their entrepreneurial initiative. Entrepreneur's exhibit some of the characteristics that are associated with resilience and tend to shine in situations that require ambiguity and change (Ayala & Manzano, 2014) as well as identifying new opportunities that were previously unexploited (Hitt et al., 2001). Additionally, entrepreneurs are thought to persevere during times of adversity (Holland & Shepherd, 2013) and they view 'dire circumstances' as a moment of opportunity (Bullough & Renko, 2013; Bullough et al., 2014) thus making them resilient in surviving the dire circumstance.

Entrepreneurialism has been frequently argued as a contributing factor for community, region or economy resilience (Boettke et al., 2007; Westley et al., 2011). Huggins and Thompson (2015) advised that entrepreneurship contributes greatly to the recovery of localities in relation to economic downturns but in order to do that the entrepreneurial activity within the locality must be resilient and innovative. Rae et al. (2012) described an entrepreneurially resilient locality as one that takes advantage of opportunities that are a result of the impacts of economic downturns, such as a reduction in new business growth rates and previously unexplored business areas that are suddenly more attractive. When an entrepreneur takes advantage of an economic change and adjusts, a positive reorientation may take place for the economy of the locality that the business resides in. Some countries and regions highly depend on SMEs, such as Northern Italy, where SMEs hold significance within the economic structure and are critically important to the locality (OECD, 2020).

Social research has suggested that resilience is linked to the capability for an entrepreneur or business to adapt in circumstances that involve crisis episodes such as natural disasters. Furthermore, resilience has been coined by researchers as a movement amongst entrepreneurs, businesses, communities and governments in order to react and recover from crisis episodes in a timely matter (Rutter, 2008; Masten 2009). Entrepreneurial resilience is essential for addressing unexpected crises such as the impacts of the COVID-19 global pandemic (Sawalha, 2020). Salisu et al. (2020) have highlighted that there is no clear indication of how to identify business/entrepreneurial resilience along with the factors that support the improvement and development of resilience. Duchek (2018) noted that previous research has not been able to conclude what entrepreneurial resilience denotes and the factors that are associated with the development and improvement of the resilience skill.

Davidson (2000) advised that resilience in entrepreneurs can be elevated by an entrepreneur networking to form a group of mentors and coaches and by the entrepreneur accepting that change is something that they will experience as a part of life and being a business owner so as they no longer see crises as overwhelming and unconquerable. Bonanno (2012) and Masten (2001) viewed resilience as a construct, conceptualising resilience as something that could be developed over a period of time. This belief highlighted that entrepreneurs, business owners and every day individuals alike have the ability to learn the ways in which they could address stress and issues that are associated with traumatic events (Luthans et al., 2006; Reivich et al., 2011; Orr et al., 2013). Psychologists have stated that the definition of resilience includes a person's ability and/or capability to be able to maintain a somewhat healthy, stable emotional and psychological state of mind even in situations where they experience trauma or loss (Bonanno, 2004, 2005; Leipold & Greve, 2009).

For the purpose of this research, we define resilience as a developmental trait where entrepreneurs and business owners of SMEs learn about handling stress for issues that they come up against over time. Rutter's (2008) belief that resilience has both a psychological and social meaning is backed up by Huggins and Thompson (2015). Rutter (2008) highlighted that resilience is more than a psychological trait, it is something that can be acquired. Resilience is considered as maintaining stability and healthy levels of emotional functioning in crisis episodes in order to react to protect their business.

Despite the fact that research has been unable to conclude how resilience is acquired, further research shows that individuals that interact with their environments (Zautra et al., 2010) and have supportive schools, communities, families and social policies are more likely to develop the skill of resilience (Leadbeater et al., 2005). Entrepreneurs with these relationships that provide support, trust, care and encouragement paired with having their own self-confidence and realistic planning are able to manage impulse decisions and strong feelings and therefore are more likely to be considered resilient (Hedner et al., 2017). This suggests that entrepreneurial resilience depends on more than internal factors as there are external factors that can impact the success of a business along with the ability to be resilient during crisis episodes and failure. Liao (2004) conducted research on entrepreneurial failure, noting the causes are a mixture of internal and external factors: the entrepreneur and their characteristics; the business structure paired with the business strategies; the micro and macro environment; and the process that lead to the failure. Entrepreneurial resilience may follow a similar suit in terms of consisting of a combination of internal and external factors.

Many researchers believe that small and medium-sized enterprises (SMEs) do not possess resilience and are impacted by external crises (Ingirige et al., 2008; Battisti & Deakins, 2012) such as severe weather, global pandemics, terrorist attacks and geopolitical instability which in turn challenges the SME's survival and success (Linnenluecke et al., 2012; May & Koski, 2013). Additionally, SMEs are considered to be more vulnerable and possess lower resilience when compared to larger firms (OECD, 2020). One of the explanations that have been explored for this lack of resilience is due to the lack of planning for a crisis (Paton et al., 2010).

A business should conduct all the necessary actions for survival if a crisis occurs and grows as quickly as COVID-19. An example of an action to take is the evaluation and investigation of missed opportunities and taking advantage of those missed opportunities by pursuing them in an act to counteract the impacts of the crisis. Timing should be prioritised during the survival stage (Ribera, 2020) of a crisis episode. One of the ways that entrepreneurs can ensure that they have adequate time to survive a crisis episode is by having a risk management plan already in place with potential innovation ideas to mitigate the risk of significant business damage.

The OECD published a report in 2020 which highlighted their results of surveys in relation to SME impacts of COVID-19. These results highlight that in the United Kingdom, 1/3 of SMEs feared being out of business within 1 month followed closely by Canada having 25% of SMEs expecting to not survive longer than 1 month. There is a mixture of reasons of SMEs not believing that they will survive such as Portugal and Germany stating that 50% of their SMEs do not possess enough resources for more than 2 months of survival and 85% of SMEs in the Netherlands expect they will be in financial difficulty due to COVID-19 with 20% expected to be at serious risk of almost irreversible financial difficulty (OECD,

2020). Though these statistics do not note if these businesses had risk management plans in place it is safe to assume that some did not as they did not have resources put by for a crisis episode that would impact their ability to get additional resources.

One of the known characteristics of entrepreneurs include the entrepreneur's willingness to take risks, which in turn makes the entrepreneur prone to experiencing failure during their business ventures. Research has suggested that entrepreneurial resilience can be developed through experiences such as struggling or failed businesses as it is a skill that is learned over time. An entrepreneur having a failed business and learning from it is an important part of the success story of many entrepreneurs as it helps to build cases on how they rebuild after failure and how that helps them become a successful entrepreneur (De Vries, 1977).

Scholars have paired entrepreneurial resilience with the entrepreneur being prepared, hardy, persistent and the entrepreneur believing that their business will be successful through means of self-efficacy. Another scholarly thought surrounding entrepreneurial resilience is the fostering and adjusting to new circumstances in order to contribute to the success of the business by adopting innovative products, services or survival strategies. As an *ex-ante*, resilience is an inherent entrepreneurial characteristic with various factors such as psychological resilience that is important for reinforcing the entrepreneur's intentions, organisational resilience behaviour and entrepreneurial SMEs and entrepreneurs attempting to enhance the community's resilience (Korber and McNaughton, 2018).

Table 1. Summary table

Author	Purpose	Summary Points
Bernard and Barbosa (2016) Bonanno (2012) Masten (2001) Luthans et al., 2006 Reivich et al., 2011 Orr et al., 2013	Definition of entrepreneurial resilience	a form of emotional and cognitive ability that is useful for the entrepreneur, especially when bouncing back after failures linked to their entrepreneurial initiative. Entrepreneurial resilience can be developed over a period of time by learning how to address stress such as what is experienced during crisis episodes.
Boettke et al. (2007) Westley et al. (2011) Huggins and Thompson (2015)	Benefits of entrepreneurs within the economy	Entrepreneurialism has been frequently argued as a contributing factor for the resilience of a community, region or economy as entrepreneurship contributes greatly to the recovery of localities.
Davidson (2000) Zautra et al. (2010) Leadbeater (2005) Liao (2004)	How can entrepreneurial resilience be elevated?	Resilience in entrepreneurs can be elevated by an entrepreneur networking to form a group of mentors and coaches and by the entrepreneur accepting that change is something that they will experience as a part of life and being a business owner so as they no longer see crises as overwhelming and unconquerable. Entrepreneurial resilience relies on internal and external factors such as interaction with communities, family and social policies along with business structure, strategy and plans such as risk management.

Risk Management

There are many things that are at risk when an entrepreneur starts a business including financial investments; personal wealth; well-being; family and friend relationships and career opportunities (Bird, 1989). Entrepreneurs have been labelled as risk-takers; however, research suggests that they do not have high levels of risk propensity. This is because entrepreneurs do not consider themselves risk takers which may be due to their over confidence that makes them believe that the risks that could result in a failed business will not happen to them, thus making them think that the risks don't actually exist. Entrepreneurs tend to start a business quickly when they think of an idea, making it almost impossible to create a risk management plan where they would consider the viability of the business. Entrepreneurs do not start their business in a sequential and methodological perspective, often approaching a new business through a process that is not completely thought out. Busenitz (1999) believes that if entrepreneurs started their business with detailed research and a risk analysis, many business ventures would never start due to the lack of sufficient information being found or being retrieved from all which would, in turn, result in research results advising that there is a low probability of success and that would lead to ventures being rarely pursued.

Entrepreneurs are thought to use bias and heuristics when making business decisions which was considered to be a possible negative aspect, however recent studies have explored the possibility that this may actually be beneficial for entrepreneurs as they will be able to handle and function more efficiently in uncertain, risky situations due to their quick thinking. Business risk is defined as the probability of major financial loss (Baird & Thomas, 1985) and Sonfield and Lussier (2000) have highlighted that while not all risks are centered around financial loss, such as the risk of a company's reputation, risk can lead to financial implications for the company if it happens. The sooner a problem or opportunity is discovered, the greater the variety of options and time there is to explore those options to consider implementation (Ribera, 2020).

Entrepreneurs and SMEs look for a stable environment to start and develop their business. There has been economic prosperity since World War two which is thought to be a good indication that there is a peaceful co-existence among countries, therefore creating a stable environment for start-ups. However, Morrison (2017) questions if the world is a safe environment for day-to-day life and business. Morrison's questioning derives from political risk and how businesses are impacted by economic uncertainties that the government have power over such as policies, taxes, restrictions and regulations. These political risks extend further than policies and restrictions but also include external forces such as political unrest and terrorist attacks. There is an assumption that political risk is generally low where there is high economic prosperity and that developing countries have a higher likelihood of facing political risks for businesses, however political risks may arise in democratic and autocratic states (Morrison, 2017).

Many crisis episodes, such as the COVID-19 pandemic, are low-probability, high-risk scenarios (Eduardsen, 2021) which often means that they take more time and consideration to evaluate, therefore decreasing the likelihood of entrepreneurs and SMEs undertaking the task of risk planning for something that is low-probability. Gunasekaren et al. (2015) stated that organisations face the challenge of being more prepared for unexpected crisis events such as terrorism, cyber-attacks, natural disasters and pandemics as a traditional risk assessment does not usually deal with unforeseeable events to that level. In risk management there is a heavy focus on risk identification through lessons learned and prior evidence, which confirms that the traditional risk approach that most companies follow will fall short as these crisis episodes are often unpredictable with unknown risks which will not be picked up in risk identification (Centeno et al., 2014). This evidence suggests that the traditional risk approach needs to be reconsidered and a new risk assessment model should be designed that considers the complexity and diversity of risks such as natural disasters, terrorist attacks, political risks, cyber-attacks and pandemics (Eduardsen, 2021).

The traditional risk assessment being re-evaluated would not only have to consider the previously mentioned areas but would additionally need to evaluate the smaller risks within them. For example, political risks are not one single risk but instead include other risks within that group such as social and ethnic tensions that may be paired with inequality and a lack of government accountability. These political tensions can escalate to civil disorder and violent clashes which may impact businesses directly if they are caught in the middle of a riot. Examples of businesses being impacted by political risks and civil unrest can be seen during the George Floyd protests in Minneapolis where small businesses were "burned, ransacked and looted" (Davis, 2020). The effects of businesses being targeted during the George Floyd rioting have caused severe economic crisis for the impacted small businesses. In Davis' 2020 article on the George Floyd protests, small business owners highlight that their insurance will not replace everything they've lost which is not something they would have considered if they had a risk management plan in place.

Political risks are not only risks for physical businesses but also online ones as terrorist groups have extended their attacks to not only include deadly injury and creating an atmosphere of fear but also include targeting states and organisations through cyber-attacks (Morrison, 2017). Zerzri (2017) discussed how terrorist organisations have started to invade cyberspace, creating a battleground through means of sabotaging online infrastructures around the world. Cyber-attacks have many motivational factors such as creating political or ideological change and physical and psychological repercussions through data theft and bank fraud. Cyber terrorism aims to manipulate and corrupt information system functions in an attempt to damage or destroy virtual and physical assets; this can be done through worms and viruses. Another motivational factor surrounds causing disruption in normal day to day life through targeting transportation, financial systems and medical utility such as what the Health Service Executive (HSE) in Ireland experienced in May 2021. All of these targets can lead to major crises for entrepreneurs and SMEs across multiple industries.

Common traits that are linked to entrepreneurs are a desire of achievement, locus for control and the readiness for risk taking (Hisrich & Peters, 1998). According to Douglas and Shepherd (2002), the level of risk aversion in an individual aids the determination of whether or not that person is likely to become an entrepreneur or not. This information highlights that entrepreneurs are more tolerant to taking risks in order to achieve their desire of being self-employed and in control of their business. Risk taking can lead to either success or failure, therefore it is important that entrepreneurs and SMEs evaluate the risks when making a decision. However, despite the risk-taking trait in entrepreneurs, the fear and risk around failure when pursuing being an entrepreneur may hinder some from either starting their own business or trying again after a failed business (Hegarty et al., 2020). In order to effectively manage risks, an entrepreneur or SME must identify the risks while reducing the vulnerability of their business in an act of preparing for these risks (Eduarden, 2021).

The attribution theory (Heider, 1958; Weiner, 1986) explores entrepreneurial resilience and how individuals use attributions between the relationships between cause and effect. The attribution theory model highlights that success or failure is attributed by three dimensions; locus of causality, stability and controllability. Entrepreneurs believe that they can influence an outcome through their own ability, skills and effort, highlighting that entrepreneurs are considered to have an internal locus control. This leads entrepreneurs to be more likely to take responsibility for their business' future thus causing them to act independently (McClelland, 1961). Entrepreneurs attempt to attribute to their success and failure through their own actions, which includes risk taking, impacting the success of their business through entrepreneurial resilience. While this suggests that entrepreneurs should know to take the time to create a risk management plan, it does not mean that they will. Entrepreneurs are confident that a risk will not happen to them, and if it does that they can control it by being re-active rather than pro-active (Busenitz, 1999).

Entrepreneurs and SMEs have been identified to not allow time outside of their main business activities for their strategic horizon. Due to this, risk assessments for economic crises and resilience agendas tend to not exist (Ingirige et al., 2008). Eduardsen (2021) claimed that spending time focusing on reducing exposure to risks would more than likely result in a decrease in efficiency, which suggests that entrepreneurs with minimal available time would have to sacrifice productive hours to plan for risks that may or may not occur. This highlights that there is a trade-off between risk management planning and business efficiency for entrepreneurs. To further this statement Schneider (2002) advised that disaster risk management is considered a reactive measure due to risk planning strategies not being considered as urgent for some entrepreneurs and SMEs.

Some of the suggested methods for risk reduction include various forms of mitigation measures to identify the development of coping mechanisms and address the potential of company behavioural changes that could help avoid or reduce the impact of the assessed risks (Bosher et al., 2007). An example of this is the entrepreneurial strategic matrix (ESM) that some businesses use to consider and decide on the appropriate strategies and tactics for different situations depending on the levels of risk and innovation required in the situation (Sonfield & Lussier, 2000). Tools such as the ESM aid business owners in making decisions when it comes to a risk management plan.

Stress is a personal reaction and unexpected events usually lead to stress in individuals which causes a higher chance of poor decisions which is why tools such as the ESM are beneficial for entrepreneurs and SMES. There are two different types of stress; positive – eustress – and negative – distress with the latter being most common in relation to reactions of crisis episodes (Phillips-Wren et al., 2020). The quality of a decision should be evaluated with the consideration of the process of reaching that decision and the outcomes that have derived from the made decision. When an individual makes a decision in a stressful environment, the quality of the decision is impacted by the individual generating less alternatives, and ignoring vital information which then results in solutions being recommended before considering all options that are available. This factor is why being proactive and having a risk management plan is more effective than being reactive and acting on impulse to try to save a business.

Phillips-Wren et al. (2020) advised that individuals have two internal systems for processing decision making; one that is fast and based on experience and one that is slower that is based on reasoning – the slower system requires more cognitive function than the faster one. In unexpected situations where there are conflicting options and opportunities that have been derived from expert advice, decision makers have a task that is almost impossible. Therefore, the decision makers can only make the best decisions possible with the information that has been provided to them at the time of making the decision which is vital as it can impact the overall success of a business overcoming a financial or global crisis. This factor is another reason why there should be risk management plans in place with good decisions already outlined for the reaction of crisis episodes in order to help reduce the financial impact to the business, making it resilient to the crisis episode that it faces.

In a situation that is constantly changing such as the COVID-19 pandemic, decision makers consult experts and confide in groups that deliver guidance. Decision makers have relied on expert opinions, judgement and expertise during the pandemic so far, allowing their actions to be influenced by the expert's advice. There are key differences between experts and decision makers – experts are expected to provide precise information that is up to date with valuable arguments, whereas decision makers have empathic qualities and anticipate the reactions of those who are impacted by assessing risks and attempting to react quickly and intuitively (Phillips-Wren et al., 2020). Despite there being a difference between experts and decision makers, decision makers rely on expert's data, advice and knowledge of a particular topic to help them make their decisions (Ferguson, 2020) in which business owners then use to help them when assessing their risks and how to mitigate those risks.

The next section of this chapter is going to review the results from an anonymous survey that specifically focuses on what entrepreneurs have experienced during the COVID-19 pandemic, how they were resilient in this crisis episode and if they had a risk management plan in place.

METHODOLOGY

A delivered and collected survey of the experience of entrepreneurs throughout the COVID-19 pandemic was undertaken for this chapter in April 2021. The research design of the study was conducted in two sections. The first section of this research consisted of detailed research and analysis of published research documents conducted by various researchers related to the chapter title. The second section consisted of an anonymous survey directed towards entrepreneurs that operated their businesses before the COVID-19 pandemic began. This part of the research outlined whether the published research documents matched the results obtained by the researcher through the anonymous survey and provided an opportunity to verify the findings by either confirming or disputing them and providing further insight.

Out of the 50 entrepreneurs that were approached to take part in the survey only 29 responded. The 50 entrepreneurs that were approached for the survey for the research of this chapter were randomly selected with the following criteria:

- They were entrepreneurs.
- They were in business before COVID-19.

This criteria was selected in order to properly evaluate if the pandemic had impacted their business and how. As the participants were randomly selected and as it was an anonymous survey, there is no way to accurately group the respondents into industries, size of business and type of business. The reason that the survey was left anonymous was to promote entrepreneur responses as they were confident that their business name was not going to be publicly linked to their experience throughout COVID-19.

The research question that this survey aims to address is "are risk management and entrepreneurial resilience linked?" in order to aid in the research of this chapter. Along with this question, there are three objectives that the researcher has developed which are:

1. How were entrepreneurial businesses impacted by the COVID-19 pandemic?
2. If businesses were required to adapt in order to be resilient, how did they do so?
3. Did the entrepreneurs have a risk management plan?

The researcher deemed a survey strategy as the most appropriate, primary data collection method for this research. The researcher used a quantitative research method as it is concerned with collecting and analysing numerical data; it concentrates on measuring the scale, range and frequency of findings. This type of research, in which is usually more difficult to design initially, is highly detailed and structured in a way that allows results to be efficiently collated and presented statistically. In order to achieve the research objectives, the researcher used different types of questions in relation to attitude and values when it comes to entrepreneurial resilience during a crisis episode and related to beliefs surrounding the benefits of risk management.

The methodology used for this research provided the means to answer the research question and objectives of the investigation of whether or not entrepreneurial resilience and risk management were linked. The next heading of this chapter will focus on the results retrieved from the survey followed by another heading that will provide a comprehensive comparison of the findings against published material from experts within this field.

FINDINGS

Extensive data was collected from the survey and only selected results are presented here. Three categories were developed from the results of the survey:

- Entrepreneurs that were impacted negatively by the COVID-19 pandemic (65.52%).
- Entrepreneurs that were impacted positively by the COVID-19 pandemic (31.03%).
- Entrepreneurs that were not impacted by the COVID-19 pandemic at all (3.45%).

The share of respondents in each of the categories is noted above but this should not make the reader assume that these percentages would be accurate for a wider sample as the entrepreneurs that took part in this survey were randomly selected. Should this study focus on specific industries of geographical areas the results would be different.

Figure 1.

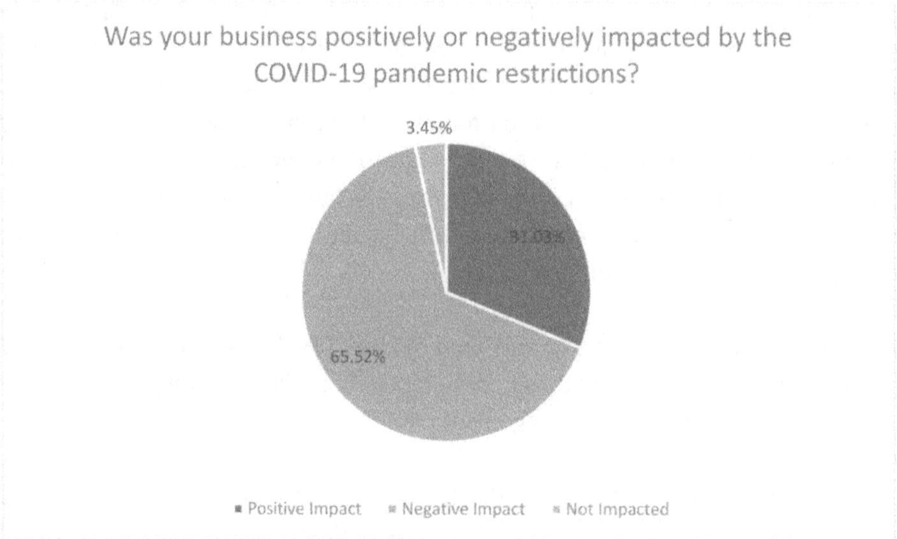

The first three questions of the survey focused on how the participants were impacted by COVID-19. 44.83% of respondents reported that their business became less busy due to lockdowns and restrictions with an additional 24.14% reporting that they could not operate at all. Conversely, 24.14% reported that their business became busier and 6.9% reported that their business did not change and was not impacted. The businesses that were not able to operate at all were impacted due to restrictions, however it is hard to specifically note why a business would have become busier or less busy. Possible reasons for more business could be due to individuals having more disposable income for the participant's product as things that the individual would usually spend their money on were closed; another possible reason is if the entrepreneur was innovative and came up with new business ideas in which we discuss further in this chapter.

Figure 2.

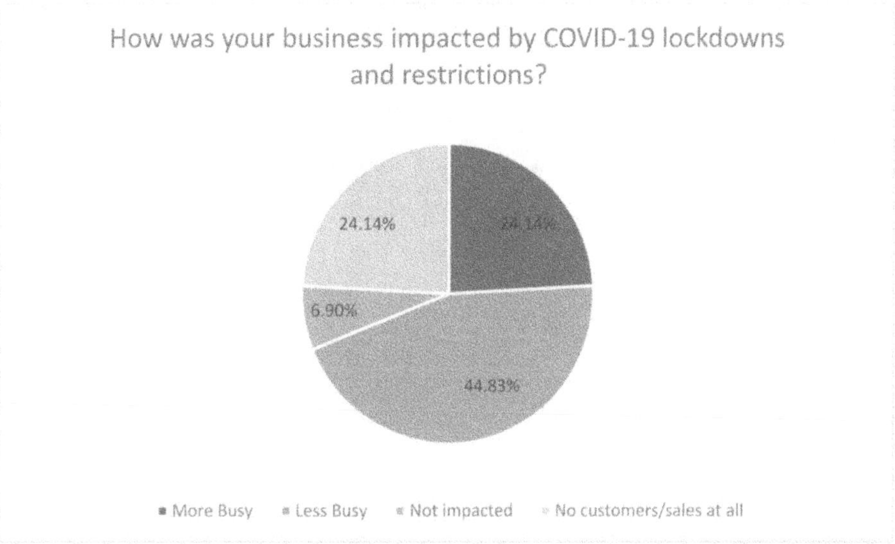

The third question surrounding how businesses were impacted by COVID-19 asks participants if they were temporarily forced to close their business due to lockdowns. 41.38% of participants stated that their businesses were forced to close and they could not operate in any way while 24.14% advised that they were forced to close but found alternative ways to operate. 34.48% did not have to close due to lockdowns. When comparing the results from this question to that of the last question, it is interesting that 34.48% of respondents did not have to close their business as lockdowns did not impact them yet only 6.9% stated that their level of business was not impacted. Further surveys and research could identify how those that were not forced to close were impacted and why.

Another three questions focused on how entrepreneurs adapted to the lockdowns and restrictions in an act of entrepreneurial resilience. The results from the survey highlighted that out of the 29 respondents, 79.31% found alternative ways to operate during the lockdowns that occurred during the first year of the COVID-19 pandemic by either moving their business online (27.59%) or starting new products and services that were allowed to be sold and conducted during the lockdowns (51.72%). These results highlight that entrepreneurs are highly likely to be innovative and find ways to adapt their business in order to survive.

These adaptations proved to be beneficial to the entrepreneurs that took part in the survey as 68.95% of respondents' that adapted are planning on keeping their adaptations post lockdowns and 65.52% feel that the adaptations were beneficial to their business as it improved their business in ways that they did not expect.

Figure 3.

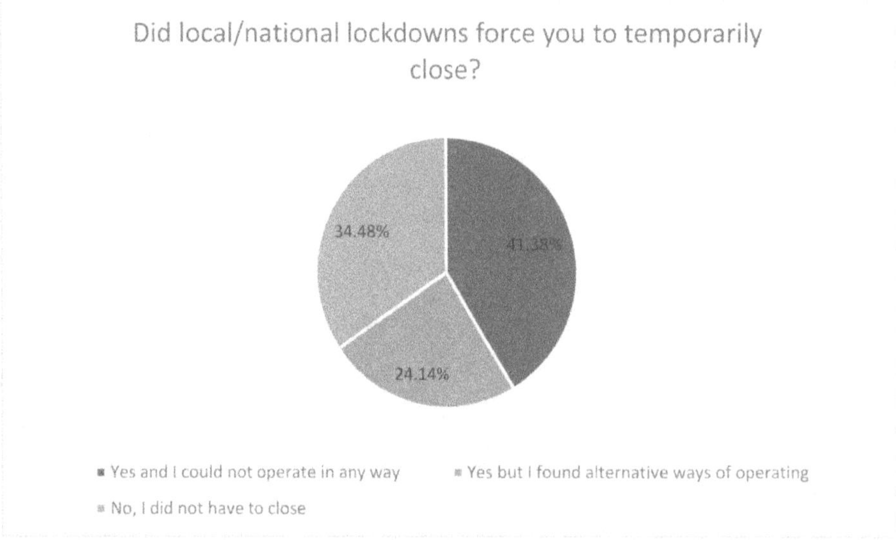

Figure 4.

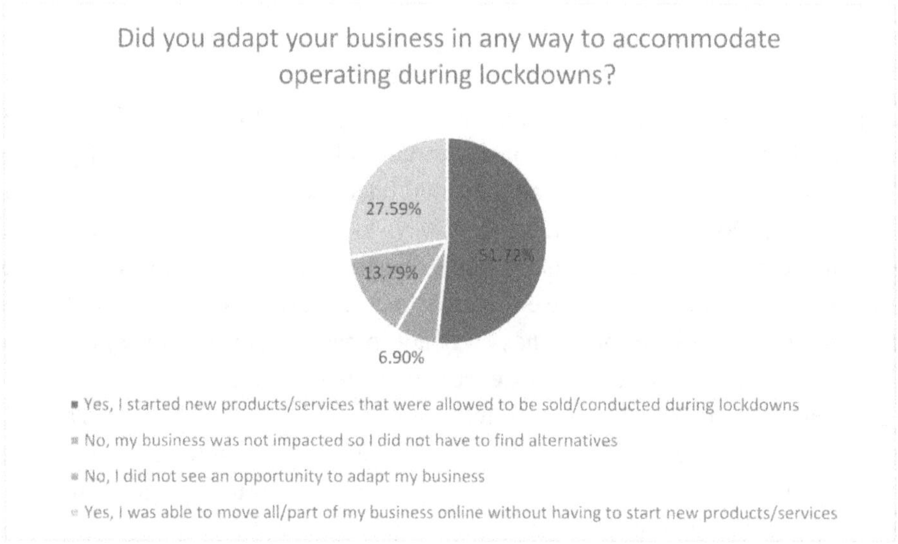

Figure 5.

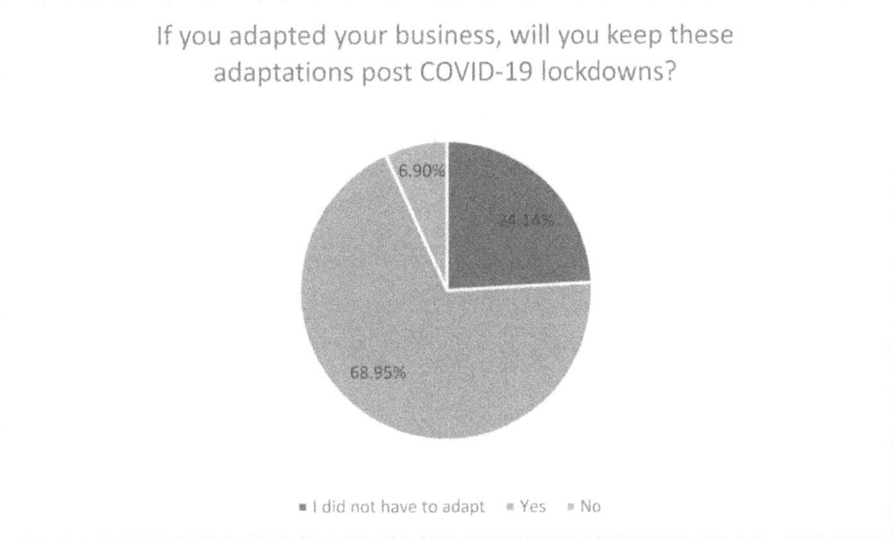

However, not all entrepreneurs felt that the adaptations were something they wanted to continue as 10.34% felt that their adaptations were a means of survival that did not benefit their business in any way. Despite there being evidence of some entrepreneurs not finding their innovations beneficial, a majority of participants reported that they did think it helped to develop their business in new ways that they had not thought of before; this suggests that innovation is a big factor in entrepreneurial resilience. This suggestion can be supported further by the evaluation of results noting that only 10.35% of the respondents that started new products and services during the lockdown had previously planned these new products and services; 6.90% reported that while they already had these plans in place, the COVID-19 lockdowns did make them act on starting these products and services sooner while only 3.45% found that the pandemic did not influence them to start these products and services sooner than already planned.

The final three questions focused on risk management and the attitude of the participants around risk management. Only 20.69% of respondents had a risk management plan in place with 3.45% of respondents having considered a global pandemic as a risk. 37.93% of participants stated that they did not know what a risk management plan was prior to taking part in the survey leaving just over half (62.07%) advising that they knew what a risk management plan was. Almost 67% of the 62.07% of entrepreneurs that stated they knew what a risk management plan was but although they knew what it was, they did not create one.

Upon further analysis, only 48.28% of respondents think that a risk management plan would have helped them to be more prepared for a crisis episode such as the COVID-19 pandemic. 17.24% of entrepreneurs did not want to determine if they thought a risk management plan would have been of assistance as they did not understand the benefits of having one and 34.48% of entrepreneurs advised they do not think that a risk management plan would be beneficial for their business.

When the survey participants were asked if they would be interested in education and training around risk management plan, 55.17% advised they would be. The additional 44.83% stated that they would not be interesting in education around risk management as they do not think that it would be beneficial to their business (27.59%) or they do not have time to learn about risk management (17.24%).

Figure 6.

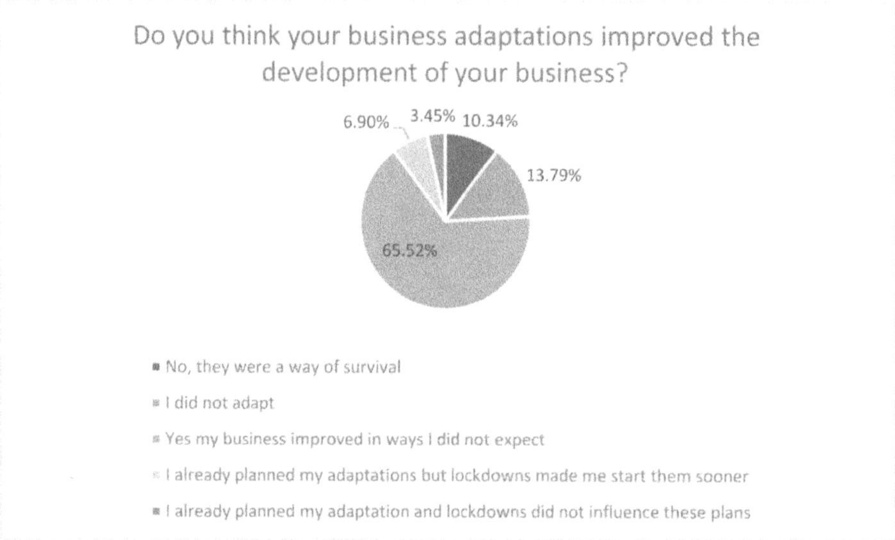

Figure 7.

DISCUSSION

The three objectives set out at the start of this chapter were investigated and will be discussed in this section.

1. How were entrepreneurial businesses impacted by the COVID-19 pandemic?

Figure 8.

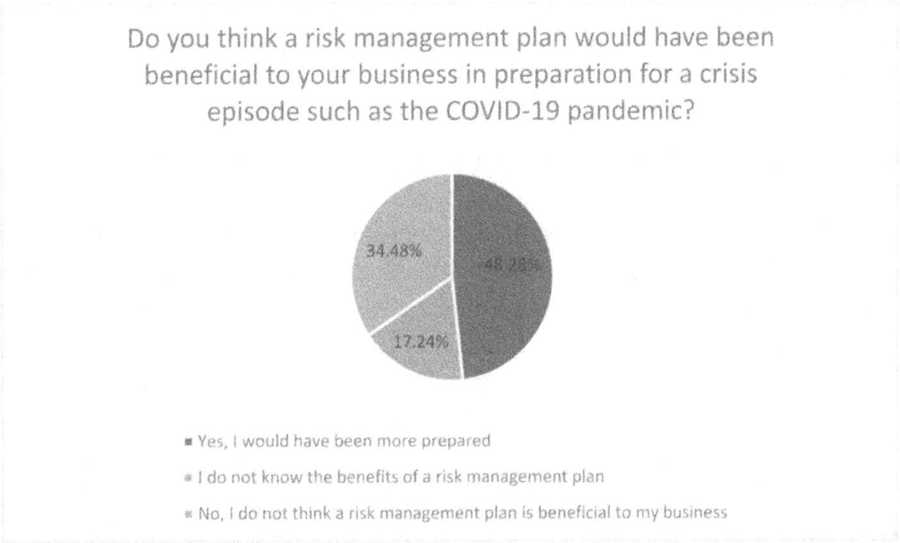

Figure 9.

The results from the survey highlight that more than half of the entrepreneurs that participated were impacted negatively by the COVID-19 pandemic whether their business was forced to shut down, resulting in no customers/sales or if the business became less busy due to lockdowns and restrictions. Very few entrepreneurs (6.9%) were not impacted in anyway by this crisis episode and less than a quarter of participants (24.14%) advised that they became busier.

Governments responded to COVID-19 being labelled as a global pandemic by implementing restrictions and lockdowns in an effort to contain the disease which in turn, impacted entrepreneurs and their SMEs. This can be seen in the survey results as 65.52% of participants advised that they had to close their business due to local and national lockdowns. Further analysis highlighted that not all entrepreneurs that closed their business were able to operate in alternative ways which may be a result of limitations due to the industry that they are in or may be due to a lack of entrepreneurial resilience and innovation traits existing within the entrepreneur.

2. If businesses were required to adapt in order to be resilient, how did they do so?

Researchers believe that entrepreneurs should be innovative and act dynamically during crisis episodes such as the COVID-19 pandemic (Ratten, 2020). An entrepreneur can be resilient if they identify new opportunities and if they are proactive and have a risk management plan in place with innovative ideas ready should they need to react to a crisis episode (Branicki et al, 2020). The results from the survey highlighted that most (79.31%) of respondents adapted their business in ways that allowed them to conduct business during lockdowns that initially closed them. When looking back at the other questions focused on how businesses were impacted by COVID-19, there is a possibility that some of the 79.31% of respondents that adapted their business to suit operating during lockdowns are more than likely some of the same respondents that reported that their business was positively impacted by COVID-19. The ways that these respondents adapted their business was by offering new products and services that were allowed during COVID-19 lockdowns (51.72%) and by moving all/part of their services online (27.59%). When these statistics are compared to past research it suggests that the respondents that adapted their business with new ways of delivering their product or entirely new products and services are entrepreneurially resilient as they had innovative ideas and put them in place as a reaction to the COVID-19 pandemic.

Only 13.79% of entrepreneurs that took part in the survey stated that they did not see an opportunity to adapt their business which may be due to a lack of entrepreneurial resilience or it may be due to industry limitations.

3. Did the entrepreneurs have a risk management plan?

The statistics surrounding the attitude around risk management plans matched that of what past researchers have suggested; that entrepreneurs are risk takers and that they have over confidence that makes them believe that the risks will not happen to them. 37.93% of respondents did not know what a risk management plan was prior to taking part in the survey and while the remaining percentage did know what it was, 41.38% did not create one. Of the 20.69% of respondents that created a risk management plan prior to COVID-19, only 3.45% had considered a global pandemic as a risk; however, crisis episodes such as global pandemics are low-probably, high-risk scenarios which requires additional time to evaluate, thus decreasing the likelihood of a global pandemic being considered during the traditional risk management plan.

Further analysis of the survey results shows that 48.28% of respondents think that a risk management plan would have helped them be more prepared for the COVID-19 pandemic but 34.48% still do not think that a risk management plan would be beneficial to them; the remaining 17.24% did not know the benefits of a risk management plan and therefore did not want to make a decision on whether or not they wish that they had one in place. When asked if they would take advantage of opportunities to learn more about risk management plans, only 55.17% were interested in education and training opportunities while 27.59% had no interest as they did not think it would be beneficial to their business and 17.24% were not interested as they did not feel that they had time to take part in risk management training. The

17.27% of respondents that do not think they have time to take part in risk management confirm previous suggestions that entrepreneurs do not allow time outside of their main business activities in order to evaluate their strategic horizon and ultimately consider and risk management plan (Ingirige et al., 2008).

CONCLUSION: ARE ENTREPRENEURIAL RESILIENCE AND RISK MANAGEMENT LINKED?

Entrepreneurs are known for adapting well to changing situations by identifying new opportunities for their business in order to either increase revenue or to survive a difficult situation. Perseverance is an important characteristic in entrepreneurs that often leads them to viewing a difficult situation as a moment of opportunity to be innovative and find new ways of doing business which has been reflected in the results for the survey conducted for this chapter. There are many factors that can contribute to an entrepreneur and SME's ability to be resilient in a time of uncertainty such as being prepared through means of risk assessment and management along with perseverance and the belief that the business will survive the difficult time. Additionally, entrepreneurial resilience depends on a mixture of internal and external factors that contribute to an entrepreneur's ability to be innovative for business survival during crisis episodes. Examples of internal factors are the entrepreneur's characteristics and the overall business structure; examples of external factors include friend and family reactions to failure along with resources available to the entrepreneur when attempting to mitigate the failure of their business. Internal and external factors do not only impact an entrepreneur's resilience and innovativeness, but also impact an entrepreneur's decision when deciding whether or not to take risks.

The research conducted for this chapter suggests that the traditional risk management plan assessments are not suitable for global crises such as pandemics, terrorist attacks and natural disasters which leads to the recommendation that the traditional risk management plan should be reassessed to be more inclusive of rare global crises that impact the financial aspects and success of entrepreneurs and their SMEs, thus potentially aiding in the development of entrepreneurial resilience due to experience in creating the risk management plan.

While the research throughout this chapter highlights that there is a linkage between entrepreneurial resilience and risk management, there are things that could improve the relationship between the two areas such as the improvement of the traditional risk management plan being more inclusive and an overall change to the attitude towards risk within the entrepreneurial community. By reassessing the traditional risk management plan, entrepreneurs and their businesses will have a better chance at surviving global crises such as what happened with the COVID-19 pandemic and changing the overall attitude towards risk within entrepreneurial communities. This creates the potential for creating more local and regional support for entrepreneurs taking risks that could result in more successful businesses that turn global. Ways of changing the attitude towards entrepreneurs taking risk involves the changing of government policies and increase of support and funding for entrepreneurs after lockdowns and restrictions such as what were implemented by governments around the world during COVID-19.

Reassessing the risk management plan is not the only recommendation that has derived from the research for this chapter. Survey results highlighted that there is a significant percentage of entrepreneurs that do not think that a risk management plan is beneficial to them and their business along with a number of entrepreneurs advising that they do not have the time to take part in learning more about risk management plans and their benefits. This attitude towards risk management is something that will impact the success of entrepreneurs and SMEs during difficult situations and crisis episodes. There should be a focus placed on providing entrepreneurs with this relevant training in entrepreneurial start up classes in order to start the conversation of the importance of risk assessment within the entrepreneurial community. It is without a doubt that if more entrepreneurs and SMEs develop risk management plans, there would be less business failure and more innovation and entrepreneurial resilience within the entrepreneurial community which would then, in turn, help localities and regions in their own economic recovery after an economic or global crisis improving the relationship between entrepreneurial resilience and risk management.

REFERENCES

Ayala, J. C., & Manzano, G. (2014). The resilience of the entrepreneur. Influence on the success of the business. A longitudinal analysis. *Journal of Economic Psychology*, *42*, 126–135. doi:10.1016/j.joep.2014.02.004

Baird, I., & Thomas, H. (1985). Toward a contingency model of strategic risk-taking. *Academy of Management Review*, *10*(2), 230–243. doi:10.5465/amr.1985.4278108

Baldwin, R., & Tomiura, E. (2020). Thinking ahead about the trade impact of COVID-19. In R. Baldwin & B. W. di Mauro (Eds.), *Economics in the Time of COVID-19* (pp. 59–72). CEPR Press.

Battisti, M., & Deakins, D. (2012). Perspectives from New Zealand small firms: crisis management and the impact of the Canterbury earthquakes. In New Zealand Centre for Small & Medium Enterprise Research (Ed.), BusinesSMEasure. Massey University.

Bernard, M. J., & Barbosa, S. D. (2016). Resilience and entrepreneurship: A dynamic and biographical approach to the entrepreneurial act. *Management*, *19*(2), 89–123.

Bird, B. J. (1989). *Entrepreneurial behavior*. Scott, Foresman.

Boettke, P., Chamlee-Wright, E., Gordon, P., Ikeda, S., Leeson, P. T., & Sobel, R. (2007). The political, economic, and social aspects of Katrina. *Southern Economic Journal*, *74*(2), 363–376.

Bonanno, G. A. (2004). Loss, trauma, and human resilience. *The American Psychologist*, *59*(1), 20–28. doi:10.1037/0003-066X.59.1.20 PMID:14736317

Bonanno, G. A. (2005). Clarifying and extending the construct of adult resilience. *The American Psychologist*, *60*(3), 265–267. doi:10.1037/0003-066X.60.3.265b PMID:15796689

Bonanno, G. A. (2012). Uses and abuses of the resilience construct: Loss, trauma, and health-related adversities. *Social Science & Medicine*, *74*(5), 753–756. doi:10.1016/j.socscimed.2011.11.022 PMID:22300714

Bosher, L., Dainty, A., Carillo, P., Glass, J., & Price, A. (2007). Integrating disaster risk management into construction: A UK perspective. *Building Research and Information*, *35*(2), 163–177. doi:10.1080/09613210600979848

Branicki, L., Sullivan-Taylor, B., & Livschitz, S. (2018). How entrepreneurial resilience generates resilient SMEs. *International Journal of Entrepreneurial Behaviour & Research*, *24*(7), 1244–1263. doi:10.1108/IJEBR-11-2016-0396

Brown & Rocha. (2020). Entrepreneurial uncertainty during the Covid-19 crisis: Mapping temporal dynamics of entrepreneurial finance. *Journal of Business Venturing Insights*. Retrieved from: https://www.ncbi.nlm.nih.gov/pmc/articles/PMC7283071/

Bullough, A., & Renko, M. (2013). Entrepreneurial resilience during challenging times. *Business Horizons*, *57*(3), 343–350. doi:10.1016/j.bushor.2013.01.001

Bullough, A., Renko, M., & Myatt, T. (2014). Danger zone entrepreneurs: The importance of resilience and self-efficacy for entrepreneurial intentions. *Entrepreneurship Theory and Practice*, *38*(3), 473–499. doi:10.1111/etap.12006

Busenitz, L. W. (1999). Entrepreneurial Risk and Strategic Decision Making: It's a Matter of Perspective. *The Journal of Applied Behavioral Science*. Retrieved from https://shareok.org/bitstream/handle/11244/24846/10.1177.0021886399353005.pdf?sequence=1

Caligirui, P., De Cierei, H., Minbaeva, D., Verbeke, A., & Zimmermann, A. (2020). International HRM insights for navigating the COVID-19 pandemic: Implications for future research and practice. *Journal of International Business Studies*, *51*(5), 697–713. Advance online publication. doi:10.105741267-020-00335-9 PMID:32836500

Centeno, M. A., Nag, M., Patterson, T. S., Shaver, A., & Windawi, A. J. (2014). The emerge of global systemic risk. *Annual Review of Sociology*, *41*(1), 65–85. doi:10.1146/annurev-soc-073014-112317

Colombo, M. G., D'Adda, D., & Quas, A. (2019). The geography of venture capital and entrepreneurial ventures' demand for external equity. *Research Policy*, *48*(5), 1150–1170. doi:10.1016/j.respol.2018.12.004

Cumming, D., & Dai, N. (2010). Local bias in venture capital investments. *Journal of Empirical Finance*, *17*(3), 362–380. doi:10.1016/j.jempfin.2009.11.001

Davidson, R. J. (2000). Affective style, psychopathology and resilience: Brain mechanisms and plasticity. *The American Psychologist*, *55*(11), 1196–1214. doi:10.1037/0003-066X.55.11.1196 PMID:11280935

Davis, T. J. (2020, June 1). Their stores were burned, ran sacked and looted. What's next for Minneapolis-area small business owners? *USA Today*. Retrieved from https://eu.usatoday.com/story/news/nation/2020/06/01/george-floyd-protests-riots-minneapolis-small-businesses/5300736002/

De Clercq, D., & Sapienza, H. J. (2006). Effects of relational capital and commitment on venture capitalists' perception of portfolio company performance. *Journal of Business Venturing*, *21*(3), 326–347. doi:10.1016/j.jbusvent.2005.04.007

De Vries, M. F. R. K. (1977). The entrepreneurial personality: A person at the crossroads. *Journal of Management Studies*, *14*(1), 34–57. doi:10.1111/j.1467-6486.1977.tb00616.x

Douglas, E. J., & Shepherd, D. A. (2002). Self-Employment as a Career Choice: Attitudes, Entrepreneurial Intentions, and Utility Maximization. *Entrepreneurship Theory and Practice*, *26*(3), 81–90. doi:10.1177/104225870202600305

Drucker, P. F. (1994). *Innovation and Entrepreneurship: Practice and Principles*. Heinemann.

Duchek, S. (2018). Entrepreneurial resilience: A biographical analysis of successful entrepreneurs. *The International Entrepreneurship and Management Journal*, *14*(2), 429–455. doi:10.100711365-017-0467-2

Eduardsen, J. S. (2021). COVID-19, Global Value Chains, Risk and Resilience. In A. Marinov & S. T. Marinova (Eds.), *COVID-19 and International Business: Change of Era*. Taylor & Francis Group.

Ferguson, N. (2020). Historian Niall Ferguson on what the pandemic means for the global economy, geopolitics – and parties. *World Economic Forum*. Retrieved from https://www.weforum.org/agenda/2020/05/niall-ferguson-economy-pandemic-coronavirus-covid/

Gilmore, T. N., & Kazanjian, R. K. (1989). Clarifying decision making in high-growth ventures: The use of responsibility charting. *Journal of Business Venturing*, *4*(1), 69–83. doi:10.1016/0883-9026(89)90034-7

Gunasekaran, A., Subramanian, N., & Rahman, S. (2015). Supply claim resilience: Role of complexities and strategies. *International Journal of Production Research*, *53*(22), 6809–6819. doi:10.1080/00207543.2015.1093667

Hambrick, D. C., & Crozier, L. (1985). Stumblers and stars in the management of rapid growth. *Journal of Business Venturing*, *1*(1), 31–45. doi:10.1016/0883-9026(85)90005-9

Hedner, T., Albouzeedan, A., & Klofsten, M. (2017). Entrepreneurial resilience. *Annals of Innovation amp; Entrepreneurship*, *2*. https://www.tandfonline.com/doi/full/10.3402/aie.v2i1.6002

Hegarty, C., Gallagher, P., Cunningham, I., & Stephens, S. (2020). *Šebestová, J. (e.d) Developing Entrepreneurial Competencies for Start-Ups and Small Business*. IGI Global. Retrieved from https://www.igi-global.com/gateway/book/237831

Heider, F. (1958). *The psychology of interpersonal relations*. Wiley. doi:10.1037/10628-000

Hisrich, R. D., & Peters, M. P. (1998). Entrepreneurship (4th ed.). Irwin/McGraw-Hill.

Hitt, M. A., Ireland, R. S., Camp, S. M., & Sexton, D. L. (2001). Strategic entrepreneurship: Entrepreneurial strategies for wealth creation. *Strategic Management Journal*, *22*(6-7), 479–491. doi:10.1002mj.196

Holland, D. V., & Shepherd, D. A. (2013). Deciding to persist: Adversity, values and entrepreneurs' decision policies. *Entrepreneurship Theory and Practice*, *37*(2), 331–358. doi:10.1111/j.1540-6520.2011.00468.x

Howell, S., Lerner, J., Nanda, R., & Townsend, R. (2020). *Financial Distancing: How Venture Capital Follows the Economy Down and Curtails Innovation*. Harvard Business School Working Paper, 20–115. Retrieved from https://www.nber.org/system/files/working_papers/w27150/w27150.pdf

Huggins, R., & Thompson, P. (2015). Local entrepreneurial resilience and culture: The role of social values in fostering economic recovery. *Cambridge Journal of Regions, Economy and Society*, *8*(2), 326. doi:10.1093/cjres/rsu035

IMF. (2020). *A Crisis Like No Other*. International Monetary Fund Annual Report. Retrieved from: https://www.imf.org/external/pubs/ft/ar/2020/eng/spotlight/covid-19/

Ingirige, M. J. B., Proverbs, D., & Joness, K. G. (2008). *Investigating SME Resilience and Their Adaptive Capacities to Extreme Weather Events: A Literature Review and Synthesis*. University of Salford. Retrieved from http://usir.salford.ac.uk/18262/1/SMEs.pdf

Kleinhans, R., Resyschke, D., Van Ham, M., Mason, C., & Syrett, S. (2017). Unravelling the nexus between entrepreneurship, neighbourhoods and commuinciites – introduction. In M. V. Ham, D. Reuschke, R. Kleinhans, C. Mason, & S. Syrett (Eds.), *Entrepreneurial Neighbourhoods*. Edward Elgar Publishing. doi:10.4337/9781785367243.00008

Korber, S., & McNaughton, R. B. (2018). *Resilience and entrepreneurship: a systematic literature review*. University of Auckland. Retrieved from https://www.researchgate.net/profile/Stefan-Korber/publication/321380097_Resilience_and_entrepreneurship_A_systematic_literature_review/links/5b63cd97aca272e3b6ac2651/Resilience-and-entrepreneurship-A-systematic-literature-review.pdf

Leadbeater, B., Dodgen, D., & Solarz, A. (2005). *The resilience revolution: A paradigm shift for research and policy?* doi:10.1007/0-387-23824-7_4

Leipold, B., & Greve, W. (2009). Resilience: A conceptual bridge between coping and development. *European Psychologist*, *14*(1), 40–50. doi:10.1027/1016-9040.14.1.40

Liao, J. (2004). *Entrepreneurial failures: Key challenges and future directions. In Entrepreneurship: The way ahead.* Routledge.

Lima, M. (2021). *Entrepreneurship and Innovation Education: Frameworks and Tools* (Vol. 32). ISTE Ltd. doi:10.1002/9781119804147

Linnenluecke, M. K., Griffiths, A., & Winn, M. (2012). Extreme weather events and the critical importance of anticipatory adaptation and organizational resilience in responding to impacts. *Business Strategy and the Environment*, *21*(1), 17–32. doi:10.1002/bse.708

Luthans, F., Vogelgesang, G. R., & Lester, P. B. (2006). Developing the psychological capital of resiliency. *Human Resource Development Review*, *5*(1), 25–44. doi:10.1177/1534484305285335

Masten, A. S. (2001). Ordinary magic: Resilience processes in development. *The American Psychologist*, *56*(3), 227–238. doi:10.1037/0003-066X.56.3.227 PMID:11315249

Masten, A. S. (2009). Ordinary magic: Lessons from research on resilience in human development. *Education Canada*, *49*(3), 28–32.

May, P. J., & Koski, C. (2013). Addressing public risks: Extreme events and critical infrastructures. *The Review of Policy Research*, *30*(2), 139–159. doi:10.1111/ropr.12012

McClelland, D. C. (1961). *The achieving society*. The Free Press. doi:10.1037/14359-000

Olson, D. L., & Wu, D. (2020). *Enterprise Risk Management Models* (Vol. 3). Springer. doi:10.1007/978-3-662-60608-7

Organisation for Economic Co-operation and Development (OECD). (2020). *Coronavirus (COVID-19): SME policy responses*. Retrieved from https://www.oecd.org/coronavirus/policy-responses/coronavirus-covid19-sme-policy-responses-04440101/

Orr, J. A., King, R. J., Hawke, P., & Dalgleish, J. (2013). Can we text you? A qualitative exploration of young unemployed jobseekers' attitudes to receiving resilience-building SMS messages. *Advances in Mental Health, 11*(3), 268–285. doi:10.5172/jamh.2013.11.3.268

Palich, L. E., & Bagby, D. R. (1995). Using cognitive theory to explain entrepreneurial risk-taking: Challenging conventional wisdom. *Journal of Business Venturing, 10*(6), 425–438. doi:10.1016/0883-9026(95)00082-J

Paton, D., Bajek, R., Okada, N., & McIvor, D. (2010). Predicting community earthquake preparedness: A cross-cultural comparison of Japan and New Zealand. *Natural Hazards, 54*(3), 765–781. doi:10.100711069-010-9500-2

Peng, M. W., & Shekshnia, S. V. (2001). *How entrepreneurs create wealth in transition economies*. Academy of Management. Retrieved from: https://www.jstor.org/stable/4165713?origin=JSTOR-pdf&seq=1

Phillips-Wren, G., Pomerol, J. C., Neville, K., & Adam, F. (2020). Supporting Decision Making During a Pandemic: Influence of Stress, Analytics, Experts, and Decision Aids. In J. Leibowitz (Ed.), *The Business of Pandemic: The COVID-19 Story*. Auerbach Publishers, Incorporated. doi:10.1201/9781003094937-12

Portuguez Castro, M., Ross Scheede, C., & Gómez Zermeño, M. (2020). Entrepreneur profile and entrepreneurship skills: Expert's analysis in the Mexican entrepreneurial ecosystem. *International Conference on Technology and Entrepreneurship - Virtual (ICTE-V),* 1-6.

Rae, D., Prince, L., Bosworth, G., & Parkinson, P. (2012). Business inspiration: Small business leadership in recovery? *Industry and Higher Education, 26*(6), 473–489. doi:10.5367/ihe.2012.0125

Ratten, V. (2020). Coronavirus and international business: An entrepreneurial ecosystem perspective. *Thunderbird International Business Review, 62*(5), 1–6. doi:10.1002/tie.22161

Reivich, K. J., Seligman, M. E. P., & McBride, S. (2011). Master resilience training in the U.S. army. *The American Psychologist, 66*(1), 25–34. doi:10.1037/a0021897 PMID:21219045

Ribera, J. (2020). Business and Management Lessons Learned from COVID-19. In J. Leibowitz (Ed.), *The Business of Pandemic: The COVID-19 Story*. Auerbach Publishers, Incorporated. doi:10.1201/9781003094937-1

Rosa, A.C.M., Rosa, A. M., Neves, J.M.S. & Santos, R.O.B.D. (2021). Innovative Entrepreneur and Creativity: A Bibliometric Analysis. *Global Scientific Journals, 9*(3). Retrieved from file:///home/chronos/u-c99ce39cb0cd0fcc8b77fc8301015dd7a2e8c6d4/MyFiles/Downloads/Innovative_Entrepreneur_ and_Creativity_ A_Bibliometric_ Analysis.pdf

Rutter, M. (2008). *Developing concepts in developmental psychopathology. Developmental psychopathology and wellness: Genetic and environmental influences*. American Psychiatric Publishing.

Salisu, I., Hashim, N., Mashi, M. S., & Aliyu, H. G. (2020). Perseverance of effort and consistency of interest for entrepreneurial career success: Does resilience matter? *Journal of Entrepreneurship in Emerging Economies, 12*(2), 279–304. doi:10.1108/JEEE-02-2019-0025

Sawalha, I. H. (2020). A contemporary perspective on the disaster management cycle. *Foresight, 22*(4), 469–482. Advance online publication. doi:10.1108/FS-11-2019-0097

Schneider, R. O. (2002). Hazard mitigation and sustainable community development. *Disaster Prevention and Management, 11*(2), 141–147. doi:10.1108/09653560210426821

Shane, S., & Cable, D. (2002). *Network ties, reputation, and the financing of new ventures.* Retrieved from https://www.researchgate.net/profile/Daniel-Cable-2/publication/227447495_Network_Ties_Reputation_and_the_Financing_of_New_Ventures_Management_Science_Jg_48_3_S_364-381/links/00b495390a82e5ca78000000/Network-Ties-Reputation-and-the-Financing-of-New-Ventures-Management-Science-Jg-48-3-S-364-381.pdf

Shapira, Z. (1995). *Risk taking: A managerial perspective.* Russell Sage Foundation.

Sonfield, M. C., & Lussier, R. N. (2000). Innovation, Risk and Entrepreneurial Strategy. *International Journal of Entrepreneurship and Innovation, 1*(2), 92–93. doi:10.5367/000000000101298586

The Organisation for Economic Co-operation and Development (OECD). (2020). Coronavirus (COVID-19): SME policy responses. *OECD Policy Responses to Coronavirus (COVID-19).* Retrieved from https://www.oecd.org/coronavirus/policy-responses/coronavirus-covid-19-sme-policy-responses-04440101/

Weiner, B. (1961). *An attributional theory of motivation and emotion.* Springer-Verlag.

Wenzel, M., Stanske, S., & Lieberman, M. (2020). *Strategic responses to crisis episodes.* Strategy Management Journal.

Westley, F. R., Tjornbo, O., Schultz, L., Olsson, P., Folke, C., Crona, B., & Bodin, O. (2013). A theory of transformative agency in linked social-ecological systems. *Ecology and Society, 18*(3), 27. doi:10.5751/ES-05072-180327

World Bank. (2020, June 8). *The Global Economic Outlook During the COVID-19 Pandemic: A Changed World.* Retrieved from: https://www.worldbank.org/en/news/feature/2020/06/08/the-global-economic-outlook-during-the-covid-19-pandemic-a-changed-world

Zautra, A. J., Hall, J. S., & Murray, K. E. (2010). *Resilience: A new definition of health for people and communities. Handbook of adult resilience.* Guilford.

Zerzri, M. (2017). *The threat of cyber terrorism and recommendations for countermeasures.* Center for Applied Policy Research. Retrieved from https://euagenda.eu/upload/publications/untitled-145478-ea.pdf

APPENDIX 1: QUESTIONNAIRE DESIGN

1. Was your business positively or negatively impacted by the COVID-19 pandemic restrictions?
   a. My business was positively impacted.
   b. My business was negatively impacted.
   c. My business was NOT impacted in any way.
2. How was your business impacted by COVID-19 lockdowns and restrictions?
   a. My business got busier.
   b. My business got less busy.
   c. My business was not impacted in any way.
   d. Lockdowns and restrictions resulted in me having no customers/sales at all.
3. Did local/national lockdowns force you to temporarily close?
   a. Yes, I had to close my business during lockdowns and could not operate in any way.
   b. Yes, I had to close my business during lockdowns but I found alternative ways to operate.
   c. No, my business did not have to close due to lockdowns.
4. Did you have a risk management plan in place?
   a. I did not know what a risk management plan was prior to participating in this survey.
   b. Yes, but I did not consider a global pandemic as a risk.
   c. Yes, and I considered a global pandemic as a risk.
   d. No, I know what a risk management plan is but did not create one.
5. Do you think a risk management plan would have been beneficial to your business in preparation for a crisis episode such as the COVID-19 pandemic?
   a. Yes, I think I would have been more prepared.
   b. I do not know the benefits of a risk management plan.
   c. No, I do not think a risk management plan is beneficial to my business.
6. Would you be interested in education/training opportunities surrounding risk management plans for your business?
   a. Yes, I am interested in learning more about risk management plans.
   b. No, I do not think they would be beneficial to me or my business.
   c. No, I do not have time to learn more about risk management plans.
7. Did you adapt your business in any way to accommodate operating during lockdowns?
   a. Yes, I started new products/services that were allowed to be sold/conducted during lockdowns.
   b. No, my business was not impacted so I did not have to find alternatives.
   c. No, I did not see an opportunity to adapt my business.
   d. Yes, I was able to move all/part of my business online without having to start new products/services.
8. If you adapted your business, will you keep these adaptations post COVID-19 lockdowns?
   a. I did not have to adapt.
   b. Yes.
   c. No.

9. Do you think your business adaptations improved the development of your business?
    a. No, my adaptations were a way of survival and did not improve my business or services in any way.
    b. I did not adapt.
    c. Yes, my adaptations have improved my business in ways that I did not expect.
    d. I already planned my new products/services prior to COVID-19, but the lockdowns made me start these new products/services sooner than originally planned.
    e. I already planned my new products/services prior to COVID-19 and the pandemic did NOT influence these plans in any way.

APPENDIX 2: SURVEY RESULTS

1. Was your business positively or negatively impacted by the COVID-19 pandemic restrictions?

Table 2.

A.	My business was positively impacted.	31.03%
B.	My business was negatively impacted.	65.52%
C.	My business was NOT impacted in any way.	3.45%

2. How was your business impacted by COVID-19 lockdowns and restrictions?

Table 3.

A.	My business got busier.	24.14%
B.	My business got less busy.	44.83%
C.	My business was not impacted in any way.	6.90%
D.	Lockdowns and restrictions resulted in me having no customers/sales at all.	24.14%

3. Did local/national lockdowns force you to temporarily close?

Table 4.

A.	Yes, I had to close my business during lockdowns and could not operate in any way.	41.38%
B.	Yes, I had to close my business during lockdowns but I found alternative ways to operate.	24.14%
C.	No, my business did not have to close due to lockdowns.	34.48%

4. Did you have a risk management plan in place?

Table 5.

A.	I did not know was a risk management plan was prior to participating in this survey.	37.93%
B.	Yes, but I did not consider a global pandemic as a risk.	17.24%
C.	Yes, and I considered a global pandemic as a risk.	3.45%
D.	No, I know what a risk management plan is but did not create one.	41.38%

5. Do you think a risk management plan would have been beneficial to your business in preparation for a crisis episode such as the COVID-19 pandemic?

Table 6.

A.	Yes I think I would have been more prepared.	48.28%
B.	I do not know the benefits of a risk management plan.	17.24%
C.	No, I do not think a risk management plan is beneficial to my business.	34.48%

6. Would you be interested in education/training opportunities surrounding risk management plans for your business?

Table 7.

A.	Yes, I am interested in learning more about risk management plans.	55.17%
B.	No, I do not think they would be beneficial to me or my business.	27.59%
C.	No, I do not have time to learn more about risk management plans.	17.24%

7. Did you adapt your business in any way to accommodate operating during lockdowns?

Table 8.

A.	Yes I started new products/services that were allowed to be sold/conducted during lockdowns.	51.72%
B.	No, my business was not impacted so I did not have to find alternatives.	6.90%
C.	No, I did not see an opportunity to adapt my business.	13.79%
D.	Yes, I was able to move all/part of my business online without having to start new products/services.	27.59%

8. If you adapted your business, will you keep these adaptations post COVID-19 lockdowns?

Table 9.

A.	I did not have to adapt.	24.14%
B.	Yes.	68.97%
C.	No.	6.90%

9. Do you think your business adaptations improved the development of your business?

Table 10.

A.	No, my adaptations were a way of survival and did not improve my business or services in any way.	10.34%
B.	I did not adapt.	13.79%
C.	Yes, my adaptation have improved my business in ways that I did not expect.	65.52%
D.	I already planned my new products/services prior to COVID-19, but the lockdowns made me start these new products/services sooner than originally planned.	6.90%
E.	I already planned my new products/services prior to COVID-19 and the pandemic did NOT influence these plans in any way.	3.45%

Chapter 4
Post-Pandemic Restorative Talent Management Strategy for SME Development

Neeta Baporikar
https://orcid.org/0000-0003-0676-9913
Namibia University of Science and Technology, Namibia & University of Pune, India

EXECUTIVE SUMMARY

Indian economy post-COVID 19 pandemic may witness a massive reengineering of all its economic activities. Some will cherish the change, while others will perish over time. The post-pandemic scenario will have a drastic impact across industries and sectors regardless of their scale or size. The magnitude of impact on SMEs and entrepreneurship is unfathomable considering the prevailing intensity of the crisis. SMEs should come up with plausible innovation and talented human force to sustain in the market. The enterprises should develop and nourish 'talent culture' and should focus on 'talent', which remains the most neglected component in Indian SMEs until today. Hence, adopting an exploratory approach with a systematic literature review, the chapter focuses on positioning the importance of talent management and its components in the SME framework to manage the post-pandemic crisis. In the process, the chapter deliberates on the key strategies for rearing SMEs through proper management of critical talent and human resources.

INTRODUCTION

Talent management has become a buzzword across Indian industries with wide recognition. Talent management acts as a major HR intervention that aims to the intrinsic develop of employee's talent. In this knowledge economy, talent management plays a vital role in the resilient process of SMEs and entrepreneurship. The various interventions of talent management will help the SME's in emerging as successful entrepreneurship in the post-pandemic era. India had until recent times neglected the potentials of talent management where talent management stands as an unknown concept in the SME context. Indian SME's which are largely struggling to meet their ends meet has not yet tested the fruitfulness of

DOI: 10.4018/978-1-7998-7657-1.ch004

this concept. The anonymity in the talent definition and identification strategies contributes to the plight of talent management in this sector. Considering talent management synonymous with human resource management is the ever greatest mistake of these millennia. Talent management emerges as a holistic concept that identified the pivotal positions in the organization filled through the successful development of the talent pool. Talent management is posited as a key element in staffing offering thoughtful insights for human and organizational development (Vaiman, Scullion, & Collings, 2012). Small and medium enterprises which were already squeezed by changing politics and academic research will become topsy-turvy post this pandemic situation. The Indian SME's are largely considered as the major source of employment and contributors to the global economy. In India, SME's represent over 90% of the country's business and captures a predominant role in the overall development index. This sector also assumes the main role in boosting employment opportunities at an estimated 30-50% of available opportunities (Krishnan & Scullion, 2017). Post this pandemic the working and configuration of SMEs require massive reengineering for both their survival and sustainability. The revival of SMEs via human resource forms is crucial. Hence, adopting an exploratory approach with a systematic literature review the chapter focuses on positioning the importance of talent management and its components in the SME framework to manage the post-pandemic crisis. In the process, the chapter deliberates on the key strategies for rearing SMEs through proper management of critical talent and human resources. The less used yet powerful lens of talent management has been explored to plan a revival and resilient mechanism for the Indian SME's.

LITERATURE REVIEW

Despite the economic importance of small- and medium-sized enterprises (SMEs), talent management in this context is under-researched. The liability of smallness and scarce resources as typical features of SMEs require a specific definition and approach to talent management. The limited knowledge about talent management in SMEs indicates major challenges in attracting and retaining talent (Festing, Harsch, Schäfer, & Scullion, 2017). Moreover, in the present day, the success and worth of businesses depend more on intellectual capital. So, knowledge is a critical resource, for any organizational growth and sustainability. For small and medium enterprises (SMEs) the latent knowledge is seen as the principal component for success and often tends to be over guarded and that sometimes becomes detrimental to the SMEs' growth (Baporikar, 2020a; 2014). This outlook towards knowledge by SMEs has to change as there is vast room for talent management.

Small and Medium Enterprises (SMEs) are the engines of economic growth, promote equitable development and create more opportunities for being innovative in providing sustainable solutions (Baporikar, 2021; 2020b; 2018b). SMEs and entrepreneurs play a crucial role in providing employment opportunities, aid industrialization in rural backward areas, reduce regional imbalances, and assure equitable distribution of national income and wealth (Baporikar, 2015; 2018c). But survival in the new environment calls not only for improved productivity but sustainability and growth through innovation on an incessant basis (Baporikar, 2014; 2018a). Business sustainability involves self-assessment to identify improvement opportunities, strengths, and ideas for future organizational development. In India, though SMEs are an important contributor to the economy, yet many face a lot of difficulties and end winding up or becoming unsustainable. Several studies have shown that factors related to poor management, less innovative approaches, short short-termism are the causes of failure or closure.

An organization is a structure, which consists of two or more people who have a deliberate objective and intention to accomplish it. Therefore, about this definition, it is easily understandable that the organization concept has roots not only in our time but also in ancient times. Management concept is also derivable from an equation in which both people and their organization exist as vital variables. Both management and organization practices stem from ancient times and survive in today's global era. The business management concept has evolved as a separate discipline during and after the industrial revolution. In connection with this development, this discipline has combined many different theories born from diverse disciplines and approaches from researchers and applications from managers and other professionals (Baporikar, 2019). This amazing development of management has reached its peak in today's business environment. Today's dynamic, chaotic and complex environment makes it a must for SMEs to adopt contemporary approaches for maximizing both individual and organizational effectiveness. Different contemporary management techniques, approaches, and implications apply to this unstable, dynamic, and knowledge-intensive environment. Among the various approaches to competitiveness, talent management strategies are at the core of organizational growth, development, and sustainability.

TALENT MANAGEMENT

'Talent management is becoming an area of growing concern in the field of human resource management. Retention of good employees and the role that various factors have in an employee's decision to stay or leave an organization is many sought-after themes of contemporary management research. Talent management is an espoused and enacted commitment to implementing an integrated, strategic, and technology-enabled approach to human resource management. This commitment stems in part from the widely-shared belief that human resources are the organization's primary source of competitive advantage; an essential asset that is available in increasingly short supply every passing day (Chitranshi, 2015). Talent management refers to the anticipation of required human capital for an organization and the planning to meet those needs. The field increased in popularity after McKinsey's 1997 research and the 2001 book on *The War for Talent*. Talent management is the science of using strategic human resource planning to improve business value and to make it possible for companies and organizations to reach their goals. Talent Management refers to the process of attracting, selecting, training, developing, and promoting employees through an organization (Baporikar, 2017a: 2017b).

SMEs owners and managers who focus on developing talent in-house ensure their employees have the tools and resources they need to perform well, receive proper compensation, and transition to leadership roles. Internally developed leaders are valuable assets because over time they have developed the necessary core competencies and internalized company values (Baporikar, 2020b). A talent-management strategy needs to link to business strategy to make sense. From a talent management standpoint, employee evaluations concern two major areas of measurement: 'performance' and 'potential'. Current employee performance within a specific job has always been a standard evaluation measurement tool of the profitability of an employee. However, talent management also seeks to focus on an employee's potential, meaning an employee's future performance, if given the proper development of skills and increased responsibility (Iles, 2013). The term "talent management" is usually associated with 'competency-based management'. Talent management decisions are often driven by a set of organizational core competencies as well as position-specific competencies. The competency set may include knowledge, skills, experience, and personal traits (Luna-Arocas, 2012).

In a post-pandemic situation due to adverse economic conditions, many SMEs need to cut expenses. This should be the ideal environment to execute a talent management system as a means of optimizing the performance of each employee and the organization. However, within many SMEs, the concept of human capital management has just begun to develop. With more SMEs in the process of deepening their global footprints, more questions have been asked about new strategies and products, but very few on the kind of talent management that will bring them success in their globalization process. "In fact, only 5 percent of SMEs say they have a clear talent management strategy and operational programs in place today."

CURRENT SCENARIO

Notwithstanding its effect on general wellbeing, COVID-19 has caused a significant monetary shock. The agony and vulnerability of the effect of the COVID-19 on entrepreneurs are faltering and liable to be considerable. Business people are being compelled to find a way to keep working and many are dreadful about their fates. A National Small Business Association part overview found that three of every four entrepreneurs are exceptionally worried about the financial effect of COVID-19. Small organizations, including proprietors and workers, are as of now confronted with troublesome, quick decisions: to remain open and face challenges with the soundness of their staff and clients or close without help. These associations as of now work on a slight net revenue, and most new organizations aren't even beneficial yet. The decision is a troublesome one, and consider all the more requesting choices will be on their way.

In this situation, the issues regarding attraction, development, and retention of employee's talent in the SMEs is a long-discussed yet still pending agenda. The relatively little attention to SME's and their vital components have deteriorated the talent culture in this sector (Park & Ghauri, 2015). When the whole world is undergoing an unprecedented transformation in the field of talent management, the SME's and their organizational framework are largely unaware of its effectiveness and implementation dilemmas. (Doh, Smith, Stumpf, & Tymon, 2011) had highlighted the turmoils of talent neglected organization structure irrespective of its nature and size compositions. Unproductive employees, undesired outcomes, and losing key employees are always neglected in times of depressed economic crisis. As Indian-based companies grow and Western companies continue to enter, expand, and hire professionals, capitalizing on outsourcing opportunities, lower labor costs, and relatively high skill levels, talent gaps constrain opportunities for growth and success. Studies have proved that talent management fosters room for creativity among organizations. Creative mindsets push innovation leading to the pooling of competitive advantages (Ingram, 2016). (Harsch & Festing, 2020) noted the role of talent management in promoting organizational agility. An agile environment creates a blend of dynamic capabilities for the organization that ultimately leads to organizational success. This study further emphasizes three dimensions of dynamic capabilities namely sensing, seizing, and transforming the organizational talent and thereby the economic opportunities. There are three magical bullets for developing talent in an organization (Ali & Hollis, 2014) that still needs to be embraced by the Indian SME's. This includes basic intelligence through the hiring process, variety of experience, and emphasis on change and innovation. While the first two ingredients are visible, the third component requires the blend of talent management. Rather than considering talent management as another palette in the HR domain, the organizations should judiciously embrace the change, deploy talent, developing talent and retain their talent post this pandemic and forever (Alziari, 2017).

After the worldwide money-related emergency, the business world has gone through radical change, and associations have gotten more globalized and innovation-driven. The administration, controllers, and organizations are dealing with fundamental issues like financial recuperation, environmental change, administration models, and innovation progression. In any case, in what manner will organizations adjust to the repercussions of the worldwide emergency and what sort of ability will they have to send in this coordinated worldwide condition? Does the incorporation of ability the board with global portability kill the issue looked at by business groups? Talent versatility is the capacity of the association to move individuals from job to job, capacity to capacity, and business to business quickly and straightforwardly to handle basic business challenges(Mishra, 2017). It is imperative to have a profoundly gifted workforce set up if such objectives are to be figured out. Certain countries contribute to creating ability at home, while others search abroad for the correct workforce. Some put their eggs in both of these baskets. Talent executives are as yet a hot issue in numerous associations. Chiefs and other top supervisors are worried about having the ability to take their organizations forward and they frequently focus on ability procurement. They may feel that they have to enroll superb individuals through the utilization of talent scouts who can poach ability from different organizations. There is no uncertainty that organizations frequently need to select senior individuals from outside. However, there have been numerous outstanding disappointments in this procedure, particularly where the approaching individual doesn't change following a culture that they have not experienced childhood in. Securing ability as opposed to developing it can appear to be a simple handy solution to issues of filling senior initiative holes. However, it may not pay off by and by. Associations progressively need to attempt to guarantee that they have somebody set up that can succeed an individual who leaves the association or gets an inner advancement. An issue is that such changes, aside from retirement, are frequently erratic. Henceforth more dynamic associations perceive that they need a pool of capable individuals who are promotable into influential positions. This implies putting resources into junior administrators, graduates, and other people who can be in a situation to assume greater liability if necessary. One approach to describe this methodology is that it is more in the idea of ''progression improvement'' than progression arranging. As opposed to endeavoring an unthinking cycle where an individual is distinguished as a replacement to their chief, the progression advancement approach perceives that associations need the adaptability to browse a scope of alternatives when somebody leaves a post. First and foremost where associations have distinguished a replacement they have been gotten out when it is the selected replacement that leaves the association first. Another factor representing a mark against progression arranging has been the inclination for prejudicial practices to happen – white male supervisors have been known to recognize potential replacements that resemble them and in this manner have disparaged the chance of a lady or ethnic minority chief having the option to take on the job.

DISCUSSION

Along with understanding the need to hire, develop, and retain talented people, organizations are aware that they must manage talent as a critical resource to achieve the best possible results. Few, if any, today have an adequate supply of talent. Talent is an increasingly scarce resource, so it must be managed to the fullest effect (Baporikar, 2017a). Are SMEs able to do more with less? The idea of managing talent is not new. Four or five decades ago, it was viewed as a peripheral responsibility best relegated to the personnel department, today talent management is an organizational function that is taken far more seriously (Baporikar, 20 17b).

Yet successful sailing in talent management is a distant dream for the majority of SME organizations. Talent differentiation, segmentation, ostensible exclusivity, subjective talent identification, and labeling process are some of the major reasons that make talent management a double-edged sword (Rotolo et al., 2018). Talent management sometimes fails and goes wrong by rooting up all the organizational efforts (Kumar, 2014). The definition of the substance 'talent' varies across industries. The talent management practices are widely rooted in exclusive management philosophies in which only top performers are labeled as talented. This will harm the psychological contract of left-out employees whose performance was not considered valuable for the organization. The effectiveness of talent management was measured based on many outdated quantitative metrics. Talent management researchers and practitioners have widely neglected the role of 'inner work life' which can never be achieved with extrinsic motivation alone. By practicing exclusive talent philosophies, workforce differentiation, and metric assessment the employees will eventually start to dislike what they do which ultimately affects the organizational performance.

This pervasive fear of failure encourages employees to pursue low-hanging fruits rather than embrace entrepreneurship and use productive mistakes to drive innovation. The major controversy existing in the body of literature pertains to the very substance of talent. What is considered to be talent?(Dalal & Akdere, 2018) (Gallardo-gallardo, Dries, & González-cruz, 2013) What is not?(Nijs, Gallardo-gallardo, Dries, & Sels, 2014) What are the circumstances and various factors that constitute talent? (Cappelli, 2008) How to identify the right talent? (Snell, 2011) Talent identified in one context may not prove fruitful in another context. The diversity brought in by the employees brings with them a variety of talent, which further needs nourishment from the organization.

Another major stigma in talent management practice revolves around the customization of the talent interventions. What appeals to one group of employees need not get approved by other peer groups? Indian SME's are the epitome of diversity. Millennials are slowly gaining momentum within the sector, which have ultimately different perspectives, views, and visions about their organization. For eg; a veteran employee will prefer mentoring over teamwork, whereas the younger generation is widely tech-savvy and prefer to work in teams. Hence the organization must ensure to customize each talent management intervention that best suits each group. Once piece and style never fit all, though customizing talent management comes at a heavy cost to the business.

The new economy has prompted reconsidered characterizations of work and the work power, comparing the immediate all-day business model to unforeseen work and an undeniably wide scope of elective work game plans to become both in type and size. Maybe it is no big surprise: laborers are carefully associated day in and day out, frightful at the possibility of a more drawn-out working life, separated, and their work profitability has not so much expanded in the course of recent years. As their business status shifts from beneficial work by an organization to different autonomous and less secure specialist modalities, they are compelled to change vocations due to (in) voluntary disturbances or mishaps, continually expecting to re-make themselves, and incorporate more noteworthy strength with their profession venture. Each modern upheaval required change and variation at the authoritative level. Jacob Morgan summed up the focal point of businesses through ensuing mechanical insurgencies. Similarly as before, when HR developed from workforce the executives to vital human asset the board - and consequently ability the board - a modern upheaval is again disturbing the current ability the executives rehearses. The fourth mechanical upset is making ready for a more dynamic ability the board later on - if HR can react to the disturbance challenges conveniently and fittingly. The new customized and altered ability to oversee management design is straightforward, legitimate, responsive, and straightforward. The new ability of the executives' esteem proposition is developing from ability procurement - grounded in approaches and systems - to creator or planner of specialist experiences. Building another authoritative ability the board engineering includes a lot of speculation to plan a gainful and important involvement with the physical, innovative, and social condition of our organizations through arrangements that are convincing, charming, basic, and tweaked for various worker personas. HR and ability the executives must escape from a ''one program fits all'' attitude and consider building an organizational ability engineering that permits modifying projects to explicit worker fragments. The design is tied in with making a representative encounter through HR arrangements that are at the crossing point of the need and desires for the workers and the ability necessities of the organization. However, HR and ability the board should at present meet existing necessities regarding being legitimately agreeable, socially proper, impartial, and reasonable. The genuine talent the board challenge is about a guarantee to have any kind of effect in the life of associations and their ability - regardless of whether they are representatives or part of the bigger unforeseen workforce.

SOLUTIONS AND RECOMMENDATIONS

Although companies around the world have made talent management a top priority, most human resource professionals and senior executives believe their organizations have not fully resolved the talent management puzzle. It is revealed that albeit being a differentiator between organizations that succeed and those that do not, talent management is saddled with uncertainties, lack of clarity, and misunderstanding, which are hurdles that need to be cleared to pave way for more effective talent programs (Oppong, 2017). To overcome these, SME organizations should avoid one common blueprint to all talent situations, but develop approaches that suit individual talent requirements as a one-fit-for-all solution is theoretically and practically impossible to face the challenges of designing, developing, and implementing talent management in the Indian SME's. The minuscule natures of organizations, changing demographic trends, and stringent HR policies have deprived the development of multiple approaches in SMEs. In other words, the Indian SME's were already hit hard by viruses that made it change to reverse. Now, since both the global and domestic business environment has hit hard and changes, it is time for these SME's to change their face in the global business footprint.

The prima facie of any talent management process lies in building and shaping well-conceived talent architecture. The discussion on the systematic approach, which includes six steps, follows in the subsequent paragraphs.

Step 1: Defining Talent

What is considered as talent in one industry/business need not constitute talent in another industry/sector. The HR manager must conceptualize and operationalize the element of talent. Talent can be innate, acquired, developable, and also hereditary (Iles, 2013). Talent is a very subjective concept and can mean potential, a specific endeavor, or a skill (Baporikar, 2017a; 2014).

Step 2: Talent Identification and Attracting Talent

The talent identification step is the foundation of strong talent management architecture (Natacha Golik & Rita Blanco, 2014). The most recommended strategies include performance management and potential identification. Talent can also be identified through a talent matrix (Bhatnagar, 2008). There are many talent identification tools in practice; however the most comprehensive among them is performance management and potential identification. Performance management is concerned with fixing attainable goals for the employees, measuring them concretely, analyzing the deviations if any, and necessary actions at proper times. But no organization can succeed only with the performance evaluation or management. The Indian SME's should embrace various potential identification or management for promoting inclusive talent development goals (Baporikar, 2014). Every individual has their potential, however small or big, important or unimportant for organizational growth. The organization should identify these potentials, nourish them and channel them for the growth of their business. The authors again reemphasize that the talent identification process should never be subjective. Talent is not a feature confined only to star performers; it is an inclusive feature that can be seen at all levels of the organization.

Step 3: Talent Development

Speaking about talent development, the major underlying fact is that there is no one-fit solution for talent development across organizational hierarchy and a particular industry/sector (Baporikar, 2017b). Researchers have opined that talent developmental interventions should be designed in a way that promotes inclusivity and boosts the psychological contract of the employees towards the organization. Talent development tools consist of a set of HR interventions that increases the necessary organizational talent among the employees. In the majority of the organizational circumstances, talent development can be classified on a three-tier basis- developmental relationship, developmental assignment, and formal education-based talent development. A developmental relationship is based on providing relationship-oriented interventions to develop employee talent. These kinds of interventions seek to manage the relationship between various employees and between the employees and the management. Two major ways to achieve this developmental relationship were through coaching and mentoring. In caching the employees are churned up and provided extensive knowledge in a particular subject matter and whereas mentoring involves a holistic process in which the employees are mentored, their inner feeling towards their organization is boosted. Effective mentoring affects the employees more psychologically than coaching and developmental assignments work on real organizational problems and dilemmas faced by the SME's. These assignments are an important part of the talent development system as they help both organizational and employee growth. Job rotations, project assignments, and international transfers are the major tools of project assignments. The employees must be continuously rotated in varieties of jobs in the organizational framework; the main notion of job rotation revolves around building good organizational expertise. The future workplace clearly demands varied skill sets, which can never be increased rather diminish by continuously engaging in monotonous jobs. The employees must be provided with various roles in the project assignment group. Project assignment roles can vary from the supervisor to project coordinator or just a project member. The employees should become part of nail-biting projects, to understand their difficulties, lagging skills, and where to improve upon. The entire work challenge must be divided into minor projects which are to be headed and managed by employee groups. The role of formal education in any sector can never be ruled out. It is the concrete fundamental knowledge in a subject that helps the business in achieving long-term success. Formal education takes place in the form of corporate programs and executive coaching. The SME's and the government should arrange many such interactions which promote vivid learning, sharing of success mantras, organizational expertise, and career development skills. The employees should always be motivated to attend these kinds of programs, which provide innovative ideas for development.

Step 4: Talent Retention

When developing retention strategies, we need to take into account demographic and other factors that influence the decision to remain with or leave an organization. Progress, demanding jobs, and career development are goals for early-career employees. Flexibility at work, the ability to adapt their tasks, and gain a sense of fulfillment from their work are goals for mid-career workers. Retention is something companies ought to be cautious about; it's important to preempt attrition. There are also other factors and variables outside the control of an entity, such as the labor market or the environment. Attrition is often beyond organizational control and is strongly affected by the dynamics of the labor market or the country's economy, etc. In the light of this discovery, it is time to redefine the conventionally accepted objectives of human resource management (that of reducing employee turnover among others) and substitute it with a new, perhaps aspirational, aim of being able to control who leaves the company and when. Retaining skilled workers ensures that the components of work satisfaction and organizational engagement need to be analyzed by organizations. For certain organizations and their workers, the reputation of the company and the sector will be relevant, while for others, it will be job satisfaction, promotional opportunities, and career management. Organizations must adopt workplace practices, which are supported strongly by staff if retention levels are to be improved (Baporikar 2017a). Given that the needs of workers vary from one organization to another, each company must communicate with its staff to determine initiatives that are likely to gain the most impact.

Step 5: Developing Inclusive Talent Culture

Talent management is commonly seen as an exclusive activity that focuses on cultivating a limited proportion of high-performing and high-potential workers. Exclusive discourses speak of talent pools and talent streams and a segregated workforce based on skill and commitment. However, the definition of inclusive talent management remains ill-defined and ambiguous and it is hard to find compelling examples. Two 'inclusive' definitions require consideration. One is that each person has the opportunity to be covered in an intelligence program and this may also require fine motion to equalize the possibilities for deprived or underrepresented agencies of humans from a variety of backgrounds to show their potential. This strategy has implications for the ways that genius is identified. The second means of 'inclusive' is that all people are deemed to have Genius of some kind and therefore have got right of entry to programs that enhance their talent. This means of inclusion is used here; we are dealing with inclusive participation, no longer inclusive opportunity. Talent management in many instances was described as the accelerated improvement of a small percentage of employees, exceptional using their above common performance and conceivable for promotion, and who can make significant in additional contributions to the enterprise and the alignment of these employees with key roles.

Step 6: Preventing Talent Derailment

Profession direction is the identical representation of progression improvement. Here the emphasis is on the individual and their vocation decisions as opposed to jobs that should be filled. Numerous individuals invite uphold in settling on professional decisions. From an improvement perspective, it very well may be useful for more youthful workers to see that they have to consider vocation decisions which will prepare them for an assortment of conceivable future jobs; the world is changing excessively quick for individuals to expect that all the current senior jobs will be later on equivalent to they are present. This may mean individuals taking sideways moves as opposed to continually searching for advancements. It can likewise mean individuals dismissing advancements if they don't see formative open doors in the job offered them. Learning and improvement professionals need to draw in with the dynamic association of the various components plot above. They may need to present a defense for an all the more learning-based way to deal with the ability of the board yet they can't guarantee that learning and advancement action alone will unravel ability the executives' issues. They have to participate in an exchange with HR associates in zones, for example, pay and advantages and enrollment to verify that all components are set up to draw in and hold capable individuals. Touchpoints are the passionate purposes of contact the worker has with the association whether through structures, frameworks, or individuals. When a representative encounter map has been structured, it is basic for the ability supervisory group to build up a stock of all the ability the executives' touchpoints the worker has with the cycles, items, and administrations that HR gives and through which channels (virtual or f2f) these touchpoints are experienced. These touchpoints are experienced either emphatically by representatives or they are seen contrarily as torment focuses. HR can give a consistent arrangement of administrations that empowers work efficiency and improves the general representative experience and handles all the touchpoints with individuals (supervisors, HR, collaborators), devices, frameworks, strategies, and techniques - from the worker's perspective as opposed to from the ability the executives' cycle and conveyance viewpoint. Since representatives are probably going to encounter the different touchpoints to some degree distinctively dependent on various bunches of needs and needs identified with their personas, it is important to utilize the focal point or superseding channel through which a specific individual is seeing the worker venture.

Figure 1 gives the systematic approach framework for developing talent management architecture.

FUTURE RESEARCH DIRECTIONS

The focus of this chapter 'talent management in SMEs' which is less researched in the HR domain in general and more so in the Indian context. The composition of each industry and underlying demographic dividend plays a rich role in shaping the future of talent management research. Conceptual and empirical research exploring the positive impact of talent management on various constructs such as organizational trust perceived justice, organizational performance already exists in the literature. Empirical studies that deal with the possible negative impact such as employee alienation, negative psychological contract, perceived injustice, imbalance in inner work life need to be conceptualized in the future. In this chapter, the researchers focused on the potentials of using talent management as a reviving mechanism for Indian SME's. Future studies can be done in the customizing talent management process for SMEs, developing non-metric-based talent assessment and talent reviews for more robust implementation of talent management across industries.

Figure 1. Systematic Approach Framework
Source: Self-Developed

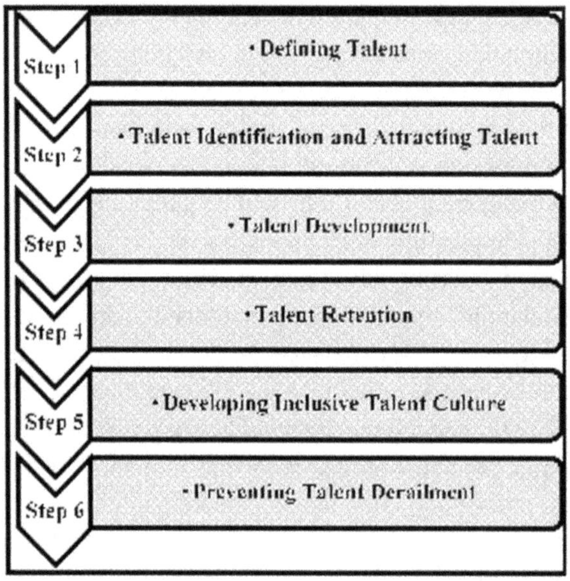

CONCLUSION

SMEs are enormously affected by the negative effect of the progressing pestilence flare-up in the COVID-19 period. Most importantly, these are more labor-oriented organizations whose working and productivity have grossly changed as the workers are in isolation, as is going on in a few states of India. Likewise, they have more slender liquidity saves. They have restricted budgetary options, and they generally depend on help from neighborhood banks. In most cases, they need resources that can be discarded, or that can be utilized as a guarantee for new credit lines. It is significant to note here that the act of ability to perform well isn't another checkbox to be ticked for the association with an organization. One must not overlook that the six phases mentioned already are essentially the unfortunate obligation, which is creating results significant to the business. Creating and holding representatives are not the endgame. The endgame is accomplishing predominant business results and competitiveness through improved ability, which the executives rehearse. One must not dismiss the genuine objective and thus, not all ability the executives rehearse is implementable in the hierarchical setting, and all expenses caused toward ability the board must be justified. The challenges related to the ability of the executives have been concentrated inside and out and indeed, are confronted each day by HR experts in companies all over the world.

Talent management is more craftsmanship than logical administration. At the point when scholastically investigating ability the management and specialists widen the idea to incorporate professional way by which the executives can long haul hierarchical procedure. Worker commitment levels henceforth impact the choices of the representatives to remain on in the association with their employers or to leave for greener fields. Subsequently, through representative commitment, associations must endeavor to support an affiliation/connection between the business and worker, provoking expectation to remain on inferable from a larger feeling of connectedness. The association must know which representatives or gatherings of representatives to focus on their maintenance endeavors. Accordingly, studies proved that reasons that starting from great ability fascination and ability the executives rehearses, the association will get drew in workers, with whom managers/associations structure a suffering relationship. Truly, for dynamic businesses, what's to come is as of nowhere and continually advancing. Without a doubt, this ability the board improvements are not just shaking the conventional and built up training of HR they likewise making a danger or potentially open door for ability the executives. The war for ability recommends that organization A recruits a first-rate worker from organization B and friends B enlists a first-rate representative from organization A - a predicament. The current ability of the executives has moved past this and the fight presently is about how to connect with and hold significant representatives by offering them convincing encounters at work. Ability securing, an essential piece of ability the board, is presently being tested to ponder the enlistment and determination of laborers. When the individual is ready, ability the board turns into the hierarchical draftsman of the worker experience where the physical condition, innovation, and culture are incorporated to create maintainability sweet detect a success for the business, the representative, and at last the customer. Workers are constrained by the transition to a mutual economy, the untethering of work from a physical area, the relocation of human work by innovation, and developing requests for assorted variety, consideration, and having a place.

Perspective changes don't nullify a portion of the valid and demonstrated accepted procedures of the old reasoning - if they despite everything include esteem - yet rather drastically change the talk. How about we outline this with a relationship of the half-vacant/half-full glass with regards to the advancing HR and ability the board rehearses. Conventional HR centers around value-based exercises identified with consistency and operational issues (glass half-empty). This kind of HR practice can even now be seen in numerous associations around the world - ordinarily in little organizations with HR offices set up fundamentally with managerial faculty. Key ability the executives plan and improves cycles to serve the serious human capital needs of the association as the essential HR client (glass half-full). As the setting is changing drastically today, there is a need to reexamine HR's incentive, update the ability of the board - to fill the half-full glass once more. This is an opportunity to limit (or right to completion) by concentrating on the representative/laborer client, experience and searching for the sweet spot where abilities and the board rehearses are useful for both the specialist and the business. That is another ability that the board is endowed with in dynamic organizations is about. The new customized and tweaked ability to oversee design is basic, valid, responsive, and straightforward. The new ability of the executive's incentive is advancing from ability procurement - grounded in strategies and methodology - to originator or draftsman of laborer encounters. Building another authoritative ability the board engineering includes a lot of speculation to structure a beneficial and significant involvement with the physical, innovative, and social condition of our organizations through arrangements that are convincing, charming, straightforward, and modified for various representative personas. HR and ability the board must escape from a ''one size fits all'' mindset and consider building an authoritative ability design that permits tweaking projects to explicit representative portions.

REFERENCES

Ali, M., & Hollis, L. (2014). Developing Talent 1. *Strategic HR Review*, *4*(2), 1–5.

Alziari, L. (2017). A chief HR officer's perspective on talent management. *Journal of Organizational Effectiveness: People and Performance*, *4*(4). doi:10.1108/JOEPP-05-2017-0047

Baporikar, N. (2014). Strategic Management Overview and SME in Globalized World. In K. Todorov & D. Smallbone (Eds.), *Handbook of Research on Strategic Management in Small and Medium Enterprises* (pp. 22–39). Business Science Reference. doi:10.4018/978-1-4666-5962-9.ch002

Baporikar, N. (2014). Innovation Strategies in SME: Global Perspective. In C. Machado & P. Melo (Eds.), *Effective Human Resources Management in Small and Medium Enterprises: Global Perspectives* (pp. 315–341). Business Science Reference. doi:10.4018/978-1-4666-4731-2.ch016

Baporikar, N. (2015). Role of Entrepreneurship in Networked Indian Economy. In P. Ordóñez de Pablos (Ed.), *Technological Solutions for Sustainable Business Practice in Asia* (pp. 36–59). Business Science Reference. doi:10.4018/978-1-4666-8462-1.ch003

Baporikar, N. (2017a). Global Perspective on Talent Management: The South African Experience. In M. Mupepi (Ed.), *Effective Talent Management Strategies for Organizational Success* (pp. 283–300). IGI Global. doi:10.4018/978-1-5225-1961-4.ch018

Baporikar, N. (2017b). Sustainable Framework to Attract, Develop, and Retain Global Talent. In K. Tamzini, T. Ayed, A. Boulanouar, & Z. Boulanouar (Eds.), *Driving Multinational Enterprises Through Effective Global Talent Management* (pp. 50–74). IGI Global. doi:10.4018/978-1-5225-2557-8.ch003

Baporikar, N. (2018a). Innovation and Sustainability in SMEs. In R. Perez-Uribe, C. Salcedo-Perez, & D. Ocampo-Guzman (Eds.), *Handbook of Research on Intrapreneurship and Organizational Sustainability in SMEs* (pp. 163–181). IGI Global. doi:10.4018/978-1-5225-3543-0.ch008

Baporikar, N. (2018b). Entrepreneurship Development and Project Management (Text & Cases). Himalaya Publishing House.

Baporikar, N. (2018c). *Knowledge Integration Strategies for Entrepreneurship and Sustainability*. IGI Global. doi:10.4018/978-1-5225-5115-7

Baporikar, N. (2019). Factors Creating Competitive Advantage for Family-Owned Business. In J. M. Saiz-Alvarez (Ed.), *Handbook of Research on Digital Marketing Innovations in Social Entrepreneurship and Solidarity Economics* (pp. 47–62). IGI Global. doi:10.4018/978-1-5225-8939-6.ch003

Baporikar, N. (2020a). Role and Room for Knowledge Management in Small and Medium Enterprises. In E. C. Idemudia (Ed.), *Handbook of Research on Social and Organizational Dynamics in the Digital Era* (pp. 115–134). IGI Global. doi:10.4018/978-1-5225-8933-4.ch006

Baporikar, N. (2020b). *Handbook of Research on Entrepreneurship Development and Opportunities in Circular Economy*. IGI Global. doi:10.4018/978-1-7998-5116-5

Baporikar, N. (2021). *Handbook of Research on Sustaining SMEs and Entrepreneurial Innovation in the Post-COVID-19 Era*. IGI Global. doi:10.4018/978-1-7998-6632-9

Bhatnagar, J. (2008). Managing capabilities for talent engagement and pipeline development. *Industrial and Commercial Training*, *40*(1), 19–28. doi:10.1108/00197850810841602

Cappelli, P. (2008). Talent management for the twenty-first century. *Harvard Business Review*, *86*(3), 74–82. doi:10.100710551-010-0541-y PMID:18411966

Chitranshi, J. (2015). Talent Management. In S. Kalia, B. Bhalla, L. Das, & N. Awasthy (Eds.), *Promoting Socio-Economic Development through Business Integration* (pp. 124–134). IGI Global. doi:10.4018/978-1-4666-8259-7.ch009

Dalal, R., & Akdere, M. (2018). Talent development: Status quo and future directions. *Industrial and Commercial Training*, *50*(6), 342–355. doi:10.1108/ICT-03-2018-0033

Doh, J. P., Smith, R. R., Stumpf, S. A., & Tymon, W. G. Jr. (2011). Pride and professionals: Retaining talent in emerging economies. *The Journal of Business Strategy*, *32*(5), 35–42. doi:10.1108/02756661111165453

Festing, M., Harsch, K., Schäfer, L., & Scullion, H. (2017). Talent management in small and medium-sized enterprises. In The Oxford handbook of talent management. OUP.

Gallardo-gallardo, E., Dries, N., & González-cruz, T. F. (2013). Human Resource Management Review What is the meaning of "talent " in the world of work? *Human Resource Management Review*, *23*(4), 290–300. doi:10.1016/j.hrmr.2013.05.002

Harsch, K., & Festing, M. (2020). Dynamic talent management capabilities and organizational agility—A qualitative exploration. *Human Resource Management*, *59*(1), 43–61. doi:10.1002/hrm.21972

Iles, P. (2013). Human Resource Management Review Commentary on "The meaning of 'talent' in the world of work". *Human Resource Management Review*, *23*(4), 301–304. doi:10.1016/j.hrmr.2013.08.002

Ingram, T. (2016). Relationships between Talent Management and Organizational Performance : The Role of Climate for Creativity. *Entrepreneurial Business and Economics Review*, *4*(3), 195–205. doi:10.15678/EBER.2016.040315

Krishnan, T. N., & Scullion, H. (2017). Human Resource Management Review Talent management and dynamic view of talent in small and medium enterprises. *Human Resource Management Review*, *27*(3), 431–441. doi:10.1016/j.hrmr.2016.10.003

Kumar, R. (2014). When talent management goes wrong. *Development and Learning in Organizations*, *28*(5), 24–26. doi:10.1108/DLO-06-2014-0046

Luna-Arocas, R. (2012). Talent Management: A New Perspective in Human Resource Management. In Human Resource Management in the Digital Economy: Creating Synergy between Competency Models and Information (pp. 50-65). IGI Global. doi:10.4018/978-1-61350-207-5.ch003

Mishra, S. (2017). Integration of talent and mobility function: Strategy for HR to manage business. *Strategic HR Review*, *16*(6), 274–278. doi:10.1108/SHR-07-2017-0043

Natacha Golik, M., & Rita Blanco, M. (2014). Talent identification and development tools. *Management Research: Journal of the Iberoamerican Academy of Management*, *12*(1), 23–39. doi:10.1108/MRJIAM-01-2013-0498

Nijs, S., Gallardo-gallardo, E., Dries, N., & Sels, L. (2014). A multidisciplinary review into the definition, operationalization, and measurement of talent. *Journal of World Business*, *49*(2), 180–191. doi:10.1016/j.jwb.2013.11.002

Oppong, N. Y. (2017). Mastering Talent Management: The Uncertainties, Lack of Clarity and Misunderstandings. In M. Mupepi (Ed.), *Effective Talent Management Strategies for Organizational Success* (pp. 31–46). IGI Global. doi:10.4018/978-1-5225-1961-4.ch003

Park, B., & Ghauri, P. N. (2015). Determinants influencing CSR practices in small and medium-sized MNE subsidiaries: A stakeholder perspective. *Journal of World Business*, *50*(1), 192–204. doi:10.1016/j.jwb.2014.04.007

Rotolo, C. T., Church, A. H., Adler, S., Smither, J. W., Colquitt, A. L., Shull, A. C., Paul, K. B., & Foster, G. (2018). Putting an End to Bad Talent Management: A Call to Action for the Field of Industrial and Organizational Psychology. *Industrial and Organizational Psychology: Perspectives on Science and Practice*, *11*(2), 176–219. doi:10.1017/iop.2018.6

Snell, A. (2011). Developing talent intelligence to boost business performance. *Strategic HR Review*, *10*(2), 12–17. doi:10.1108/14754391111108301

Vaiman, V., Scullion, H., & Collings, D. (2012). Talent management decision-making. *Management Decision*, *50*(5), 925–941. doi:10.1108/00251741211227663

ADDITIONAL READING

Atiku, S. O., & Fapohunda, T. (2021). *Human Resource Management Practices for Promoting Sustainability*. IGI Global. doi:10.4018/978-1-7998-4522-5

Baporikar, N. (2016). *Handbook of Research on Entrepreneurship in the Contemporary Knowledge-Based Global Economy*. IGI Global. doi:10.4018/978-1-4666-8798-1

Baporikar, N. (2017). *Innovation and Shifting Perspectives in Management Education*. IGI Global. doi:10.4018/978-1-5225-1019-2

Baporikar, N. (2017). *Management Education for Global Leadership*. IGI Global. doi:10.4018/978-1-5225-1013-0

Baporikar, N. (2018). *Global Practices in Knowledge Management for Societal and Organizational Development*. IGI Global. doi:10.4018/978-1-5225-3009-1

Collings, D. G., Mellahi, K., & Cascio, W. F. (Eds.). (2017). *The Oxford handbook of talent management*. Oxford University Press. doi:10.1093/oxfordhb/9780198758273.001.0001

Cui, W., Khan, Z., & Tarba, S. Y. (2018). Strategic talent management in service SMEs of China. *Thunderbird International Business Review*, *60*(1), 9–20. doi:10.1002/tie.21793

Hughes, C. (2020). *Strategies for Attracting, Maintaining, and Balancing a Mature Workforce*. IGI Global. doi:10.4018/978-1-7998-2277-6

Kaliannan, M., Abraham, M., & Ponnusamy, V. (2016). Effective talent management in Malaysian SMEs: A proposed framework. *Journal of Developing Areas*, *50*(5), 393–401. doi:10.1353/jda.2016.0071

Mupepi, M. (2017). *Effective Talent Management Strategies for Organizational Success.* IGI Global. doi:10.4018/978-1-5225-1961-4

Niu, Y. (2020). Improving the Employability of Mature Workers: Career Learning. In C. Hughes (Ed.), *Strategies for Attracting, Maintaining, and Balancing a Mature Workforce* (pp. 28–60). IGI Global. doi:10.4018/978-1-7998-2277-6.ch002

Perez-Uribe, R. I., Largacha-Martinez, C., & Ocampo-Guzman, D. (2021). *Handbook of Research on International Business and Models for Global Purpose-Driven Companies.* IGI Global. doi:10.4018/978-1-7998-4909-4

Tamzini, K., Ayed, T. L., Boulanouar, A. W., & Boulanouar, Z. (2017). *Driving Multinational Enterprises Through Effective Global Talent Management.* IGI Global. doi:10.4018/978-1-5225-2557-8

KEY TERMS AND DEFINITIONS

Business: Pertains broadly to commercial, financial, and industrial activities.

Competitive Advantage: An advantage that firms have over their competitors, allowing them to generate greater sales or margins and/or retain more customers than their competition. There can be many types of competitive advantages including knowledge, skills, structure, product offerings, distribution network, and support.

Competitiveness: Act of competing for some honor, or advantage. A rivalry between two or more persons or groups for an object desired in common, usually resulting in a victor and a loser but not necessarily involving the destruction of the latter. The need for global competitiveness is much important for any industry to sustain in this competitive world.

Decision-Making: A rational and logical process of choosing the best alternative or course of action among the available options.

Development: Means "steady progress" and stresses effective assisting in hastening a process or bringing about the desired end, a significant consequence or event, the act or process of growing, progressing, or developing.

Dynamic Capabilities: This represents the touchpoints in the organization that the management focuses on talent development. These are the specific talent development centers of the organization.

Enterprises: The act or process of organizing; a structure through which individuals cooperate systematically to conduct business and/or the administrative personnel of such a structure.

Government: The organization, machinery, or agency through which a political unit exercises authority and performs functions and which is usually classified according to the distribution of power within it and usually refers to a political system.

Innovation: Something new or different introduced, is the act of innovating, which includes the introduction of new things or methods. Innovation is also the introduction of a new idea into the marketplace in the form of a new product or service, or an improvement in an organization or process. The process of translating an idea or invention into a good or service to create value for which customers are will to pay.

Policy: Refers to guidelines as issued by the governance.

Small and Medium Enterprises (SMEs): This is a term for segmenting businesses and other organizations that are somewhere between the "small office-home office" size and the larger enterprise.

Country to country this term may vary, but the basis usually is on the criteria of investment, the number of employees, and turnover, etc.

Talent: The innate or acquired quality of an individual to excel in a particular job is called talent.

Talent Architecture: The structure of any talent management system in an organization that is built to enhance employee and organizational performance.

Talent Derailment: A negative impact of talent management characterized by the excessive outflow of organization talent costing both money and time of the organization.

Talent Development: The formal and informal initiatives taken by the organizations that result in the holistic development of individual talent is called talent development.

Chapter 5
Small Business Survival of Onslaughts of Boko Haram Insurgency, COVID-19 Pandemic, and Economic Crisis in Yola, North-East Nigeria:
Leveraging Entrepreneurial Marketing

Lukman Raimi
https://orcid.org/0000-0002-5329-8715
School of Business and Economics, Universiti Brunei Darussalam, Brunei

Theoneste Manishimwe
https://orcid.org/0000-0002-6771-0918
American University of Nigeria, Nigeria

EXECUTIVE SUMMARY

Underpinning this chapter on vulnerability and resilience theoretical views, the authors examine the survival strategy of small businesses (SBs) facing triple crises. They adopted a descriptive survey research design as the most appropriate strategy while relying on the primary data collected through structured questionnaires. In the absence of a sample frame for the target population, a sample size of 400 managers of SBs was selected purposively based on objective eligibility criteria. Out of the sample, 257 managers of SBs returned their completed questionnaires. The findings support largely the resilient view and also affirmed the vulnerability view because the four entrepreneurial marketing (EM) dimensions, namely entrepreneurial orientation, market orientation, innovation orientation, and customer orientation, have mixed impacts on the financial and non-financial performance of SBs facing triple crises. The study recommends that vulnerable SBs, when faced with economic crises, should be resilient and leverage the four EM dimensions for business continuity.

DOI: 10.4018/978-1-7998-7657-1.ch005

INTRODUCTION

The emergence of COVID-19 pandemic and associated public health crisis expose the global economy to unprecedented exogenous shocks with negative ripple effects on the wellness and lifestyles of countries, people, and businesses (Sarkar & Clegg, 2021; Raimi, 2021). The report of the OECD (2020) posits that the pandemic triggered a major economic crisis, leading to a halt in production of basic goods and delivery of services, as well as engendering loss of confidence, and heightened uncertainties in the stock exchanges across the globe. To sustainably reduce the adverse effects of the pandemic on public health and enhance business continuity, the global governments imposed stringent measures ranging from complete or partial lockdowns, fiscal stimulus packages, and other economic interventions to mitigate the spread of the disease and keep afloat business operations (Chibueze, Mairami, Ugwu, Agwu & Lawal, 2020; Raimi, 2021).

Across all sectors, the micro, small and medium enterprises (MSMEs) have become vulnerable to the exogenous shocks caused by the pandemic; and they require sustainability interventions from the national governments and international development agencies to speed up the recovery process considering their important roles as drivers of economic growth and development (Ghosh, 2020; Jha & Kumar, 2020; Alonso et al., 2021). In the midst of the pandemic, the vulnerable small businesses (SBs) are responding proactively and innovatively to the changing times by creating new products, services, and technologies, hence they have strategically turned the crisis situation into economic opportunities (Sarkar & Clegg, 2021). The survival of the SBs is imperative because of their significant contributions to the national and global economies (Megersa, 2020). In Nigeria, the crucial roles of SBs are undeniable, as they represent the hub for wealth creation, economic opportunities and contribute a large component to the GDP (Eniola & Entebang, 2015). According to the 2013 collaborative survey of the Small and Medium Enterprises Development Agency of Nigeria and National Bureau of Statistics, the SBs contribute 48% of Nigeria's GDP and 7.27% of the export earnings (SMEDAN/NBS, 2013). The report of Price Waterhouse and Coopers (2019) stated the SBs in Nigeria constitute 96% of the businesses and provide 84% of employment in the country. Moreover, the World Bank through the Development Bank of Nigeria (DBN) supported the SBs with a cumulative sum of US $243.7 million (World Bank, 2019). The steady growth of SBs in Nigeria as explicated above has been terribly curtailed by the pandemic, and that justifies the need for government interventions to support the vulnerable SBs and improve their performance. In this study, the SBs are operationally defined as independent businesses with 1- 49 employees. This operational definition accommodated the micro and small businesses as defined by SMEDAN-NBS (2013).

Empirical studies on the vulnerability and resilience of SBs are few. Most of the contemporary studies on vulnerability and resilience are in the field of macro-economics, and the level of analysis is national with a focus on macro-economic variables such as the gross domestic products (GDPs) and/or per capita GDPs (Buckle, Mars & Smale, 2000; Briguglio, 2004; Briguglio, et al.,2009; Proag, 2014; Briguglio, 2014). For instance, the effect of economic recession was found to be strongly linked to a country's resources and productivity, hence, vulnerability challenges created by economic shocks more often have negative effect on a country's per capita GDP (Cordina, 2004a; Cordina, 2004b). Furthermore, the negative impact of economic vulnerability was confirmed to be largely dependent on the degree of diminishing marginal productivity (DMP), which is also influenced by the national policy measures that are consistent with the notion of resilience (Briguglio, et al.,2009). However, on the effect of global COVID-19 pandemic on how businesses adapt and survive while coping with the crisis, there is very little guidance from extant literature (Sarkar & Clegg, 2021). This paper, therefore, attempts to fill the knowledge gap created by the paucity of literature on the survival strategies of SBs in recessionary and crisis periods.

Based on the foregoing, this chapter examines the impact of entrepreneurial marketing (EM, henceforth) as a resilient strategy on the financial and non-financial performance of SBs in the period of crisis in Yola, Nigeria. In specific terms, what is the impact of the four dimension of EM on the financial and non-financial performance of the SBs. The research location is Yola, the capital of Adamawa state. The research location is Yola, the capital of Adamawa state. Adamawa is one of the states in the North-East of Nigeria ravaged by insecurity, unemployment, and poverty. The state maintains proximity to Boko Haram's stronghold of Sambisa forest, and that seven of the state's local governments - Madagali, Michika, Mubi North and South, Maiha, Gombi, and Hong were fully controlled by the terror group at a point in time (Audu & Bristone, 2020). In spite of the existential threat posed to lives and businesses, the owner-manager of SBs have innovatively developed resilient strategies to cope with the vulnerable and hostile business environment.

Despite the fact that EM research is still in its infancy and growing, it is apt to note that more than 95% of the reviewed works are from developed countries. However, in developing countries like Nigeria, research on EM at both national and organisational levels is still very few but emerging. The anticipated findings from this inquiry would therefore be of immense benefits to the small business owner-managers, the governments, and the academic community.

Apart from the introduction (Section 1) above, there are other seven sections in this chapter. Section 2 provides a theoretical foundation through a critique of the vulnerability and resilience perspectives of economic shocks. Section 3 focuses on the review of the literature with emphasis on conceptual and empirical reviews. Section 4 explains the research methods. Section 5 presents the results/findings of the study. Section 6 discusses the findings in relation to previous studies. Section 7 contextualises the findings, practical implications, and limitations. Section 8 concludes with recommendations.

THEORETICAL PERSPECTIVES

In recessionary and crisis periods, the two dominant perspectives for explaining how the exogenous shocks affect the economy are vulnerability and resilience views (Kitching et al., 2009; Smallbone et al., 2012). Both vulnerability and resilience are terms used in the field of emergency management, but adopted and integrated into multidisciplinary fields such as community development, social psychology, development economics and environmental management among others (Buckle et al., 2000; Martini & Vespasiano, 2015; Papathoma-Köhle, Thaler & Fuchs, 2021).

Vulnerability View

The term vulnerability is deeply rooted in the field of poverty and development studies based on the understanding that the first reality of poverty-induced underdevelopment is vulnerability of the citizens to hopelessness and helplessness (Carter & Barrett, 2006; Editorial, 2006). Vulnerability therefore refers to a current condition, where humans, animals, and inanimate objects are susceptibility to harm, powerlessness, and marginality in the physical and socio-ecological systems (Paul, 2013). Scholars explained that when the term vulnerability is viewed as an attack on infrastructure, on which humans and businesses depend, then there are structural and functional vulnerabilities (Ouyang et al., 2009). But when viewed broadly, vulnerability has four dimensions, namely: physical, social, economic and institutional (Fuchs & Thaler, 2018). Other scholars extended the scope of vulnerability adding attitudinal, cultural and environmental vulnerability dimensions (M & E Studies, 2021; Papathoma-Köhle et al., 2021).

Figure 1.

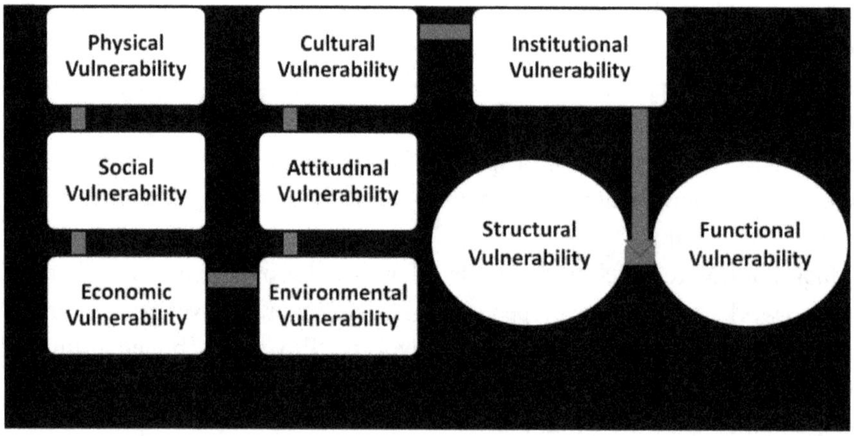

The vulnerability perspective of economic recession posits that the SBs are highly vulnerable to external shocks in the economy because they have limited resources, limited product lines, and limited customers, which tend to restrict their ability and capacity to survive the competitive pressures imposed on their operations by harsh economic conditions (Kitching et al., 2009). Besides, Smallbone et al. (1997) observed that over time, the economic downturn has affected sales, profitability, and survivability of the SBs because they operate under unfavourable conditions and shocks. From an empirical standpoint, Barbhuiya & Chatterjee (2020) investigated the impact of natural disasters and political conflicts on domestic and foreign tourist arrivals in the tourism sector in India including the degree of vulnerability and resilience. The study found that severe conflicts in the region negatively affect domestic tourist arrivals because of the high vulnerability, but natural disasters do not because of the resilience to cope. However, natural disasters negatively affect international tourist arrivals because they are vulnerable to risks and threats to lives, but political conflicts do not because of their high resilience to cope with such events. Overall, domestic tourists are more resilient compared to international tourists, obviously because they are more familiar with the terrain in India. From the foregoing, the SBs are often vulnerable to social risks, physical threats, economic shocks and political crises because they lack coping capacities (USP, 2013). But, the vulnerability view, that explains the helplessness and hopelessness of the SBs in recessionary and crisis periods has been challenged by the proponents of the resilience viewpoint.

Resilience View

The term resilience refers to a measure of how quickly individuals, groups, communities and systems recover from physical risks, economic shocks, dangerous situation and system failures based on their coping capacities that vary over time (Emergency Management Australia 1998; Buckle et al., 2000).

Additionally, resilience connotes the ability of an organisation or a system to cope with, and adapt to unusual/unplanned situations by continually carrying out its mission (Caralli et al., 2010; Marrella et al., 2019). Resilience is also a process of developing countermeasures against failures, by conceptualising what to do in time of failures, developing a timely and flexible reactive approach to mitigate and move on sustainably (Maco et al.., 2018; Marrella et al., 2019). With regards to operational management, resilience includes the individual and organisational responses to turbulence and discontinuities (Bhamra, Dani & Burnard, 2011). In reality, resilience emerges when cognition and behaviour of business leaders work together by seeing public health crisis as a business opportunity rather than a disaster; and extends to providing radical responses, services and products that helped to deal with the crisis situation (Sarkar & Clegg, 2021).

The resilience perspective explicates that small enterprises have the ability and capability to survive exogenous shocks resulting from economic recessions that hit the national economy, if they can adopt proactive and innovative strategies that would make them resilient (Wedawatta & Ingirige, 2012; Kitching, et al., 2009). In the UK, the SBs are highly resilient and adaptive to the frequent flood events in recent years, through the implementation of varieties of property-level protection measures and generic business continuity plans including risk management measures to keep their businesses afloat (Wedawatta and Ingirige, 2012). Resilience is particularly effective, if SBs are flexible in adapting processes, inputs, products, and prices to improve their situations (Wedawatta & Ingirige, 2012). In disaster-prone regions, it has been found that resilient SBs that survived crisis situation in the long run, are those with a business continuity plans (Sarmiento et al., 2016).

Not all recessionary situations are harmful to businesses. For instance, Stangler (2009) found that economic recessions may precipitate short-term declines in the formation of businesses, but in the long run, it does not have a significant negative effect on new business formation and their survival. Furthermore, Espiner & Becken (2014) applied the concepts of vulnerability and resilience to examine the effect of environmental issues on tourist attractions in Westland National Park, New Zealand; they found that both concepts are highly compatible, because despite the geographic isolation, threats of flooding, earthquake, rising fuel prices and climate change and glacier melting, the tourism industry in New Zealand still attracts 600,000 visitors annually.

The various findings above indicate that recessionary periods triggered economic activities in some sectors as well as stimulated the growth of certain types of businesses (Savrul & Kılıç, 2011). For example, when customers shift to products that are cheaper so as to reduce expenditure, this can benefit suppliers of low-cost products and have a negative effect on the providers of highly-priced products (Kitching et al., 2009). In recessionary periods, researchers underscored the importance of resilient strategies such as improved revenue generation activities (Latham, 2009; Latham & Braun, 2011), use of diverse innovation (Smallbone et al., 2012), exploring exports in foreign markets (Burger, et al., 2017; Jaclik & Burger, 2020), new marketing techniques (Kashmiri & Mahajan, 2014), investment in HRIS or human resource management systems (Iwu & Benedict, 2013) nd revenue diversification strategies (Hussain et al., 2013).

From the foregoing, relationship between vulnerability and resilience is complementary. While vulnerability poses serious disadvantages and threats on economic development by magnifying the element of risk in the growth process for the economy and the organisations ((Briguglio, et al.,2009), resilience on the other hand is the remediation processes, procedures, and technical mechanism for redressing and remedying vulnerabilities (Hatton, Seville & Vargo, 2012; Sarmiento et al., 2016). For this study, the economic vulnerability and economic resilience are the focus, and both have operationally been defined. Economic vulnerability is the exposure of an economy to exogenous shocks, arising out of economic openness imposed by internationalisation, globalisation, and export concentration, while economic resilience is defined as the policy measures that boost the capacities and abilities of individuals, groups, communities, and other economic agents to withstand, cope and recover from the ripple effects of the shocks (Briguglio, et al.,2009).

EMPIRICAL REVIEW

Business Survival and Coping Strategies During COVID-19 Pandemic

A number of empirical studies have started emerging in different parts of the world explaining the novel strategies and interventions used by the governments and businesses to mitigate environmental and economic shocks. To revamp Sri Lanka's tourism industry at the peak of the pandemic, the Porter's Diamond model with six facets was adopted and innovatively applied to the operations of the tourism-oriented SBs in the following ways: (a) minimizing economic leakages, (b) re-branding of destination, (c) product differentiations (d) entrepreneurship development, (e) creating domestic eco-friendly travels, (f) developing special interest tourism (SIT) and (g) exploring e-promotions (Fernando, 2021). In Nigeria, the government provided fiscal stimulus to the vulnerable SBs as part of business sustainability and continuity measures. The fiscal stimulus includes relief materials and cash assistance, tax reliefs, debt rescheduling, and non-monetary support incentives (Raimi, 2020). For Namibia however, the vulnerable commercial banks have innovatively reinvented CSR as resilient strategy for business sustainability through improved CSR reporting, stakeholder engagement, and preferential pricing strategies for vulnerable customers in the pandemic-ravaged communities (Randa, 2020).In Portugal and Brazil, the use of a combination of strategic approaches such as co-creation, entrepreneurship, holistic thinking, and creativity have been reported as helpful to businesses and the people in trying to cope with the vulnerable situation created by COVID-19 pandemic (Dieguez, 2020). In spite of recurring crises facing the SBs in New Zealand, they enhanced business resumption within few weeks through collaboration, cooperation and innovation (Hatton, Seville & Vargo, 2012). Phil O'Reilly, affirmed that: "Christchurch businesses are like weeds, they grow out of the cracks of the pavement, they are hard to kill, they may be pretty ugly, but gosh they are still there" (Hatton et al., 2012:25).

The survival and coping strategies explicated above clearly demonstrated how the SBs have become more resilient in their operations, by merging entrepreneurship and marketing. The SBs have deployed innovation in the marketing of existing and new products and services in recessionary periods. The concepts of innovation and strategy are both entrepreneurship and knowledge management strategies (Morgan & Berthon, 2008; Bettiol, Di Maria & Grandinetti, 2011). In the Five-P of strategy, Mintzberg (1987) explained that strategy can be viewed as a plan, as a ploy, as a position, as a pattern, and as a perspective, and that each of these five perceptions of strategy is crucial for the application of strategy. Therefore, entrepreneurial marketing (EM) is a strategy that falls with the domains plan, ploy, position, pattern and perspective. The EM is crucial in a recessionary period or crisis situation to strengthen the capabilities of the SBs to be able to leverage the three dimensions of the EM (entrepreneurial orientation (EO), market orientation (MO), innovation orientation (IO), and customer orientation (CO) to enhance organisational performance (Jones &Rowley, 2009; Kowalik & Danik, 2019). What then is EM?

According to Schindehutte and Morris (2010), the term EM refers to the proactive identification and the exploitation of opportunities by entrepreneurial marketers purposely to acquire and retain profitable customers (including prospects) through the deployment of innovative approaches to risk management, resource leveraging, and value creation. Therefore, EM is a new marketing approach, which emphasises that opportunities are continually co-created by entrepreneurs or entrepreneurial organisations through the development and communication of value propositions (Whalen and Akaka., 2015). It is also described as a form of marketing aimed at growth and innovation (Kraus et al., 2012; Mwangi and Bwisa, 2013).

From the different perspectives above, EM is an entrepreneurial practice that extends beyond the traditional marketing practices because it is change-focused, proactive, reactive and change-oriented. EM deals with several issues such as severe resource constraints, a limited geographic market presence, lack of economies of scale, a limited market image, little market shares or brand loyalty, inadequate specialized management expertise, time scarcity with a given task, a mixture of personal and business goals, which traditional marketing does not take in consideration (Whalen and Akaka, 2015).

Comparatively, the EM is linked with marketing activities that challenge the existing market conventions (Babor and Robaina, 2013), whereas, traditional marketing is more customer-centered rather than opportunity-driven like the EM (Crick, 2018). The EM is seen as an alternative technique for improving the effectiveness of traditional marketing (Ahmadi and O'Cass, 2015). For the EM, marketing is integrated with innovativeness, and this is the hallmark of entrepreneurship. The mechanism for EM value creation is also regarded as innovative because it deviates from traditional marketing practices. Also, EM takes risk-taking, customer interface and resource utilisation into consideration (Morrish et al., 2010).

The EM is also very useful for SBs in recessionary and crisis situation because they face more intense entrepreneurial challenges related to cashflows, fall in demand, disruption of the supply chain, and other shocks. The situation of SBs is worrisome because they operate in a very dynamic environment consisting of decreased ability to forecast, increased risk, and small business boundaries (Schmengler and Kraus, 2010). Traditional marketing is therefore inadequate and inappropriate to strengthen the competitiveness of the SBs amidst rivalry.

Summing up the discourse, the EM represents a resilient strategy that strengthens the capacities and abilities of the vulnerable SBs to gain competitive advantage and improve performance while coping with the economic shocks and operational challenges imposed by economic recession and other crises. The significant positive impact of EM on the performance of SBs was affirmed in Bangladesh (Hoque and Awang, 2019). In Saudi Arabia, the EM dimensions were found to have a positive effect on organisational performance (Rashad, 2018). Luo (2014) explained that there is a shift from traditional marketing strategy to EM because the latter impacts more effectively on performance of businesses. Considering the fact that marketing is strategic to the success businesses, the adoption of EM helps the SBs overcome the issues related to opportunities, resources, innovation, and risk (Hoque and Awang, 2019). From the foregoing, it could be hypothesised that:

H_0: Entrepreneurial marketing as a resilient strategy has no significant positive impact on the performance of SBs in the period of crisis in Yola, Nigeria.

Entrepreneurial Orientation (EO) and Organisational Performance

A number of scholarly articles focused on the impact of EO components on organisational performance (Azhar et al., 2010; Verma & Sarkar, 2018). For instance, Osei-Bonsu (2020) found that innovations, proactiveness, and risk-taking help firms to attract and retain loyal customers and to lead the market. Due to the positive influence of EO on the effectiveness and efficiency of an organization, different organizations encourage entrepreneurial attitudes among their employees in order to exploit opportunities in the operating environment (Brettel et al, 2014). Furthermore, Azhar et al (2010) stated that proactiveness, innovativeness, and readiness to take risks are vital factors for an organization to gain a competitive advantage. The need for EO strategy is becoming more serious because it is one of the aptitudes needed by business enterprises to cope with numerous challenges in the dynamic, uncertain, and turbulent business environment **(Verma & Sarkar, 2018).** Also, EO affects the growth of Turkish small businesses (Gürbüz & Aykol, 2009). Based on previous empirical findings above, it could be hypothesised that:

H_1: Entrepreneurial orientation as a resilient strategy has no significant positive impact on the performance of SBs in the period of crisis in Yola, Nigeria.

Innovation Orientation (IO) and Organisational Performance

Different studies reported the relationship between IO and organisational performance (see Dobni, 2010; Zhang and Duan, 2010). The higher the IO of an organization, the higher the growth, customer satisfaction, and profitability/return on investment (Dobni, 2010). Similarly, Azar and Ciabuschi (2017) found a significant positive impact of technological innovation, market and distribution innovation on product innovation, the performance of sales, and the level of profit. Talke et al., (2011) reported that new products with higher technologies and market newness have the highest performance. In Chinese manufacturing firms, it was found that innovation orientation has a positive moderating impact on new product performance (Zhang and Duan, 2010). Based on the outcomes of the empirical studies above, it could be hypothesised that:

H_2: Innovation orientation as a resilient strategy has no significant positive impact on the performance of SBs in the period of crisis in Yola, Nigeria.

Market Orientation (MO) and Organisational Performance

Different researches have emphasised the crucial impact of MO on organisational performance (Ellis, 2006; Eibe Sørensen, 2009). The findings are mixed and inconclusive, but most researchers agreed that MO has a significant positive impact on performance (Azizi and Sudhartio (2020; Wurjaningrum & Hartami, 2020). Wurjaningrum & Hartami (2020) found that MO had no significant positive impact on return on investment, market share, and return on equity. But some recent studies found a significant positive impact of different measures of MO on organisational performance. Osuagwu (2015) stated that, in other African developing countries other than Nigeria, MO is one of the strategies implemented by SBs for leveraging and achieving efficiency and effectiveness. He added that MO is used in developed countries to access relevant global markets, reduce product development periods and beneficial interactions with relevant stakeholders especially clients/customers and to improve their productivity. In Indonesia, Azizi and Sudhartio (2020) found that competitor orientation, customer orientation, and inter-functional coordination have a significant impact on ventures' performance. Relying on the empirical insights above, it could be hypothesised that:

H_3: Market orientation as a resilient strategy has no significant positive impact on the performance of SBs in the period of crisis in Yola, Nigeria.

Customer Orientation (CO) and Organisational Performance

The MO and CO dimensions are similar but different concepts. Jones and Rowley (2009) and Yadav and Bansal (2020) argued that there is a clear distinction between the MO and CO dimensions of EM; the CO is customer-focused, while MO is market-focused, and both have powerful effects on marketing, hence must be given equal considerations. Christensen and Bower (1996) noted that focus on CO significantly contributed to the failure of leading firms during a period of industry discontinuity (innovation). In other words, the CO has been found to inhibit innovation because the research and development (R&D) departments listen too closely and carefully to their customers (customer-led marketing philosophy), thereby making the firms maintain the status quo instead of benefiting from emergent technologies and new materials (Matsuo, 2006). In spite of the limitations and cautions, the CO has been found to influence organisational performance and long-term profitability of businesses (Mateias and Brettel, 2016). Organizations adopted a customer-oriented approach to gain customers' trust and loyalty, which leads to organization comfort and growth (Mukerjee, 2013). Another study found that proactive customer orientation (PCO) positively influences cross-buying (CB), but there is no significant relationship between PCO and word-of-mouth (WoM). Similarly, responsive customer orientation (RCO) positively influences WoM and CB (Mukerjee & Shaikh, 2019). Organisational capabilities that are associated with the application of a CO are customer response, customer relating, and market sensing. Many empirical studies have examined the relationship between CO and organisational performance. Wang et al (2019) found that CO enhances organisational performance in organisations that instills effective organisational leadership. Moreover, Mateias and Brettel (2016) found a positive impact of CO on firm performance. In Nigeria, Asikhia, (2010) found a significant positive impact of CO on organisational performance in the SBEs, when moderated by marketing information system and managerial attitude. Based on the above empirical findings, it could be hypothesised that:

H_4: Customer orientation as a resilient strategy has no significant positive impact on the performance of SBs in the period of crisis in Yola, Nigeria.

RESEARCH METHODS

The quantitative research method was adopted while relying on a survey as the strategy for conducting the study. In the absence of a sample frame detailing the demographics of the target population, a sample size of 400 registered and full-time operating SBs was selected using a non-random purposive sampling technique. Using purposive sampling technique is justified when randomization is impossible and where the population is very large or unknown (Etikan, Musa & Alkassim, 2016). Thereafter, questionnaires were self-administered physically and using the google form. The questions were measured using Likert scale measurement. A total of 257 responses were obtained from owner-managers, marketers, and senior officers of SBs involved in marketing activities. Data collected through structured questionnaires were analysed using descriptive and inferential statistics. The reliability coefficients of the EM measures and organizational performance measures were 0.817 and 0.803 respectively. Similarly, the Kaiser Meyer Olkin (KMO) and Bartlett's test of sphericity showed alpha coefficients of 0.817 for EM measures and 0.803 for organizational performance, which indicated good internal consistency.

FINDINGS AND DISCUSSION

Construct Analysis

The research used fifteen components of EO, IO, MO, and CO. These include (EO: pro-activeness, risk-taking, autonomy, and competitive aggressiveness; IO: product innovation, technology innovation, processes innovation channels/networks distribution innovation; MO: competitor orientation, inter-functional coordination, market intelligence generation and networks and relationship; and CO: customer responsiveness, customer intensity and customer value creation). The factor loadings for all the fifteen components range from 0.6 to 0.8. The performance of EM practices of the selected SBs was grouped into non-financial performance (NFP) with 7 components (market share, marketing effectiveness, employee's commitment, competitive image/reputation, job satisfaction, competitive position, and customer satisfaction) and financial performance (FP) with 5 components (profitability, customer growth, turnover, return on assets, and efficiency). Similarly, the factor loadings for the FP and NFP range from 0.5 to 0.7. Relevant questions were framed around the 12 EM factors and 12 performance metrics.

Regression Analysis

In the model summary (Table 1 and 2) below, R-values that explain the causality between EM and financial performance (FP) is 0.32 (32%), while the causality for EM and non-financial performance (NFP) is 0.409 (40.9%). The two values indicated good predictability of the two models.

Table 1. Model Summary

Model	R	R Square	Adjusted R Square	Std. Error of the Estimate
1	.320[a]	.103	.099	1.573
a. Predictors: (Constant), Entrepreneurial Marketing				

Table 2. Model Summary

Model	R	R Square	Adjusted R Square	Std. Error of the Estimate
2	.409[a]	.168	.164	3.140
a. Predictors: (Constant), Entrepreneurial Marketing				

The ANOVA results in Table 3vand 4 below also showed a good fit for the data:

- For EM and FP, the ANOVA is $F(1, 254) = 29.015$ at p-value $(0.00) < 0.05$.
- For EM and NFP, the ANOVA $F(1, 254) = 51.113$ at p-value $(0.00) < 0.05$.

Both results indicate that EM practices statistically and significantly predict the FP and NFP measures of the SBs in Yola, North-East Nigeria.

Table 3. Result of the ANOVA

Model	Sum of Squares	df	Mean Square	F	Sig.
Regression	71.768	1	71.768	29.015	.000[b]
Residual	628.260	254	2.473		
Total	700.027	255			
a. Dependent Variable: Financial Performance b. Predictors: (Constant), Entrepreneurial Marketing					

Table 4. Result of the ANOVA

Model	Sum of Squares	df	Mean Square	F	Sig.
Regression	503.923	1	503.923	51.113	.000[b]
Residual	2504.198	254	9.859		
Total	3008.121	255			
a. Dependent Variable: Non-financial performance b. Predictors: (Constant), Entrepreneurial Marketing					

With regards to causality, the unstandardized coefficient B in Tables 3a and 3b below showed that FP and NFP increases by 0.245 and 0.649 respectively when the SBs improve EM by 1 unit. Therefore, the regression equations for both could be written as: FP = 0.245 EM and NFP = 0.649EM. It could be inferred therefore that: *Entrepreneurial marketing as a resilient strategy has a significant positive impact on the financial and non-financial performance of SBs in the period of crisis in Yola, Nigeria.*

Table 5. Coefficients for financial performance

Model	Unstandardized Coefficients		Standardized Coefficients	T	Sig.	95.0% Confidence Interval for B	
	B	SE	Beta			Lower Bound	Upper Bound
Constant	15.865	.920		17.241	.000	14.053	17.677
Entrepreneurial Marketing (EM)	.245	.045	.320	5.387	.000	.155	.334
a. Dependent Variable: Financial Performance							
Model	**Unstandardized Coefficients**		**Standardized Coefficients**	**T**	**Sig.**	**95.0% Confidence Interval for B**	
	B	**SE**	**Beta**			**Lower Bound**	**Upper Bound**
Constant	30.883	1.837		16.811	.000	27.265	
Entrepreneurial Marketing (EM)	.649	.091	.409	7.149	.000	.470	
a. Dependent Variable: Financial Performance							

With regards to the result of the regression in Table 6, it was found that the unstandardized B coefficients for CO, EO, MO and IO were -0.060, 0.020, 0.90, and 0.152 respectively. This means that the strategic effort made by SBs to improve financial performance resulted in mixed outcomes. Both MO and IO as resilient strategies have significant positive impacts on the financial of SBs with p-values of 0.90, and 0.152 respectively. Whereas, EO and CO as resilient strategies have significant negative impacts on the financial of SBs with p-values of 0.020 and -0.060 respectively. The negative impact of EO and CO on financial performance measures may be due to ineffective implementation of EO and CO dimensions of EM by employees of the SBs. Below is the regression equation:

$$FP = 12.778 - 0.060x + 0.02y + 0.90z + 0.152w$$

This is the regression line, with all variables whether significant and non-significant plotted where:

FP = Financial performance

X = CO

Y = EO

Z = MO

W = IO

Table 6. Coefficients for Financial performance

Model	Unstandardized Coefficients		Standardized Coefficients	T	Sig.	95.0% Confidence Interval for B	
	B	Std. Error	Beta			Lower Bound	Upper Bound
Constant	12.778	1.469		8.697	.000	9.884	15.671
CO	-.060	.039	-.123	-1.536	.126	-.138	.017
EO	.020	.013	.117	1.518	.130	-.006	.047
MO	.090	.033	.186	2.741	.007	.025	.154
IO	.152	.042	.254	3.637	.000	.070	.235

For the result of the regression in Table 7, it was found that the unstandardized B coefficients for CO, EO, MO, and IO dimensions were -0.216, -0.047, 0.236, and 0.446 respectively. The implication of the finding above is that, for every strategic effort made by the SBs to improve non-financial performance resulted in mixed outcomes. Both MO and IO as resilient strategies have significant positive impacts on the non-financial of SBs with p-values of 0.236, and 0.446 respectively. Whereas, CO and EO dimensions have significant negative impacts on the non-financial of SBs with p-values of -0.216 and -0.047 respectively. The respondents who are mostly managers indicated strong commitment towards CO and

EO in their organizations, the inadequacies may be from the employees in the process of implementation of these vital dimensions of the EM. Below is the regression equation:

$$NFP = 30.557 - 0.216x + 0.047y + 0.236z + 0.446w$$

This is the regression line, with all variables whether significant and non-significant plotted where:

NFP = Non-Financial Performance

X = CO

Y = EO

Z = MO

W = IO

Table 7. Coefficients for non-financial performance

Model	Unstandardized Coefficients		Standardized Coefficients	t	Sig.	95.0% Confidence Interval for B	
	B	Std. Error	Beta			Lower Bound	Upper Bound
Constant	30.557	2.561		11.930	.000	25.512	35.601
CO	-.216	.069	-.211	-3.152	.002	-.351	-.081
EO	-.047	.023	-.130	-2.002	.046	-.093	-.001
MO	.236	.057	.236	4.149	.000	.124	.348
IO	.446	.073	.359	6.112	.000	.303	.590

DISCUSSIONS

Overall, the chapter found that that the EM as a resilient strategy has a significant positive impact on the financial and non-financial performance of SBs in the period of crisis in Yola, Nigeria. However, the four EM dimensions (that is, EO, MO, IO, and CO) showed some similar, but varied findings. The MO and IO dimensions have significant positive impacts on both the financial and non-financial performance, but the EO dimension has no significant positive impact on financial performance, but has a significant positive impact on non-financial performance. The CO dimension also has no significant positive impact on financial performance, but has a significant positive impact on non-financial performance.

The findings from the current study are consistent with previous studies in several respects. Filser et al. (2014) and Rank et al., (2013) found a positive influence of EO on the effectiveness and efficiency of organizations because managers imbibed entrepreneurial attitudes in their employees which helped to explore and exploit opportunities around them. A recent study of Rank and Strenge (2018) affirmed the EO positively influences on the ability of firms to obtain brokerage positions in their external collaboration networks with partners. Similarly, Zhang and Duan (2010) found a significant positive impact of IO on the organisational performance of SBs. The result of this study is also in line with Osuagwu's (2015) argument, that MO is one of the strategies used by small business enterprises in achieving effectiveness and efficiency. Overall, the study affirmed that EM is a crucial marketing strategy in recessionary and crisis situations required to strengthen the capabilities of businesses be able to leverage EM, EO, MO, IO, and CO to enhance operational performance (Jones &Rowley, 2009; Kowalik and Danik, 2019). Therefore, not all recessionary situations are harmful to businesses, a fact that Stangler (2009) had long confirmed; It was found that economic recession may precipitate short-term declines in the formation of businesses, but in the long run, it may not have a negative effect on new business formation and their survival. Also, Espiner & Becken (2014) found that vulnerability and resilience are highly compatible because high levels of vulnerability during a crisis do not necessarily determine low levels of resilience and vice versa.

Table 8. Summary of Results of the hypotheses

Research Hypotheses		P-Value	Conclusions
H_0: Entrepreneurial orientation as a resilient strategy has no significant positive impact on the performance of SBs in the period of crisis in Yola, Nigeria	**$H_{0(a)}$:** Entrepreneurial orientation as a resilient strategy has no significant positive impact on the financial performance of SBs in the period of crisis in Yola, Nigeria	0.130 >5%)	$H_{0(a)}$ was supported.
	$H_{0(b)}$: Entrepreneurial orientation as a resilient strategy has no significant positive impact on the non-financial performance of SBs in the period of crisis in Yola, Nigeria	0.046 <5%)	$H_{0(b)}$ rejected.
H_1: Innovation orientation as a resilient strategy has no significant positive impact on the performance of SBs in the period of crisis in Yola, Nigeria	**$H_{1(a)}$:** Innovation orientation as a resilient strategy has no significant positive impact on the financial performance of SBs in the period of crisis in Yola, Nigeria	0.000 <5%	$H_{0(a)}$ rejected
	$H_{1(b)}$: Innovation orientation as a resilient strategy has no significant positive impact on the non-financial performance of SBs in the period of crisis in Yola, Nigeria	0.000 < 5%	$H_{0(b)}$ rejected
H_2: Market orientation as a resilient strategy has no significant positive impact on the performance of SBs in the period of crisis in Yola, Nigeria	**$H_{2(a)}$:** Market orientation as a resilient strategy has no significant positive impact on the financial performance of SBs in the period of crisis in Yola, Nigeria	0.007< 5%	$H_{0(a)}$ rejected.
	$H_{2(b)}$: Market orientation as a resilient strategy has no significant positive impact on the non-financial performance of SBs in the period of crisis in Yola, Nigeria	0.000 < 5%	$H_{0(b)}$ rejected
H_3: Customer orientation as a resilient strategy has no significant positive impact on the performance of SBs in the period of crisis in Yola, Nigeria	**$H_{3(a)}$:** Customer orientation as a resilient strategy has no significant positive impact on the financial performance of SBs in the period of crisis in Yola, Nigeria	0.126 >5%	$H_{0(a)}$ supported.
	$H_{3(b)}$: Customer orientation as a resilient strategy has no significant positive impact on the non-financial performance of SBs in the period of crisis in Yola, Nigeria	0.002 < 5%	$H_{0(b)}$ rejected

CONCLUSION, IMPLICATIONS AND LIMITATIONS

The chapter sets out to investigate the impact of EM on the organisational performance of SBs facing triple crises in Yola, a region in Northeast Nigeria. At the end, it was found that EM dimensions (used as resilient strategies in the period of triple crises) have significant positive impacts on the financial and non-financial performance of the SBs. From the eight formulated null hypotheses, two were accepted, while six were rejected. Specifically, it was found that EO, IO, MO, and CO have significant positive impacts on the non-financial performance of SBs. Similarly, IO and MO have significant positive impacts on the financial performance of SBs. However, EO and CO do not have significant positive impacts on the financial performance of SBs. The reasons for the negative impact of EO and CO on financial performance during the period of crisis may be context-specific. The logical explanation for the divergence among EO, CO and financial performance is that, the owner-managers of SBs are more market-oriented and innovation-oriented during the triple crises than being entrepreneurial. The managerial implication of this is that, the owner-managers of SBs and their officers in marketing units need to focus on EO measures, namely; proactiveness, risk-taking, competitive aggressiveness in their marketing activities in order to boost their financial performance measures (profitability, growth, turnover, return on assets, and efficiency). Also, the owner-managers of SBs in Yola should be more customer-oriented in their marketing activities by strengthening their CO measures such as customer responsiveness, customer intensity, and customer value creation.

In spite of the insightful managerial implications, this study has three research limitations. Firstly, the study focused on the SBs in Yola, Adamawa, hence the scope of the study is limited to the small businesses as it left out micro and large businesses, hence the findings cannot be generalised as representative of micro, small, and medium enterprises (MSMEs), as the term MSMEs has its own unique definition and measurement. Secondly, the finding on the impact of EM on the organisational performance of SBs in Yola, Northeast of Nigeria cannot be generalised as representing the trends in Nigeria. Finally, the use of purposive sampling constitutes another limitation because such sampling technique is viewed as non-random and subjective. For this study, it was found appropriate because there was no sample frame for SBs in Yola. Secondly, the study required practitioner-based opinions, and the owner-managers of SBs and their senior officers in charge of marketing are the most qualified in recessionary and crisis periods to provide such opinions. In spite of the three limitations explicated above, the study is unique and distinct, as it opens the space for further empirical studies on gaps left behind. Overall, we contribute to the literature on the survival strategies of SBs in recessionary and crisis periods. We also contribute to theory by validating the vulnerability and resilience views.

RECOMMENDATIONS

Based on the above findings, we offer the following recommendations as interventions for improving EM practices of the SBs currently struggling with triple crises in Yola, North-East, Nigeria:

1. The owner-manager of SBs should review their EO measures especially proactiveness, risk-taking, competitive aggressiveness in relation to the financial performance measures in order to keep their businesses afloat and competitive in the long run.

2. The managers are advised to put more emphasis on CO measures, especially customer responsiveness, customer intensity, and customer value creation in their marketing activities in relation to non-financial performance.
3. It is expedient for owner-managers of SBs to train all their employees on EM practices as resilient mechanisms required to boost financial and non-financial performance.

REFERENCES

Ahmadi, H., & O'Cass, A. (2015). The role of entrepreneurial marketing in new technology ventures first product commercialisation. *Journal of Strategic Marketing*, *24*(1), 47–60. doi:10.1080/0965254X.2015.1035039

Alonso, A. D., Bressan, A., Kok, S. K., Sakellarios, N., Koresis, A., O'Shea, M., . . . Santoni, L. J. (2021). Facing and responding to the COVID-19 threat–an empirical examination of MSMEs. European Business Review. ahead-of-print. doi:10.1108/EBR-09-2020-0231

Asikhia, O. (2010). Customer orientation and firm performance among Nigerian small and medium scale businesses. *International Journal of Marketing Studies*, *2*(1), 197–212. doi:10.5539/ijms.v2n1p197

Audu, I. M., & Bristone, W. T. (2020). The Socio-Economic Effects of Boko Haram Insurgency in Hong Local Government Area of Adamawa State, Nigeria. *International Journal of Academic Research*, *2*(1), 40–63.

Azar, G., & Ciabuschi, F. (2017). Organizational innovation, technological innovation, and export performance: The effects of innovation radicalness and extensiveness. *International Business Review*, *26*(2), 324–336. doi:10.1016/j.ibusrev.2016.09.002

Azhar, A., Javaid, A., Rehman, M., & Hyder, A. (2010). Entrepreneurial intentions among business students in Pakistan. *Journal of Business Systems, Governance and Ethics*, *5*(2), 13–21. doi:10.15209/jbsge.v5i2.181

Azizi, M., & Sudhartio, L. (2020). The influence of entrepreneurial and marketing orientation to strategic learning capability and SME performance automotive industry in Indonesia - a conceptual framework. *Contemporary Research on Business and Management*, 118-122.

Babor, T. F., & Robaina, K. (2013). Public health, academic medicine, and the alcohol industry's corporate social responsibility activities. *American Journal of Public Health*, *103*(2), 206–214. doi:10.2105/AJPH.2012.300847 PMID:23237151

Barbhuiya, M. R., & Chatterjee, D. (2020). Vulnerability and resilience of the tourism sector in India: Effects of natural disasters and internal conflict. *Tourism Management Perspectives*, *33*, 100616. doi:10.1016/j.tmp.2019.100616

Bettiol, M., Di Maria, E., & Grandinetti, R. (2011). Market extension and knowledge management strategies of knowledge-intensive business services. *Knowledge Management Research and Practice*, *9*(4), 305–314. doi:10.1057/kmrp.2011.35

Bhamra, R., Dani, S., & Burnard, K. (2011). Resilience: The concept, a literature review and future directions. *International Journal of Production Research*, *49*(18), 5375–5393. doi:10.1080/00207543.2011.563826

Brettel, M., Bendig, D., Keller, M., Friederichsen, N., & Rosenberg, M. (2014). Effectuation in Manufacturing: How Entrepreneurial Decision-making Techniques can be used to Deal with Uncertainty in Manufacturing. *Procedia CIRP*, *17*, 611–616. doi:10.1016/j.procir.2014.03.119

Briguglio, L. (2004). *Economic vulnerability and resilience: concepts and measurements*. University of Malta. Islands and Small States Institute & The Commonwealth Secretariat.

Briguglio, L. (2014). *A vulnerability and resilience framework for small states*. Working Paper, University of Malta, 1-02.

Briguglio, L., Cordina, G., Farrugia, N., & Vella, S. (2009). Economic vulnerability and resilience: Concepts and measurements. *Oxford Development Studies*, *37*(3), 229–247. doi:10.1080/13600810903089893

Buckle, P., Mars, G., & Smale, S. (2000). New approaches to assessing vulnerability and resilience. *Australian Journal of Emergency Management*, *15*(2), 8–14.

Burger, A., Damijan, J. P., Kostevc, Č., & Rojec, M. (2017). Determinants of firm performance and growth during economic recession: The case of Central and Eastern European countries. *Economic Systems*, *41*(4), 569–590. doi:10.1016/j.ecosys.2017.05.003

Caralli, R. A., Allen, J. H., & White, D. W. (2010). *CERT resilience management model: A maturity model for managing operational resilience*. Addison-Wesley Professional.

Carter, M. R., & Barrett, C. B. (2006). The economics of poverty traps and persistent poverty: An asset-based approach. *The Journal of Development Studies*, *42*(2), 178–199. doi:10.1080/00220380500405261

Chibueze, O. O., Mairami, F. F., Ugwu, D. O., Agwu, A. N., & Lawal, H. B. (2020). *Implications of COVID-19 on Nigeria's Economy*. Connected Development.

Christensen, C., & Bower, J. (1996). Customer power, strategic investment, and the failure of leading firms. *Strategic Management Journal*, *17*(3), 197–218. doi:10.1002/(SICI)1097-0266(199603)17:3<197::AID-SMJ804>3.0.CO;2-U

Cordina, G. (2004a). Economic Vulnerability, Resilience and Capital Formation. In L. Briguglio & E. J. Kisanga (Eds.), Economic Vulnerability and Resilience of Small States. Malta: Islands and Small States Institute and London: Commonwealth Secretariat.

Cordina, G. (2004b). 'Economic Vulnerability and Economic Growth: Some Results from a Neo-Classical Growth Modelling Approach'. *Journal of Economic Development*, *29*(2), 21–39.

Crick, J. M. (2018). The facets, antecedents and consequences of coopetition. *Qualitative Market Research*, *21*(2), 253–272. doi:10.1108/QMR-11-2016-0109

Dieguez, T. (2020). Cultural Approach to Mitigate COVID-19's Impact: Comparative Perspective. In N. Baporikar (Ed.), *Handbook of Research on Strategies and Interventions to Mitigate COVID-19 Impact on SMEs*. IGI Global.

Dobni, C. B. (2010). The relationship between an innovation orientation and competitive strategy. *International Journal of Innovation Management*, *14*(02), 331–357. doi:10.1142/S1363919610002660

Editorial. (2006). Resilience, vulnerability, and adaptation: A crosscutting theme of the International Human Dimensions Programme on Global Environmental Change. *Global Environmental Change*, *16*(3), 237–239.

Eibe Sørensen, H. (2009). Why competitors matter for market orientation. *European Journal of Marketing*, *43*(5/6), 735–761. doi:10.1108/03090560910947025

Ellis, P. D. (2006). Market orientation and performance: A meta-analysis and cross-national comparisons. *Journal of Management Studies*, *43*(5), 1089–1107. doi:10.1111/j.1467-6486.2006.00630.x

Emergency Management Australia. (1998). *Australian Emergency Management Glossary*. Author.

Eniola, A. A., & Entebang, H. (2015). Government policy and performance of small and medium business management. *International Journal of Academic Research in Business & Social Sciences*, *5*(2), 237–248. doi:10.6007/IJARBSS/v5-i2/1481

Espiner, S., & Becken, S. (2014). Tourist towns on the edge: Conceptualising vulnerability and resilience in a protected area tourism system. *Journal of Sustainable Tourism*, *22*(4), 646–665. doi:10.1080/09669582.2013.855222

Etikan, I., Musa, S. A., & Alkassim, R. S. (2016). Comparison of convenience sampling and purposive sampling. *American Journal of Theoretical and Applied Statistics*, *5*(1), 1–4. doi:10.11648/j.ajtas.20160501.11

Fernando, I. (2021). Assessing the Competitiveness of Sri Lanka's Tourism in the COVID Period by Porter's Diamond Model. In N. Baporikar (Ed.), *Handbook of Research on Strategies and Interventions to Mitigate COVID-19 Impact on SMEs*. IGI Global. doi:10.4018/978-1-7998-7436-2.ch001

Filser, M., Eggers, F., Kraus, S., & Málovics, É. (2014). The effect of financial resource availability on entrepreneurial orientation, customer orientation and firm performance in an international context: An empirical analysis from Austria and Hungary. *Journal for East European Management Studies*, *19*(1), 7–30. doi:10.5771/0949-6181-2014-1-7

Fuchs, S., & Thaler, T. (Eds.). (2018). *Vulnerability and resilience to natural hazards*. Cambridge University Press. doi:10.1017/9781316651148

Ghosh, S. (2020). Examining the Covid-19 relief package for MSMEs. *Economic and Political Weekly*, *55*(22), 10–68.

Gürbüz, G., & Aykol, S. (2009). Entrepreneurial management, entrepreneurial orientation and Turkish small firm growth. *Management Research News*, *32*(4), 321–336. doi:10.1108/01409170910944281

Hatton, T., Seville, E., & Vargo, J. (2012). *Improving the resilience of SMEs: policy and practice in New Zealand.* Christchurch, New Zealand: Asia Pacific Economic Co-operation (APEC). https://www.resorgs.org.nz/wp-content/uploads/2019/04/apec-sme-resilience-policy-final-report.pdf

Hoque, A.S.M.M., & Awang, Z.B. (2019). Does gender difference play moderating role in the relationship between entrepreneurial marketing and Bangladeshi SME performance? *Accounting*, 35–52.

Hussain, S., Khattak, J., Rizwan, A., & Latif, M. A. (2013). ANSOFF matrix, environment, and growth-an interactive triangle. *Management and Administrative Sciences Review*, *2*(2), 196–206.

Iwu, C., & Benedict, H. (2013). Economic recession and investment on human resource information systems (HRIS): Perspectives on some South African firms. *Journal of Management Development*, *32*(4), 404–418. doi:10.1108/02621711311326383

Jaklič, A., & Burger, A. (2020). Complex Internationalisation Strategies During Crises: The Case of Slovenian Exporters During the Great Recession and COVID-19 Pandemic 1. *Teorija in Praksa*, *57*(4), 1018–1041.

Jha, S. K., & Kumar, A. (2020). Revitalizing MSME Sector in India: Challenges and the Road Ahead. *Journal of Politics & Governance*, *8*(5), 4–10. doi:10.47914/jpg.2020.v08i10.001

Jones, R., & Rowley, J. (2009). Presentation of a generic "EMICO" framework for research exploration of entrepreneurial marketing in SMEs. *Journal of Research in Marketing and Entrepreneurship*, *11*(1), 5–21. doi:10.1108/14715200911014112

Kashmiri, S., & Mahajan, V. (2014). Beating the recession blues: Exploring the link between family ownership, strategic marketing behavior and firm performance during recessions. *International Journal of Research in Marketing*, *31*(1), 78–93. doi:10.1016/j.ijresmar.2013.08.003

Kim, Han, & Oh. (2014). Historical review of market orientation: Generation, refinement, differentiation, and debates of the concept. *The Review of Business History*, *29*(1), 5–25. doi:10.22629/kabh.2014.29.1.001

Kitching, J., Smallbone, D., & Xheneti, M. (2009) *Have small businesses beaten the recession?* In 32nd Institute for Small Business and Entrepreneurship (ISBE) Conference: Celebrating 3 decades of excellence in education, research and practice: at the cutting edge of international entrepreneurship, Liverpool, UK.

Kowalik, I., & Danik, L. (2019). Marketing activity of international new ventures – application of the EMICO framework. *Journal of Business and Industrial Marketing*, *34*(4), 779–791. doi:10.1108/JBIM-02-2018-0079

Kraus, S., Filser, M., Eggers, F., Hills, G. E., & Hultman, C. M. (2012). The entrepreneurial marketing domain: A citation and Co-citation analysis. *Journal of Research in Marketing and Entrepreneurship*, *14*(1), 6–26. doi:10.1108/14715201211246698

Latham, S. (2009). Contrasting strategic response to economic recession in start-up versus established software firms. *Journal of Small Business Management*, *47*(2), 180–201. doi:10.1111/j.1540-627X.2009.00267.x

Latham, S., & Braun, M. (2011). Economic recessions, strategy, and performance: A synthesis. *Journal of Strategy and Management*, *4*(2), 95–115. doi:10.1108/17554251111128592

Luo, J. (2014). Entrepreneurial marketing- How marketers can satisfy customers' needs when applying entrepreneurial marketing approaches. *International Journal of Advances in Management Science*, *3*(4), 109–112. doi:10.14355/ijams.2014.0304.02

Maco, B., Bardos, P., Coulon, F., Erickson-Mulanax, E., Hansen, L. J., Harclerode, M., ... Wick, W. D. (2018). Resilient remediation: Addressing extreme weather and climate change, creating community value. *Remediation Journal*, *29*(1), 7–18.

Marrella, A., Mecella, M., Pernici, B., & Plebani, P. (2019). A design-time data-centric maturity model for assessing resilience in multi-party business processes. *Information Systems*, *86*, 62–78.

Martini, E., & Vespasiano, F. (2015). The Spaces of Resilience: Learning and Adaptation. *Italian Sociological Review*, *5*(1), 21–38.

Mateias, M., & Brettel, M. (2016). Effects of customer interaction orientation on customer satisfaction and firm performance: A longitudinal study. *Global Marketing Conference at Hong Kong*, 147-148.

Matsuo, M. (2006). Customer orientation, conflict, and innovativeness in Japanese sales departments. *Journal of Business Research*, *59*(2), 242–250.

M&E Studies. (2021). *Types of Vulnerabilities in Disaster Management*. http://www.mnestudies.com/disaster-management/vulnerability-types

Megersa, K. (2020). *Improving SMEs' Access to Finance Through Capital Markets and Innovative Financing Instruments: Some Evidence from Developing Countries. K4D Helpdesk Report 733*. Institute of Development Studies.

Mintzberg, H. (1987). The strategy concept I: Five P's for strategy. *California Management Review*, *30*(1), 11–24.

Morgan, R. E., & Berthon, P. (2008). Market orientation, generative learning, innovation strategy and business performance inter-relationships in bioscience firms. *Journal of Management Studies*, *45*(8), 1329–1353.

Morrish, S. C., Miles, M. P., & Deacon, J. H. (2010). Entrepreneurial marketing: Acknowledging the entrepreneur and customer-centric interrelationship. *Journal of Strategic Marketing*, *18*(4), 303–316.

Mukerjee, K. (2013). Customer-oriented organizations: A framework for innovation. *The Journal of Business Strategy*, *34*(3), 49–56.

Mukerjee, K., & Shaikh, A. (2019). Impact of customer orientation on word-of-mouth and cross-buying. *Marketing Intelligence & Planning*, *37*(1), 97–110.

Mwangi, H. W., & Bwisa, H. (2013). The Effects of Entrepreneurial Marketing Practices on the Growth of Hair Salons. *International Journal of Academic Research in Business and Social Sciences*, *3*(5), 467–480.

OECD. (2020). *Coronavirus (COVID-19): SME Policy Responses*. OECD Policy Responses to Coronavirus (COVID-19), July 15 Edition. https://www.oecd.org/coronavirus/policy-responses/coronavirus-covid-19-sme-policy-responses-04440101/

Osei-Bonsu, N. (2020). Entrepreneurial orientation and internationalization of SMEs –empirical evidence from developing markets. *Journal of Management Research*, *12*(2), 1–13.

Osuagwu, L. (2015). Market Orientation in Small Business Enterprises (SBES) in North-Eastern Nigeria: A Research Agenda. *Proceedings of 11th International Business and Social Science Research Conference*.

Ouyang, M., Hong, L., Mao, Z. J., Yu, M. H., & Qi, F. (2009). A methodological approach to analyze vulnerability of interdependent infrastructures. *Simulation Modelling Practice and Theory, 17*(5), 817–828.

Papathoma-Köhle, M., Thaler, T., & Fuchs, S. (2021). An institutional approach to vulnerability: Evidence from natural hazard management in Europe. *Environmental Research Letters, 16*(4), 044056.

Paul, S. K. (2013). Vulnerability concepts and its application in various fields: A review on geographical perspective. *Journal of Life and Earth Science, 8*, 63–81.

PricewaterhouseCoopers. (2010). *Nigeria SME survey*. https://www.pwc.com/ng/en/events/nigeria-sme-survey.html

Proag, V. (2014). The concept of vulnerability and resilience. *Procedia Economics and Finance, 18*, 369–376.

Raimi, L. (2021). Innovative Government-Backed Policy Measures in Nigeria for Sustaining MSMEs Post Pandemic (290820-071327). In N. Baporikar (Ed.), *Handbook of Research on Strategies and Interventions to Mitigate COVID-19 Impact on SMEs*. IGI Global.

Randa, I. (2020). Corporate Social Responsibility Interventions for Namibia's Post-COVID-19 Sustainable Banking Sector. In N. Baporikar (Ed.), *Handbook of Research on Strategies and Interventions to Mitigate COVID-19 Impact on SMEs*. IGI Global.

Rank, O. N., & Strenge, M. (2018). Entrepreneurial orientation as a driver of brokerage in external networks: Exploring the effects of risk taking, proactivity, and innovativeness. *Strategic Entrepreneurship Journal, 12*(4), 482–503.

Rank, O. N., Strenge, M., & Brennecke, J. (2013). Entrepreneurial orientation, Interfirm networks, and organisational performance. *Academy of Management Proceedings, 1*, 11433–11433.

Rashad, N. M. (2018). The impact of entrepreneurial marketing dimensions on the organizational performance within Saudi SMEs. *Eurasian Journal of Business and Management, 6*(3), 61–71.

Sarkar, S., & Clegg, S. R. (2021). Resilience in a time of contagion: Lessons from small businesses during the COVID-19 pandemic. *Journal of Change Management*, 1–26.

Sarmiento, J. P., Hoberman, G., Jerath, M., & Ferreira Jordao, G. (2016). Disaster risk management and business education: The case of small and medium enterprises. *AD-Minister*, (28), 73–90.

Savrul, M., & Kılıç, C. (2011). E-commerce as an alternative strategy in recovery from the recession. *Procedia: Social and Behavioral Sciences, 24*, 247–259.

Schindehutte, M., & Morris, M. (2010). Entrepreneurial marketing strategy: Lessons from the Red Queen. *International Journal of Entrepreneurship and Innovation Management, 11*(1), 75–94.

Schmengler, K., & Kraus, S. (2010). Entrepreneurial marketing over the internet: An explorative qualitative empirical analysis. *International Journal of Entrepreneurial Venturing, 2*(1), 56–71.

Smallbone, D., Deakins, D., Battisti, M., & Kitching, J. (2012). Small business responses to a major economic downturn: Empirical perspectives from New Zealand and the United Kingdom. *International Small Business Journal, 30*(7), 754–777.

Smallbone, D., North, D., & Kalantaridis, C. (1997). *Growth and Survival of Small Rural Manufacturing Firm*. Rural Research Report Number 32, Rural Development Commission, London and Salisbury.

SMEDAN - NBS MSMEs Survey. (2013). *Small Medium Enterprises Development Agency and National Bureau of Statistics Collaborative Survey: Selected Findings*. https://www.smedan.gov.ng/images/PDF/2013-MSME-Survey-Summary-Report.pdf

Stock, R. M., & Zacharias, N. A. (2010). Patterns and performance outcomes of innovation orientation. *Journal of the Academy of Marketing Science, 39*(6), 870–888.

Talke, K., Salomo, S., & Kock, A. (2011). Top Management Team Diversity and Strategic Innovation Orientation: The Relationship and Consequences for Innovativeness and Performance. *Journal of Product Innovation Management, 28*(6), 819–832.

USP. (2013). *Vulnerability Mapping*. University of the South Pacific. https://www.usp.ac.fj/index.php?id=10045

Verma, D. C., & Sarkar, R. (2018). Towards a better understanding of business models of social enterprise in an uncertain institutional environment. *Social Entrepreneurship and Sustainable Business Models*, 119-140.

Wang, Z., Huang, Y., Luo, J., & Feng, X. (2019). *Customer orientation and brand performance: A study of ROBAM*. China Branding.

Wedawatta, G., & Ingirige, B. (2012). Resilience and adaptation of small and medium-sized enterprises to flood risk. *Disaster Prevention and Management, 21*(4), 474–488.

Whalen, P. S., & Akaka, M. A. (2015). A dynamic market conceptualization for entrepreneurial marketing: The co-creation of opportunities. *Journal of Strategic Marketing, 24*(1), 61–75.

World Bank. (2019). *Small and Medium Enterprises (SMEs) Finance: Improving SMEs' Access to Finance and Finding Innovative Solutions to Unlock Sources of Capital*. World Bank. https://www.worldbank.org/en/topic/smefinance

Wurjaningrum, F., & Hartami, B. (2020). The intervening effect of market orientation on entrepreneurial orientation, operations strategy, and business performance. *Proceedings of the 3rd Global Conference On Business, Management, and Entrepreneurship (GCBME 2018)*.

Yadav, A., & Bansal, S. (2020). Viewing marketing through entrepreneurial mindset: A systematic review. *International Journal of Emerging Markets, 16*(2), 133–153.

Zhang, J., & Duan, Y. (2010). Empirical study on the impact of market orientation and innovation orientation on new product performance of Chinese manufacturers. *Nankai Business Review International, 1*(2), 214–231.

Chapter 6
Resilient Entrepreneurial Strategies Adopted by Zimbabwean Small and Medium Enterprises During Economic Crisis

Mufaro Dzingirai
https://orcid.org/0000-0002-1518-8275
Midlands State University, Zimbabwe

Rodgers Ndava
Midlands State University, Zimbabwe

EXECUTIVE SUMMARY

Resilient entrepreneurial strategy is a concept of great importance as it captures how entrepreneurs can ensure business sustainability in the face of harsh economic conditions of a market. In the wake of the economic crisis induced by the COVID-19 pandemic, it is not surprising to observe that scholars and practitioners are shifting their attention towards entrepreneurial resilience especially in the context of SMEs. With this in mind, this chapter focuses on the resilient entrepreneurial strategies adopted by Zimbabwean SMEs during the COVID-19 pandemic. The study established five strategies, namely strategic alliance, product differentiation, cost containment, innovation, and product differentiation. It is, therefore, recommended that SMEs should harness online technology and constantly re-evaluate entrepreneurial strategies in order to augment their agility to shocks emanating from the business environment.

DOI: 10.4018/978-1-7998-7657-1.ch006

INTRODUCTION

Recently, the global health crisis induced by the outbreak of coronavirus had created a spillover to an economic crisis that threatens the existence of many Small and Medium Enterprise (SMEs) across the globe (Brown & Rocha, 2020; Dzingirai, Chagwesha, & Mudzurandende, 2021; Kuckertz et al., 2020). It is an open secret that crisis is not a new phenomenon since the world had experienced numerous crises in the past such as the great depression of the 1930s, the global economic crisis of 2008, and the recent COVID-19 crisis (Tsilika, Kakouris, Apostolopoulos, & Dermatis, 2020). Despite the relevance of organizational resilience in the face of challenging times, it is discouraging to observe sparse crisis-oriented entrepreneurial research (Bullough et al., 2014; Doern, Williams, & Vorley, 2019; Monllor & Murphy, 2017).

According to Fatoki (2018), SMEs have a significant role to play in the sustainable development initiatives in most African countries including South Africa. Unavailability or inadequacy of financial capital in most developing countries is a challenge hence SMEs with little capital constitute a greater proportion of contribution towards sustainable development and economic growth hence the sustainability and thriving of these enterprises is crucial for job creation, poverty alleviation, and economic growth (Blundell & Machin, 2020; Fatoki, 2018). Escalating SMEs' failure rate is worrisome for South Africa and Zimbabwe among other countries in the region as these failures negatively impacted sustainable development (Odero, 2016). Fatoki (2018) reported that SMEs contribute significantly to the South African economy constituting approximately a whopping 90% proportion of all formal businesses in the country. Gross Domestic Product contribution by SMEs is estimated to be between 51% and 57%. More so, SMEs in South Africa provide approximately 60% of the country's employment population. The contribution to GDP as well as poverty alleviation by SMEs makes it crucial for due attention to be given to the worrisome and continued failure rates of these businesses especially after the COVID-19 outbreak and lockdown restrictions in Zimbabwe just like everywhere else around the globe. These experiences call for the emergence to analyze and understand how SMEs survive in times of uncertainty.

Pursuit of entrepreneurship by individuals or corporates is by no means an easy task due to multiple obstacles and unforeseen impediments such as the pandemic outbreak. Entrepreneurs should continuously keep tabs on global changes and changing contingencies in order to come up with resilient strategies and then align their goals (Korber & McNaughton, 2018; Odero, 2016). Entrepreneurial resilience should be the focal point for researchers and businesses yet to the best of the researcher's knowledge no satiable empirical study in the past has been done to satisfy the effect of entrepreneurial resilience on SMEs in Zimbabwe. This is witnessed by the continued increase in the number of SME failures. Some of the reasons behind the failure of SMEs include technological inadequacies (Dzingirai et al. 2021; UNDP, 2020).

Despite voluminous adoption prototypes of the technology across the globe, there is still a slow uptake of the technology by SMEs in Zimbabwe hence low drive is being witnessed towards adopting smart technologies (UNDP, 2020, Odero, 2016). Decision-making obstacles are faced, mainly influenced by the fear as well as the uncertainty of acquiring the technology. This situation arises as a result of a lack of planning and evaluation when considering the technology (Reynolds, Fourie, & Erasmus, 2019). SMEs need to plan and evaluate the technology alongside their business strategies, processes, and then embrace innovation as a strategy to overcome technology chasm (OECD, 2019a).

Worryingly, the research that captures issues of entrepreneurial resilience during the COVID-19 pandemic is scarce (Giones et al., 2020; Kuckertz et al., 2020; Thorgren and Williams, 2020). Notably, SMEs are more likely to be negatively affected by crises due to their weak financial muscles as compared to large organizations (Dzingirai et al., 2021). Given this state of affairs, some SMEs managed to come up with resilient entrepreneurial strategies so as to survive. In the context of Sweden, many SMEs embarked on cost-minimization strategies at the expense of entrepreneurial strategies as substantiated by the fact that less than 7% of the SMEs in Sweden engaged in innovation or revenue-generating activities during the COVID-19 pandemic (Thorgren & Williams, 2020). This heightens the need to broaden our understanding of resilient entrepreneurial strategies with the context of SMEs since they play a significant role in terms of employment creation, poverty alleviation, innovation, and economic growth. Consequently, this chapter's objective is to establish the resilient entrepreneurial strategies adopted by Zimbabwean SMEs during the COVID-19 pandemic.

BACKGROUND

Although the world has experienced many crises in the past, the issue of COVID-19 has attracted much policy and scholarly attention due to its acute negative socio-economic effects induced by lockdown measures. In addition to the serious health crisis, the coronavirus disease outbreak caused serious economic shocks globally (Bartik et al., 2020). In the United States (US), unprecedented lockdowns, closures, and mass layoffs caused massive dislocations for SMEs prior to government assistance through Relief and Coronavirus Aid. Notably, a sharp decline in business activity was recorded in Australia, Canada, New Zealand as well as in the USA where 54% of businesses closed in New York and employment decreased by 47%. The arrival of the COVID-19 pandemic in March 2020 in the United States witnessed a widespread economic disruption, illness, and death, leading to escalating levels of unemployment and business closures more than the Great depression levels (Wilmoth, 2021). Fairlie (2020) also confirmed that small business owners were struggling to keep their businesses viable as a result of the spread of the pandemic in the USA just like elsewhere globally. Wilmoth (2021) further proclaimed that the effects of the pandemic outbreak are ongoing hence the federal government started to roll out billions of dollars in emergency funds such as the Paycheck Protection Program, the Economic Injury Disaster Loan Program and the Coronavirus Aid, and Relief and Economic Security (CARES). SMEs struggles with survival and a substantial number of closing down enterprises in Australia was alarming just like in Asia and the rest of Europe. In the US, a report on SMEs by Bartik et al., (2020) confirmed that 43% of businesses had closed down temporarily and 40% had downsized their workforce as a result of the COVID-19 pandemic.

In the Indian context, the negative effects of Coronavirus did not spare Indian SMEs just like every business worldwide as the majority of Indian SMEs temporarily closed especially during the early months of the COVID-19 news outbreak (OECD, 2020; ITC, 2020). As the pandemic spread, not only death problems were at the hand of the Indian business community but many SMEs went out of business as the little finance could not sustain the viability of the businesses under lockdown. Contribution to GDP and employment drastically fell hence the Indian government had to rollout multiple schemes and programs in a bid to resuscitate the collapsing SMEs and the economy (UNDP, 2020; OECD, 2020) The government reduced the interest rates on loans from 5.15% to 4% so as to avail special credit facilities for SMEs (OECD, 2020).

In the African context, continental supply shock affected many businesses in Africa especially SMEs since they rely mostly on imports from Europe, America, and Asia (UNDP, 2020; Wilmoth, 2021). Supply chain lines are disturbed by the global pandemic and SMEs find it difficult to adjust to the global turbulence forcing many to go out of business. Even the giant corporates in the African continent just like elsewhere in the world find it difficult to survive the disastrous Coronavirus disturbances. The shutting down of SMEs in Africa as a result of the COVID-19 outbreak not only caused decreases in tax revenue, and increases in unemployment but also severely led to increases in poverty and a fall in the standard of living in Africa (UNDP, 2020; IMF, 2020).

The efforts of the Debt Relief Fund in South Africa focused on debt relief and assistance to help SMEs that were struggling as a result of the Coronavirus outbreak. SMEs affected only need to demonstrate a direct link on how the pandemic outbreak has impacted or could affect the business operations. This is done through the centralized registration platform (www.smmesa.go.va) managed by the relevant ministry. More so, the Business Growth or Resilience Facility has shown a remarkable effort to assist SMEs in South Africa, particularly those in the supply value-chain businesses (OECD, 2020; Wilmoth, 2021). The Solidarity Fund also provides seed capital to the business, individuals, and the international community as supported by R150 million that has been availed (ITC, 2020; OECD, 2020).

In the context of Zimbabwe, stressed that the economy of Zimbabwe has been characterized by macroeconomic volatility and turbulence for the past two decades (Dzingirai, 2020; UNDP, 2020). The outbreak of the COVID-19 pandemic has exacerbated the economic hardships in the country. Heavily taxed and burdened SMEs in the country face another war battle to fight for survival and success due to the disruptions emanating from the spread of coronavirus. Liquidity crisis, economic and political tussles have led to the closure of many giant corporates or relocation to neighboring countries leaving the country on the verge of collapse and a sorry state. The emergence of SMEs was witnessed in the past two decades as they sustain the economy and fill in the gaps left by large multinational corporates (UNDP, 2020; ZELA, 2020; Odero, 2016; UNDP, 2020).

The business sector in the country is composed of many SMEs, few viable state-owned enterprises, and few large companies hence there is an outcry among the SME sector as a result of stringent lockdown restrictions coupled with a harsh economic environment. Zimbabwe Statistical Agency concurs with the World Bank on the declining GDP in Zimbabwe as a result of the pandemic outbreak hence calling for the need to enact robust SMEs turnaround and resilience strategies that could turnaround or sustain the economy. Despite the need for assistance in terms of finance to SMEs affected by coronavirus, the government has instituted an array of operational measures and policies to combat the spread of the virus but has fallen short of the much-needed financial assistance to the troubled SMEs. Hence, UNDP (2020) proclaimed that the growth of the economy is most likely to be depressed if the fiscus stimulus and the macroeconomic environment are not addressed.

According to Fatoki (2018) the word “Resilience” does not possess a universally prescribed definition. The term originates from a Latin verb “resilire”, which generally means “to leap back”. Hedner et al., (2017) proclaimed that the concept of “Resilience” though complex is very common in Geman, Spainish, English, and French referring to the ability to recover. Hence, it is used as a characteristic of an individual who is willing to defy all the odds and challenges to prosper. Korber & McNaughton (2018) explains that resilience is a very important construct in entrepreneurship. The survival and success of entrepreneurs thus depend on the resilient characteristics of individuals owning the business. Literature does not show consensus on the definition of Entrepreneurial resilience as scholars offer various definitions for the subject. However, the essential feature synonymous with many descriptions includes adaptation to suit challenging environment for the purpose of survival or success of businesses (Hedner et al., 2017). Awotoye & Singh (2017) describes entrepreneurial resilience as the ability to overcome detrimental and high-impact business challenges and persevere in the entrepreneurial process.

Entrepreneurial resilience refers to business entrepreneurial mindset in a diversity of settings including SMEs or individual entrepreneurs or even corporate entrepreneurship (Hedner et al., 2017). High-Impact challenges in business are those events that are capable of impeding business success leading to bankruptcy, loss of clients, and business collapse (Awotoye & Singh, 2017). These events come in different forms including poor implementation or execution of business strategies, limited access to finance capital, climatic changes, intense competition from established firms, and global crisis including the outbreak of pandemics such as the COVID 19. Awotoye & Singh (2017) argue that high-impact challenges such as pandemic outbreaks impact firms' survival negatively. Surviving such high-impact events calls upon the need for robust strategies or resilient entrepreneurial strategies if SMEs are to thrive in such turbulent and detrimental business environments.

RELEVANCE OF ENTREPRENEURIAL RESILIENCE

Challenging and difficult times in business determine whether the business is going to survive or collapse (Portuguez-Castro & Gomez-Zermeno, 2020). Entrepreneurial resilience allows managers and entrepreneurs to become optimistic when facing tough conditions and unexpected challenges in an effort to ensure the survival and success of the business venture. It is interesting to note that Awotoye & Singh (2017) proposed that there is a strong relationship between business survival and entrepreneurial resilience. Non-resilient entrepreneurs are generally less adaptive to changes that occur in the business environment. Linnenluecke (2017) emphasized that entrepreneurial resilience helps to deal with high-impact challenges and come up with adaptive strategies that remedy the challenges. Resilience focuses on eliminating or limiting adverse effects of challenges and impediments for firms' survival and ultimately success. Put simply, it is the ability to manage challenges that increase the chances of venture failure (Portuguez-Castro & Gomez-Zermeno, 2020).

Going forward, Korber & McNaughton (2018) described resilience as synonymous with persistence, preparedness, self-efficacy, firmness of the entrepreneur. This explains why some firms perform better than others. More so, resilience in the context of SMEs explores the cognitive and behavioral business traits' ability to adjust swiftly to new circumstances. Entrepreneurial resilience does not solely rely on internal characteristics but more so on external facets such as the entrepreneur's ability to establish relationships in the social networks (Hedner et al., 2017). Based on the above perspectives and descriptions it is vital to note that entrepreneurial resilience focus on the preparedness of businesses in light of the existing and potential damning disruptions.

It is important at this juncture to note that there is no universally agreed definition of Small and Medium Enterprises (SMEs) since various scholars and institutions put forward various definitions. The Bureau of Economic Research (2016) defined SME as any business that employs up to 100 employees with annual revenue of US$25 million. Fatoki (2018) defined small businesses as separate legal entities that include cooperatives and other businesses managed by a single owner or more. A quantitative perspective or definition concentrates on the number of workers, sales revenue or turnover, and the value of assets owned by the business. Classification of businesses differs across the world but turnover, numbers of workers and assets value are the general yardsticks used for classification purposes. The number of employees is one indicator that used to classify SMEs in Southern Africa where small enterprises are widely regarded as entities that employ fewer than 50 workers, micro-enterprises usually in the retail business have less than 5 employees while very small businesses have less than 20 employees and medium businesses have less than 250 employees.

RESILIENT STRATEGIES

Despite the challenges encountered by SMEs from global pandemics and economic crises, entrepreneurs always thrive to come up with resilient strategies so as to ensure the survival and success of their enterprises. The development of a strategy is regarded as one of the most important decisions in any business setup. SMEs' ability to simultaneously overcome today's dynamic global environment challenges and exploit the opportunities that may arise even in times of trouble is highly significant in today's world. This is generally termed strategic entrepreneurship (Chumphong, et al., 2020). SME owner-managers are entrusted to come up with resilient strategies especially in this turbulent business environment that is characterized by an unfavorable economic atmosphere and COVID-19 disturbances. A number of strategies have been adopted in different countries and regions hence resilient strategies are becoming widely acknowledged as the appropriate framework of representing ways of business survival, value creation, and success. Tshwete (2020) reiterates that as SMEs face many challenges from different frontier they need visionary leaders that are skilled to craft the best strategies needed to navigate the turbulent waters of today's dynamic environment. Turner & Endres (2017) states that 50% of small businesses in America fail within the first 5 years of their creation hence resilient strategies are necessary. These small businesses, according to the Small Business and Entrepreneurial Council (2016), account for a significant percentage of job creation in the USA.

According to Lum (2017), most small businesses fail to succeed during the first years of their formation owing to poor planning and strategies. Hence, it is important for managers of SMEs to develop effective and robust resilient entrepreneurial strategies. These strategies may need aggressive approaches as well as defensive approaches depending on the situation or business environment. Strategies should set the tone and pattern for the goals and objectives of the entity. In this respect, strategies should be well communicated to everyone taking part in the venture. Environmental scanning and analysis are some of the most crucial activities before coming up with a strategy. Strategies should be crafted with an understanding of the business environment in which the entity operates. The economic crisis in Zimbabwe has made it difficult for entrepreneurs to stick to one strategy hence multiple resilient strategies are available for selection and these include cost leadership strategies, strategic alliances, growth strategies, differentiation strategies, competitive strategies, and diversification strategies.

Strategic Alliances

Turner & Endres (2017) asserted that interpersonal ties and social alliances and networking create new connections essential for the sustainability of businesses involved. Alliances aid networking and sustainability that is crucial for business operations. Turner & Endres (2017) further claims that 50% of small businesses exploit knowledge management from networking and alliances to perfect their business operations. The government can also facilitate strategic alliances between SMEs and large companies so as to ensure that some costs are shared. For instance, the Malaysian government provides a facilitative and supportive role through its ministries to link SMEs and transnational companies as well as local large companies. Strategic alliances create a network of connections that helps to share information and resources. According to Lum (2017), strategic alliances are cooperative arrangements between small entities for the purpose of working together to improve performance and competitive advantages. These alliances are not only limited to small businesses but can also include cooperation between small and large entities for the purpose of sharing costs or other resources (Hashim, 2018).

Entrepreneurs are perfect potential candidates for strategic alliances as a way to ensure sharing of information and resources. The ministry of Mining, Industry and Commerce in Zimbabwe encourages strategic alliances for the purpose of sharing other costs. For instance, the collaboration of small-scale miners to share acquisition of mining equipment that is very expensive for small-scale miners. These miners can as well collaborate with established miners and use their resources from exploration to mining. However, strategic alliances between SMEs in Zimbabwe with the established giants do not always bring fruitful results as established giants attempt to take over artisanal small-scale mines. In the end, owners of these small mines lose control of their entities due to acquisition. For instance, the failed attempts by ZMDC to take over King Mine was reported by ZELA (2020). Despite these setbacks, some small-scale miners have done extremely well in this COVID-19 era as reported by Zimbabwe Environmental Law Association (ZELA) (2020). The success of small-scale miners where large mines failed to prove that the strategic alliances between small scale miners can bring positive results during the economic crisis.

Differentiation Strategies

According to Lum (2017), differentiation as a business strategy is the uniqueness of the product as compared to other similar products and services from the competitors. The product or service might basically be the same but the entrepreneur may try to make the product or service look slightly different and this is usually done through extensive research and product development. Differentiation, hence, goes hand in hand with product improvement or development (Bose, 2016). Most basic commodities are basically the same across the market, what makes the difference is the way the product or service is delivered either through packaging or excellent service provision. Differentiation is, however, risky in some circumstances as differentiation initiatives can result in unnecessary costs making the product or service more expensive (Hashim, 2018). SMEs can ensure that their products or services are unique and not so easy to replicate by rival competitors. It is within this context that Lum (2017) stressed that most successful SMEs use differentiation as a strategy to outperform large companies.

Cost Leadership Strategies

Cost leadership strategies are based on operational efficiencies and these can be achieved by using advanced technology to improve processes and economies of scale (Lum, 2017). Learning organizations, be it SMEs or large corporates, can enjoy low-cost production benefits as long as they invest in innovation and improvements of their production processes or keep abreast with technological advancements that take place in this global society where new and less costly ways of production are being invented. According to Turner & Endres (2018), cost leadership strategies are positively correlated to business performance. Turner & Endres (2018) also confirm that SMEs that use cost leadership strategies are conservative and less vulnerable to new entrants and existing competitors. Despite the existence of competitors, economic crises also require businesses to employ effective cost leadership strategies to deal with economic instabilities that may halt business success.

Innovation

Innovativeness of the entrepreneur is an absolute leading phenomenon among successful businesses. Burns & Dewhurst (2016) described innovativeness as the willingness to introduce novelty through research and experimentation aiming at developing new lucrative products and services. SMEs innovativeness is thus regarded as the first and most important dimension of entrepreneurship ahead of competitive aggressiveness, risk-taking or proactiveness (Mueller, 2017; Burns & Dewhurst, 2016). Innovation by no doubt has become the leading strategy for businesses to achieve competitive advantages even in times of economic crisis (Pearce & Robinson, 2019).

Empirical evidence has shown that as businesses increase their innovativeness, their chances of success also increase together with competitive advantage (Blundell & Machin, 2020). The challenge for SMEs, however, is financial resources to invest in innovation and product improvement or research and development. In this regard, Odero (2016) confirmed that most SMEs in Zimbabwe need financial assistance when it comes to innovation agenda. The establishment of the Small Enterprises Development Corporation (SMEDCO) way back in the 1980s was an initiative to support SMEs with both financial and non-financial assistance (UNDP, 2020; World Bank, 2019; Odero, 2016).

Product Reengineering

Product reengineering is somehow related to innovation except that reengineering does not include the invention or creation of a new product (Turner & Endres, 2018). Innovation can include coming up with a new product or a new way of doing things when the firms continuously lose the market or decline in sales. Product reengineering involves the recapture and modification of product mechanisms to preserve the competitiveness of the products or services (Blundell & Machin, 2020). During economic crises, customers switch to cheap alternative products that are perfect substitutes for expensive products. Hence, SMEs as active participants in the market with immediate adaptation are the first to notice these changes and can opt for product reengineering in a bid to come up with a relatively cheap, affordable, and lucrative product that may recapture the lost market (Blundell & Machin, 2020). However, this may result in the production of inferior products as producers simply want to reduce the costs and come up with a product that is affordable to the customers and survive competition (Alberti et al., 2018).

Product reengineering is always thwarted by some impediments surrounding the Zimbabwean economy and other third-world economies. SMEs face challenges in trying to sustain and create new ventures due to a lack of resources and a constantly changing business environment (Dzingirai et al., 2021; UNDP, 2020; Odero, 2016). Falkner & Hiebl (2015) emphasized that both financial and non-financial resources are necessary for businesses to survive although small businesses mainly face financial resources especially during their elementary stages or when faced with a constantly changing environment. Non-financial resources include planning expertise which includes strategic management and entrepreneurial ideas to explore opportunities that are available.

Joseph Schumpeter's entrepreneurship theory describes an entrepreneur as an agent of change within an economy that resembles the ability to manage change (Lum, 2017; OECD, 2019). Entrepreneurs should, therefore, come up with resilient strategies for managing change to ensure the survival and success of SMEs during the economic crisis. Zimbabwean entrepreneurs are accustomed to economic crises that have rocked the country for the past two decades. First was the hyper-inflationary 2008 period year where inflation escalated beyond imaginable levels and the liquidity crisis resurfacing in 2016 until the

COVID-19 crisis worsening the already sorry state of the economy (UNDP, 2020; World Bank, 2019; Odero, 2016). Frequent trade restrictions and changes in legislation on trade worsen the situation in the country where an array of statutory instruments was enacted, reversed, and then reapplied on several occasions forcing entrepreneurs to always be alert of these changes (UNDP, 2020). These scenarios always call upon entrepreneurs in the country to always be innovative and come up with resilient strategies to suit every situation as it arises. Dzingirai et al., (2021) concurred with Lum (2017) on the idea that managers or entrepreneurs should always keep their tabs on the change mode and come up with entrepreneurial strategies that align the business and the new environment.

RESEARCH METHODOLOGY

Research Philosophy

This research adopted an interpretivism approach. This approach has been used by other researchers on entrepreneurial-related studies in an attempt to gather entrepreneurs' perspectives and experiences (Doern, 2017). More so, this philosophical approach is mainly used in qualitative research since it is appropriate to conduct an in-depth analysis of the resilient entrepreneurial strategies employed by SMEs in times of economic crisis (Creswell, 2014; Doern, 2017; Taylor, Bogdan, & DeVault, 2016). Interpretivism was, therefore, more relevant in exploring the strategies used by Zimbabwean Small and Medium Enterprises during the economic crisis accelerated by the COVID-19 pandemic.

Research Design

The interpretivism philosophy allowed the adoption of exploratory research design so as to explore the resilient strategies employed by SMEs in Zimbabwe. A research design is generally a plan on how research is conducted to answer the research question and address the research objectives (Creswell, 2014). In this regard, exploratory was appropriate since the study is qualitative and supported by interpretivism philosophy.

Sample

The research sample consisted of 10 SME owner-managers in Gweru who were directly affected by the economic crisis amid the Coronavirus pandemic outbreak period. Hence, the sample size was small allowing for a profound level of analysis of the resilient strategies (Doern, 2017). SMEs selected were identifies through referral, business news on SMEs in the city of Gweru and observation of enterprises closure and scaling down of business operations in the CBD, Mkoba, and Senga. These SMEs were into retail businesses selling groceries, clothing boutiques, electrical gadgets including cell phones and accessories. The majority of these enterprises had fewer than 25 employees except for only 3 businesses with close to 50 employees including family members working on part-time and college students on work-related learning. Seventy percent of the owner-managers were male between 40 and 60 years of and the other 30% female owner-managers fall within the same age range as the male counterparts.

Going forward, a judgmental sampling technique was used for sampling where specific retail SMEs particularly in the retail business were selected. This sampling technique was used for the purpose of selective sampling on the particular sect, that is, SMEs in Gweru. Researchers concur on the use of judgemental sampling emphasizing that this technique is used where the researcher's judgment is used to provide the best information basing on homogeneous participants (Sharma, 2017; Etikan & Bala, 2017).

Data Collection Techniques

In-depth or comprehensive semi-structured interviews were used to collect data as the main research instruments and observations were also used as complementary. Interviews were conducted under strict and careful COVID-19 restrictions. In this respect, interviews were conducted when the lockdown restrictions were relaxed allowing careful interaction with the participants to prevent the chances of spreading the virus. Respondents were asked to give a brief background about their entrepreneurial journey, the strategies they used to sustain the economic crisis, and what motivate them to pursue their trade. The interviews lasted between 50 minutes and 108 minutes. Open-ended questions were asked during the interviews as they allow the participants to give lengthy answers so as to clarify all the aspects (Leedy & Ormrod, 2016; Thomas, 2017). Interviews also help to solicit retrospective and real-time accounts from occurrences. Notably, the quality of interviews determines the quality of the research (Vaughn & Turner, 2016; Silverman, 2017).

Data Analysis

Thematic analysis was used for data analysis as a qualitative method of analyzing data. (Braun & Clarke, 2012). Thematic analysis is increasingly becoming popular because of its flexibility in analyzing data. This makes it easy for the themes to emerge from the data and allows an analysis of qualitative data systematically. Thematic analysis, therefore, makes it simple to make sense of collected data from SME owner-managers' perspectives and experiences.

RESULTS AND DISCUSSIONS

This section captures the findings and discussions related to the resilient entrepreneurial strategies adopted by SMEs. The purpose of the study was to understand the resilient strategies adopted by the SMEs in the face of the economic crisis exacerbated by the outbreak of coronavirus. Five key patterns emerged from data analysis, that is, strategic alliances, product differentiation, cost containment, innovation, and product reengineering. These themes are presented as follows.

Strategic Alliances

Respondents expressed their feelings and perceptions on the relevance and usefulness of strategic alliances as a resilient strategy. However, the minority of the respondents expressed that although strategic alliances offer an opportunity to gain a competitive advantage as well as utilizing other entities' resources, it is not always a win-win situation. Some of the responses are captured below:

Although we managed to embark on alliances in an effort to survive operational challenges during COVID-19 pandemic, sometimes strategic alliances fail halfway if the other parties discover that they are not benefiting from the alliance. This state of affairs affects the benefiting parties who are already counting on the alliance for the overall completion of certain project. (R10)

Strategic alliances are not really a merger so they cannot be trusted. Certainly, I arranged with my suppliers for an alliance so as to ensure a constant supply of products so that my small business remains relevant during the lockdown. (R2)

We have managed to reduce our transport costs by more than 68% as a result of the alliances that we have with other retailers. (R4)

These alliances have been helpful for us especially when it comes to sharing the transport costs but who knows how long is this going to last. (R6)

As highlighted in some of the responses on the resilient entrepreneurial strategies as captured above, strategic alliance emerged as of the strategies that were used by SMEs. Respondents generally agree that strategic alliances are mutually beneficial for all parties involved although other respondents could not count on these alliances for a long period of time. Several studies confirm that strategic alliances are fruitful but cannot be relied upon solely by SMEs that wish to continue operating as single entities due to the risky of takeover (Lum, 2017; Turner & Endres, 2017; Hashim, 2018).

Product Differentiation

Differentiation was also mentioned as a strategy that was adopted by SMEs in an effort to survive in the face of an economic crisis emanating from the emergence of the COVID-19 pandemic. Notably, it emerged that the respondents in the cell phone and accessories business confirmed that differentiation has sustained their businesses for a long period of time:

Customers always want the latest and top-class phones especially nowadays when smartphones are replacing the traditional cameras. In short, we offer our valued clients latest brands in town as compared to our rivals. (R3)

Unique and latest phones are always a preference especially for millennials so we have to constantly bring different cell phones from the last order batch. This generation always wants to try new things so we give them new cell phones and computers often but with cell phones, you never go wrong. (R7)

Four respondents, however, mentioned that product differentiation is a bit tricky but worthy trying so as to capture the constantly changing consumer tastes and preferences:

Product differentiation has been helpful but it has to be closely similar to the common products otherwise sales drop and then takes time for customers to familiarise with the new product. (R9)

If there is a new opportunity we opt for product differentiation but if the current products are performing well then we stick to current products. (R5)

In light of the above responses, all participants generally agree that product differentiation is at play among other survival strategies. The only difference is the frequency of differentiation which also depends upon the nature of products or services being offered. Technological products such as cell phones require frequent differentiation than basic commodities such as food and other groceries. Other studies on entrepreneurial studies also confirm the need for differentiation of firms' products for survival and success (Lum, 2017; Hashim, 2018).

Cost Containment

Cost containment is another theme that emerged from the data. Seven participants confirmed the cost containment was one of the key resilient strategies they applied in order to survive during the economic crisis period linked to the COVID-19 pandemic. Improving operational efficiencies is the way to go in the face of a hash economic crisis. Some of the quotes are mentioned as follows:

Cost leadership strategy always keep us ahead of others in this business. (R1)

Similar to innovation, operational efficiencies always help us to keep up with the changes even in developed countries. (R10)

Not only do we survive the competition but we also reduce unnecessary costs as we improve our operations. (R7)

The other three participants also confirmed that cost leadership strategy is relevant but expensive for them due to the financial incapacity to invest in improvements. Some of the quotes are as follows:

Although we are embarking on cost minimization, it appears that this strategy is mainly used by large firms with financial resources. (R4)

There is no much difference between innovation and cost leadership strategies, they both need financial resources for research and development and that is what we cannot afford at the moment. (R5)

Despite the confirmation by many respondents that they were focusing on cost containment, a few respondents further highlighted that there was a need for financial resources to effectively contain operational costs. Previous studies also confirm the relevance of cost leadership strategies to business survival in times of economic distress (Lum, 2017; Turner & Endres, 2018).

Innovation

All participants in the study concur with the idea of innovation and creativity to sustain the threatening effects of economic crisis except for one who hesitates to commit resources on innovation arguing that it is too risky but admitted that it is a requirement for businesses to survive. Respondents reported that the products offered are basically the same. Hence, there is a need for an entrepreneur to be more creative and be innovative when it comes to delivering the products to the customers. The most pertinent quote (R7) is as follows: *"There is no much variation when it comes to basic products offered by many grocery and retail businesses as the suppliers are basically the same. It is up to the entrepreneur to come up with ways of attracting customers through innovative ways such as repackaging the products into small different quantities to suit the affordability expectations of the customers"*. Some studies carried out on entrepreneurial strategies confirm the use of innovation and growth strategies. (Lum, 2017; Turner & Endres, 2017; Doern, 2017).

However, all participants emphasized that being innovative also involves some kind of financial risk as they sometimes lose substantial volumes of products testing the markets. Some customers are loyal to certain brands. Despite the lucrativeness of innovation to business survival, owner-managers agreed that innovative marketing needs careful planning otherwise businesses risk accelerating the already tough economic situation:

Innovation is the way to go but we have to be careful about introducing the right products that are needed by the customers. (R1)

Innovation is well provided the financial muscles permit. At this point in time, we cannot afford radical innovations due to limited financial resources. If innovation is about other non-financial resources then it is fine but if it involves risking financial resources it is not worth it in times like these. (R8)

The majority, nevertheless, of the respondents admitted that innovation has been their prime strategy as far as surviving the turbulent and business environment. All participants also proclaimed that internal innovation is more important than strategic alliances. Hence, innovation is thus undoubtedly an important strategy for SMEs' survival and also an imperative dimension of corporate entrepreneurship.

Product Reengineering

Product reengineering was another strategy that emerged from the data. The respondents recognized the essence of this strategy when it comes to entrepreneurial resilience. The only way they could partake in product reengineering is by giving feedback to the manufactures concerning customers' preferences. In this respect, some of the quotes are as follows:

Reengineering sounds like manufacturing but it is an option if we could divert to manufacturing. (R9)

We always try to negotiate with our suppliers so that we get products that are relatively cheap to suit pockets of our customers. (R3)

Last time we made recommendations to our supplier they responded swiftly and the products increased our sales volume by 26%. (R8)

Based on the above quotes, product reengineering is widely adopted as a relevant strategy for entrepreneurial survival and success during an economic crisis. Recent studies support the need for resilient entrepreneurial strategies in times of crisis among which product reengineering is an important strategy that can be adopted by businesses. (Bjorklund et al., 2020; Kuckertz, 2020).

RECOMMENDATIONS

Based on the findings presented in the previous section, the following recommendations were suggested.

Adoption of Several Resilient Entrepreneurial Strategies

Overreliance on a single or two strategies is not the way to go about since the Zimbabwean economic crisis intensified by the COVID-19 pandemic. Therefore, SMEs could adopt product reengineering together with strategic alliances. In such setups, SMEs could get opportunities to control the production processes and come up with the actual products that meet customers' expectations.

Diversification

Given that the economic crisis has made it difficult for some entrepreneurs to continue with one line of business, it is hereby recommended that SMEs in the retail business could diversify in an attempt to provide health-related products that are much needed by everyone for health reasons.

Harnessing Online Technology

Despite voluminous adoption prototypes of the technology across the globe, there is still a slow uptake of the technology by SMEs in Zimbabwe. Therefore, it is recommended that SMEs should harness online technology so as to augment product or service differentiation. SMEs need to plan and evaluate the technology alongside their business strategy, processes, and embrace innovation as a strategy to overcome technology chasm and uphold attractiveness.

Constant Re-Evaluation of Strategies

The dynamic economic environment is constantly changing, so is the economic crisis status. Accordingly, SMEs should re-evaluate their strategies and see if they are still relevant to the present and probably future changes.

RECOMMENDATIONS FOR FURTHER RESEARCH

This study only focused on the resilient entrepreneurial strategies used by Zimbabwean SMEs during the economic crisis. Therefore, future research work could focus on the challenges faced by SMEs in implementing resilient entrepreneurial strategies during the economic crisis. Having noticed that SMEs always strive to come up with resilient strategies, a number of impediments continue to resurface making it difficult for SMEs to successfully implement their strategies or turn around their business facing the impasse of collapse. Moreover, future research can focus on the business resilient strategies adopted by large companies during the economic crisis accelerated by the COVID-19 pandemic.

CONCLUSION

This chapter extends the scarce literature on entrepreneurial resilience during crises by focusing on the resilient entrepreneurial strategies adopted by SMEs during the economic crisis with special reference to the COVID-19 pandemic. Clearly, the most common strategies adopted by SMEs particularly in the retail sector include strategic alliances, innovation, product reengineering, differentiation, and cost leadership strategies. The recommendations suggested were submitted as remedies to the loopholes of the way in which the adopted strategies were being implemented. Recommendations were also offered as complementary approaches to the adopted strategies. Empirical evidence from this study clearly shows that SMEs in Zimbabwe a faced with a challenging economic crisis exacerbated by the outbreak of Coronavirus. Hence, the entrepreneurial resilient strategies should constantly be reviewed and applied for the SMEs to survive and succeed in this economic dilemma. It is concluded that SMEs can focus on sustainable business performance by embracing resilient entrepreneurial strategies in an effort to survive economic crises.

REFERENCES

Alberti, F. G., Ferrario, S., & Pizzurno, E. (2018). Resilience: Resources and strategies of SMEs in a new theoretical framework. *International Journal of Learning and Intellectual Capital, 15*(2), 165–188. doi:10.1504/IJLIC.2018.091969

Awotoye, Y., & Singh, R. P. (2017). Entrepreneurial Resilience, High Impact Challenges, and Firm Performance. *Journal of Management Policy and Practice, 18*(2).

Bartik, W., Bertrand, M., Cullen, Z., Glaeser, E. L., Luca, M., & Stanton, C. (2020). The impact of COVID-19 on small business outcomes and expectations. *Proceedings of the National Academy of Sciences of the United States of America, 117*(3), 17656–17666. doi:10.1073/pnas.2006991117 PMID:32651281

Bjorklund, T. A., Mikkonen, M., Mattila, P., & Van-Der-Marel, F. (2020). Expanding entrepreneurial solution spaces in times of crisis: Business model experimentation amongst packaged food and beverage ventures. *Journal of Business Venturing Insights, 14*, e00197. doi:10.1016/j.jbvi.2020.e00197

Blundell, J., & Machin, S. (2020). *Self-employment in the Covid-19 crisis: CEP COVID-19 analysis.* Retrieved May 15, 2021, from https://cep.lse.ac.uk/pubs/download/cepcovid-19-003.pdf

Braun, V., & Clarke, V. (2012). Thematic analysis. In H. Cooper (Ed.), *APA handbook of research methods in psychology: research design: quantitative, qualitative, neuropsychological and biological* (Vol. 2, pp. 57–71). American Psychological Association. doi:10.1037/13620-004

Brown, R., & Rocha, A. (2020). Entrepreneurial uncertainty during the Covid-19 crisis: Mapping the temporal dynamics of entrepreneurial finance. *Journal of Business Venturing Insights, 14*, e00174. doi:10.1016/j.jbvi.2020.e00174

Bullough, A., Renko, M., & Myatt, T. (2014). Danger zone entrepreneurs: The importance of resilience and self–efficacy for entrepreneurial intentions. *Entrepreneurship Theory and Practice, 38*(3), 473–499. doi:10.1111/etap.12006

Bureau of Economic Research. (2016). *The small, medium, and micro-enterprise sector of South Africa.* University of Stellenbosch. Retrieved May 10, 2021, from http://www.seda.org.za/

Burns, P., & Dewhurst, J. (2016). *Small Business and Entrepreneurship* (4th ed.). Palgrave. doi:10.1007/978-1-137-43034-2

Chumphong, O., Srimai, S., & Potipiroon, W. (2020). The Resource-Based View, Dynamic Capabilities and SME Performance for SMEs to Become Smart Enterprises. *ABAC ODI Journal Vision, 7*(2), 129–146.

Creswell, J. W. (2014). *Research design: Qualitative, quantitative, and mixed-method approaches* (4th ed.). Sage.

Doern, R. (2017). Strategies for resilience in entrepreneurship: Building resources for small business survival after a crisis. In T. Vorley & N. Williams (Eds.), *Creating resilient economies: Entrepreneurship, growth and development in uncertain times*. Edward Elgar. doi:10.4337/9781785367649.00008

Doern, R., Williams, N., & Vorley, T. (2019). Special issue on entrepreneurship and crises: Business as usual? An introduction and review of the literature. *Entrepreneurship and Regional Development, 31*(5–6), 400–412. doi:10.1080/08985626.2018.1541590

Dzingirai, M. (2020). Demographic determinants of youth entrepreneurial success. *International Journal of Sustainable Entrepreneurship and Corporate Social Responsibility, 5*(2), 1–16. doi:10.4018/IJSECSR.2020070101

Dzingirai, M., Chagwesha, M., & Mudzurandende, F. (2021). Challenges and opportunities from covid-19 vis-à-vis informal cross-border women entrepreneurs scenario in Zimbabwe. In N. Baporikar (Ed.), *Handbook of research on sustaining SMEs and entrepreneurial innovation in the post-COVID-19 Era* (pp. 40–59). IGI Global. doi:10.4018/978-1-7998-6632-9.ch003

Etikan, I., & Bala, K. (2017). Sampling and sampling methods. *Biometrics and Biostatistics International Journal, 5*(6), 215–217. doi:10.15406/bbij.2017.05.00149

Fairlie, R. W. (2020). *The Impact of COVID-19 on Small Business Owners: Continued Losses the Partial Rebound in May 2020.* National Bureau of Economic Research Working Paper 27462.

Falkner, E. M., & Hiebl, M. R. W. (2015). Risk management in SMEs: A systematic review of available evidence. *The Journal of Risk Finance, 16*(2), 122–144. doi:10.1108/JRF-06-2014-0079

Fatoki, O. (2018). The Impact of Entrepreneurial Resilience on the Success of Small and Medium Enterprises in South Africa. *Sustainability, 10*(7), 2527. doi:10.3390u10072527

Giones, F., Brem, A., Pollack, J. M., Michaelis, T. L., Klyver, K., & Brinckmann, J. (2020). Revising entrepreneurial action in response to exogenous shocks: Considering the COVID-19 pandemic. *Journal of Business Venturing Insights, 14*, e00186. doi:10.1016/j.jbvi.2020.e00186

Hashim, N. B., Raza, S., & Minai, M. S. (2018). Relationship between entrepreneurial competencies and small firm performance: Are dynamic capabilities the missing link? *Academy of Strategic Management Journal, 17*(2), 1–2.

Hedner, T., Adli Abouzeedan, A., & Klofsten, M. (2017). Entrepreneurial resilience. *Annals of Innovation amp; Entrepreneurship*, *2*(1), 7986. doi:10.3402/aie.v2i1.6002

IMF. (2020). *World economic outlook update, June 2020: A crisis like no other, an uncertain recovery*. Retrieved May 16, 2021, from https://www.imf.org/en/Publications/WEO/Issues/2020/06/24/WEOUpdateJune2020?utm_medium=emailandutm_source=govdelivery

ITC. (2020). *SME competitiveness outlook 2020: COVID-19: the great lockdown and its impact on small business*. ITC. Retrieved May 18, 2021, from http://www.intracen.org

Korber, S., & McNaughton, R. B. (2018). Resilience and entrepreneurship: A systematic literature review. *International Journal of Entrepreneurial Behaviour & Research*, *24*(7), 1129–1154. doi:10.1108/IJEBR-10-2016-0356

Kuckertz, A., Brandle, L., Gaudig, A., Hinderer, S., Reyes, C. A. M., Prochotta, A., Steinbrink, K., & Berger, E. S. (2020). Startups in times of crisis–A rapid response to the COVID-19 pandemic. *Journal of Business Venturing Insights*, *13*, e00169. doi:10.1016/j.jbvi.2020.e00169

Leedy, P. D., & Ormrod, J. E. (2016). *Practical research: Planning and design* (11th ed.). Pearson Education Inc.

Linnenluecke, M. K. (2017). Resilience in business and management research: A review of influential publications and a research agenda. *International Journal of Management Reviews*, *19*(1), 4–30. doi:10.1111/ijmr.12076

Lum, B. W. (2017). Business Strategies for Small Business Survival. Walden Dissertations and Doctoral Studies. Walden University.

Monllor, J., & Murphy, P. J. (2017). Natural disasters, entrepreneurship, and creation after destruction: A conceptual approach. *International Journal of Entrepreneurial Behaviour & Research*, *23*(4), 618–637. doi:10.1108/IJEBR-02-2016-0050

Mueller, P. (2017). *Exploiting entrepreneurial opportunities: The impact of entrepreneurship on growth.* Retrieved May 20, 2021, from https://www.econstor.eu/obitstream/10419/27104/1/518488292.PDF

Odero, K. K. (2016). *Small and Medium Enterprises Support System in Zimbabwe*. Paper presented at IDS Seminar, University of Nairobi, Kenya.

OECD. (2019). *OECD SME and Entrepreneurship Outlook 2019 Policy Highlights*. OECD.

OECD. (2020). *COVID-19 in Africa: Regional Socio-Economic Implications and Policy Priorities.* OECD Publishing.

OECD. (2020). *Financing SMEs and Entrepreneurs 2020: An OECD Scoreboard.* OECD Publishing.

Pearce, J. A., & Robinson, R. B. (2019). *Formulation, implementation, and control of competitive strategy* (12th ed.). McGraw-Hill/Irwin.

Portuguez-Castro, M., & Gómez-Zermeno, M. G. (2020). (Forthcoming). Being an entrepreneur post-COVID-19 – resilience in times of crisis: A systematic literature review. *Journal of Entrepreneurship in Emerging Economies.* Advance online publication. doi:10.1108/JEEE-07-2020-0246

Reynolds, A., Fourie, H., & Erasmus, L. (2019). A Generic Balanced Scorecard for Small and Medium Manufacturing Enterprises in South Africa. *The Southern African Journal of Entrepreneurship and Small Business Management, 11*(1), 1–15. doi:10.4102ajesbm.v11i1.193

Salisu, I., Hashim, N., Mashi, M. S., & Aliyu, H. G. (2020). *Perseverance of effort and consistency of interest for entrepreneurial career success: Does resilience matter? Journal of Entrepreneurship in Emerging Economies*. doi:10.1108/JEEE-02-2019-0025

Sharma, G. (2017). Pros and Cons of Different Sampling Techniques. *International Journal of Applied Research, 3*(7), 749–752.

Silverman, D. (2017). How was it for you? The interview society and the irresistible rise of the (poorly analyzed) interview. *Qualitative Research, 17*(2), 144–158. doi:10.1177/1468794116668231

Taylor, S. J., Bogdan, R., & DeVault, M. L. (2016). *Introduction to qualitative research methods* (4th ed.). John Wiley & Sons Ltd.

Thomas, D. R. (2017). Feedback from research participants: Are member checks useful in qualitative research? *Qualitative Research in Psychology, 14*(1), 23–41. doi:10.1080/14780887.2016.1219435

Thorgren, S., & Williams, T. A. (2020). Staying alive during an unfolding crisis: How SMEs ward off impending disaster. *Journal of Business Venturing Insights, 14*, e00187. doi:10.1016/j.jbvi.2020.e00187

Tshwete, L. M. (2020). Strategies for the Growth and Survival of Small- and Medium-Sized Businesses. Walden Dissertations and Doctoral Studies Collection. Walden University.

Tsilika, T., Kakouris, A., Apostolopoulos, N., & Dermatis, Z. (2020). Entrepreneurial bricolage in the aftermath of a shock. Insights from Greek SMEs. *Journal of Small Business and Entrepreneurship, 32*(6), 635–652. doi:10.1080/08276331.2020.1764733

Turner, S., & Endres, A. (2017). Strategies for Enhancing Small-Business Owners' Success Rates. *International Journal of Applied Management and Technology, 16*(1), 34–49. doi:10.5590/IJAMT.2017.16.1.03

UNDP (2020). *A Preliminary Assessment of the Socio-economic Impact of Coronavirus (COVID -19) on Zimbabwe*. Policy Brief 001/2020.

Vaughn, P., & Turner, C. (2016). Decoding via coding: Analyzing qualitative text data through thematic coding and survey methodologies. *Journal of Library Administration, 56*(1), 41–51. doi:10.1080/01930826.2015.1105035

Wilmoth, D. (2021). The Effects of the COVID-19 Pandemic on Small Businesses. U.S. Small Business Administration. Office of Advocacy Brief Number 16.

World Bank. (2019). *Small and Medium Enterprises (SMEs) Finance*. Retrieved May 20, 2021, from https://www.worldbank.org/en/topic/smefinance

Zimbabwe Environmental Law Association (ZELA). (2020). State of Closed Large- and Small-Scale Mines and their Relationship with Artisanal Mining. Mining Sector Situational Report. Harare.

ADDITIONAL READING

Bose, T. K. (2016). Critical success factors of SME internationalization. *Journal of Small Business Strategy*, *26*(2), 87–109.

Exposito, A., & Sanchis-Llopis, J. A. (2019). The relationship between types of innovation and SMEs 'performance: A multi-dimensional empirical assessment. *Eurasia Business and Economics Society*, *9*(2), 115–135. doi:10.100740821-018-00116-3

Jegede, O. O., Ilori, M. O., Olorunfemi, M. O., & Oluwale, B. A. (2016). On the link between human capital, innovation and performance: Evidence from a resource-based economy. *International Journal of Learning and Intellectual Capital*, *13*(1), 27–49. doi:10.1504/IJLIC.2016.074344

Kamalahmadi, M., & Parast, M. M. (2016). A review of the literature on the principles of enterprise and supply chain resilience: Major findings and directions for future research. *International Journal of Production Economics*, *171*(1), 116–133. doi:10.1016/j.ijpe.2015.10.023

Kitsos, A., & Bishop, P. (2018). Economic resilience in Great Britain: The crisis impact and its determining factors for local authority districts. *The Annals of Regional Science*, *60*(2), 329–347. doi:10.100700168-016-0797-y

Wellalage, N. H., & Fernandez, V. (2019). Innovation and SME finance: Evidence from developing countries. *International Review of Financial Analysis*, *66*, 101370. Advance online publication. doi:10.1016/j.irfa.2019.06.009

Yoshino, N., & Taghizadeh-Hesary, F. (2019). Optimal credit guarantee ratio for small and medium-sized enterprises' financing: Evidence from Asia. *Economic Analysis and Policy*, *62*(C), 342–356. doi:10.1016/j.eap.2018.09.011

Zaki, I. M., & Rashid, N. H. (2016). Entrepreneurship impact on economic growth in emerging countries. *The Business and Management Review*, *7*(2), 31–39.

KEY TERMS AND DEFINITIONS

COVID-19: A deadly disease that is linked to severe respiratory problems that can be spread from one individual to the other by contact with infected droplets or materials.

Economic Crisis: Financial catastrophe including inflation, high interest rates, unavailability of financial resources or unstable financial status.

Entrepreneur: Is an individual who takes risks associated with establishing a new business so as to make a profit.

Entrepreneurial Resilience: The ability of the entrepreneur to sustain business in the face of toughness or difficulties.

Entrepreneurship: Refers to the economic activity associated with risks is undertaken to generate a return on investment.

Gross Domestic Product (GDP): The monetary value of all goods and services produced within an economy over a given period of time usually a year.

SMEs: The business organizations that employ 5-40 employees.

Strategy: A unique plan devised to remedy a situation or create a favorable outcome.

Chapter 7
The Market of Fertilizers in Mexico During the Pandemic Crisis:
The Case of a Comprehensive Entrepreneurship Model for Organic Fertilizer Businesses

José G. Vargas-Hernández
https://orcid.org/0000-0003-0938-4197
University Center for Economic and Managerial Sciences, University of Guadalajara, Mexico

EXECUTIVE SUMMARY

This chapter aims to analyze the market of fertilizers in México during the pandemic crisis. This analysis of the fertilizer market in Mexico points out that the consumption of fertilizers has undergone a change in the structure in favor of consumers with the highest concentration and diversification. The method used is the analytical-descriptive and the critical reflexive based on the quantitative data obtained from secondary sources. This situation has contributed to a drop in the consumption of fertilizers because the farmer's real income has fallen during the pandemic crisis. To take advantage of the opportunities arising from the crisis, it analyzes the functioning of an integral model of entrepreneurship in green innovation business (GIB) that is currently emerging and in the process of internationalization. This chapter analyzes a particular company that specializes in ecological biomineral organic fertilizer, where no chemical product is used to produce the composition; everything that is marketed is made up of a base of organic minerals and other organic compounds.

DOI: 10.4018/978-1-7998-7657-1.ch007

INTRODUCTION

The Mexican Government's National Fertilizer Program aims to address the problem of low availability of national fertilizers at competitive prices for small producers. It includes both chemical fertilizers and biofertilizers. The National Fertilizer Plan aims to reduce dependence on the import of these fertilizers. To achieve this, the Cosoleacaque Petrochemical Complex plants and the Pajaritos plant are reactivated to produce ammonia, an input to produce urea, which Mexico imports mainly from Ukraine. In the case of phosphates, in the Pacific, the Lázaro Cárdenas plant is operational and is the largest in Latin America.

The National Biofertilizer Program shows incipient progress. The fertilizer production in Mexico estimated for 2019 was 1.85 million tons, reflecting an annual reduction of 2%; while demand continues to rise, with a record estimate of around 5.5 million mt. However, by July 2020, the production volume of nitrogen fertilizers in Mexico almost reaches 48,800 metric tons, which represents a decrease of 32.7% compared to that reported during the same month in 2019. The production volume of phosphate fertilizers in Mexico exceeded 75,600 metric tons, which represents a decrease of 29.1% compared to that reported during the same month in 2019 (Burgueño-Salas, 2020).

Currently, there is a new business model which has as the objective to be eco-efficient. Eco-efficiency is defined as the production of goods and services at competitive prices that meet human needs and provide quality of life, while the ecological consequences and the use of numerous resources during the life cycle are progressively reduced at the equivalent level at least to the estimated capacity of the planet (World Business Council for Sustainable Development, 1991).

On the other hand, it is mentioned that eco-efficiency has the purpose of establishing production of manufactured products of high durability, reducing the intensity in the application of energy for the production of goods and services, maximizing the use of raw materials, managing and disposing of hazardous materials and waste in an efficient and environmentally acceptable manner. Eco-efficient companies have management systems supported by environmental quality, as well as procedures in occupational safety and health, among other provisions, that will bring them financial benefits and competitiveness (Cantú, 2008).

In both definitions, the authors agree that eco-efficient companies should have as their main objective, to develop quality products at competitive prices, as well as to reduce the environmental impact of producing or offering their products and services. Castro (1998) mentions that eco-efficiency aims to address three relevant aspects that correspond to 1) the total quality, which involves productivity and quality in the company, 2) the preservation of the environment, which is related to sustainable development; 3) occupational health and safety (Castro, 1998). State the chapter's objective(s) so as to guide the reader.

FERTILIZER DEMAND IN MEXICO

A recent analysis of the fertilizer market in Mexico has pointed out that the consumption of fertilizers has undergone a change in the structure in favor of consumers with the highest concentration and diversification (UACH). This situation has contributed to a drop in the consumption of fertilizers because the farmer's real income has fallen.

On the changes in the consumption pattern, it has been documented already the use of mixed and compound fertilizers, considered as the mixture of two or more straight fertilizer materials of the three primary nutrients--N, P_2O_5, and K_2O (Hignett 1985; Rajani, 2019). From experience in the field, it can be stated that there has been a growth in the use of physical fertilizer mixtures where the distributor makes certain formulations, mixing fertilizers and thus the producer only buys one product. Regarding those of high concentration, it is well understood, if possible because there has been significant growth in protected agriculture and around strawberries and high-value vegetables where drip irrigation is used and through its fertilizers are applied and for this, highly soluble sources with minimal impurities are usually used, which are not normally traditional sources.

However, with more recent data reported by Instituted Trusts in Relation to Agriculture (FIRA 2020), in the agricultural year 2019, 71.8% of the sown area was fertilized. This represents the seventh consecutive year with increases in the percentage of fertilized area. According to this report, the consumption of fertilizers in Mexico grew by 5.8%. Add more information.

In an interview with a FIRA fertilizer specialist analyst, Gallegos Cedillo (2021) asking about the trend in fertilizer consumption and asked about the demand and supply of fertilizers in Mexico, he warned that the lack of information with hard data does not always support trends in which the market moves. Regarding the consumption of fertilizers, the production information indicates that production has fallen: 15.4% from 2013 (2.06 million tons) to 2020 (1.75 million tons) for the period January-September. However, between 2014 and 2019 increased compared to the previous years.

Now, if we consider the fertilized area, it has increased, as a percentage of the sown area. This proportion has increased from 2013 to 2019, the last reported year, going from 65.3% in 2012 to 71.8% in 2019. However, if we look at the apparent consumption, it increased from 5 million tons in 2013 to 6.7 in 2018, in 2019 (January-December) it does drop to 5.8 and in September 2020 it is 5.2 (Graph in quarterly report). There are no elements to attribute the drop in consumption from 2018 to 2019 to the decrease in producers' income, but if someone affirms this, it is difficult to prove otherwise. Given the above information, it appears that there is no link with the emergence of the pandemic and how the pandemic crisis affected the production of fertilizer in Mexico.

Figure 1. Production and consumption of fertilizer in Mexico (Millions of tons)

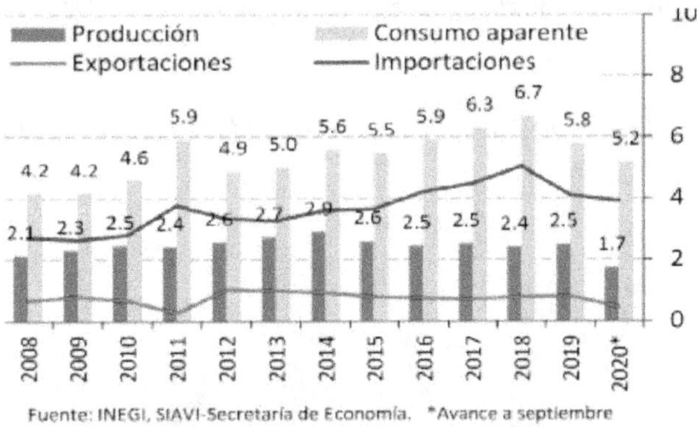

Fuente: INEGI, SIAVI-Secretaría de Economía. *Avance a septiembre
Nota: En marzo 2019 se cambió la base SCIAN de la EMIM, que resultó en cambios en el volumen de producción reportada a partir de 2013.

FERTILIZER PRODUCTION IN MEXICO

The increase in Mexican fertilizer production during the last years is attributed, in part, to the reforms made to the Pemex Law since 2008. These had the objective of promoting the production and productivity of the Mexican fertilizer industry through the supply of raw materials, such as ammonia, at competitive prices for national manufacturers._In 2018, national production contributed 30.7% of apparent national consumption, which is estimated at 6.2 million dollars and represents an annual increase of 7.9%. The foregoing shows the country's high dependence on fertilizer imports.

With data from 2019, the national production of fertilizers is mainly composed of: Phosphate fertilizers (diammonium and others) with 55.7%. Nitrogen fertilizers (ammonium sulfate and nitrate and others) with 32.2% Acidic fertilizers (phosphoric, sulfuric, and nitric) with 10.9%. The estimated value of the fertilizer industry in Mexico in 2019 is 13,616.4 million pesos, 2% lower than that registered in 2018.

Fertilizer production processes in Mexico are not integrated, a situation that has an impact on domestic producers, especially urea and nitrate, being at a disadvantage compared to producers of international competition (UACH). According to data from the latest Quarterly Report on Fertilizers from the Directorate of Research and Economic Evaluation of the Instituted Trusts in relation to Agriculture (FIRA, 2020), the production of fertilizers in Mexico decreased at an annual rate of 8.4% in the first nine months of the year compared to the same period in 2019. Add more information.

Regarding the fact that the national producers of urea and ammonium nitrate are at a disadvantage with international competition, as a consequence of the lack of integration of their production processes. If the statement is well understood, especially the reason that is manifested by the lack of integration of their production processes, in general, it would be expected that greater integration greater profitability. However, this is not considered to be the main reason for the disadvantage of domestic producers. It can affect but is not the main reason.

More weight would be given to the characteristics of the Mexican farmer, small areas and little specialized, he grows various products, as well as the dependence to a large extent on the import of fertilizers that expose him to have fertilizers without due quality control, lack of weight in the containers (49 kg bags instead of 50 for example), exchange rate, etc. Gallegos-Cedillo, 2021). Add more information.

*Figure 2. Acid fertilizer production in Mexico, 2013-2020 * (Thousands of tons)*

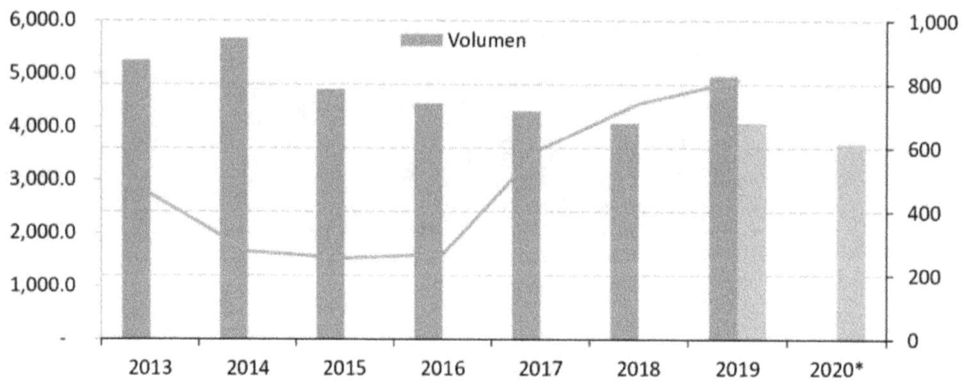

*Figure 3. Fertilizer production in Mexico, 2013-2020 * (Millions of tons)*

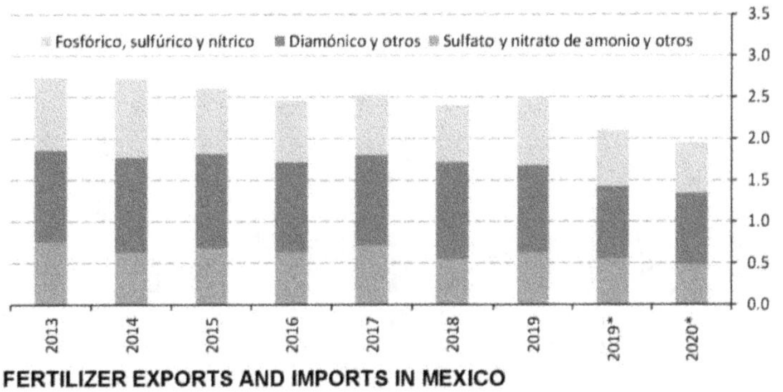

FERTILIZER EXPORTS AND IMPORTS IN MEXICO

In this regard, with information from the Ministry of Economy, imports of fertilizers in Mexico, during 2018, registered a volume of 5.06 million dollars and represented an annual increase of 12.6 percent. In said year, imports came from Russia (30.9%), the United States (14.3%), Norway (12.1%) and China (11.1%), mainly. In the last five years, these countries participated with 69.5% of the national fertilizer imports. In the case of exports, these stood at 0.79 million pesos and registered an annual growth of 10.5%. Between 2008 and 2018, consumption and imports grew on average at an annual rate of 6.3 percent.

Imports in 2019 are estimated at around 2.9 million tons, of which an advance of 92% was recorded as of November. Of the total imported, 67.2% corresponded to nitrogenous, 15.5% to phosphate, 12.5% to potash and others with 4.8%. The commercial value of these imports was 807.8 million dollars, reflecting a reduction of 14.3% in relation to the record of 943.1 million dollars registered in 2018. The main supplying countries were Russia 30.6%, China 16.9%, United States 11.3%, Algeria 7.9%, Malaysia 3.8%, Chile 2.9%, Canada 2.1%, Egypt 1.4%, and others 23.1%.

Between January and September 2020, Mexican fertilizer imports grew 9.9%, while exports decreased 16.6% at an annual rate, totaling 3.9 and 0.46 million dollars, respectively.

*Figure 4. Mexican Fertilizer Exports, 2003-2020 * (Millions of dollars)*

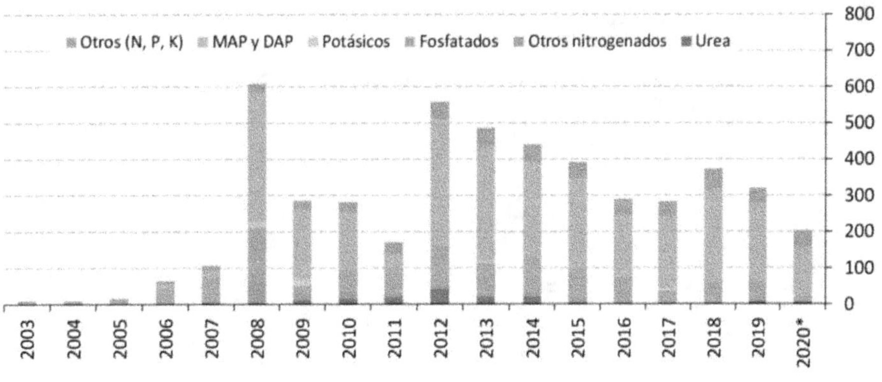

*Figure 5. Mexican Fertilizer Imports, 2003-2020 * (Millions of dollars)*

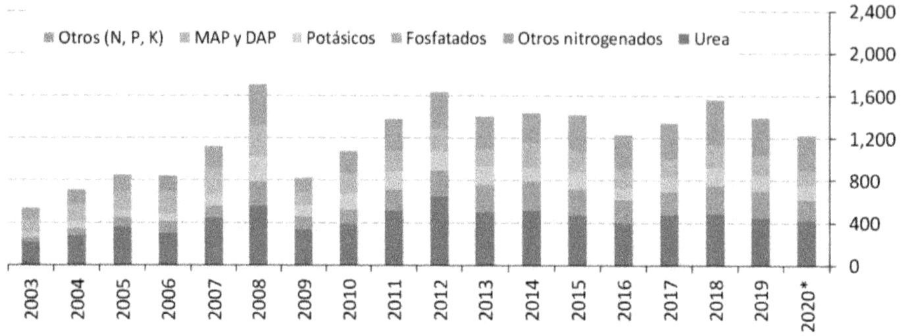

*Figure 6. Balance of the fertilizer trade balance, 2003-2020 * (Millions of dollars)*

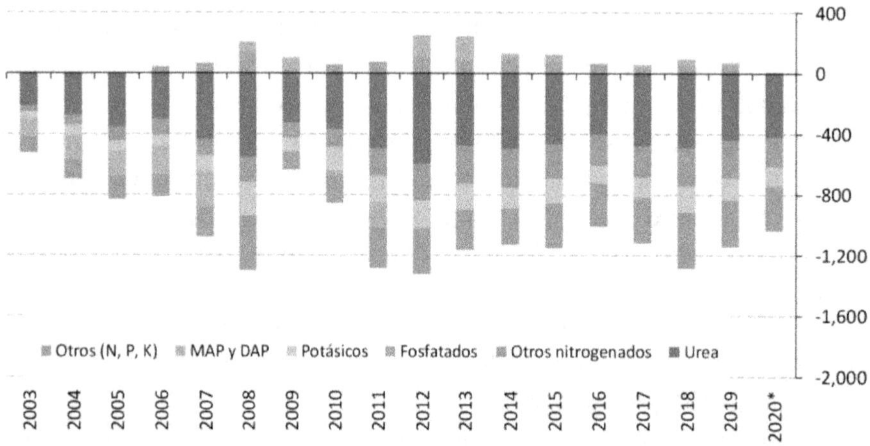

Figure 7. Trade balance (Millions of tons)

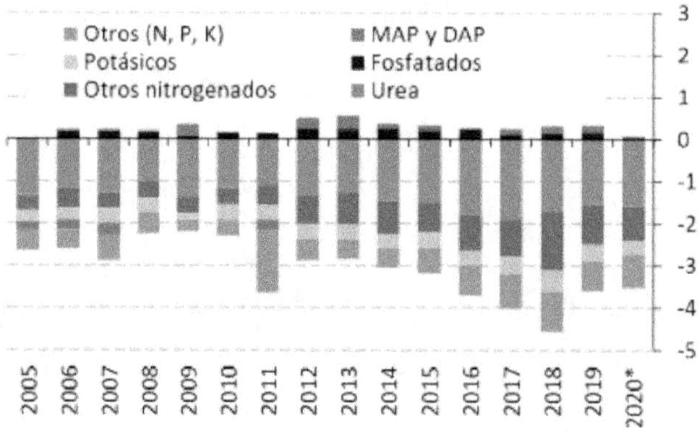

Fuente: SIAVI-Secretaría de Economía. *Avance a septiembre de 2020.

THE FERTILIZER MARKET

The implicit price of fertilizer imports in Mexico in 2018 was $ 322.3 per ton and represented an annual increase of 6.7%. The implicit price of imports from Russia was 283.4 dollars per ton, 387.2 for those from China and 416.1 for those from the United States, and showed an annual growth of 10.8, 24.2, and 9.7%, respectively. Regarding the average price level of fertilizers in Mexico, since 2014 the behavior has been on the rise. In 2018, a ton of fertilizer, in distribution centers, was quoted on average at 10,254 pesos, which represents an increase of 3.5% compared to 2017.

The fertilizers with the highest annual increases in prices were, diammonium phosphate (DAP) (10.4%), Triple 17 (10%) and potassium nitrate (9.4 percent). In January and February 2019, the average price was reduced by 2.0 and 1.3% compared to December 2018, so it would be expected that the average price in 2019 will be at levels like those registered during 2018. Add more information.

In the domestic market, urea prices increased 7.3% from 2018 to 2019; while those of diammonium phosphate rose 4.8%. The average price of fertilizers in the country maintains an upward trend. In November 2020, it registered growth of 2.7% at an annual rate and 3.3% from December 2019 to date. As of November, the price increases of triple 17 (12.2% annually), ammonia (9.9%), ammonium sulfate (8.3%) and ammonium nitrate (7.9%) stand out. The prices of simple superphosphate and potassium chloride were the ones that showed the greatest annual decrease, at rates of 7.1 and 4.6%, respectively.

Figure 8. Prices in the national market (In Mexican pesos per ton)

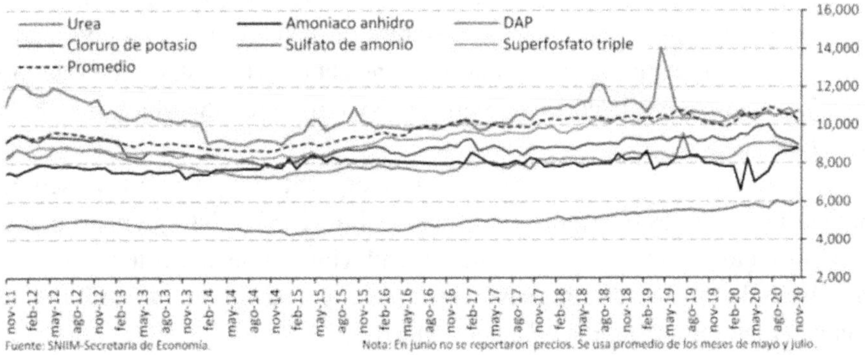

CHALLENGES AND OPPORTUNITIES: A COMPRENHENSIVE ENTREPRENEURSHIP MODEL OF GREEN BUSINESS INNOVATION (GBI).

Fertilizers are an input of fundamental importance in primary agricultural activity. The rehabilitation of fertilizer producing plants in the country is not economically viable in the short term, because the reactivation of activities in the plants takes time, it is necessary to invest more resources for the qualification and the import of ammonia gas continues, an input necessary in the production of fertilizers. The importation of fertilizers will continue, since the national production of 2020 only covers 33.7% of the total demand, and the remaining 66.3% is brought from the foreign market.

*Figure 9. Production, foreign trade, and apparent consumption of fertilizers in Mexico, 2013-2020 * (Millions of tons)*

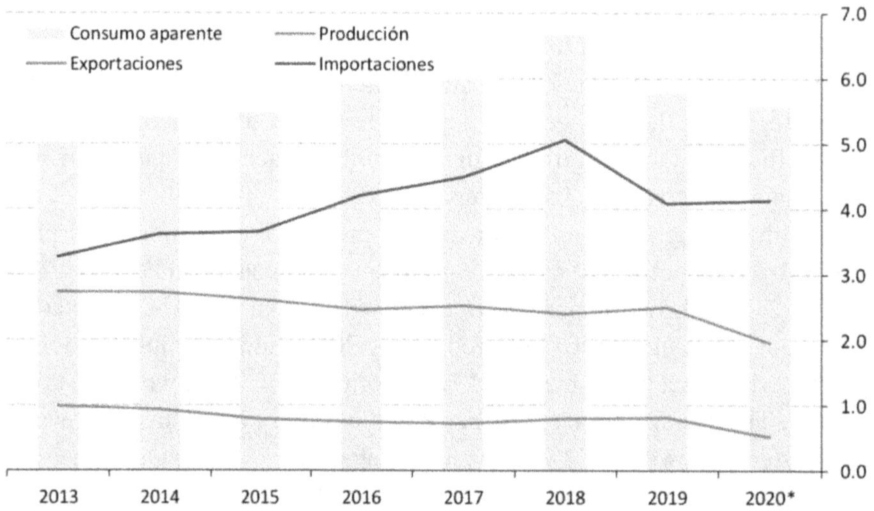

Entrepreneurship, inclusiveness, civil and culture are variables that have complex but straightforward linkages and processes among them and much is still unknown. The last few years have witnessed the generation of extensive theoretical and empirical literature on entrepreneurship and its impact at the levels of regional and firm economic performance (Holmes & Schmitz, 1990; Evans & Leighton, 1989). However, when linking entrepreneurship to the variables of inclusiveness and civil culture, the literature is inexistent. There is a relative void, despite some recent efforts to study the relationship between entrepreneurship in some other related fields beyond economic growth, which may be attributable to the lack of theoretical frameworks.

However, some studies conducted in economic development have shown reversed causality influencing entrepreneurial activities (Ortega-Anderezand & Lai, 2017). Entrepreneurial activities tend to be overestimated in regions where there are start-ups playing a relevant role while entrepreneurship activities tend to be underestimated in regions where there is a new entrepreneurial formation and the startups are relatively few (Baptista, Escária, and Madruga, 2017).

The role of entrepreneurship in economic development has received attention from researchers showing the impact of entrepreneurship on employment and social development. Entrepreneurial intentions promote entrepreneurial behaviors (Krueger et al., 2000; Veciana et al., 2005; Souitaris et al., 2007). Entrepreneurship activity can be associated with human necessity providing an opportunity to earn money for living, until better alternative opportunities are found on the labor market (Carree and Thurik, 2010).

The concept of entrepreneurship is multidimensional and related to individual willingness, abilities, and activities on their own, in teams and in organizations to make decisions facing obstacles and uncertainty on the use of institutions and resources to create and develop new opportunities (Wennekers and Thurik, 1999). Entrepreneurial opportunities are the result of unemployment the influences start-up activity, the effect of a thriving economy and experience in entrepreneurial activities (Lin, Manser and Picot, 1998; Pfeiffer and Reize, 2000).

Entrepreneurship is the recognition and exploitation of opportunities leading to the creation and development of a firm (Aragon-Sanchez, Baixauli-Soler, Carrasco-Hernandez, 2017). Moreover, entrepreneurial intentions predict entrepreneurial behaviors, according to the theory of planned behavior (Ajzen, 1991). Entrepreneurial activity creates opportunities to influence economic performance (van Stel, Carree and Thurik, 2005) such as entering the markets with new production processes and products (Acs and Audretsch, 2003). Among the entrepreneurial models there is evidence that the entrepreneurial intentional models (Krueger et al., 2000) supports the theory of planned behavior.

The theory of planned behavior has been used in the analysis of entrepreneurial intentions (Shook et al. 2003). The determinants have significant positive relationships with behavior intention (Armitage and Conner 2001). Do Paço et al. (2011) found a positive and significant influence between entrepreneurial intentions, attitudes, and perceived behavior control. However, subjective norms have an indirect impact on entrepreneurial intentions.

The determinants of entrepreneurial intentions are linked with access to financial, natural, human, and cultural capital and resources through the influence of attitudes, individual subjective norms, perceived social control, and self-efficacy. The attitude is the individual favorable evaluation to start a new opportunity. Individual subjective norms are the perceived social pressure to start a new opportunity and perceived social control and self-efficacy is the perceived ease to start a new opportunity. Based on the Shapero and Sokol 1982) model, attitudes and subjective norms are linked to desirability and perceived behavioral control or self-efficacy with feasibility (Krueger et al., 2000).

METHODOLOGY OF RESEARCH

Green innovation in urban areas is a neglected issue in terms of urban planning and policing. Still, more neglected is a concern for changes in urban green areas toward the implementation of green innovation initiatives to revitalize the cities, increase the economic growth, improve the social justice and inclusiveness, as well as the improvement of environmentally sustainable development, strengthen the biodiversity and socio-ecosystems. To achieve these goals, it is necessary to implement some actions following the design and implementation of a comprehensive entrepreneurship model.

The research methodology used was based on the analysis of secondary data sources to obtain the main tendencies in production and consumption of fertilizers. After obtaining the main niches of the market fertilizers in México, it was considered the need to expand the bio-organic production of fertilizers and the opportunities to develop an eco-efficient business entrepreneurship model

This new eco-efficient business entrepreneurship model will be analyzed in the context of the integral model, analyzing in this way the tripod of the strategy, which integrates considerations based on industry, resources, and institutions. This paper begins with the assumption that the companies of ecological base present major difficulty at the time of wanting to internationalize, in comparison to the companies of the industrial base.

Instrument and Procedures

This analysis is based on the specific case study of an eco-efficient company using the methodological tools proposed for each one of the theoretical approaches.

For the analysis industry-based considerations are employed in the model of the five forces, also called the diamond model proposed by Porter (1980). The method for analyzing competition derives from the five forces framework that determine the competitive intensity and the attractiveness of an industry in terms of its profitability. The resource and capabilities analysis of the eco-efficient company is employed the model proposed by Barney (2001) based on the value, rarity, inimitability and organizations, complemented with the SWOT analysis of strengths, weaknesses, opportunities and threats. Finally, the eco-efficient company is also analyzed in terms of the institutional considerations considered as the "rules of the game", formal and informal, that frame the entrepreneurial activities and the creation and development of companies according to the territorial environment.

Data Analysis: Use of fertilizers in Mexico

The National Development Plan 2019-2024 establishes among the priority actions for food self-sufficiency and the rescue of the field the Fertilizer Program for the benefit of agricultural producers. The data analysis tools used are the time series analysis, to determine the tendencies of growth in production and consumtion.

BIO ORGANIC FERTILIZERS IN MÉXICO

The use of organic fertilizers in Mexico is not very common, this is because industrial-based companies need chemical products that make plants grow at a faster rate due to market demand. But these fertilizers damage the soil causing it to become unusable after a time for the harvest, as a result, the food absorbs these fertilizers that are harmful to the human being in the long run.

On the other hand, organic fertilizers bring many benefits to the soil along with plants and food. According to a study carried out by SAGARPA, organic fertilizers favorably influence the physical characteristics of the soil (physical fertility); These characteristics are structure porosity, air action, water retention capacity, infiltration, hydraulic conductivity, and stability of aggregates. The following table 1 shows a comparison made by the National Agricultural Survey (ENA) in which there is an increase in the use of chemical fertilizers in Mexico and a decrease in organic fertilizers.

Table 1. Comparison of the use of chemical and organic fertilizers in Mexico

Employed technology	**Percentage**	
	ENA 2012	**ENA 2014**
Type of seed	60.9%	82.2%
Creole	29.7%	29.2%
Improved	Na	Na
Certified	Na	Na
Transgenic	Na	Na
Seedling	Na	21.0%
Chemical fertilizers	65.5%	68.8%
Natural fertilizers	40.4%	27.5%
Herbicides	61.7%	62.7%
Insecticides	45.3%	48.2%

The sum does not give 100 because each production unit can use more than one technology
Na Not available
Source: INEGI: National Agricultural Survey (ENA 2014)

THEORETICAL-CONCEPTUAL FRAMEWORK

The theoretical framework applied in this study is based on the analysis of the coefficient company using the main three theories of strategic design and implementation: The industry-based considerations, the resource and capabilities considerations, and the institutions-based considerations, as shown below in figures 10 and 11.

Figure 10. Model of strategic analysis

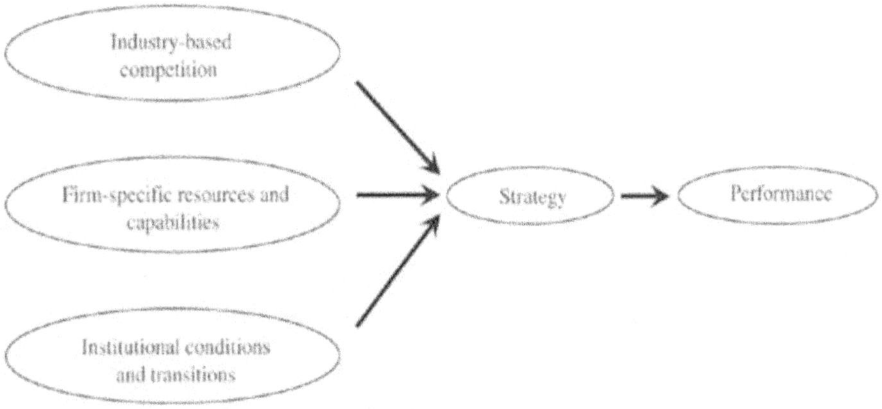

Source. Own elaboration based on Peng (2012).

Figure 11. A comprehensive entrepreneurship model for the internationalization of green innovation business (GIB) and eco efficient companies

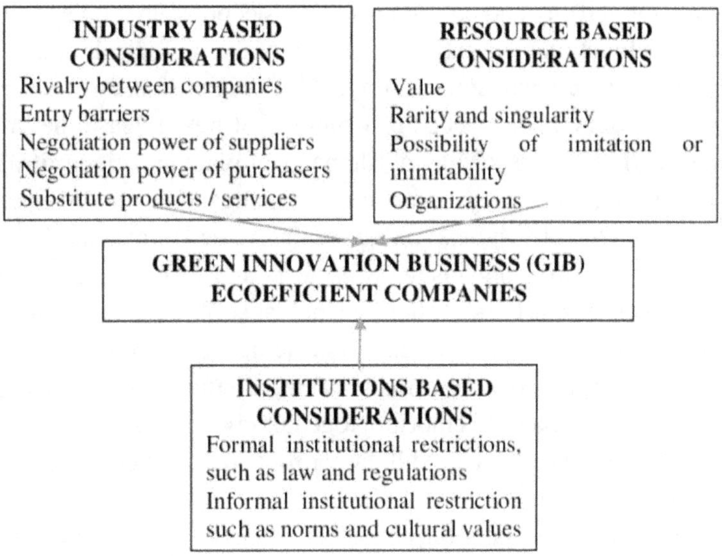

Source: Own elaboration

THE GREEN INNOVATION BUSINESS (GIB): BIO-FOM

BIO-FOM is a green innovation business (GIB) also characterized as an eco-efficient company to promote sustainable, profitable, and inclusive development through highly competitive Mexican seeds with fair prices. Using organic mineral bio-fertilizers healthily increased the profitability of the producers. It is in the metropolitan area of Guadalajara (Figure 12).

Figure 12. Localization of BIO-FOM a green innovation business (GIB)

Source: Web page of the company.

BIO-FOM is the most complete Organic Mineral Bio-fertilizer available on the market, which is made from the interaction of elements: biological, organic, and mineral. It is a mineral organic bio-fertilizer for plant nutrition. The interaction of the BIO-FOM elements forms a Functional Plant Nutrition System; its results reflect: improving seed germination and initiation, healthy and adequate growth, larger roots, greater flowering, and tie, increase in the quality of the fruits, and provide resistance to pests and diseases. BIO-FOM increases soil fertility and contributes to the decontamination and regeneration of the soil.

BIO-FOM bases its functionality on the interaction of the biological, organic, and mineral elements that compose it: A Poly-Functional Consortium of Microorganisms, among them: antagonists to pests and diseases, nitrogen fixers, and; mycorrhizal fungi; that help release the nutrients provided by the BIO-FOM blend itself. The 17 Basic Mineral Elements of plant nutrition (nitrogen, phosphorus, potassium, calcium, magnesium, sulfur, iron, boron, copper, manganese, silicon, zinc, iodine, sodium, cobalt, molybdenum, selenium) Organic Matter, Amino Acids, Acids Humic, and Fulvi.

BIO-FOM contains live microorganisms: 8 bacteria and mycorrhizal fungi that help unblock the chemical components that exist in the soil allowing their absorption, in addition to an important contribution of organic matter, amino acids, humic and fulvic acids, this, together with its content of 16 mineral elements (nitrogen, phosphorus, potassium, magnesium, calcium, iron, boron, copper, manganese, silica, zinc, iodine, sulfur, sodium, cobalt and chlorine) together give rise to a molecular dialogue that results in a functional plant nutrition system, fertile soil, larger root size and helps improve pH, which is essential for proper and healthy plant growth.

Among other benefits, it potentiates the chemical fertilizers that complement the application of BIO FOM as:

1. It recovers the soil fertility, unlocking mineral nutrients present but not available, favoring their absorption due to their bio-organic profile.
2. Increases the specific weight of grains, resulting in higher production.
3. Increases the Br ix degrees of the fruit, having better sales possibilities.
4. Stimulates the immune system, so healthy, vigorous, and productive plants are achieved. Strengthens the root system of the plant, thereby improving the use of water and mineral nutrients available in the soil.
5. Respect the ecosystem, avoiding the contamination of the water table.
6. 100% assimilable, achieving a greater expression of the genetic potential of plants.
7. Retains and conserves moisture in soils.

EMPIRICAL RESULTS AND CONCLUSIONS

Industry-Based Considerations

When analyzing industry-based considerations, the framework of Porter's five forces is used, which considers factors such as rivalry between firms, barriers to entry, the power to negotiate with suppliers and buyers, as well as substitute products.

The Rivalry Between Companies

When talking about the rivalry of companies, it refers to the struggle that companies face every day to obtain a position before consumers. These battles can be for prices, quality in products, advertising battles, etc. On the other hand, the author Huyghebaert Van de Gucht mention that the rivalry between firms generates a direct impact on the likelihood that a business will be successfully undertaken, as well as having an impact on the existence of barriers to entry since fewer firms exist in one industry more complicated will be the entry of new firms (Huyghebaert and Van de Gucht, 2004).

The company to analyze is dedicated to organic fertilizers made from organic minerals. As it is an innovative product, it does not have much competition, nonetheless, there is competition with the substitute products that would be all chemical fertilizers, due to a great variety of substitute products that are available in the market. It is difficult to compete for price in the same way as being a medium-sized company is not even positioned in the consumer's mind when thinking of organic fertilizer.

Nowadays fertilizers and other chemical products for the treatment of the soil represent 15.7% of the income of the Nurseries and gardens industry in 2019. The industry has experienced a rapid growth in recent years, thanks to the constant increase in disposable income per capita and the consumer segment strengthened.

A decent part of the US market has been occupied by large companies such as Scotts Miracle-Gro Company, Walmart, and Lowe's. Because economies of scale, as well as large corporations can maintain a low cost while offering affordable prices. Price competition among large companies has led to slow growth throughout the sector and low profit margins. Some less profitable companies have been forced to leave the industry. Successful companies are those able to compensate the highest prices by offering a deeper knowledge of the product and superior customer service.

Over the next five years, the nursery and garden store industry are expected to continue to grow, as economic conditions are expected to remain stable. As the disposable income per capita increases, the consumer will be able to invest more time and money in the appearance and operation of their gardens. It is also expected that the industry will benefit from a growing demographic interest in small plants, gardening, and organic horticulture.

Below is a list of companies with which Mary's Poop competes in the United States.

Scotts Miracle-Gro Company (OH, USA)

Founded in 1868, Scotts Miracle-Gro Company is a multinational corporation and industry leader in the lawn and garden market. Its products include the infamous Miracle-Gro and a complete line of plant foods. The most popular Miracle-Gro fertilizers are inorganic, which are much less expensive than organic fertilizers.

PacaProGro (CA, USA)

The PacaProGro farm is in Somis, California, with an estimated 180 alpacas producing alpaca fiber and alpaca manure. Not only sell alpaca fertilizers, but also merchandise made of alpaca fiber, such as hats, gloves, scarves, and stuffed animals.

Alpaca Grow (VT, USA)

Alpaca Grow is a small family business operated in Vermont that began in 2014. Like Mary's Poop, Alpaca Grow sells only alpaca fertilizers.

Isolated wood farm (British Columbia, Canada)

Secluded Wood Farm is headquartered in British Columbia, Canada. They sell alpaca fiber and manure products.

Alpaca Island Company of Martha's Vineyard (MA, USA)

Island Alpaca Company has more than 15 acres and around 50 alpacas. They sell alpaca fiber and manure products, and they are charging higher prices.

Camelot Haven Alpacas (British Columbia, Canada)

Founded in 2002, Camelot Haven Alpacas produces and sells alpaca clothing, accessories, gifts, and alpaca fertilizers.

Entry Barriers

As already mentioned before, BIO-FOM faces competition from large chemical and organic fertilizer companies. Due to this, there are difficulties when it comes to wanting to enter the foreign markets, as the big brands are doing well positioned in the market, and it would be complicated to unseat them or compete for prices so that the company, in this case, could compete for product quality as well as innovation and for the benefits that its product provides.

It is also important to consider the transaction cost and the transportation cost if working with foreign currencies. If the costs become too high, BIO-FOM products would be less competitive in the foreign market. An alternative to export is the franchise, which allows local business units to produce BIO-FOM products for a fee.

One of the competing companies of Mary's poop is already positioned in 10 states of North America, and has large sales volumes, being this way, the products of Mary's poop and other small alpaca farms cannot compete by prices and volume, as already mentioned previously, which makes it be handled as an oligopoly market among large companies. These in turn set entry barriers when playing with prices since, if they see that a new product wants to enter the market, they lower their prices to continue to have an advantage over others or use promotions which makes them more attractive. the purchase of their products to the final consumer.

It is also important to consider the transaction cost and the transportation cost if working with foreign currencies. If the costs become too high, Mary's Poop products would be less competitive in the foreign market. An alternative to export is the franchise, which allows local alpaca farms to produce Mary's Poop products for a fee.

Substitute Products or Services

In the global marketplace and more specifically, North America, large, medium-sized, and small competitors produce similar products. Geographically, most of the production plants are in rural areas and seem to serve only local markets. The competitive advantage of BIO-FOM is that it is the company with the highest social awareness among all its competitors. And although its product is easy to imitate, it gives it a plus by mixing it with some other ingredients that make the compost a better quality. It is also easy to use as they pack the product inside disposable pod-made biodegradable materials that only must be deposited in a container with water waiting for it to dissolve and starts to water in a normal way.

But there is a high range of substitute products that, although they are not organic, the final use is the same (serve as fertilizer to the plants), sharing with substitute products is complicated since the raw material they are made with are very economical and this it makes the prices of the products accessible to all types of publics. On the other hand, the organic products that Mary's poop handles are of a slightly higher price, this is due to the handmade process with which they are manufactured.

Bargaining Power with Buyers

According to Porter, at this point, it is defined as the ability of customers to impose prices and conditions of sale (Porter, 1980). This force can be established by customers directly, whether negotiating a discount or financing model, demanding delivery forms, or indirectly which is summarized with competitive purchases.

The bargaining power of buyers may depend on some variables such as a high supply of products and/or services and low demand for them. Another may be that the products offered have no differentiation among themselves, etc. At this point, the customer has the option to choose any product or service that is presented to them and that they consider to be the best and meet their expectations. As well as defining what is the maximum price customers are willing to pay for a product or service, as well as some other requirements that could be delivery times, product quality, etc. All this has an impact on the company's profits.

Mary Forte, the owner of Mary's Poop, manages and operates the company and interacts with customers and other interested parties through social networks. Nowadays, online / digital marketing is the most important marketing tool, especially in social networks. For example, use "Pinterest" to communicate with the company's audience. This social networking platform is popular with many users who share images that can be easily shared. Therefore, she can approach her audience and attract their attention and thus know what customers need and adapt to the needs of the market.

Bargaining Power with Buyers

In one of his writing papers, Peng mentions that when the bargaining power of suppliers becomes too great, business solutions must be found that can reduce it (Peng, 2012, page 127); this is since many options must be available to purchase inputs at reasonable prices.

The organic fertilizer based on organic minerals requires many inputs because of a lot of raw materials are used for its elaboration, so it is necessary to have many suppliers. But if it is necessary that with few suppliers that have contact make and establish the negotiation agreements and delivery times among many other things, in this way can reduce and to a certain extent eliminate transaction costs.

Considerations based on resources and capabilities

The resources are any input in a productive system in which an output is generated. These can be classified as financial, physical, human, technological, organizational, knowledge, management team experience, and customer service, among others. The consideration based on resources groups some indispensable factors for entrepreneurship, some of them are creating value, being unique through the rarity factor among other aspects. For example, in an analysis Peng mentions that it is important to consider the resources of the company, they must be oriented to create value, they must have rarity, they must be difficult to imitate and finally business resources must be immersed in the organization (Peng, 2012).

On the other hand, Barney dogmatizes that the heterogeneity of organizations is due to the possession of resources: i) valuable, which must respond to environmental threats and take advantage of their opportunities; ii) rare or scarce, those that cannot allow obtaining competitive advantages with competitors; iii) difficult resources to imitate, without substitutes and organizational, which means that the company has aspects of order (Barney, 2001, page 41).

The company BIO-FOM offers the market an innovative product because it is taking the greatest benefit to a product that people see as a waste and transformed it into a product with added value; the strengths which this product provides are that they are organic, have a higher performance compared to other fertilizers, are favorable to the environment, are not expensive to produce. Something that gives a higher value is that the packaging is biodegradable by which makes the whole product itself is ecological and there is no waste of plastic or any other material that is difficult to decompose, the product is safe for children and pets so anyone can use it.

Therefore, for the considerations based on resources, a SWOT analysis was carried out to analyze both: the internal and external factors that provide added value to the firm, as the positive and negative factors that can cause the company not to grow as rapidly as expected.

Table 2. SWOT Analysis

Strengths	Opportunities
Organic products / products without chemicals Excellent performance compared to other inorganic fertilizers environment friendly It is not expensive to produce The packaging is biodegradable No toxic, safe for children and pets It is not easy to imitate	Growing trend in organic products Market development Product development Product differentiation
Weaknesses	**Threats**
Lack of advertising + visibility Small production capacity-challenge for the company at scale The products have limited functions The products are not standardized Hard to forecast production Limited capital and strategic partners Do not go alone Expensive compared to inorganic fertilizers	Regulations that exist for exports Animal diseases Environmental factors may affect production Breach of demand levels Low market level

Source: Prepared by the Authors

In this table, it is shown that the firm has many strengths that make its product different but also has many threats. This is due to the same rarity of the product that makes it somewhat complicated for sale, likewise, the product is easy to imitate, so at any time it could have a lot of competition, which can quickly get to the market firm. In his essay, Porter states that the competitive advantage comes from the value that a company manages to create for its customers, by offering special benefits that compensate a higher price of the product (Porter, 1980).

Considerations Based on Institutions

When talking about considerations based on institutions, we are talking about the rules of the game of these, in which the behavior of the company is determined and how they are developed around the world. Peng points out 5 strategies for an entrepreneurial company to be successful, which can be applied together, and they are growth, innovation, networks, financing/government, and harvest/output (Peng, 2012).

The BIO-FOM company integrates some of these strategies such as innovation in their products, as well as networks since they try to have a wide network to get known as well as to obtain advice and keep growing as the company participates in a program called X-culture where companies are assigned a group of people from different parts of the world, advising companies so they can expand or internationalize at the time the company uses all the networks that are possible for be able to expand. Peng mentions that there is evidence that networks, personal and organizational, represent significant resources and opportunities and that the successful creation of networks can lead to the efficient performance of firms (Peng, 2012, page 13).

Instead, McDougall notes that network analysis builds a very solid foundation and helps identify international opportunities, as well as establish credibility, provide access to critical resources, as well as knowledge, and lead strategic and cooperative partnerships (McDougall and Oviatt, 2000).

CHALLENGES AND OPPORTUNITIES

Green innovation business (GIB) is in the field of organic fertilizers are contributing with an input of fundamental importance in primary agricultural activity. The rehabilitation of organic fertilizer-producing plants in the country is not economically viable in the short term, because the reactivation of activities in the plants takes time. Besides, it is not common to find these kinds of producer units in urban areas.

It is necessary to invest more resources in the qualification and to reduce the import of organic inputs and other ingredients necessary in the production of fertilizers. The importation of chemicals as well as organic fertilizers will continue, since the national production of 2020 only covers 33.7% of the total demand, and the remaining 66.3% is brought from the foreign market.

CONCLUSION

When analyzing the green innovation business (GIB) and eco-efficient company through the comprehensive method of entrepreneurship, it is observed that just as the company has some advantages in the product also with many threats that are the large companies that are already positioned and that also compete with competitive prices. It is also determined that although the green innovation business (GIB) has a wide network that is using the best way possible, it is necessary to increase the international network of contacts so that the business can grow quickly.

Although BIO-FOM has been positioned in the local, regional, and national markets for a short time and has grown steadily, it has the challenge to enter the international markets in a very competitive position. The company Mary's poop has a competitive advantage that differentiates it from other firms, and that is that its product is innovative and ecological, as well as its processes are carried out in an ecological way which makes it an eco-efficient company.

Likewise, due to the culture of planting in Mexico, this company faces problems to become highly competitive in the country, since most farmers prefer chemical fertilizers and thus produce more in less time than caring for the land and having a product of a higher quality with organic fertilizers.

It is necessary to implement a culture of conscience in Mexico when we talk about caring for the land since the use of organic fertilizers would not only help the environment but also people, this is because the foods that are consumed will have better nutrients and they would not be contaminated with pesticides. Today some people started to make their gardens at home, so they grow their food, this is a good technique because they can be sure that the consumption of food is one hundred percent organic. Here is the importance of the topic for green innovation in urban areas.

REFERENCES

Acs, Z. J., & Audretsch, D. B. (2003). Innovation and Technological Change. In Z. J. Acs & D. B. Audretsch (Eds.), *Handbook of Entrepreneurship Research* (pp. 55–79). Kluwer Academic Publishers. doi:10.1007/b105789

Ajzen, I. (1991). The theory of planned behavior. *Organizational Behavior and Human Decision Processes*, *50*(2), 1–63. doi:10.1016/0749-5978(91)90020-T

Aragon-Sanchez, A., Baixauli-Soler, S., & Carrasco-Hernandez, A. J. (2017). A missing link: The behavioral mediators between resources and entrepreneurial intentions. *International Journal of Entrepreneurial Behaviour & Research, 23*(5), 752–768. doi:10.1108/IJEBR-06-2016-0172

Armitage, C. J., & Conner, M. (2001). Efficacy of the theory of planned behavior: A meta-analytic review. *British Journal of Social Psychology, 40*(4), 471–499. doi:10.1348/014466601164939 PMID:11795063

Barney, J. (2001). Is the resource-based "view" a useful perspective for strategic management research? *Academy of Management Review, 26*(1), 41–56.

Burgueño-Salas, E. (2020). Volumen de producción mensual de fertilizantes fosfatados en México de enero de 2019 a julio de 2020 (en toneladas métricas). *Statista.* Retrieve on the 2 of July 2021 from https://es.statista.com/estadisticas/594554/volumen-de-produccion-de-fertilizantes-superfosfatados-en-mexico/

Cantú, P. (2008). *Desarrollo sustentable: conceptos y reflexiones.* Universidad Autónoma de Nuevo León. Colección: Tendencias Científicas.

Carree, M. A., & Thurik, A. R. (2010). The impact of entrepreneurship on economic growth. In J. Zoltan & D. Audretsch (Eds.), *Handbook of entrepreneurship research* (pp. 557–594). Springer. doi:10.1007/978-1-4419-1191-9_20

Castro, A. (1998). *Hacia el desarrollo sostenible y la ecoeficiencia: integración de las normas ISO 9000, ISO 14000 e ISO 18000 diseño de un sistema de gestión ambiental certificable. (Tesis de maestría inédita).* Obtenido de Facultad Regional de Buenos Aires: http://posgrado.frba.utn.edu.ar/investigacion/tesis/MIA-1998-Castro.pdf

Consejo Mundial Empresarial para el Desarrollo Sostenible. (1991). Ecoeficiencia y sustentabilidad. *Ciencia UANL, 35*, 15–28.

Do Paço, F., Arminda, M., Ferreira, J. M., Raposo, M., Gouveia, R., & Dinis, A. (2011). Behaviours and entrepreneurial intention: Empirical findings about secondary students. *Journal of International Entrepreneurship, 9*(1), 20–38. doi:10.100710843-010-0071-9

Evans, D. S., & Leighton, L. S. (1989). Some empirical aspects of entrepreneurship. *The American Economic Review, 79*, 519–535.

FIRA (2020). *Reporte trimestral de fertilizantes, Dirección de Investigación y Evaluación Económica del Fideicomisos Instituidos en relación con la Agricultura.* FIRA, Diciembre 2020.

Gallegos-Cedillo, G. (2021). Working paper *Agronegocios FIRA.*

Hignett, T. P. (1985). Compound Fertilizers. In T. P. Hignett (Ed.), *Fertilizer Manual. Developments in Plant and Soil Sciences, (15).* Springer. doi:10.1007/978-94-017-1538-6_19

Holmes, T. J., & Schmitz, J. A. Jr. (1990). A theory of entrepreneurship and its application to the study of business transfers. *Journal of Political Economy, 98*(2), 265–294. doi:10.1086/261678

Huyghebaert, N., & Van de Gucht, L. M. (2004). Incumbent strategic behavior in financial markets and the exit of entrepreneurial start-ups. *Strategic Management Journal, 25*(7), 669–688. doi:10.1002mj.415

Krueger, N. F. Jr, Reilly, M. D., & Carsrud, A. L. (2000). Competing models of entrepreneurial intentions. *Journal of Business Venturing*, *15*(5-6), 411–432. doi:10.1016/S0883-9026(98)00033-0

Lin, Z., Manser, M. E., & Picot, G. (1998), T*he Role of Self-Employment in Job Creation in Canada and the U.S. OECD-CERF-CILN International Conference on Self-Employment*, Burlington, Ontario, Canada.

McDougall, P., & Oviatt, B. M. (2000). International entrepreneurship: The intersection of two research paths. *Academy of Management Journal*, *43*(5), 902–906.

Ortega-Anderezand, D., & Lai, E. (2017). The Main Factors Influencing Entrepreneurial Activities and Intentions within a Country—A Case Study of Spain. *International Journal of Innovation, Management and Technology*, *8*(1), 32–37. doi:10.18178/ijimt.2017.8.1.698

Peng, M. (2012). *Global Strategy*. Thomsom South-Western.

Pfeiffer, F., & Reize, F. (2000). Business Start-ups by the Unemployed - an Econometric Analysis Based on Firm Data. *Labour Economics*, *7*(5), 629–663. doi:10.1016/S0927-5371(00)00016-6

Porter, M. (1980). *Competitive Strategy*. Free Press.

Rajani, A. V. (2019). *Chapter: 8 Fertilizer mixtures (mixed fertilizers)*. DOI., doi:10.13140/RG.2.2.23850.36801

Shapero, A., & Sokol, L. (1982). The social dimensions of entrepreneurship. In C. A. Kent, D. L. Sexton, & K. H. Vesper (Eds.), *Encyclopedia of Entrepreneurship* (pp. 72–90). Prentice Hall.

Shook, C. L., Priem, R. L., & McGee, J. E. (2003). Venture creation and the enterprising individual: A review and synthesis. *Journal of Management*, *29*(3), 379–399. doi:10.1016/S0149-2063(03)00016-3

Souitaris, V., Zerbinatib, S., & Al-Lahamc, A. (2007). Do entrepreneurship programmes raise entrepreneurial intention of science and engineering students? The effect of learning, inspiration and resources. *Journal of Business Venturing*, *22*(4), 566–591. doi:10.1016/j.jbusvent.2006.05.002

Van Stel, A., & Suddle, K. (2007). The Impact of New Firm Formation on Regional Development in the Netherlands. *Small Business Economics*, *30*(1), 31–47. doi:10.100711187-007-9054-1

Veciana, J. M., Aponte, M., & Urbano, D. (2005). University students' attitudes towards entrepreneurship: A two countries comparison. *The International Entrepreneurship and Management Journal*, *1*(2), 165–182. doi:10.100711365-005-1127-5

Wennekers, A. R. M., & Thurik, A. R. (1999). Linking entrepreneurship and economic growth. *Small Business Economics*, *13*(1), 27–55. doi:10.1023/A:1008063200484

Chapter 8
Advancing SME Sustainability:
Rising Above the Atrocities of Crisis

Meng Kui Hu
https://orcid.org/0000-0001-5009-1105
Universiti Sains Malaysia, Malaysia

Daisy Mui Hung Kee
Universiti Sains Malaysia, Malaysia

EXECUTIVE SUMMARY

The world has been struck by multiple crises that crippled the socio-economy of nations in the past. The impact of these crises was so significant that they initiated numerous policy changes worldwide. The radical crises in this context refer to the Spanish flu, the Asian financial crisis, the global financial crisis, and the current COVID-19 pandemic. Due to their small capital structure with limited resources and fragile nature, SMEs were severely impacted by these crises. Many SMEs were forced to close down their business operations. Somehow, the remaining SMEs managed to persist and survive through the crises. Moving forward, SMEs can better prepare for future crises by understanding and learning from the predicaments of these past crises. Consequently, SMEs must also be adaptive to new business environments and responding promptly to crises by realigning their strategies to achieve business sustainability in the long term.

INTRODUCTION

Nineteen-eighteen was when the deadliest influenza pandemic, often known as the Spanish flu, struck the world. This disease infected one-third of the world population, estimated at 500 million, and wiped out 50 million lives during the 18 months pandemic (CDCP, 2020). The impacts of the pandemic were severe due to the lack of critical care measures, such as intensive care support and mechanical ventilation, which were not available in 1918. Influenza vaccines did not exist at that time, and even antibiotics had not been developed yet (Jordan et al., 2019). Besides, the global magnitude and spread of the pandemic were exacerbated by World War I, which itself is estimated to have killed roughly 10 million civilians

DOI: 10.4018/978-1-7998-7657-1.ch008

and 9 million troops (Garrett, 2007). Fast forward to 2020; the world is confronted with another virus pandemic, namely the Covid-19 crisis. Since its formal declaration as a global pandemic by the World Health Organisation (WHO) on 11th March 2020, this pandemic has infected more than 190 million people with over 4 million deaths worldwide. The Covid-19 pandemic has caused numerous socio-economic issues to nations, businesses, and people. Although the current pandemic might not be as deadly as the Spanish flu a century ago, its economic consequences are undoubtedly much worse. While the economic condition of the countries is critical at all times, people's well-being and livelihood are equally important. This situation has put tremendous stress on the governments.

Between the Spanish flu and Covid-19 pandemics, the world has experienced various other crises, impacting most parts of the world in different magnitudes and dimensions. In the past three decades, the other most critical global crises that severely affected the nation's socio-economy were the Asian financial crisis in 1997, followed by the global financial crisis in 2007. Many businesses – both large and small, new and established ones, were severely impacted during these crises, with many forced to close down due to various financial-related obstacles. SMEs, in particular, were not spared from the devastating effects due to their small capital structure with limited resources. The extent of the impacts on businesses varied in each crisis due to dissimilarity nature and root causes. Moreover, the progressive globalisation among businesses has initiated an innovation-driven era characterised by intense competition, shorter product life cycles, and high product varieties. This has led to a complex-globalised supply chain (Dietrich et al., 2020). These crises nevertheless have caused considerable damages to businesses at large. Only a handful of business sectors continued to survive throughout the challenging period. In hindsight, valuable lessons from these crises can be adopted to tackle issues in the current situation and future.

This chapter aims to understand the implication and root causes of each crisis. The diagnosis of each crisis will assist SMEs in identifying and learning from the challenges. With this, SMEs can adopt some of the practical solutions applied by businesses during the past crises, in tackling the crisis that may arise in the future. Consequently, this chapter will also deliberate and discuss practical approaches that SMEs need to strive to recover from the current Covid-19 pandemic and any other crises in the future. Some of the crucial questions to be answered here would be: How have SMEs approached the problems encountered during the past crises? What were the constraints faced by SMEs then? How could SMEs survive the crises? What have they done right? What else can SMEs learn from these crises? If a similar challenging situation is to recur in the future, can SMEs handle them more effectively? What do SMEs need to do more and better in tackling business challenges during the current Covid-19 pandemic? More importantly, what kind of business strategy must SMEs implement in ensuring business sustainability in the long term? The chapter will also focus on the impacts and approaches in addressing these crises, specifically for SMEs operating in Malaysia.

BACKGROUND

No matter how well a crisis is handled and overcame, new crises will continue to occur in the future, albeit in different forms and magnitude. When thoroughly understood and leveraged, valuable lessons learned from past crises can provide helpful guidance to handle future crises. For instance, many of the measures implemented during the Spanish flu pandemic a century ago are remarkably similar to those applied in the current Covid-19 pandemic (Bishop, 2020). During the Spanish flu era, seven main precautions against influenza were recommended as effective containment measures, namely the avoidance of crowded public spaces, the airing and drying of mattresses and clothes, restraint from spitting, frequent disinfection of houses, and even the limited consumption of quinine once a day (Liew, 2007). Social distancing, donning of face masks, lockdown measures, upkeeping of personal hygiene and quarantining those showing signs of the disease, keeping minor cases separate from those suffering more severe illness, and limiting people's movements were among the critical practices implemented during the Spanish flu pandemic until the condition burn itself out (Dowling & Stephen, 2020). While the Spanish flu experience offered helpful guidance on public health policy, there are limited studies on its implication on businesses, particularly on the performances of SMEs. The SMEs term was not even been coined in 1918. Without a digital platform for consideration, companies had limited options but to temporarily close down their business operations during the pandemic. On the other hand, a more meaningful lesson can be uncovered for adoption from the Asian financial crisis and global financial crisis in 1997 and 2007, respectively. During these crises, many SMEs were forced to cease their business operations due to numerous reasons. On the contrary, there were SMEs that have successfully manoeuvred themselves out of the crises. Some even emerged stronger from the crises. There must be valuable lessons to be captured from these incidences.

Somehow, the financial crises pointed out many relevant and critical lessons where SMEs can benefit. When business revenue was adversely impacted, businesses have to respond rapidly in ensuring business continuity. No business can survive for long when business revenue is lower than operating expenses. Companies need to be flexible and dynamic in realigning their business strategy in fulfilling customer's expectations in light of changing consumer behaviours. They need to respond promptly and act fast on remedial measures to minimise the impact of the crisis. Consequently, the lessons on business failure and subsequent business recovery can be valuable sources for possible adoption in mending SME impacts caused by the Covid-19 pandemic. In addressing some of the issues faced during the Covid-19 pandemic, SMEs need to fully comprehend the pandemic's impacts, hence developing and implementing a sound business strategy to overcome the challenges towards business sustainability in the long run (Hu & Kee, 2021). In short, the common causes that affected SMEs in the past crises and the present pandemic relate to the significant drop in business, deteriorated financial position, difficulties handling supply chain disruption, and changing consumer behaviours. SMEs must react speedily by shifting and adapting their existing business strategies to the new normal. This realignment must also be accommodated by a dynamic approach in driving business sustainability in the long term. SMEs must not be complacent with their past successes but remain energised and driven in striving for further business growth in the future.

METHODOLOGY

This chapter draws upon the literature on SMEs' recovery and business continuity from the past crises that impacted the world and Malaysia, specifically with further deliberation on the standard measures that saved SMEs from destruction. It also discusses the measures and approaches SMEs can execute to achieve sustainable business growth in the future. The reflection in this chapter involves a discussion of findings from secondary research. This chapter also includes the author's views based on accumulated evidence, observation, and critical arguments on the implication of various crises faced by the SMEs, with a specific focus on SMEs operating in Malaysia.

Figure 1. Consequences of Crises and Execution of Critical Measures in Driving SME Sustainability

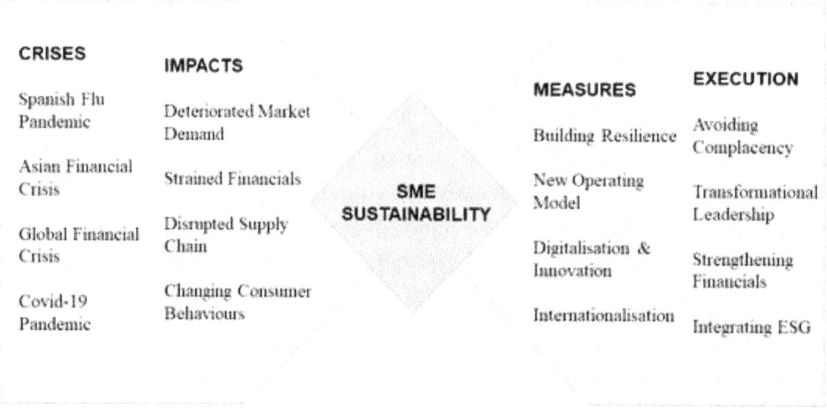

IMPLICATIONS OF MAJOR CRISES

In this chapter, four distinct global crises are in focus and discussed at length. In light of differences in root causes and magnitude of impacts, the implication of each crisis on the nation, people, and business is not the same. The consequences of the crises can be skewed to specific segments, impacting different community clusters with varied intensity. Being small by capitalisation with limited resources, SMEs were severely affected in the past crises. Following are the implications of four global crises that occurred since 1918:

Spanish Flu Pandemic (1918-1920)

The Spanish flu is known to be the deadliest pandemic ever struck the world. Started in 1918, it infected approximately 500 million people worldwide with a 10% fatality rate (CDCP, 2020). Whilst numerous studies were carried out on the public health policy in addressing the disease, the records on business impacts are quite limited. Studies related to economic consequences pointed mainly to the general effects on country performances globally. The real capita incomes were also affected significantly due to the pandemic. Bodenhorn (2020) explained that manufacturing activity was severely impacted during the pandemic due to high worker absenteeism. Many workers became sick after contracting the flu virus, causing a massive labour supply to carry business activities. Consequently, production output was severely affected. As the mortality rate continued to rise, more businesses were forced to close down. Business failures due to the excessive mortality rate were more intense than the mandated closures of business.

Back in British Malaya, where Malaysia was known to be in 1918, the Spanish flu pandemic killed at least 40,000, slightly above 1% of the nation's population of 3.6 million population then. The hardest-hit community was the rubber plantation workers, where many of them were either infected or succumbed to the disease. This incident caused a massive shortage of workers in the plantations, leading to the disruption of rubber outputs. The share of rubber in the export market of British Malaya expanded rapidly in the early 1900s to cater to the exponential increase in demand for rubber-based products (Liew, 2010). Being a rubber exporting nation, British Malaya's economy was impacted by the pandemic. Back in 1918, rubber production contribution to the national GDP declined sharply to 29.5% (1917: 61.1%), and its share of total exports dropped to 44.7% (1917: 80.5%) (Shah, 2016). The declined rubber output led to hardship among businesses in the rubber and rubber-related sectors (Liew, 2007).

Asian Financial Crisis (1997-1999)

Started as a currency crisis in Thailand in 1997, the Asian financial crisis spread rapidly across the neighbouring countries in south-east Asia and beyond. This crisis was caused by the massive capital outflow from the Asian region, resulted in the collapse of foreign currency exchange systems in a few Asian countries, particularly Thailand, Malaysia, the Philippines, Indonesia, and South Korea. The impact of this crisis was not limited to Asia but gradually spread to other parts of the world. Businesses, particularly those involved in international trades, were severely impacted due to the sudden weakening of the domestic currencies against other major currencies. The drastic and rapid changes in foreign currency rates led to some cancellation of orders, leaving the businesses to absorb currency exchange losses. Many companies, including SMEs, collapsed as a result of the sudden and unexpected financial impact.

Sitting right at the heart of Southeast Asia, Malaysia was traumatically impacted by the Asian financial crisis. The stock market, currency, and property market were at the brink of collapse. In short, this crisis affected Malaysia's economy, where the liquidity crunch resulted in a general loss of confidence in the Malaysian economy. Eventually, it precipitated a massive contraction in the Malaysian economy from 7.3% growth in 1997 to a low of -7.4% in 1998 (Lee & Tham, 2007). Many businesses, particularly those that borrowed excessively, were forced to fold up their operations due to financial constraints. Somehow, some companies, particularly the prudently managed SMEs, were spared from the worst crisis due to fewer bank financing exposures. Lee and Tham (2007) added that some SMEs even benefited from the devaluation of the Malaysian currency, which aided the competitiveness of their products in the international arena. SMEs that practised prudent financial management and did not borrow excessively from banks managed to survive through the crisis. In 1997, SMEs in Malaysia were predominantly involved in manufacturing activities with less than 150 full-time employees and an annual business turnover below RM25 million. They made up about 84% of the total business establishment during the period (Asia-Pacific Economic Cooperation, 2002).

Global Financial Crisis (2007-2008)

The global financial crisis was triggered by the massive magnitude of non-performing subprime loans owned by financial institutions in the United States in 2007. The extreme stress on the economic and banking system gradually spread and impacted other countries worldwide. It was the worst global crisis after Great Depression in the 1930s. The impact of this crisis gradually spread to other ASEAN countries through the reduction of foreign direct investment and trade flows. This event resulted in a significant decline in ASEAN trade. The intensity of the impact on trade activities became more potent in the post-crisis period (Kabir et al., 2018). Consequently, the drastic and rapid drop in demand from customers coupled with supply chain disruption has impacted SMEs. When banks became more stringent on their credit, SMEs felt pressurised, forcing many to cease business operations.

During this global financial crisis, Malaysia suffers a deep downturn in private consumption. It was almost impossible for Malaysia to shift their industries from export-oriented to focus on the domestic market since the domestic demand is weak. The government has no choice but to extend economic stimulus packages in driving consumption in the domestic market (Setyawan, 2011). The drastic drop of the ringgit-US dollar exchange rate, from RM2.48 per US$1 in March 1997 to RM3.77 per US$1 by the end of 1997, caused severe damage to the national economy. The ringgit-US dollar exchange rate touched a historical low of 4.88 per US$1 in early 1998. The share market was not spared when the Kuala Lumpur Composite Index (KLCI) also fell sharply from 1,216 points at the end of January 1997 to merely 594 points by December of that year. Market capitalisation contracted from RM826 billion in January 1997 to RM200 billion in August 1998. The dramatic deterioration of economic activities created massive challenges across business sectors. SMEs that have grown over the years were also impacted during this crisis. Based on the census in 2005, SMEs in Malaysia contributed 32% to the nation's GDP, 56.4% of employment, and 19% of total exports (Bank Negara Malaysia, 2008).

Covid-19 Pandemic (Started in 2020)

When the Covid-19 infections were discovered and subsequently spread in China in 2020, many people expected it to cease within the next few months, just like the severe acute respiratory syndrome (SARS). This disease (SARS) started in China in November 2002 and subsequently spread to 24 countries before the health authorities contained it in July 2003. SARS infected 8,098 cases with 774 deaths (McIntosh, 2020). The Covid-19 crisis turned out to be much fierce than SARS. After more than a year affecting more than 190 million casualties and over 4 million deaths, the world continues to battle infections. Many countries have imposed various movement restriction measures to contain the disease. The implementation of such efforts led to other socio-economic problems. Like in the previous crises, SMEs are severely impacted during the Covid-19 pandemic. Many SMEs were compelled to adjust their business models to be more adaptive to the changing environment in the new normal. Those that failed to respond fast enough have to face the worst consequence of closing down their businesses.

The Malaysian economy slumped by 17.1% in the second quarter of 2020 following the first movement control order (MCO) beginning 18th March 2020. The country has yet to achieve positive quarterly growth since the spread of the Covid-19 disease in Malaysia (Kana, 2021b). Nearly a year later, the country's economy continues to contract, having registered a decline of 0.5% for the first quarter of 2021. The growth of Malaysia's labour productivity, measured in terms of value-added per employment, has been negative for five consecutive quarters. Businesses, including SMEs, suffered relentlessly during this crisis. Over 32,000 companies in Malaysia, comprising mainly micro and SMEs, shuttered from March to September 2020 (Kana, 2021a). SMEs continued to contribute positively to the Malaysian business environment, performed relatively stronger, and contributed 38.9% to GDP, 48.4% to employment, and 17.9% to exports in 2019. According to the 2016 Economics Census, almost 98.5% of establishments are SMEs (Department of Statistics Malaysia, 2021).

Whilst these four major crises caused massive damage to the socio-economic conditions of the nations, SMEs were among the most significant casualties. Drawing from the consequences and experiences from these crises, SMEs can leverage by creating and implementing specific measures based on the lessons learned in handling future situations more effectively.

IMPACTS ON SMEs

As the nature and causes of each crisis are different, the degree of impacts on countries' socio-economy can vary accordingly. In contrast, some of the consequences that impacted SMEs during each crisis can be similar in nature. For instance, during the Spanish flu and Covid-19 pandemics, the public health system was severely stretched, and businesses suffered due to containment measures imposed by the government. During the Asian and global financial crises, the nation's overall economic performance was impacted. Companies with excessive bank borrowing and less prudent in financial management suffered the most during these crises. In hindsight, it is essential and beneficial for SMEs to fully use past experiences by comprehending the root causes and steps undertaken by businesses during crises. The valuable lessons learned can be effectively applied to develop practical measures in assisting SMEs on their road to recovery post-Covid-19 pandemic (Hu & Kee, 2021b). Following are the common and significant consequences faced by SMEs during the past crises:

Deteriorated Market Demand

During the Spanish flu, the governments implemented various containment measures to control the spread of the virus infections. This situation forced people to stay home and only spent on essential goods, causing a significant slump in market demand for other non-essential goods and services (Bodenhorn, 2020). These circumstances are similar to some of the critical measures implemented by the governments during the Covid-19 pandemic. During both crises, many people lost their jobs, and those who were still keeping their jobs continued to worry about possible retrenchment. The overall economic sentiment was rather worrisome. This situation led to a severe drop in demand for goods and services. Besides, people are not frequenting as much to shops due to movement restrictions. When this happened, shops started to close down. SMEs that are flexible and dynamic have rapidly realigned their business models by including online platforms to spur business transactions. Delivery services and online orders of foods and products have saved many businesses from ceasing to operate. Similarly, market demand for various products and services was also affected by Asian and global financial crises. Although the consequence was rather similar in these crises, the root cause of the drop in market demand during the financial crises was mainly attributed to deterioration in consumption power. The consumers' incomes were impacted by a drastic decline in business activities, leading to lower take-home pay and employment issues.

During these financial crises, consumer spending was affected by the loss of employment and uncertainties that prevented people from spending excessively. Many people preferred to spend prudently on necessities, hence the drop in market demand for various products and services. However, the situation is slightly different during the Covid-19 pandemic. In addition to concern over job loss and worries about the future, the containment measures implemented by the government during the Covid-19 pandemic have prevented people from going out to spend. When the market demand deteriorated, business communities would suffer. As Malaysia has become more globalised now, the overall economic performance was impacted by slower international trade that declined by 4.6% from January to November 2020. In 2019, Malaysia's export and imports of goods and services accounted for 63.7% and 56.7% of GDP, respectively (Department of Statistics Malaysia, 2021). Therefore, SMEs that continue to operate during the pandemic could only capture a fraction of their usual business volumes.

Strained Financials

One common and trying consequence of the crises relates to the financial adversity of companies. The slowdown of business activities in general with consistent operating costs often strained business cash flow. When the situation is not promptly addressed through innovative approaches in lifting business performance and cost rationalisation, the business would soon suffer. During the global financial crisis, the financial impact on SMEs was amplified when banks scaled-down the financing limit granted to them. SMEs that retrenched their employees were made to compensate fairly according to the requirements under the respective country's labour laws. During the Covid-19 pandemic, SMEs are compelled to incur extra on incidental expenses such as sanitisation of the workplace, providing face masks and hand gloves to employees, mass testing of factory workers for possible contraction of the Covid-19 disease. All these activities consume time and attract additional costs to the business. Many SMEs have voiced their concern about strained financials that may bring them down if the pandemic is prolonged.

When the Malaysian government imposed the first wave of movement restriction on 18th March 2020, many SMEs expressed their deep concern in keeping their business relevant and operational during the challenging period. Like in the earlier crises, SMEs' financials were also severely strained during the Covid-19 pandemic. The Department of Statistics Malaysia (2021) reveals that 67.8% of SMEs and large corporations did not capture any sales during the complete-lockdown period. Over two-thirds (68.9%) used their internal cash reserves to accommodate operating costs and working capital during the full-lockdown period. The rest survived an existing bank loan (19.8%) and fresh capital injection (11.3%). 42.5% of SMEs reckoned that the business would take at least six months to recover from the pandemic. Another 28.7% to take between 4-6 months.

Disrupted Supply Chain

When the whole nation faces an economic crisis, more so when the entire region and world face similar issues, goods and services are often disrupted. The breakdown of the global logistics added pain to the situation. During the Covid-19 pandemic, the closing of borders caused a severe problem to the supply chains. Many businesses run out of essential goods to meet demands. Logistics between the domestic and foreign countries were impacted due to the closure of international borders as part of the containment measures (OECD, 2020). When the international borders were opened at the later stage of the pandemic, logistics costs increased massively because of the trade imbalance between the developed and the less developed ones. In both instances, the supply chains were disrupted, causing a wide array of challenges for companies to continue with their normal business activities. However, during the Asian and global financial crises, supply chain disruption was less impactful as the crises impacted mainly companies with excessive bank borrowings and those that transact in foreign currencies. The international borders and trades continued to operate during the crises. Some companies suffered when the banks scaled down their bank financing coupled with customer cancellation due to irregular foreign currency exchange rates. Consequently, SMEs dealt with the affected companies were also impacted.

In the Spanish flu era, many workers in British Malaya were infected and succumbed to the disease, causing severe shortages of workers in the production and agricultural sectors. While the supply chain disruption was also affected but to a lesser extent during the Spanish flu pandemic in British Malaya, the impact was confined mainly to the rubber exporters. British Malaya was a net exporter of rubber during that time. The subsequent financial crises rendered limited effect on the supply chains. The financial impacts were mainly confined to companies with excessive bank borrowing and those with foreign currency exposure. However, the situation was different during the Covid-19 pandemic. The imposition of containment measures and the closure of international borders created massive shortages of materials in various countries worldwide. Consequently, the shortage of containers at Port Klang caused myriad supply chain problems for local businesses relying on these services. The imbalance of trade and willingness to pay higher freight rates by certain countries led to a severe shortage of containers for intra-Asian trades and other trade routes (The Star, 2020b). Many SMEs were caught in the entanglements, resulting in business failures.

Changing Consumer Behaviours

In the wake of a crisis, the business environment changes, forcing consumers to alter their buying behaviours. When this happens, businesses that are rigid and fail to change their business approach and model will face the consequences of business failures in the worst-case scenario. Somehow, they will likely lose out to their competitors that are more adaptive to the changes. During the financial crises, consumers were forced to adjust their spending patterns due to a drastic drop in income. Many became jobless during crises when the overall economies were impacted. Those who remain in employment were concern about the future. More drastic changes in consumer behaviours can be observed during the current Covid-19 pandemic. Many opted for online transactions to procure merchandise when people are forced to stay home due to movement restrictions. This option was impossible during the Spanish flu pandemic in the absence of advanced technology. In the current progressive technology era, online transactions have become a reality, allowing business transactions to be conducted without face-to-face interactions. Online transactions have picked up tremendously during the Covid-19 pandemic.

In Malaysia, many businesses, including SMEs, adopt online transactions as a new channel to attract customers for continuous sales during the Covid-19 pandemic. Many SMEs were indeed new to this electronic channel in reaching out to their customers. The outcome of this new initiative was encouraging. The online retail sales in Malaysia increased significantly by 28.9% in April 2020, one month after the enforcement of movement restrictions during the Covid-19 pandemic (The Star, 2020a). Many consumers opted to transact online, a large proportion for the first time, to shop for essential goods. When the lockdown period was extended, consumers continued to use online platforms for shopping, including other non-essential products and services. This strong surge reflects the changing consumer behaviour of shopping online. SMEs that are reluctant to change to a new online approach to trade are at a losing end.

Having evaluated the common impacts caused by various crises in the past, SMEs should gain a clear understanding of possible issues that can arise in a crisis. With this knowledge, they can now develop practical measures in handling these common issues should a similar crisis recur in the future. SMEs need to shift their strategy in rising above atrocities proactively. It is only with sound and effective business strategy that SMEs can recover strongly from the crisis.

RISING ABOVE ATROCITIES

Post-crises, SMEs must essentially execute proactive measures to accelerate business recovery in the immediate term and sustainable growth in the long run. While organisational resources are critical in times of crisis, the temporary growth setback during the crisis can provide space and time for companies to identify a new opportunity for the next phase of growth. To be successful, companies need to realign and regain the balance and fit within their company's resource system (Lim et al., 2020). However, this is easier said than done. The highly unpredictable environment during crises allows for only a few feasible strategic approaches regarding an SME's decision to follow incumbents, become a challenger, or reinvent themselves based on their transformation drivers and readiness to apply digital technologies (Gregurec et al., 2021). While globalisation can be challenging for SMEs, it can be overcome by increasing the company's supply chain resilience against global environmental impacts. By doing so, SMEs will be able to leverage opportunities in expanding their global reach for better business performances (Milovanovic et al., 2017). Having exhausted most of the resources during the crises, SMEs would find it tough to rebound and recover from the crises. They need to implement the following critical measures to be more adaptive in the new normal and ready to charge forward for business recovery and growth in the new normal:

Building Resilience

Business resilience is a critical fundamental of SMEs that would allow them to withstand the impacts of a crisis. It will also permit SMEs to survive and recover well from a crisis. In this context, SMEs must not lose time and start rebuilding resilience to accelerate their business performance. Resilience can be addressed systematically by strengthening the overall business functions to withstand external forces during crises. The critical operations involve financial management, supply chain management, and digitalisation, including cybersecurity and talent management. Sound financial management enables SMEs to maintain adequate capital and can be a valuable buffer during challenging moments. The other aspects of financial management involve a dynamic risk management framework and prudent financial execution. Ramachandran (2021) reiterates that supply chain management is also critical towards SME sustainability by adopting digital technology enablers like big data, blockchain, supply chain analytics, IoT, artificial intelligence. The execution of the advanced technology would simplify processes resulting in faster turnaround time, provide flexibility and reduce production costs in the long run.

Besides structural reformation, SMEs must also emphasise talent management which is essential in building business resilience. In this context, SMEs must develop suitable ways to improve their approach and image in attracting and retaining talent (Hu, 2017). Education and proper training are the essential and effective measures provided to SME owners and the workforce. The resilience attributes of SME owners can significantly influence and contribute to SME resilience. Through their resilience characteristics, the SME owners create a culture or climate within their businesses that fosters resilience beyond their direct influence (Branicki et al., 2018). As such, initiatives that promote the personal strength of entrepreneurs or entrepreneurial approaches to small businesses should be implemented in building business resilience

New Operating Model

The world and business environment have changed dramatically during the Covid-19 era. This unprecedented situation has brought significant changes to the way business is conducted and customers' buying behaviours. While employers and their employees may deal more virtually, customers may choose to transact online for goods and services. In this aspect, businesses, including SMEs, need to find a new and practical approach in dealing with these changes. A recent Ipsos MORI survey in the UK found that pre-Covid-19, 79% of employers said their staff was entirely office-based, but just 28% expect that to be the case in the future, and 47% expect to operate a hybrid working model where people split their working time between work and home (Page, 2020). This survey indicates that more people are expected to work from home, resulting in less face-to-face interactions with both the employers and customers. In light of these changes, businesses need to realign their business operating model to remain relevant and sustainable in the new normal. New techniques and strategies are essential in lifting their business to the next level. In terms of work culture, SMEs must be ready to adopt advanced technology and allow their workforce to work from home and continue to undertake a thorough cost rationalisation.

Working from home may expose SMEs to cyber threats that could damage the entire operating system. Failing to advise, enforce and train the workforce about the severity of cyber-crimes would put the companies at risk. Therefore, SMEs must also proactively make security adjustments required by different business domains and corporations toward the virtual office envision, which is necessary nowadays. Greater focus is requested on individual security characteristics such as behaviour, attitude, awareness and compliance, and research is mandated on quantifying these mainly quality indicators for having a reliable cultural approach toward cybersecurity. The human factor is the key to information security progress and remains uncharted (Georgiadou et al., 2021). Besides cybersecurity, SMEs must also take steps to keep track of work productivity. Morikawa (2020) pointed out that many employees who work from home during the Covid-19 pandemic registered lower productivity than those working at the workplace. The mean of work-from-home productivity was about 60% to 70% of working at the usual workplace. The main reasons for such lower productivity relate to poor communication due to the lack of face-to-face interactions, poor telecommunication environment at home, and restriction to access certain documents from home due to security and compliance requirements. If this inferior output is not addressed properly, it can affect the effective operating costs.

Digitalisation and Innovation

Moving forward, digitalisation in business is inevitable and essential. Companies must invest in digitalisation to improve performance efficiency, product quality, cost management, and improved delivery system. The entire operational chain can be enhanced through this digitalisation process. More importantly, the process of technology implementation enhances the consumer experience. Łobejko (2020) pointed out that digitalisation does not only involves the transfer of all functions to the digital format but, above all, a significant change in thinking about the company's functioning, its processes, products and services, partners and consumers. Consequently, SMEs must be technologically adaptive, enabling them to develop and execute a clear digital strategy in ensuring smooth transformation in the digital aspects. A dynamic and digitalised operating system would also help SMEs gain better control and monitor the employees' overall work performances. Some critical internal functions like human resources, finance, sales, and marketing, should be prioritised. A comprehensive strategy framework outlining the overall digitalisation development plans is essential and can be included in an Industry 4.0 framework for the respective business (Ghobakhloo, 2018). This framework will serve as a roadmap for the execution of the digitalisation plans.

SMEs must be able to blend in digital capabilities to enhance innovation capabilities critical in improving performance and competitive advantage. They need to raise the entrepreneurial spirit, optimise market analysis, network with various stakeholders and empower employees to promote innovation capabilities. These measures would increase performance and achievement of competitive advantage (Sulistyo & Siyamtinah, 2016). In Malaysia, the government strongly encourages SMEs to adopt advanced technology in their business operations. Under the newly launched Malaysia Digital Economic Blueprint (EPU, 2021), the digital economy is expected to contribute 22.6% of the nation's GDP by 2025. The government would encourage 875,000 micro, small and medium enterprises to accept the use of e-commerce. This blueprint also serves as a digital transformation direction plan in improving business competitiveness in the global arena by enhancing the expediency and efficiency of their operations. In this context, SMEs must leverage government assistance in lifting their digital capabilities to optimise their business performance.

Internationalisation

During the current Covid-19 pandemic, when containment measures prevented people from frequenting shops, most companies suffered due to a lack of business activities. Many SMEs were compelled to innovate and offer their products and services through online platforms. Besides generating revenues, this response has created a fresh avenue for SMEs to expand their business beyond international borders. Riding on a good start, SMEs need to depend on the momentum in leveraging cross-border opportunities. However, to successfully tapping the global markets, SMEs need to improve their products and services quality, delivery systems, and performance management. Bose (2016) suggested that for proper internationalisation, SMEs need to be innovative, possess the appropriate capacities, be backed by governmental policies, and get membership of critical business networks or clusters. Therefore, SME owners must develop networking, innovation, and internationalisation capacities. Besides, human capital is equally essential in bringing SMEs to international platforms. Foreign language skills and international experience were also significant predictors of the internationalisation of the firm. With such knowledge, they will deal more smoothly with the local stakeholders like suppliers, transportation companies, and the authorities (Kim, 2017).

In Malaysia, exporting SMEs contribute their competitive advantages to three essential critical capabilities: market intelligence capability, product innovation capability, and pricing capability. Exporting SMEs must emphasise their pricing capability that has a significant indirect effect on international performance. Continuous process improvement and tight cost control coupled with eliminating unnecessary operational wastages could be effective options to enhance pricing capability. Consequently, exporting SMEs rely on both product advantages and price advantages to excel in international markets (Falahat et al., 2020). In addition, SMEs in Malaysia are strongly encouraged by the government to jump on the digital bandwagon to tap into the global market through domestic and international digital platforms and accelerate the export of high-quality Malaysian products globally (The Star, 2021).

As part of the recovery acceleration process, SMEs must shift some of their business strategies to adapt to the new business environment. Besides, they must also develop and work on new initiatives to circumvent the challenges of achieving business sustainability. However, the whole process of driving the business towards sustainable business growth in the long term can only be achieved through the effective implementation of the new and realigned business strategies. SMEs must place adequate resources and effort in this aspect in ensuring success.

DRIVING SME SUSTAINABILITY

Knowing the past and putting up detailed business plans for the future may not necessarily lead to business sustainability. SMEs need to establish a sound approach in executing the set business plans. The approach needs to be dynamic with precise tracking and monitoring mechanism. It is through consistent drive and perseverance that SMEs can achieve their long-term business sustainable goals. This session aims to elaborate on the essence of discipline and action that SMEs need to succeed in sustainable business growth post-crisis. Following are the critical approaches SMEs should strictly adhere to when executing their revised strategic plans during and post-crisis:

Avoiding Complacency

Staying put and waiting for things to improve will not augur well for businesses during crises. SMEs must not be complacent with the comfort of past performances, which can be quickly diminished in a crisis. The lack of desire and drive to grow business would do more harm to the companies. SMEs need to remain dynamic and agile and continue to thrive for improvement during a challenging time. However, many SMEs can easily fall into the trap of being complacent and let the crisis take their business away. SMEs must remain forceful and strive to excel in multiple priorities and innovations in their market rather than concentrate on a single operations priority and innovation type. When integrated effectively in business operations, innovations would enhance company performance (Kilic et al., 2015). Besides, business leaders, managers, and entrepreneurs must also challenge themselves to contribute positively to sustainable development on the individual, organisational, and societal levels (Schaltegger et al., 2016). Therefore, SMEs owners and the workforce must be driven and continue to strive for business growth. They must possess the right attitude and energy to beat the market competition that can be fierce due to affected market demand during the crisis.

Transformational Leadership

Changes often start from the top, hence the importance of outstanding leadership. When drastic changes are critical, particularly during crisis, to manoeuvre the business into a new direction, transformational leadership becomes crucial. Companies that are severely impacted during the crisis need dynamic leadership to rebound and recover from the challenging time. Transformational leadership engenders the higher innovative work behaviour of the employees through trust in leaders and work engagement. When the employees observe that their leaders are caring, helpful, and fulfil their promises, their performance improves (Li et al., 2019). The critical dimensions of transformational leadership that comprise idealised influence/inspirational motivation, intellectual stimulation, and individualised consideration could produce intermediate outcomes such as shared vision, team commitment, an empowered team environment and functional team conflict. All these intermediate outcomes may positively affect team communication, cohesion and conflict management (Dionne et al., 2004). Simply put, transformational leadership, when embraced diligently and smoothly in the organisations, can hold together critical resources through people and work engagement in lifting business performances.

Given the significance of transformational leadership, SME owners should adopt this leadership style in lifting their companies out of the current crisis. Subsequently, they can continue to drive essential changes in enhancing the overall efficiency of their business operations. In the longer term, they can drive strategic moves that would place them on a firmer footing to leverage any growth opportunities that may arise in the future.

Strengthening Financials

The financial capabilities can determine the survival of SMEs during the crisis. With adequate financial resources, SMEs will be able to chart and implement various plans to ensure continued improvement post-crisis. During crisis, SMEs have little choice but to take drastic actions to remain relevant and continue to survive. Thorgren and Williams (2020) pointed out that SMEs are generally more willing to reduce negative cash flow and possibly file for bankruptcy than to increase their debt-to-equity ratio and propel financial problems on to the future. During the crisis, SMEs' survival strategies are focused on better cost management. Many would also act immediately by deferring investments, reducing labour costs, reducing expenses, and negotiating contracts and terms to stay relevant and make it out of the crisis. In short, SMEs need to prioritise their allocation of funds for productive usage by practising prudent financial management during crisis time. Karadag (2015) reiterates the importance of a strategic perspective for the efficient and effective conduct of financial management in contributing to the success of SME performance. The crucial financial functions relate to strategic financial planning, strategic working capital management, strategic fixed-asset management, and strategic financial reporting and control.

Cash reserves, being one essential item in business, must be prioritised as part of SMEs' financial management. Cash reserves will provide an operational buffer to the company in crisis time. Consequently, SMEs must also work on other functional areas in enhancing their financial resilience. With substantial financial stability, SMEs will be able to charge forward and achieve sustainable business growth in the new normal.

Integrating ESG

The ESG adoption among SMEs is generally low at the moment. This response, however, should not compromise the significance of ESG in the future. SMEs must allocate adequate resources to comprehend and gradually integrate ESG principles in their businesses. The lack of in-depth understanding of the ESG approach is partly explained by the fact that over two-thirds of companies are at a very early stage of the journey (51%) or are only planning to start the journey over the next one to two years (16%). Despite being early on in the journey, and the piecemeal approach being taken to ESG as evidenced by interviews and confirmed by many investors, 92% of survey participants confirm that they are moderately (69%) to very knowledgeable (23%) about ESG, with smaller companies tending to be less knowledgeable (Ward & MacKenzie, 2020). By adopting ESG principles, businesses have positively correlated with the companies' overall financial performances (Friede et al., 2015). Therefore, it is essential and beneficial for SMEs to proactively integrate ESG factors in their companies to remain sustainable in the long run. ESG adoption is vital and will likely be a prerequisite when dealing with large and established corporations globally.

As part of the ESG integration process, SMEs must ensure that the leadership team walks the talk by observing the good practices and taking the necessary steps to preserve the environment. By simply adapting to the 3R concept – reduce, reuse, and recycle, SMEs can raise their resource efficiency and make reasonable progress in supporting the environmental factor in their business operations. Besides, SMEs must also place the adequate resource on the social principle that involves people and the community where the companies are operating. People, be they employees or family members who work in the business, must be treated with respect and reasonably according to labour standards and human rights. SMEs must maintain good policies in dealing with people issues in the companies. In terms of governance, SMEs must adhere to the rules and regulations when carrying out their business operations. Internally, they must be fair and transparent to the employees, directors. This means SMEs must conduct their business operations professionally and ethically. They must embrace accurate and transparent reporting about their business activities. Importantly, SMEs must not involve bribery and corruption activities.

In business recovery, SMEs must realign and execute their strategic plans with firm discipline and the right attitude. They must adopt transformational leadership and walk the talk in strengthening business resilience, enabling them to register sustainable business growth in the long term.

CONCLUSION AND RECOMMENDATIONS

Economic crises are unavoidable and will continue to recur globally in the future. The implications of each crisis can be different, its root causes and magnitude. However, some of the impacts on businesses, particularly SMEs, can be common and universal. The experience can provide valuable lessons to the present SMEs, offering them some clear hints in developing relevant measures to counter future crises. Understanding and learning from past crises is a practical approach for SMEs in enhancing business foundation and sharpening resilience. Besides building business resilience, SMEs must be receptive to innovate their business models and operating procedures to be successful in the new normal. Digitalisation and internationalisation are two critical initiatives that can help SMEs lift their business to the next level. SMEs must be prepared to execute relevant and practical action plans to drive business progression in the right direction. They must realign their business strategies to remain relevant and sustain continued business growth in the longer term. SMEs must not forget to place adequate emphasis on the way these strategies are executed in ensuring success. Given the dynamism and agility of SMEs, many would rebound and recover from the current Covid-19 pandemic, and poise to business growth in the near future.

FUTURE RESEARCH DIRECTIONS

This chapter elaborates on the general impact caused by various critical crises in the past and the respective implications on SMEs. This research can be narrowed down to focus on the manufacturing or services sectors in Malaysia. Further study can be carried out to understand any mediating effects on the relationship between the critical imperative factors and SME business sustainability. This research's findings would assist SMEs operating in the relevant industry sectors to understand the focused areas better, allowing them to address issues more effectively in a future crisis.

REFERENCES

Asia-Pacific Economic Cooperation. (2002). *Profile of SMEs and SME Issues in APEC 1990-2000.* https://www.apec.org/Publications/2003/12/Profile-of-Small-and-Medium-Enterprises-SMEs-and-SME-Issues-in-APEC-19902000-Published-in-2003

Bank Negara Malaysia. (2008). *SME Annual Report 2007.* https://www.bnm.gov.my/-/sme-annual-report-2007

Bishop, J. (2020, June). Economic effects of the Spanish Flu. *Reserve Bank of Australia,* 8–17. https://www.rba.gov.au/publications/bulletin/2020/jun/economic-effects-of-the-spanish-flu.html

Bodenhorn, H. (2020). Business in a time of Spanish influenza. *National Bureau of Economic Research, N11*(July). https://www.nber.org/system/files/working_papers/w27495/w27495.pdf

Bose, T. (2016). Critical success factors of SME internationalization. *Journal of Small Business Strategy, 26*(2), 87–109. https://libjournals.mtsu.edu/index.php/jsbs/article/view/614

Branicki, L. J., Sullivan-Taylor, B., & Livschitz, S. R. (2018). How entrepreneurial resilience generates resilient SMEs. *International Journal of Entrepreneurial Behaviour & Research, 24*(7), 1244–1263. doi:10.1108/IJEBR-11-2016-0396

Center for Disease Control and Prevention (CDCP). (2020). Influenza (Flu) 1918 Pandemic (H1N1 virus). *1918 Pandemic Webpage, 2019,* 1918–1920. https://www.cdc.gov/flu/pandemic-resources/1918-pandemic-h1n1.html#:~:text=It is estimated that about,occurring in the United States.

Department of Statistics Malaysia. (2021). *Malaysian Economic Statistics Review.* https://www.dosm.gov.my/v1/index.php?r=column/cthemeByCat&cat=481&bul_id=U05RQmY4cU1MK1FQdDRMSmNURlVrdz09&menu_id=azJjRWpYL0VBYU90TVhpclByWjdMQT09

Dietrich, F., Palm, D., & Louw, L. (2020). Smart contract based framework to increase transparency of manufacturing networks. *Procedia CIRP, 91,* 278–283. doi:10.1016/j.procir.2020.02.177

Dionne, S. D., Yammarino, F. J., Atwater, L. E., & Spangler, W. D. (2004). Transformational leadership and team performance. *Journal of Organizational Change Management, 17*(2), 177–193. doi:10.1108/09534810410530601

Dowling & Stephen. (2020). *Coronavirus: What can we learn from the Spanish flu?* https://www.bbc.com/future/article/20200302-coronavirus-what-can-we-learn-from-the-spanish-flu

Economic Planning Unit Malaysia (EPU). (2021). *Malaysia Digital Economy Blueprint.* EPU.

Falahat, M., Ramayah, T., Soto-Acosta, P., & Lee, Y. Y. (2020). SMEs internationalization: The role of product innovation, market intelligence, pricing and marketing communication capabilities as drivers of SMEs' international performance. *Technological Forecasting and Social Change, 152*(June), 119908. doi:10.1016/j.techfore.2020.119908

Friede, G., Busch, T., & Bassen, A. (2015). ESG and financial performance: Aggregated evidence from more than 2000 empirical studies. *Journal of Sustainable Finance and Investment, 5*(4), 210–233. doi:10.1080/20430795.2015.1118917

Garrett, T. A. (2007). Economic effects of the 1918 influenza pandemic: Implications for a modern-day pandemic. *Federal Reserve Bank of St. Louis.* www.stlouisfed.org/community/other_pubs.html.%0Ahttp://199.169.201.166/community_development/assets/pdf/pandemic_flu_report.pdf

Georgiadou, A., Mouzakitis, S., & Askounis, D. (2021). Working from home during COVID-19 crisis: A cyber security culture assessment survey. *Security Journal*. Advance online publication. doi:10.105741284-021-00286-2

Ghobakhloo, M. (2018). The future of manufacturing industry: A strategic roadmap toward Industry 4.0. *Journal of Manufacturing Technology Management, 29*(6), 910–936. doi:10.1108/JMTM-02-2018-0057

Gregurec, I., Furjan, M. T., & Tomičić-pupek, K. (2021). The impact of covid-19 on sustainable business models in smes. *Sustainability (Switzerland), 13*(3), 1–24. doi:10.3390u13031098

Hu, E. (2017). *SME Challenges and Solutions* (1st ed.). MPH Group Publishing. https://www.mphonline.com/en/productdetails/books/business-and-management/9789674152208

Hu, M. K., & Kee, D. M. H. (2021a). SMEs and business sustainability: Achieving sustainable business growth in the new normal. Handbook of Research on Sustaining SMEs and Entrepreneurial Innovation in the Post-COVID-19 Era, 331–351. doi:10.4018/978-1-7998-6632-9.ch016

Hu, M. K., & Kee, D. M. H. (2021b). Strategic measures and tactical interventions for COVID-19 impact relief on SMEs. Handbook of Research on Strategies and Interventions to Mitigate COVID-19 Impact on SMEs, 522–541. doi:10.4018/978-1-7998-7436-2.ch026

Jordan, D., Tumpey, T., & Jester, B. (2019). The deadliest flu: The complete story of the discovery and reconstruction of the 1918 pandemic virus. *Centers for Disease Control and Prevention (CDC), 2019*, 1–2. https://www.cdc.gov/flu/pandemic-resources/reconstruction-1918-virus.html#references

Kabir, S., Bloch, H., & Salim, R. A. (2018). Global financial crisis and southeast Asian trade performance: Empirical Evidence. *Review of Urban and Regional Development Studies, 30*(2), 114–144. doi:10.1111/rurd.12080

Kana, G. (2021a). A necessary but painful move. *The Star Malaysia*. https://www.thestar.com.my/business/business-news/2021/05/31/a-necessary-but-painful-move

Kana, G. (2021b). Employment dilemma. *The Star Malaysia*. https://www.thestar.com.my/business/business-news/2021/05/21/labour-productivity-value-added-per-employment

Karadag, H. (2015). Financial management challenges in small and medium-sized enterprises: A strategic management approach. *EMAJ: Emerging Markets Journal, 5*(1), 26–40. doi:10.5195/EMAJ.2015.67

Kilic, K., Ulusoy, G., Gunday, G., & Alpkan, L. (2015). Innovativeness, operations priorities and corporate performance: An analysis based on a taxonomy of innovativeness. *Journal of Engineering and Technology Management, 35*, 115–133. doi:10.1016/j.jengtecman.2014.09.001

Kim, K. (2017). Factors affecting the internationalization of small and medium-sized enterprises in South Korea: Entrepreneurial Orientation, Human Capital and Technological Capabilities. *International Journal of Economics and Financial Issues, 7*(5), 371–379.

Lee, P. P., & Tham, S. Y. (2007). Malaysia ten years after the Asian financial crisis. *Asian Survey, 47*(6), 915–929. doi:10.1525/as.2007.47.6.915

Li, H., Sajjad, N., Wang, Q., Ali, A. M., Khaqan, Z., & Amina, S. (2019). *Influence of transformational leadership on employees' innovative work behavior in sustainable organizations: Test of mediation and moderation processes.* Sustainability. doi:10.3390u11061594

Liew, K. K. (2007). Terribly severe though mercifully short: The episode of the 1918 influenza in British Malaya. *Modern Asian Studies, 41*(2), 221–252. doi:10.1017/S0026749X05002180

Liew, K. K. (2010). Planters, Estate Health & amp ; Malaria in British Malaya (1900 – 1940). *Journal of the Malaysian Branch of the Royal Asiatic Society.*

Lim, D. S. K., Morse, E. A., & Yu, N. (2020). The impact of the global crisis on the growth of SMEs: A resource system perspective. *International Small Business Journal: Researching Entrepreneurship, 38*(6), 492–503. doi:10.1177/0266242620950159

Łobejko, S. (2020). Digital transformation and innovativeness of enterprises. *Optimum. Economic Studies, 2*(2(100)), 36–46. doi:10.15290/oes.2020.02.100.03

Milovanovic, G., Milovanovic, S., & Radisavljevic, G. (2017). Globalization: The key challenge of modern supply chains. *Ekonomika (Nis), 63*(1), 31–40. doi:10.5937/ekonomika1701031M

Morikawa, M. (2020). Productivity of working from home during the COVID-19 pandemic: Evidence from an employee survey. In *Covid Economics* (Issue 49, pp. 123–147). https://econpapers.repec.org/RePEc:eti:rpdpjp:20020

OECD. (2020). *Tackling the coronavirus (COVID-19) crisis together: OECD policy contributions for co-ordinated action.* OECD Website of Coronavirus Collection.

Page, B. (2020). CBI / Ipsos MORI survey : COVID-19 provides pathway to future of carbon reduction, flexible working & local shopping. *Ipsos Mori*, 1–9. https://www.ipsos.com/ipsos-mori/en-uk/cbi-ipsos-mori-survey-covid-19

Ramachandran, R. (2021). Leadership during COVID Crisis-Part 1. SSRN *Electronic Journal.* doi:10.2139srn.3791574

Schaltegger, S., Lüdeke-Freund, F., & Hansen, E. G. (2016). Business models for sustainability. *Organization & Environment, 29*(3), 264–289. Advance online publication. doi:10.1177/1086026616633272

Setyawan, A. A. (2011). Global crisis and country's competitiveness: Lessons from Indonesia and Malaysia. *European Research Studies Journal, 14*(3), 103–118. doi:10.35808/ersj/329

Shah, S. N. (2016). *Historical GDP Accounts.* Economic History of Malaya. https://www.ehm.my/data/historical-gdp-accounts

Sulistyo, H., & Siyamtinah. (2016). Innovation capability of SMEs through entrepreneurship, marketing capability, relational capital and empowerment. *Asia Pacific Management Review, 21*(4), 196–203. doi:10.1016/j.apmrv.2016.02.002

The Star. (2020a). Malaysia's online retail sales up 28. 9% in April. *The Star Malaysia*, 1–8. https://www.thestar.com.my/business/business-news/2020/06/11/malaysia039s-online-retail-sales-up-289--in-april

The Star. (2020b). Transport Minister: Container shortage issue to be discussed Monday. *The Star Malaysia,* 1–7. https://www.thestar.com.my/news/nation/2020/12/25/transport-minister-container-shortage-issue-to-be-discussed-monday-dec-28

The Star. (2021). A chance to tap into the global market. *The Star Malaysia*, 1–7. https://www.thestar.com.my/business/business-news/2021/04/14/a-chance-to-tap-into-the-global-market

Thorgren, S., & Williams, T. A. (2020). Staying alive during an unfolding crisis: How SMEs ward off impending disaster. *Journal of Business Venturing Insights*, *14*(May), e00187. doi:10.1016/j.jbvi.2020.e00187

Ward, T., & MacKenzie, J. (2020). *Research Report ESG in small and mid-sized quoted companies : Perceptions, Myths and Realities*. Quoted Companies Alliance.

ADDITIONAL READING

Caballero-Morales, S. O. (2021). Innovation as recovery strategy for SMEs in emerging economies during the COVID-19 pandemic. *Research in International Business and Finance*. Elsevier BV, 57(May), 101396. . doi:10.1016/j.ribaf.2021.101396

Cepel, M., Gavurova, B., Dvorsky, J., & Belas, J. (2020). The impact of the covid-19 crisis on the perception of business risk in the SME segment. *Journal of International Students*, *13*(3), 248–263. doi:10.14254/2071-8330.2020/13-3/16

Deshpande, M. (2021). Strategies for Entrepreneurial Innovation and Sustainability. In N. Baporikar (Ed.), *Handbook of research on sustaining SMEs and entrepreneurial innovation in the post COVID-19 era* (pp. 465–483). IGI Global. doi:10.4018/978-1-7998-6632-9.ch022

Hansen, E., & Nybakk, E. (2018). Response to the global financial crisis: A follow-up study. *Journal of Innovation and Entrepreneurship. Journal of Innovation and Entrepreneurship*, *7*(1), 7. Advance online publication. doi:10.118613731-018-0087-2

Nieh, C. C. (2002). The effect of the Asian financial crisis on the relationships among open macroeconomic factors for Asian countries. *Applied Economics*, *34*(4), 491–502. doi:10.1080/00036840110046827

World Business Council for Sustainability Development (WBCSD). (2020). *Building long-term business resilience*. Available at: https://docs.wbcsd.org/2020/09/WBCSD_Vision_2050_Building_long-term_business_resilience

KEY TERMS AND DEFINITIONS

Business Sustainability: Relates to the establishment of long-term value within a business by integrating adequate measures in ensuring the processes, products, and manufacturing activities are operated well within an ecological, social and economic environment while maintaining a profit.

COVID-19 Pandemic: Relates to the prevalent global crisis that is caused by a newly discovered strain of coronavirus, a type of virus known to cause respiratory infections in humans.

ESG: Refers to the environmental, social, and governance factors used to measure sustainability and ethical impact of business operations.

Financial Crisis: Often associated with sudden or unexpected impact on significant financial assets such as substantial changes in stocks, real estate or oil, resulting in substantial losses of the asset values.

Small and Medium Enterprises (SMEs): Enterprises that are smallish by capital, business turnover, and the number of employees and operate in various industries. The magnitude of each parameter varies by country globally.

Strategies: A plan of action that determines the direction, scope of an organisation and configuration of resources, skills, and competencies in creating competitive advantage, leading to the attainment of the overall goals in the long term.

Chapter 9
Struggling for Survival:
Internationalization Drivers in Family SMEs – A Strategic Guideline to Overcome the Crisis Based on the Literature

Rafael Luís Castro
https://orcid.org/0000-0001-9698-5243
Universidade de Aveiro, Portugal

Joana Costa
https://orcid.org/0000-0001-7514-9836
Universidade de Aveiro, Portugal

EXECUTIVE SUMMARY

Family SMEs are embedded with unique characteristics of family ownership and management and the attributes of resource constraints and smallness in SMEs. At present, these firms are struggling for survival due to the pandemic crisis. Fast and assertive policy strategies need to be implemented to promote resilience, raising survival propensity. To better understand and recognize internationalization patterns in family SMEs, the authors conduct a systematic literature review with theoretical and empirical articles in the last 15 years. The study contributes to the literature by identifying and clustering state of the art regarding family SMEs in their internationalization strategies; moreover, they provide a theoretical basis for future guidelines of empirical research regarding the used frameworks, most predominant strategies, managerial determinants, and the elements that may lead these firms to their long-term survival and their success and prosperity in international markets.

DOI: 10.4018/978-1-7998-7657-1.ch009

INTRODUCTION

Family-owned SMEs (hereafter family SMEs) are inserted in most economies; they embody a substantial share of income and provide significant support for employment (Anderson & Reeb, 2003). The latest report of the European Commission (2009) shows that FBs symbolize more than 60% of all enterprises in Europe.

The body of research regarding family SMEs and their internationalization is still developing (Pukall & Calabrò, 2014). Moreover, the literature still fails to provide a clear and unique definition regarding family businesses (hereafter FBs); nevertheless, most empirical studies perceive FB when a family has at least 50% ownership (Sharma, Chrisman and Chua, 1999).

There seems to be widely recognized that FBs are highly oriented towards the family dimension, meaning that other than the economic goals present in all business organizations, they also pursue non-economic goals that are more oriented and centered on the family dynamics (Gómez-Mejía et al., 2007). Thus, FBs must reach an equilibrium between the aspiration to grow and exploit new international opportunities (Arregle et al., 2012) and preserve their family legacy, family values, and control (Gomez-Mejia et al., 2010).

The family involvement in the decision-making process is detrimental to their internationalization. In family SMEs, there is overlapping between ownership, management, and board of directors, meaning that family members might have an involvement in all the processes (Segaro, 2012). Thus, family involvement in the business can create a unique set of determinants, positive or negative, in the firm´s internationalization strategies.

Engaging in internationalization strategies is a valid endeavor towards competitive advantage. Recent changes in the world economy have led all types of firms to partake in global expansion; however, international expansion can also expose firms to higher risks (Westhead, 2008).

Internationalization in family SMEs can be perceived in multiple forms; positively, managers can engage international strategies to gain competitive advantages and expand their activities abroad; thus, creating more value for the business (Lahiri et al., 2020). Nevertheless, managers in family SMEs tend to be risk-averse and conservative towards the adoption of new strategies; conversely, they may perceive internationalization as a threat to their family wealth, family legacy and socio-emotional wealth (Arregle et al., 2012). The Socioemotional-Wealth concept encapsulates the non-economic goals present in FB, such as their exercise of authority, the perpetuation of family values through the business, and the conservation of the firm´s legacy (Gómez-Mejía et al., 2007).

The dominant view among FB scholars is that family SMEs move along in their international strategies differently than non-FB (e.g., Arregle et al., 2012; Nieto & Fernandez, 2012; Pukall & Calabrò, 2014). FBs have in their nature to be risk-averse; they want to maintain their family control and ownership, and their SEW (Claver et al., 2007; Gomez-Mejia et al., 2011). Consequently, in order to expose the firm to the lowest risk possible, they start internationalizing more slowly and gradually; thus, exporting to closer countries allows them to retain knowledge and experience, which in turn will be applied as they further progress in their international strategies (Kontinen & Ojala, 2010b; Boellis et al., 2016).

Besides family involvement, family SMEs have embedded in the unique characteristics of SMEs. As a consequence of their size, these institutions have more restrictions regarding their resources; furthermore, constraints in their organizational capabilities can also hinder and negatively disturb their internationalization prospects (Fernandez & Nieto, 2005). Nonetheless, family SMEs are more adaptable and have lower levels of organizational inertia; thus, they can react to fast changes in the market and seize more international opportunities than large firms with higher levels of organizational inertia (Lahiri et al., 2020).

The level of family ownership can also be an important aspect for strategies like internationalization. According to Sciascia et al. (2012), businesses in which the family detains 100% of the ownership have a lower degree of internationalization. Nonetheless, according to Fernández and Nieto (2005) there is a positive relationship between internationalization and firms´ ownership from members outside the family. Moreover, Sciascia et al. (2012) found that firms with moderate family ownership levels have better export intensity. Although family SMEs are regarded as having risk aversion and opposed to change, they favor internal factors more than being open to new ventures and taking advantage of new market opportunities; thus, this traditional mindset can jeopardize their future and existence (Lim et al., 2010).

FBs have present in their nature a long-term orientation. According to Claver et al., (2008), this attribute positively affects internationalization (Pukall & Calabrò, 2014). Internationalization can provide numerous benefits to family SMEs; nevertheless, it can also provide adverse outcomes (D'Angelo et al., 2016). On the positive side, internationalization can provide financial benefits (De Massis et al., 2018a), create competitive advantage (Zahra, 2003), increase the reputation of the firms (Scholes et al., 2016), and organizational learning and knowledge (Kontinen & Ojala, 2011a). Internationalization can affect negatively family SMEs through the fear of losing family control and ownership (Fernandez & Nieto, 2005), adjustment to new business surroundings (Hennart et al., 2019), organization conflicts within the family (D'Angelo et al., 2016), and the loss of investments and reputation if the strategy fails (Boellis et al., 2016). In light of the above, internationalization can be a dilemma for family SMEs; nevertheless, many decide to internationalize; even though, they tend to be labeled risk-aversion and conservative, some are very successful in foreign markets (Lahiri et al., 2020).

The first blueprint of research on FBs and their internationalization is from Gallo and Sveen (1991). The authors first explained the differences that institutions like FB have in their foreign expansion and the restrains limiting them from pursuing internationalization. The influential work of Gallo and Sveen, (1991), brought a new light into the FB research field. Although, at the time, many studies focused on the uniqueness in FB, few regarded their internationalization strategies and involvement. Following the steps of Gallo and Sveen, (1991), the turning of the new millennium brought a more in-depth look into internationalization processes in FB (e.g., Zahra, 2003; Fernández and Nieto, 2005; Graves and Thomas, 2006). Moreover, in the last decade, there has been a great interest to study the impact of family involvement, market entry mode and the speed in which FB develop their internationalization (e.g., Claver, Rienda and Quer, 2009; D'Angelo, Majocchi and Buck, 2016; Kraus et al., 2016; De Massis et al., 2018). Nevertheless, with a closer look, we can find a lack of unanimity regarding the findings. On one side, some authors reveal a positive relationship between FB and internationalization (e.g., Zahra, 2003), while others argue a negative relationship between the two dimensions (e.g., Fernandez and Nieto, 2005; Graves and Thomas, 2006). While the literature fails to provide clear evidence regarding the effect of family ownership and family involvement in internationalization, the inconsistency raises a critical need to explain the determinants that can benefit and restrain FBs in their international expansion.

A recent study by Lahiri et al. (2020) adopted a strategy tripod synthesis to provide a clearer vision regarding the internationalization of family SMEs. The use of the strategy tripod framework (Peng et al., 2008) can shed some light on the uncertain findings in the literature (Lahiri et al., 2020). This framework accounts for industry-based, institution-based, and resource-based factors to mutually impact the firm's strategic decision (Peng et al., 2008); moreover, applying this framework in family SMEs internationalization is essential to understand the full scope of their strategies. According to Lahiri et al. (2020), the firm-family-specific resources, institutional frameworks, and industry conditions are crucial to drive family SMEs in their expansion abroad. Moreover, how family SMEs access, face, and deal with these elements can be essential towards their strategies (Lahiri et al., 2020).

The research field regarding family SMEs and internationalization has been increasingly growing in the last years (e.g., Pukall and Calabrò, 2014; Calabrò, Brogi and Torchia, 2016; D'Angelo, Majocchi and Buck, 2016; De Massis et al., 2018a; Ray, Mondal and Ramachandran, 2018). The main contribution of this study is not only to synthesis the current state of the art regarding family SMEs internationalization but provide theoretical evidence for future guidelines of empirical research regarding the most predominant strategies, the effect of ownership, management and governance, and the impact of public policies in their support.

FBs are embedded in almost every economic sector across the world (Anderson & Reeb, 2003). These institutions represent a crucial source of employment, sustainability, and development for national, regional, and international economies (Basco, 2015). Humanity is at a crossroads in the present moment; the post-pandemic aftermath threatens numerous businesses worldwide. Although family SMEs are a source of inclusive and sustainable development, public institutions disregard their distinctiveness when designing their policies. As pledge by the United Nations agenda for 2030, no one must be left behind; for these reasons' policymakers and governmental institutions must regard these firms with a different set of lenses, helping them to survive in a crisis period. The present chapter is a forward step towards understanding their uniqueness and the lessons we can learn from the past; we aim to provide a clearer picture of these institutions in international markets, not only for scholars but also for managers, policymakers, and governmental institutions.

The study is organized as follows: After the description of the method used in the selection process, we proceed to do a quantitative study of the body of the literature. The following section provides an in-depth qualitative analysis of the literature regarding the main determinants in family SMEs internationalization. The study ends with a discussion of the results and directions towards further research.

Method

This study has employed a systematic literature review methodology, where it is proposed to synthesize and evaluate literature, identify patterns, trends, and gaps in the literature (Tranfield et al., 2003). According to Tranfield and Denyer (2009): "Systematic review is a specific methodology that locates existing studies, selects and evaluates contributions, analyses and synthesizes data, and reports the evidence in such a way that allows reasonably clear conclusions to be reached about what is and is not known.". The main objective of a systematic literature review is to identify articles using objective search criteria and a systematic reproducible method to examine relevant literature on a given subject (Gough et al., 2012).

We proceeded to do the data search on May 15th, 2021, in the Scopus Database. In order to ensure relevant articles in our search, we combine the following keywords in the title or abstract: "family business" OR "family involvement" OR "family firm" AND "internationalization" AND "SME". To improve the review process, we only included published articles in indexed Journals and written in English. Due to the nature of the study, we only took into account articles under the Business, Management, and Accounting area. Table 1 presents an overview of the methodology adopted in gathering the articles for our analysis.

Table 1. Database Search Methodology

<table>
<tr><th>Criteria</th><th>Search string in the Scopus Database</th><th>Articles</th></tr>
<tr><td>Keyword</td><td>"family business" OR "family involvement" OR "family firm" AND "internationalization" AND "SME"</td><td rowspan="2">75</td></tr>
<tr><td>Restriction</td><td>Title, Keywords, Abstract</td></tr>
<tr><td></td><td></td><td></td></tr>
<tr><td></td><td>Selection of articles</td><td></td></tr>
<tr><td>Language</td><td>English</td><td>74</td></tr>
<tr><td>Document Type</td><td>Articles</td><td>61</td></tr>
<tr><td>Source Type</td><td>Journals</td><td>54</td></tr>
<tr><td>Subject Area</td><td>Business, Management and Accounting</td><td>48</td></tr>
</table>

We gathered a total number of 48 published articles. All the selected articles were analyzed in-depth following a coding structure: (1) Country of the study; (2) Method used; (3) Theoretical framework; (4) Variables used to measure internationalization and FB; (4) Main conclusions; and (5) Policy Recommendations.

In order to provide the best results and insights, we followed a two-step analysis in the study. Firstly, we conducted a quantitative analysis according to the research objective and followed by the characterization of the articles selected. Secondly, we have a qualitative analysis in which we discuss and report the relevant findings in the literature. Both analyses have their advantages and disadvantages; thus, to better acquire an overall better understanding of the subject, we combine both.

FINDINGS

Despite the prominence of FB in the economic fabric, there is no clear, supportive understanding of their distinctiveness when it comes to internationalizing; moreover, due to recent changes in the world economy, it is of most importance to try and fully understand the determinants that make them survive and prosper in international markets. There has been a growing interest in studying the relationship between family SMEs and their internationalization. Nevertheless, researchers and scholars are still trying to fully comprehend what factors influence their behavior and their strategic choices regarding internationalization (Pukall & Calabrò, 2014). In the following section, we present the main findings in the literature.

QUANTITATIVE ANALYSIS

Descriptive Results

Table 2 presents an overview of the distribution of the articles retained in the study; we adopted the framework as used by Pukall & Calabrò (2014), but with some changes. Besides exploring the journals distribution, we also conducted a survey in SCImago Journal & Country Rank (SJR), which measures the impact, influence, and prestige of the Journals.

Table 2. Articles distribution by Journal, time period and Scimago country ranking

		Number of publications in time period							
Journal	**QuartilI HFactor**	**2005-2007**	**2008-2010**	**2011-2013**	**2014-2016**	**2017-2019**	**2020-2021**	**Total**	**Percentage**
International Business Review	Q1 I 87			1	2	2		5	10,4%
Journal of International Entrepreneurship	Q1 I 41			2	1		1	4	8,3%
Journal of World Business	Q1 I 104	1		1	1	1		4	8,3%
Journal of Management and Governance	Q2 I 47			3				3	6,3%
Family Business Review	Q1 I 96	1			1			2	4,2%
International Journal of Business and Globalisation	Q3 I 14			1	1			2	4,2%
Journal of Globalisation and Small Business	Q3 I 16	2						2	4,2%
International Marketing Review	Q1 I 83			2				2	4,2%
Journal of Business Strategy	Q2 I 36			1		1		2	4,2%
Journal of Evolutionary Studies in Business	n.a						2	2	4,2%
Journal of International Business Studies	Q1 I 184	1				1		2	4,2%
Journal of Small Business and Enterprise Development	Q1 I 61		1	1				2	4,2%
World Review of Entrepreneurship and Sustainable	Q3 I 14				1	1		2	4,2%
Africa Journal of Management	Q2 I 10				1			1	2,1%
Asia Pacific Journal of Management	Q1 I 74						1	1	2,1%
Baltic Journal of Management	Q2 I 25	1						1	2,1%
Central European Business Review	Q3 I 3					1		1	2,1%
Engineering Economics	Q2 I 27			1				1	2,1%
European Management Review	Q2 I 29					1		1	2,1%
Global Strategy Journal	Q1 I 18						1	1	2,1%
International Journal of Entrepreneurship and Innovation	Q2 I 22					1		1	2,1%
Journal of Management	Q1 I 208	1						1	2,1%
Journal of Small Business Management	Q1 I 103				1			1	2,1%
Management Science Letters	Q2 I 13					1		1	2,1%

continues on following page

Table 2. Continued

		Number of publications in time period							
Journal	**QuartilI HFactor**	**2005-2007**	**2008-2010**	**2011-2013**	**2014-2016**	**2017-2019**	**2020-2021**	**Total**	**Percentage**
Multinational Business Review	Q1 I 26				1			1	2,1%
Polish Journal of Management Studies	Q2 I 17						1	1	2,1%
Problems and Perspectives in Management	Q3 I 17					1		1	2,1%
Total		7	1	13	10	11	6	48	100%

As we can observe, the prominent journal for research on family SMEs internationalization is the International Business Review (5 articles). In general, most of the articles are published in journals with significant impact factors, which leads us to conclude the growing significance and prestige of the topic among scholars. The number of articles has been evolving and increasing over time, reaching a peak in 2011-2013 of 13 articles.

Table 3 shows the ten most-cited Journals. Although the journal with most articles in our study is the International Business Review (5 articles), analyzing Table 3, it is possible to verify that the Journal of World Business is the most cited (404 citations). This journal has an impact factor of Q1 (Table 2); thus, we can reinforce our previous comment in the sense that the topic under study is of growing importance, leading prestigious journals and researchers to yield quality articles with a significant number of citations.

Table 3. Most cited Journals

Journal	Number of Citations
Journal of World Business	404
Family Business Review	364
Journal of International Business Studies	352
Journal of Management	316
International Business Review	278
Journal of Management and Governance	273
International Marketing Review	155
Journal of International Entrepreneurship	85
Journal of Small Business and Enterprise Development	69
Baltic Journal of Management	68

Figure 1 gives an overview of the country of analysis; most articles focused on Finland (8 articles) and Italy (8 articles). According to the Finnish Family Firms Association (2017), family SMEs represent 75% of small-sized firms and embody 30% of total business sector value; while in Italy, these firms symbolize 58% of the total number of businesses and contribute to 3 million workplaces (AIDAF, 2021).

Figure 1. Country of Analysis

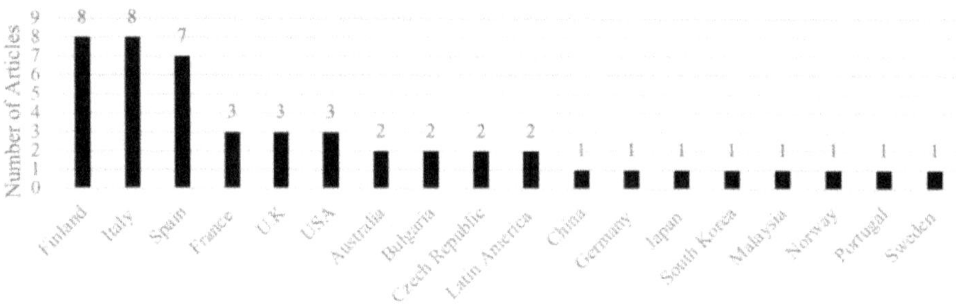

The findings above reveal the importance of family SMEs in the economic environment of a country. Due to the nature of family SMEs, many may lack the resources needed to promote their international expansion (Fernandez & Nieto, 2005). Thus, it is essential to consider the role of policy in providing the mechanisms that can help them build resources to start their international expansion (Wright et al., 2007). As mentioned by Fernández-Olmos et al. (2016), practitioners and policymakers must be aware of FB in their policies; moreover, government assistance can play a crucial role towards the survival of FB in international markets (Jeong, 2016) as firms with more significant international revenue have superior performance in both return of investment and market share (McDougall & Oviatt, 1996).

Taking into account the methodological approaches, the articles in our sample use a quantitative analysis (69%), qualitative case studies (22%), or conceptual methodology (9%). This finding leads us to conclude that most of the literature regarding family SMEs internationalization is empirical. Thus, theoretical contributions are limited in this area, which can hinder the development of empirical studies. Moreover, we also found literature reviews that reinforce the need for further theoretical development.

Theoretical Approaches

Most of the early frameworks and theories regarding internationalization focused on large companies (Saarenketo et al., 2004). These studies highlighted the struggle of expanding into foreign markets, significant entry barriers, and the costly investment that made internationalization a rare occurrence (Saarenketo et al., 2004). Nonetheless, the literature dismissed the importance and the contribution of SMEs in international contexts (Fillis, 2001; Game & Apfelthaler, 2016). Due to their resource constraints, family ownership, and control, family SMEs develop their internationalization in a differently than larger firms bundle with more resources (Claver et al., 2009).

The articles in our study use different theoretical frameworks in their empirical research design. As it can be observed in Table 4, the most prevalent approach is the resource-based view (e.g., Nieto & Fernandez, 2006; Kansikas et al., 2014; Eddleston et al., 2019). The resource-based view regards the firm as a collection of tangible and intangible assets such as their resource, capital, knowledge, and capabilities (V. M. Sharma & Erramilli, 2004). According to this framework, firms in order to reach a good stake they must depend on their resources to gain advantageous positions (Kathleen, 1991). Besides the significance of the firm's resources, resource-based models also address the importance and the ability of organizational learning to foster and create new resources (Canabal & White, 2008).

International competitiveness relies on the availability of resources and human capital (Kansikas et al., 2014); nevertheless, family SMEs are characterized as having fewer financial resources than non-family SMEs (Fernández-Olmos et al., 2016). Nonetheless, practices like the inclusion of external ownership and management can lead these firms to gain access to more resources (Davidkov & Yordanova, 2016)

Also present in the sample is the social-capital theory (e.g., Kontinen & Ojala, 2012; Bika & Kalantaridis, 2019). The social-capital theory states that firms create relationships that can offer access to resources and opportunities of different natures (Coleman, 1988; Rodrigues & Child, 2012). According to Kontinen & Ojala (2012), family SMEs must gain access to social capital; ultimately, enabling them to start their internationalization.

Another fundamental theoretical approach in the sample is the Network-theory (e.g., Eberhard & Craig, 2013; Kontinen & Ojala, 2011b). The Network-theory focuses on the creation of business networks in order to cement and be more successful internationally; moreover, businesses networks collaborate among themselves to obtain international experience and knowledge (Bužavaitė et al., 2019; Kunday & Şengüler, 2015). According to Kontinen & Ojala, (2011b), networks can play a crucial role in family SMEs internationalization, providing new international business opportunities and exclusive resources for firms within the network.

One of the foundations in internationalization theories is the Uppsala model, also known as the Stage Theory (Johanson & Vahlne, 1977); the central tenet of this theory is that internationalization is a gradual process. This theory proposes that the knowledge and experience of the market determine commitment decisions and ongoing business behaviors (Johanson & Vahlne, 1977). Scholars have widely adopted the Uppsala stage theory to explain internationalization among FB (e.g., Casillas & Acedo, 2005; Pukall & Calabrò, 2014). According to this theory, family SMEs follow their internationalization in line with the Uppsala stage model; first they gather knowledge in domestic markets and then apply it to international markets incrementally (Anand, 2013; Casillas & Acedo, 2005).

Risk-taking, innovativeness, and proactiveness define entrepreneurial orientation (EO) (Miller, 1983; Covin & Slevin, 1989). Entrepreneurial behavior is characterized as a proclivity of an organization, or individual, towards capitalizing on new opportunities and creating innovation (Kuratko et al., 2015). Family SMEs are characterized as having unique features that help them to remain innovative and entrepreneurial (Dibrell et al., 2008), such as long-term orientation and family involvement in multiple generations (Calabrò et al., 2019). As we can observe in the sample, entrepreneurial orientation started to gain traction among family SMEs scholars recently (e.g., Zapletalová, 2017; Alayo et al., 2019).

QUALITATIVE ANALYSIS

In order to synthesis the current state of the literature and therefore contribute to the literature in family SMEs internationalization, we proceeded to encapsulate the main theoretical findings in the following section. After analyzing all articles, we acknowledged four different dimensions in the literature regarding internationalization in family SMEs: (1) The nature of family ownership; (2) Governance determinants; (3) Internationalization pathways; and (4) Public Policies. Dividing the literature into four distinct dimensions provides a clear view of the current state of the art and helps us identify avenues for further research.

Table 4. Theoretical approaches used in the articles sample

Theoretical Approach	Number of articles
Not mentioned	10
Resource-based view	7
Social Capital Theory	5
Network Theory	4
Uppsala Stage model	4
Entrepreneurial orientation	4
Stewardship Orientation	3
Knowledge-Based View	3
Agency Theory	2
Upper Echelon	2
Socioemotional Wealth	2
International Performance	1
Transaction Cost	1

The Nature of Family Ownership

Ever since the first body of research regarding FBs, scholars have been trying to portray better these institutions and the unique characteristics that make them different from non-FB. Nonetheless, scholars concluded that FBs have unique features that differentiate them from one another (e.g., Sharma et al., 1999; Anderson & Reeb, 2003; Gómez-Mejía et al., 2007). Thus, studying their heterogeneity represents a crucial step to understanding these companies better (Daspit et al., 2021).

Family ownership is the most prevalent type of governance in the world (La Porta et al., 1999); still, the literature claims that FBs have lower levels of internationalization (e.g., Fernández & Nieto, 2005; Graves & Thomas, 2006); this finding is common in our sampled articles. Recent research pointed to the fact that 100% of family ownership negatively influences internationalization (e.g., Sciascia et al., 2012). Risk avoidance, conservatism, lack of financial resources, and lack of specialized management with international knowledge can be attributed to the low levels of internationalization in these companies (e.g., Nieto & Fernandez, 2006; Basly, 2007; De Massis et al., 2018). Thus, they pursue strategies more focused on their home markets, and when they internationalize, they prefer closer countries to their home (De Massis et al., 2018). Nonetheless, attributes like the strength of the family, altruism, human capital, stewardship orientation, long-term orientation, and lower agency costs can lead them to pursue successful international strategies (e.g., Sirmon & Hitt, 2003; Zahra, 2003; George et al., 2005; De Massis et al., 2018a). Nonetheless, Sciascia et al., (2012) found that firms with moderate levels of family ownership can achieve better export intensity than having 100% family ownership.

According to some studies in this review, the SEW goals of the firm can play a crucial role in the pursued strategies (e.g., Basly & Saunier, 2020; Yang et al., 2020). In Miller & Le Breton-Miller (2014) work, the authors found that FBs can follow two types of SEW: extended and restricted. Firms that have an extended SEW tend to be more open to new ventures and alliances; while, restricted SEW firms have more focus on the family needs; thus, being more conservative, risk-averse, and cautious towards their strategies (Miller & Le Breton-Miller, 2014; Daspit et al., 2021). SEW aspirations and goals can have a significant influence on internationalization. As found in Yang et al. (2020), restricted SEW aspirations can negatively impact internationalization. Moreover, SEW goals are related to the firm´s characteristics like their size, age, legacy, and culture, as seen in the work of Basly & Saunier (2020).

While some individualities of FBs seem to nurture internationalization while others prevent it (Mitter & Emprechtinger, 2016). FBs have in their nature a stewardship orientation leading them to have long-term survival and conservation of the family legacy; the altruistic behavior among family members can provide strategic flexibility, trust, and commitment which can be essential in strategies like internationalization (Arregle et al., 2007; Sciascia et al., 2012; Mitter & Emprechtinger, 2016). Stewardship behavior encourages trustworthiness among its members, which can be essential to develop more capable personnel at identifying international opportunities (Mitter & Emprechtinger, 2016; Sciascia et al., 2012). In our research sample, we found that higher levels of stewardship moderate the positive relationship between international experience and internationalization (Segaro, 2012; Segaro et al., 2014).

Family involvement is an essential factor in FBs; it dictates the company's and the pursued strategies (Zahra, 2003). According to the seminal work of Zahra (2003), family involvement can cause mixed effects on internationalization. According to our sample, a higher concentration of family involvement moderates the negative relationship of internationalization, leading these institutions to focus more on their home markets (e.g., Zulima Fernández & Nieto, 2005; Baronchelli et al., 2016). Nonetheless, the literature still requires further research to understand the full effect of family involvement on business behaviors and the outcomes for strategies like internationalization (De Massis et al., 2018b).

FBs embedded culture can moderate internationalization propensity; nonetheless, the inclusion of younger generations, core competencies, and long-term orientation can enhance international expansion to a greater extent than non-family-businesses. Some studies in this review suggest that family SMEs can invigorate their internationalization prospects with the succession of younger generations (e.g., Fernandez & Nieto, 2005; Calabrò & Mussolino, 2012; Alvarado, 2020). According to Petrů et al. (2019), younger generations can provide knowledge and diversification in international strategies; moreover, the authors found that companies in the first generation follow a more traditional process, only exporting to closer countries inside the European Union (EU). However, the involvement of younger generations leads the firm to be more diversified and exploring more riskier strategies, like exporting to more distant countries (Petrů et al., 2019).

Although many of the studies find that family ownership, involvement, and control influence internationalization, there is still room to explore further the role of family heterogeneity, as mentioned in the work of (De Massis et al., 2018).

Table 5 allows us to observe some of the articles regarding the dimension of family ownership in our sample.

Management and Governance Capability

Internationalization can be seen as a platform for economic growth, increase competitiveness, and source of more significant revenue; nonetheless, it is a milestone challenge for all types of intuitions, remarkably for family SMEs due to their organizational and financial nature. Concerning the management capabilities in family SMEs, most studies support that family SMEs management has a negative relationship with internationalization (e.g., Ortiz et al., 2012; Cerrato & Piva, 2012; Davidkov & Yordanova, 2016).

Table 5. Articles in the nature of family ownership dimension

Authors	Title	Journal	Objective
(Basly & Saunier, 2020)	*"Familiness, socio-emotional goals and the internationalization of French family SMEs"*	Journal of International Entrepreneurship	Explain the role of family's socio-emotional goals in the level of exports SMEs.
(Alvarado, 2020)	*"Perdurability, families, and internationalization processes: Approaches from business history in Latin America"*	Journal of Evolutionary Studies in Business	Describe the history of family businesses from multiple approaches in Latin America.
(Yang et al., 2020)	*"How family firm characteristics affect internationalization of Chinese family SMEs"*	Asia Pacific Journal of Management	Investigate the effect of family characteristics on the internationalization activities of Chinese family SMEs, using a socioemotional wealth perspective.
(Petrů et al., 2019)	*"Diversification of export territories of family businesses as a tool of their further development"*	Problems and Perspectives in Management	Identify the involvement of generation successors in export activities of family business.
(Baronchelli et al., 2016)	*"The impact of family involvement on the investments of Italian small-medium enterprises in psychically distant countries"*	International Business Review	The impact of family involvement on the investments of Italian small-medium enterprises in psychically distant countries
(Segaro et al., 2014)	*"Internationalisation of family small and medium sized enterprises: The role of stewardship orientation, family commitment culture and top management team"*	International Business Review	Investigate how aspects of organizational culture, typical to family businesses, influence internationalisation.
(Graves & Shan, 2014)	*"An Empirical Analysis of the Effect of Internationalization on the Performance of Unlisted Family and Nonfamily Firms in Australia"*	Family Business Review	Study and compare the performance of family and nonfamily SMEs and the effect of internationalization on their performance.
(Calabrò & Mussolino, 2012)	*"How do boards of directors contribute to family SME export intensity? The role of formal and informal governance mechanisms"*	Journal of Management & Governance volume	Analyze family SME export intensity by showing how the board of directors could provide assistance in the selection and implementation of this strategy.
(Segaro, 2012)	*"Internationalization of family SMEs: The impact of ownership, governance, and top management team"*	Journal of Management and Governance	Examine the determinant factors that may explain the internationalization of family SMEs and the relationship between ownership, governance, top management team and internationalization.
(Kontinen & Ojala, 2011c)	*"Social capital in the international operations of family SMEs"*	Journal of Small Business and Enterprise Development	Study how social capital is developed in the internationalization process family SMEs.
(Basly, 2007)	*"The internationalization of family sme an organizational learning and knowledge development perspective"*	Baltic Journal of Management	Study the specificities of family SMEs in their internationalization process.
(Nieto & Fernandez, 2012)	*"Impact of ownership on the international involvement of SMEs"*	Journal of International Business Studies	Study the relationship between the internationalization strategies of SMEs and types of ownership.

continues on following page

Table 5. Continued

Authors	Title	Journal	Objective
(George et al., 2005)	*"Ownership and the internationalization of small firms"*	Journal of Management	Analyze how ownership structures on SMEs influence their proclivity to take risk and expand the scale and scope of their internationalization efforts.
(Fernández & Nieto, 2005)	*"Internationalization strategy of small and medium-sized family businesses: Some influential factors"*	Family Business Review	To study internationalization strategies in family SMEs.

FBs and SMEs are described as having unique corporate governance (Shleifer & Vishny, 1997). The ownership structure and management in FBs have a substantial influence on internationalization, as family institutions have a more conservative approach towards their investments in international strategies (Anderson & Reeb, 2003; George et al., 2005). Nevertheless, the careful behavior of family businesses towards internationalize resides in their risk-aversion, fear of losing ownership, and family control (Gómez-Mejía et al., 2007; Nieto & Fernandez, 2012).

The most common finding in the analyzed articles is that management plays a crucial role in internationalization strategies; moreover, family SMEs generally lack the managerial capabilities to conduct successful internationalization processes as found in the work of Jorge et al. (2017) due to the lack of international knowledge and qualified personnel with experience in international markets.

One of the main contributions of top management members (hereafter TMT) is to establish and provide the necessary conditions within the firm in order to produce maximum competitiveness (Ortiz et al., 2012). TMT members play a crucial role in constructing the firm's strategy (Lubatkin et al., 2006). In family SMEs, it is usual for family members to be part of TMT; nonetheless, they provide family´s ideals and behaviors influencing strategic choices (Alayo et al., 2019). According to the work of Alayo et al., (2019), FB-specific TMT characteristics shape the EO of the firm; thus, impacting the degree of internationalization. An excessive family TMT ratio will lead to a negative relationship between EO and the degree of internationalization; meaning, an excessive level of family involvement can limit the perspectives about internationalization processes (Alayo et al., 2019). Some studies in this review reveal that higher levels of family involvement can negatively influence internationalization (e.g., Cerrato & Piva, 2012; Davidkov & Yordanova, 2016; Ortiz et al., 2012). So how can family SMEs managers address this issue?

Family employees are a valuable resource in family SMEs; nonetheless, most FBs face restrictions regarding their knowledge and skills (Daspit et al., 2021). Family SMEs can overcome the problems associated with high levels of family involvement by including of external managers (D'Angelo et al., 2016). Nonetheless, the decision to recruit external managers must be perceived in the whole governance body of the family SME, as mentioned by Huse (2000).

FBs are in their nature, intertwined with the family dimension, giving them a more excellent capability to create social capital (Segaro, 2010). According to Graves & Thomas (2008), stewardship orientation can provide family SMEs the commitment required once they internationalize. Thus, family SMEs with built-up social capital are more likely to pursue international strategies (Segaro, 2010). There are two forms of social capital in FBs, the business and the family; these two dimensions can overlap; thus, creating managerial and organizational tensions (Arregle et al., 2007; D'Angelo et al., 2016). In FBs where the family dimension is more dominant than the business side, it can hinder the efficiency of the firm (D'Angelo et al., 2016); moreover, the inclusion of external managers or external ownership in this situation can lead to potential conflict within the organization (J. Arregle et al., 2007).

Additionally, in the presence of greater family ownership concentration, the benefits relating to the presence of external managers can decline (Calabrò et al., 2013). Family SMEs can benefit in multiple ways if they embrace external managers and ownership into their structure (Compagno et al., 2005). According to some studies in this review, external managers bring a new set of values, knowledge, managerial capabilities, and valuable resources that positively impact the firm to pursue internationalization (e.g., Cerrato & Piva, 2012; Davidkov & Yordanova, 2016; Majocchi et al., 2018).

According to Majocchi et al. (2018), the presence of external managers and the interaction between family members has a positive relationship in internationalization. Although members outside the family do not have the same altruistic values as a family member, they presence might counteract risk avoidance and conservatism found in family SMEs (Lahiri et al., 2020; Minichilli et al., 2010).

Although family SMEs want, above all, to maintain their control and ownership, hiring external members can be of added value towards their internationalization strategies. The managerial capabilities in FBs are lower than non-FBs, as they pursue international strategies (Graves & Thomas, 2006); nonetheless, if they are capitalizing their EO along with managerial expertise, they can reach more successful stages than their non-family counterparts.

In Table 6, it can be observed some of the articles regarding the dimension of management competences in our sample.

Internationalization Pathways

The seminal work of Bell et al. (2003) carve the way to understand SMEs internationalization pathways better. The model developed by the authors has been vastly integrated into the articles of our sample as it serves to better understand pathways not only in SMEs but also in family SMEs. According to Bell et al. (2003), internationalization in SMEs follows three typical pathways. The first pathway encompasses traditional companies that start their internationalization incrementally and in psychically closer countries. The traditional pathway follows the same tenet as portrayed in the Uppsala model. As observed in our sample (e.g., Kontinen & Ojala, 2010; Anand, 2013; D´Angelo et al., 2013), some family SMEs follow a traditional pathway in their internationalization and are cautious regarding their growth objectives (Kansikas et al., 2014). As Kontinen & Ojala (2010) mentioned, psychical distance can be a crucial factor in internationalization strategies; moreover, the authors found that family SMEs prefer to follow a sequential process and preferred to start their expansion in closer countries.

As previously found in the literature, FBs tend to start their internationalization in more traditional frameworks, starting with lower commitment and increasing it as their knowledge and experience grows (Claver et al., 2007). According to Kontinen & Ojala (2010), family SMEs in their founder-manager generation are more inclined to implement internationalization in incremental pathways following traditional internationalization pathways.

Born-Globals embrace the second pathway of internationalization (Bell et al., 2003). Born-global firms start their international journey from the moment of their inception (Tanev, 2012). Their internationalization processes are different from more traditional firms, as they pursue to gain advantages of moving faster and exploiting their proprietary knowledge in international markets to the fullest (Bell et al., 2003).

Table 6. Articles in management competences dimension

Authors	Title	Journal	Objective
(Kolarov & Georgieva, 2020)	*"Management features in Bulgarian SMEs as determinants of business internationalization"*	Polish Journal of Management Studies	Study management features in SMEs as determinants in internationalization.
(Bika & Kalantaridis, 2019)	*"Organizational-Social-Capital, Time and International Family SMEs: An Empirical Study from the East of England"*	European Management Review	Adopt a social capital perspective in order to decipher case study data from the East of England.
(Majocchi et al., 2018)	*"Bifurcation bias and exporting: Can foreign work experience be an answer? Insight from European family SMEs"*	Journal of World Business	Examine if bifurcation bias and exporting can be the answer for family SMEs in their internationalization strategies.
(Jorge et al., 2017)	*"When family businesses go international: management sets the path"*	Journal of Business Strategy	Analyze the influence of family management on SME internationalization process.
(Zapletalová, 2017)	*"International management of Czech family enterprises: Decisions on international entrepreneurial activities"*	Central European Business Review	Investigate the impact of internal factors, particularly human resources, in international entrepreneurial activities in Czech family SMEs.
(D'Angelo et al., 2016)	*"External managers, family ownership and the scope of SME internationalization"*	Journal of World Business	Explain the scope of family SMEs internationalization and find if professional managers are important to the process.
(Davidkov & Yordanova, 2016)	*"Exploring the Bulgarian family SMEs' reluctance to internationalise"*	International Journal of Business and Globalisation	Explore the reason why family SMEs are reluctant to internationalize in the context of Bulgaria.
(Merino et al., 2015)	*"Family SMEs' Internationalization: Disentangling the Influence of Familiness on Spanish Firms' Export Activity"*	Journal of Small Business Management	Study the relationships between family involvement and internationalization of family SMEs.
(Cerrato & Piva, 2012)	*"The internationalization of small and medium-sized enterprises: The effect of family management, human capital and foreign ownership"*	Journal of Management and Governance	Examine the effect of family management, human capital and foreign ownership in the internationalization process of family SMEs.
(Ortiz et al., 2012)	*"How Does Management Perceive Exporting? An Empirical Study of SMEs"*	Engineering Economics	Analyze how management impact exporting behavior in SMEs.
(Zucchella et al., 2007)	*"The drivers of the early internationalization of the firm"*	Journal of World Business	Examine drivers of early internationalization of family and non-family firms.
(Compagno et al., 2005)	*"Corporate governance and advanced forms of internationalisation in Italian SMEs"*	International Journal of Globalisation and Small Business	Study the role of corporate governance system in providing small firms with resources and competences and promoting changes in entrepreneurial culture.
(Casillas & Acedo, 2005)	*"Internationalisation of Spanish family SMEs: an analysis of family involvement"*	International Journal of Globalisation and Small Business	Analyze the influence of family involvement on a company in the context of the firm´s internationalization.

Like the Uppsala model, existing internationalization theories failed to fully comprehend the extend of born-global firms' internationalization (Mort & Weerawardena, 2006). Moreover, the use of networks in internationalization plays a crucial role in understanding the determinants of the process in born-globals (Idris & Saridakis, 2018). Networks, formal and informal, can help firms access resources by developing existing or new ties (Idris & Saridakis, 2018). Family SMEs are challenged with more significant entry barriers than larger companies; thus, networks can provide them access to a broader range of resources (Zahra, 2005); as perceived in our sample, networks are crucial for the international development of family SMEs (e.g., Kontinen & Ojala, 2011b; Eberhard & Craig, 2013; Jeong, 2016; Idris & Saridakis, 2018).

According to Bell et al. (2003), the final pathway of internationalization are the born-again globals. Born-again globals have the main goal to gain resources after "critical events" (Bell et al., 2003). Internationalization for these firms represents an opportunity to survive, as they only internationalize after the sudden result of critical episodes, such as change of ownership or management (Kontinen & Ojala, 2010a). Family SMEs following the pathway of born-again global have their ownership structure more concentrated; thus, opposite to traditional pathways, their internationalization is more radical and intense, as found in Kontinen & Ojala (2010).

Internationalization pathways are mainly determined by the ownership and management structure of the company. In contrast, more fragmented ownership will lead to a more radical and drastic internationalization process (born globals and born-again globals), concentrated ownership will result in more traditional pathways (Kontinen & Ojala, 2010a). Table 7 allows us to observe some of the articles regarding the dimension of internationalization pathways in our sample.

Public Policies

Theoretical research emphasizes the importance of family SMEs on local and international markets. At present, these businesses have been struggling for their survival due to the recent Covid-19 pandemic crisis. According to the latest IMF paper of Ebeke et al. (2021), almost 3 million firms that were solvent pre-COVID pandemic have become insolvent in 2020. Therefore, it is essential to emphasize that policy measures need to be implemented to reduce solvency risk in family SMES and help them survive in a crisis.

Some of the studies in our review provide recommendations for policy makers towards family SMEs and their internationalization. According to Zucchella et al. (2007), public and governmental entities must provide educational resources, such as teaching foreign languages and training potential entrepreneurs with an international mindset. Moreover, according to Fernández-Olmos et al. (2016), to promote and assist family SMEs in their internationalization, policymakers should help these firms in the early stages of their processes. The authors also suggest creating informal cooperation networks between firms that operate in the same sector, which can help them improve and promote export capability and commitment towards internationalization (Fernández-Olmos et al., 2016).

Formal institutions, such as governments, can shape family SMEs internationalization activity (Carney et al., 2017). Policy strategies need to be employed to promote resilience; therefore, raising survival propensity. Some of the studies present in this review consider the importance of public policies for the survival and development of family SMEs internationalization (e.g., Casillas & Acedo, 2005; Zucchella et al., 2007; Kuivalainen et al., 2013). Thus, Practitioners must seek to provide supportive frameworks for SMEs seeking to internationalize (Wright et al., 2007). Family SMEs are seminal institutions for the economic fabric; nevertheless, public policies do not consider their uniqueness (Eberhard & Craig, 2013). Thus, the designed policies may fail to provide them the adequate resources to help them survive (Casillas & Acedo, 2005).

Table 7. Articles in internationalization pathway dimension

Authors	Title	Journal	Objective
(Anand, 2013)	*"Internationalisation of the small and medium family firm in Japan"*	International Journal of Business and Globalisation	Study the internationalisation path for small and medium family firms in Japan and strategic determinants in the process.
(Kontinen & Ojala, 2010a)	*"Internationalization pathways among family-owned SMEs"*	International Marketing Review	Understand internationalization pathways among family-owned SMEs and identify patterns taken by these types of firms.
(D´Angelo et al., 2013)	*"Geographical pathways for SME internationalization: Insights from an Italian sample"*	International Marketing Review	Examine the determinants of two distinct geographic pathways to internationalization for SMEs.
(Idris & Saridakis, 2018)	*"Local formal interpersonal networks and SMEs internationalisation: Empirical evidence from the UK"*	International Business Review	Examine the existing relationship between local (formal and informal) interpersonal networks and exporting behavior.
(Jeong, 2016)	*"Types of foreign networks and internationalization performance of Korean SMEs"*	Multinational Business Review	Analyze how various types of foreign networks can influence the internationalization performance of Korean SMEs.
(Kansikas et al., 2014)	*"Family firm prerequisites for international business operations: A production and marketing capabilities approach"*	World Review of Entrepreneurship, Management and Sustainable Development	Study and compare family and non-family SMEs in their organizational prerequisites for international business operations.
(Kontinen & Ojala, 2011b)	*"Network ties in the international opportunity recognition of family SMEs"*	International Business Review	Investigate how network ties impacts the international recognition in family SMEs.
(Kontinen & Ojala, 2010a)	*"Internationalization pathways of family SMEs: Psychic distance as a focal point"*	Journal of Small Business and Enterprise Development	Investigate how psychic distance affects the internationalization, foreign market entry, and entry mode choice of Finnish family SMEs.
(Alayo et al., 2019)	*"Internationalization and entrepreneurial orientation of family SMEs: The influence of the family character"*	International Business Review	Analyze the moderating effects of the family's influence on the relationship between entrepreneurial orientation and internationalization with the involvement of top management team and generational involvement.
(Olejnik & Swoboda, 2012)	*"SMEs' internationalisation patterns: descriptive, dynamics and determinants"*	International Marketing Review	Identify internationalization patterns in SMEs and describe how they follow different patterns over time.

As found in the work of Idris & Saridakis (2018) and Jeong (2016), government assistance and adequate policy frameworks can provide family SMEs with the help to overcome the initial barriers of internationalization and provide them the resources that can help them to survive in international markets.

Table 8 allows us to observe some of the articles regarding the dimension of public policies in our sample.

Table 8. Articles in public policies dimension

Authors	Title	Journal	Objective
(Lahiri et al., 2020)	*"Behind the internationalization of family SMEs: A strategy tripod synthesis"*	Global Strategy Journal	Review and synthesize the growing literature concerning the internationalization of small and medium-sized family enterprises (family SMEs) around a strategy tripod framework.
(Fernández-Olmos et al., 2016)	*"Internationalisation and performance in Spanish family SMES: The W-curve"*	Business Research Quarterly	Investigate the impact of family dimension on the internationalisation and performance in Spanish family SMEs.
(Denicolai et al., 2015)	*"Be international or be innovative? Be both? The role of the entrepreneurial profile"*	Journal of International Entrepreneurship	Study the impact of the entrepreneurial behavior, demography, background, and experience strategic choices, like innovation and internationalization in FB.
(Eberhard & Craig, 2013)	*"The evolving role of organisational and personal networks in international market venturing"*	Journal of World Business	Investigate the relationship between networking, international market venturing and family ownership.
(Zucchella et al., 2007)	*"The drivers of the early internationalization of the firm"*	Journal of World Business	Examine drivers of early internationalization of family and non-family firms.

DISCUSSION AND FUTURE RESEARCH

The literature argues that internationalization in family SMEs requires a great determination from their managerial capabilities and experiential knowledge in international markets (e.g., Pukall & Calabrò, 2014; De Massis et al., 2018b; Hennart et al., 2019). The prevalent view among researchers is that family ownership and involvement hinder their expansion to foreign markets. International strategies require a tremendous number of resources and capital and excellent skills from managers and personnel (e.g., De Massis et al., 2018a; Hennart et al., 2019).

In order to illustrate all the relevant findings in the literature and following the steps of Segaro (2010), we created an integrative model (Fig. 2) regarding the internationalization process in family SMEs. The model illustrates the relationship among the dimensions previously mentioned in Table. 5,6,7,8: ownership; management and governance; pathways; and public policies. As portrayed in our chapter, we consider these four dimensions the most decisive for the degree and pursuit of internationalization in family SMEs. Our framework synthesizes some of the main topics in previous theoretical and empirical research.

Nonetheless, and despite all the effort, there is still a significant gap of knowledge. We believe that further research is required to understand the idiosyncrasies in family SMEs internationalization efforts. In light of our findings, two future streams of research seem to require further consideration. First, there is minute research regarding the impact of public policies in these institutions. Many of the studies reviewed mentioned the importance of public policies towards their support and survival; nonetheless, and despite the contribution, the literature lacks to provide clearer and practical frameworks. Although some scholars have been trying to reinforce the importance of family SMEs in the economic fabric and the importance of policies towards their survival in a crisis (De Massis & Rondi, 2020; Pieper et al., 2021). Following Lahiri et al. (2020) suggestions, little is known about how "home country institutions" help these firms and their strategies. We suggest that future, empirical and theoretical, studies must provide the adequate frameworks to change the perceived notion of family SMEs. Policymakers and governmental institutions must design their policies according to the uniqueness of family SMEs. This step could represent a fundamental change towards the support of these businesses for their international expansion activities and their survival on the long run.

Figure 2. Model of internationalization in family SMEs
Source: Adapted from Segaro (2010)

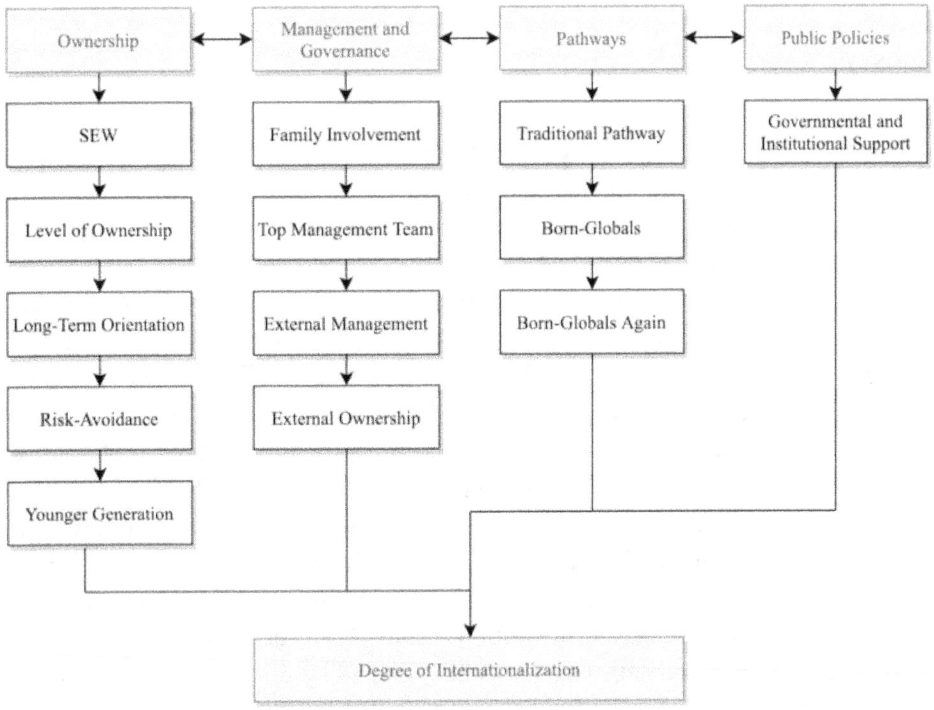

Second, we believe that managerial and governance capabilities are crucial for international orientation, as mentioned by Alayo et al. (2019). Nonetheless, the fragmented and heterogeneous findings in the literature do not provide a conclusive answer on how family SMEs managers must direct their efforts to improve their internationalization strategies. Although some studies suggest the inclusion of specialized managers in international markets and educating managers with international orientational, these efforts might not provide the best basis for their managerial capabilities on the long run. Thus, further investigation can provide more conclusive recommendations and assertive behaviors for managers in their pursue of foreign markets.

At present, these businesses are faced with significant challenges. Moreover, in light of the recent Covid-19 pandemic, changes in consumer behavior have fueled the usage of e-commerce by 17% in 2020 (UNCTAD, 2021). The adoption of e-commerce can be a significant strategic change to the development of family SMEs competitive advantages. According to Grandon & Pearson (2004), e-commerce can help smaller firms to gain competitive advantages bringing them closer to larger firms.

The gradual replacement of traditional avenues of shopping towards digital-based ones changes the paradigm and the position of these firms in international markets. Consequently, the concept of being local or global is shifting; the ever-growing usage of digital markets, challenges the accepted notion of internationalization, leading firms to trade in a "no man´s land" where geographical barriers are no longer the challenge they once were.

In light of the above, we believe that the unique attributes present in family SMEs must be addressed not only in future research but in future policy design and theoretical frameworks. Family SMEs managers and owners must take into account lessons from the past in their strategies, while policymakers and governmental institutions must perceive the distinctive and unique nature of family SMEs in their policies.

CONCLUSION

The main objective of this chapter is to synthesize and analyze the existing literature through a systematic review on family SMEs internationalization; the primary purpose is to examine the relationship of these businesses in their pursuit of international strategies. Our objective is threefold: (1) we examine the ownership and governance structures in family SMEs; (2) We analyze the pathways their pursue; (3) we present the public policies towards their support. The contribution of our study is related to the identification of the main determinants behind family SMEs internationalization; hoping it can provide basis not only for future research but for practitioners, policymakers, and managers to help these institutions survive in international markets in times of crisis. The research literature regarding FBs and family SMEs and their internationalization is vast; nonetheless, the body of literature is not homogenous. The heterogeneity of family ownership constitutes a complex research field; while scholars have been trying to fully understand the influence of family governance in a business for the last decades, these firms' unique characteristic and idiosyncrasies make them a challenging to understand. Nonetheless, in light of recent pandemic events, it is essential to regard the significance of these firms in regional and national economic environments. Governments and institutional actors must act to their support and provide them the basis for their development and survival. This study, like all systematic reviews, has its limitations. Although, some essential articles might have been disregarded due to the use of a single database, our goal was to provide the maximum transparency and easy replication of our method. We tried to use the best combination of keywords in order to achieve the most important articles in the research body; systematic reviews largely depend on the viewpoint of the researcher, which affects the bias of the study; nonetheless, we tried to our best knowledge provide a clearer picture of the state of the art and suggest the path for future avenues of research.

REFERENCES

Alayo, M., Maseda, A., Iturralde, T., & Arzubiaga, U. (2019). Internationalization and entrepreneurial orientation of family SMEs: The influence of the family character. *International Business Review*, *28*(1), 48–59. doi:10.1016/j.ibusrev.2018.06.003

Alvarado, A. A. (2020). Perdurability, families, and internationalization processes: Approaches from business history in latin america. *Journal of Evolutionary Studies in Business*, *5*(2), 1–32. doi:10.1344/jesb2020.2.j075

Anand, R. (2013). Internationalisation of the small and medium family firm in Japan. *International Journal of Business and Globalisation*, *11*(2), 117–135. doi:10.1504/IJBG.2013.055598

Anderson, R. C., & Reeb, D. M. (2003). Founding-Family Ownership and Firm Performance: Evidence from the S&P 500. *Journal of Finance, JSTOR, 58*(3), 1301–1328. doi:10.1111/1540-6261.00567

Arregle, J., Hitt, M. A., Sirmon, D. G., & Very, P. (2007). The development of organizational social capital: Attributes of family firms. *Journal of Management Studies, 44*(1), 73–95. doi:10.1111/j.1467-6486.2007.00665.x

Arregle, J. L., Naldi, L., Nordqvist, M., & Hitt, M. A. (2012). Internationalization of Family-Controlled Firms: A Study of the Effects of External Involvement in Governance. *Entrepreneurship Theory and Practice, 36*(6), 1115–1143. doi:10.1111/j.1540-6520.2012.00541.x

Baronchelli, G., Bettinelli, C., Del Bosco, B., & Loane, S. (2016). The impact of family involvement on the investments of Italian small-medium enterprises in psychically distant countries. *International Business Review, 25*(4), 960–970. doi:10.1016/j.ibusrev.2016.01.011

Basco, R. (2015). Family business and regional development-A theoretical model of regional familiness. *Journal of Family Business Strategy, 6*(4), 259–271. doi:10.1016/j.jfbs.2015.04.004

Basly, S. (2007). The internationalization of family sme an organizational learning and knowledge development perspective. *Baltic Journal of Management, 2*(2), 154–180. doi:10.1108/17465260710750973

Basly, S., & Saunier, P. L. (2020). Familiness, socio-emotional goals and the internationalization of French family SMEs. *Journal of International Entrepreneurship, 18*(3), 270–311. doi:10.100710843-019-00265-0

Bell, J., McNaughton, R., Young, S., & Crick, D. (2003). Towards an Integrative Model of Small Firm Internationalisation. *Journal of International Entrepreneurship, 1*(4), 339–362. doi:10.1023/A:1025629424041

Bika, Z., & Kalantaridis, C. (2019). Organizational-Social-Capital, Time and International Family SMEs: An Empirical Study from the East of England. European Management Review, Boellis, A., Mariotti, S., Minichilli, A., & Piscitello, L. (2016). Family involvement and firms' establishment mode choice in foreign markets. *Journal of International Business Studies, 47*(8), 929–950.

Bužavaitė, M., Ščeulovs, D., & Korsakienė, R. (2019). Theoretical approach to the internationalization of SMEs: Future research prospects based on bibliometric analysis. *Entrepreneurship and Sustainability Issues, 6*(3), 1497–1511. doi:10.9770/jesi.2019.6.3(31)

Calabrò, A., Brogi, M., & Torchia, M. (2016). What Does Really Matter in the Internationalization of Small and Medium-Sized Family Businesses? *Journal of Small Business Management, 54*(2), 679–696. doi:10.1111/jsbm.12165

Calabrò, A., & Mussolino, D. (2012). How Do Boards of Directors Contribute to Family SME Export Intensity? The Role of Formal and Informal Governance Mechanisms. SSRN *Electronic Journal.*

Calabrò, A., Torchia, M., Pukall, T., & Mussolino, D. (2013). The influence of ownership structure and board strategic involvement on international sales: The moderating effect of family involvement. *International Business Review, 22*(3), 509–523. doi:10.1016/j.ibusrev.2012.07.002

Calabrò, A., Vecchiarini, M., Gast, J., Campopiano, G., De Massis, A., & Kraus, S. (2019). Innovation in Family Firms: A Systematic Literature Review and Guidance for Future Research. *International Journal of Management Reviews*, *21*(3), 317–355. doi:10.1111/ijmr.12192

Canabal, A., & White, G. O. III. (2008). Entry mode research: Past and future. *International Business Review*, *17*(3), 267–284. doi:10.1016/j.ibusrev.2008.01.003

Carney, M., Duran, P., van Essen, M., & Shapiro, D. (2017). Family firms, internationalization, and national competitiveness: Does family firm prevalence matter? *Journal of Family Business Strategy*, *8*(3), 123–136. doi:10.1016/j.jfbs.2017.06.001

Casillas, J. C., & Acedo, F. J. (2005). Internationalisation of Spanish family SMEs: An analysis of family involvement. *International Journal of Globalisation and Small Business*, *1*(2), 134–151. doi:10.1504/IJGSB.2005.008010

Cerrato, D., & Piva, M. (2012). The internationalization of small and medium-sized enterprises: The effect of family management, human capital and foreign ownership. *The Journal of Management and Governance*, *16*(4), 617–644. doi:10.100710997-010-9166-x

Chong, P. L., Onga, T. S., Abdullah, A., & Choo, W. C. (2019). Internationalisation and innovation on balanced scorecard (BSC) among Malaysian small and medium enterprises (SMEs). *Management Science Letters*, *9*(10), 1617–1632. doi:10.5267/j.msl.2019.5.025

Claver, E., Rienda, L., & Quer, D. (2007). The internationalisation process in family firms: Choice of market entry strategies. *Journal of General Management*, *33*(1), 1–14. doi:10.1177/030630700703300101

Claver, E., Rienda, L., & Quer, D. (2008). Family firms' risk perception: Empirical evidence on the internationalization process. *Journal of Small Business and Enterprise Development*, *15*(3), 457–471. doi:10.1108/14626000810892283

Claver, E., Rienda, L., & Quer, D. (2009). Family Firms' International Commitment: The Influence of Family-Related Factors. *Family Business Review*, *22*(2), 125–135. doi:10.1177/0894486508330054

Coleman, J. S. (2009). Social capital in the creation of human capital. *Knowledge and Social Capital,* 17–42.

Compagno, C., Pittino, D., & Visintin, F. (2005). Corporate governance and advanced forms of internationalisation in Italian SMEs. *International Journal of Globalisation and Small Business*, *1*(2), 168–182. doi:10.1504/IJGSB.2005.008012

Covin, J. G., & Slevin, D. P. (1989). Strategic management of small firms in hostile and benign environments. *Strategic Management Journal*, *10*(1), 75–87. doi:10.1002mj.4250100107

D'Angelo, A., Majocchi, A., & Buck, T. (2016). External managers, family ownership and the scope of SME internationalization. *Journal of World Business*, *51*(4), 534–547. doi:10.1016/j.jwb.2016.01.004

Daspit, J. J., Chrisman, J. J., Ashton, T., & Evangelopoulos, N. (2021). Family Firm Heterogeneity: A Definition, Common Themes, Scholarly Progress, and Directions Forward. *Family Business Review*. Advance online publication. doi:10.1177/08944865211008350

Davidkov, T. P., & Yordanova, D. I. (2016). Exploring the Bulgarian family SMEs' reluctance to internationalise. *International Journal of Business and Globalisation*, *17*(1), 123–148. doi:10.1504/IJBG.2016.077570

De Massis, A., Frattini, F., Majocchi, A., & Piscitello, L. (2018a). Family firms in the global economy: Toward a deeper understanding of internationalization determinants, processes, and outcomes. *Global Strategy Journal*, *8*(1), 3–21. doi:10.1002/gsj.1199

De Massis, A., Frattini, F., Majocchi, A., & Piscitello, L. (2018b). Family firms in the global economy: Toward a deeper understanding of internationalization determinants, processes, and outcomes. *Global Strategy Journal*, *8*(1), 3–21. doi:10.1002/gsj.1199

Denicolai, S., Hagen, B., & Pisoni, A. (2015). Be international or be innovative? Be both? The role of the entrepreneurial profile. *Journal of International Entrepreneurship*, *13*(4), 390–417. doi:10.100710843-015-0143-y

Dibrell, C., Davis, P. S., & Craig, J. (2008). Fueling innovation through information technology in SMEs. *Journal of Small Business Management*, *46*(2), 203–218. doi:10.1111/j.1540-627X.2008.00240.x

Ebeke, C., Jovanovic, N., Valderrama, L., & Zhou, J. (2021). Corporate Liquidity and Solvency in Europe during COVID-19. *IMF Working Papers, 21*(278).

Eberhard, M., & Craig, J. (2013). The evolving role of organisational and personal networks in international market venturing. *Journal of World Business*, *48*(3), 385–397. doi:10.1016/j.jwb.2012.07.022

Eddleston, K. A., Sarathy, R., & Banalieva, E. R. (2019). When a high-quality niche strategy is not enough to spur family-firm internationalization: The role of external and internal contexts. *Journal of International Business Studies*, *50*(5), 783–808. doi:10.105741267-018-0199-8

Fernandez, Z., & Nieto, M. J. (2005). Internationalization Strategy of Small and Medium-Sized Family Businesses. *Family Business Review*, *18*(1), 77–89. doi:10.1111/j.1741-6248.2005.00031.x

Fernández, Z., & Nieto, M. J. (2005). Internationalization strategy of small and medium-sized family businesses: Some influential factors. *Family Business Review*, *18*(1), 77–89. doi:10.1111/j.1741-6248.2005.00031.x

Fernández, Z., & Nieto, M. J. (2005). Internationalization strategy of small and medium-sized family businesses: Some influential factors. *Family Business Review*, *18*(1), 77–89. doi:10.1111/j.1741-6248.2005.00031.x

Fernández-Olmos, M., Gargallo-Castel, A., & Giner-Bagües, E. (2016). Internationalisation and performance in Spanish family SMES: The W-curve. *BRQ Business Research Quarterly*, *19*(2), 122–136. doi:10.1016/j.brq.2015.07.001

Fillis, I. (2001). Small firm internationalisation: An investigative survey and future research directions. *Management Decision*, *39*(9), 767–783. doi:10.1108/00251740110408683

Gallo, M. A., & Sveen, J. (1991). Internationalizing the Family Business: Facilitating and Restraining Factors. *Family Business Review*, *4*(2), 181–190. doi:10.1111/j.1741-6248.1991.00181.x

Game, R., & Apfelthaler, G. (2016). Attitude and its role in SME internationalisation: Why do firms commit to advanced foreign market entry modes? *European Journal of International Management, 10*(2), 221–248. doi:10.1504/EJIM.2016.074473

George, G., Wiklund, J., & Zahra, S. A. (2005). Ownership and the internationalization of small firms. *Journal of Management, 31*(2), 210–233. doi:10.1177/0149206304271760

Gomez-Mejia, L. R., Cruz, C., Berrone, P., & de Castro, J. (2011). The Bind that ties: Socioemotional wealth preservation in family firms. *The Academy of Management Annals, 5*(1), 653–707. doi:10.5465/19416520.2011.593320

Gómez-Mejía, L. R., Haynes, K. T., Núñez-Nickel, M., Jacobson, K. J. L., & Moyano-Fuentes, J. (2007). Socioemotional Wealth and Business Risks in Family-controlled Firms: Evidence from Spanish Olive Oil Mills. *Administrative Science Quarterly, 52*(1), 106–137. doi:10.2189/asqu.52.1.106

Gomez-Mejia, L. R., Makri, M., & Kintana, M. L. (2010). Diversification decisions in family-controlled firms. *Journal of Management Studies, 47*(2), 223–252. doi:10.1111/j.1467-6486.2009.00889.x

Gough, D., Thomas, J., & Oliver, S. (2012). Clarifying differences between review designs and methods. *Systematic Reviews, 1*(1), 28. doi:10.1186/2046-4053-1-28 PMID:22681772

Grandon, E. E., & Pearson, J. M. (2004). Electronic commerce adoption: An empirical study of small and medium US businesses. *Information & Management, 42*(1), 197–216. doi:10.1016/j.im.2003.12.010

Graves, C., & Shan, Y. G. (2014). An Empirical Analysis of the Effect of Internationalization on the Performance of Unlisted Family and Nonfamily Firms in Australia. *Family Business Review, 27*(2), 142–160. doi:10.1177/0894486513491588

Graves, C., & Thomas, J. (2006). Internationalization of Australian family businesses: A managerial capabilities perspective. *Family Business Review, 19*(3), 207–224. doi:10.1111/j.1741-6248.2006.00066.x

Graves, C., & Thomas, J. (2008). Determinants of the internationalization pathways of family firms: An examination of family influence. *Family Business Review, 21*(2), 151–167. doi:10.1111/j.1741-6248.2008.00119.x

Hennart, J. F., Majocchi, A., & Forlani, E. (2019). The myth of the stay-at-home family firm: How family-managed SMEs can overcome their internationalization limitations. *Journal of International Business Studies, 50*(5), 758–782. doi:10.105741267-017-0091-y

Huse, M. (2000). Boards of directors in smes: A review and research agenda. *Entrepreneurship and Regional Development, 12*(4), 271–290. doi:10.1080/08985620050177912

Idris, B., & Saridakis, G. (2018). Local formal interpersonal networks and SMEs internationalisation: Empirical evidence from the UK. *International Business Review, 27*(3), 610–624. doi:10.1016/j.ibusrev.2017.10.010

Jeong, S. W. (2016). Types of foreign networks and internationalization performance of Korean SMEs. *Multinational Business Review, 24*(1), 47–61. doi:10.1108/MBR-08-2015-0039

Johanson, J., & Vahlne, J.-E. (1977). The internationalization process of the firm - a model of knowledge development and increasing foreign market commitments. *Journal of International Business Studies, 8*(1), 23–32. doi:10.1057/palgrave.jibs.8490676

Jorge, M., Couto, M., Veloso, T., & Franco, M. (2017). When family businesses go international: Management sets the path. *The Journal of Business Strategy, 38*(1), 31–38. doi:10.1108/JBS-01-2016-0006

Kansikas, J., Huovinen, J., & Hyrsky, K. (2014). Family firm prerequisites for international business operations: A production and marketing capabilities Approach. *World Review of Entrepreneurship, Management and Sustainable Development, 10*(4), 435–448. doi:10.1504/WREMSD.2014.064949

Kathleen, R. (1991). A Historical Comparison of Resource-Based Theory and Five Schools of Thought Within Industrial Organization Economics: Do We Have a New Theory of the Firm. *Journal of Management, 17*(1), 121–154. doi:10.1177/014920639101700109

Kolarov, K., & Georgieva, S. (2020). Management features in bulgarian smes as determinants of business internationalization. *Polish Journal of Management Studies, 22*(1), 279–294. doi:10.17512/pjms.2020.22.1.18

Kontinen, T., & Ojala, A. (2010a). Internationalization pathways of family SMEs: Psychic distance as a focal point. *Journal of Small Business and Enterprise Development, 17*(3), 437–454. doi:10.1108/14626001011068725

Kontinen, T., & Ojala, A. (2010b). The internationalization of family businesses: A review of extant research. *Journal of Family Business Strategy, 1*(2), 97–107. doi:10.1016/j.jfbs.2010.04.001

Kontinen, T., & Ojala, A. (2011a). International Opportunity Recognition among Small and Medium-Sized Family Firms. *Journal of Small Business Management, 49*(3), 490–514. doi:10.1111/j.1540-627X.2011.00326.x

Kontinen, T., & Ojala, A. (2011b). Network ties in the international opportunity recognition of family SMEs. *International Business Review, 20*(4), 440–453. doi:10.1016/j.ibusrev.2010.08.002

Kontinen, T., & Ojala, A. (2011c). Social capital in relation to the foreign market entry and post-entry operations of family SMEs. *Journal of International Entrepreneurship, 9*(2), 133–151. doi:10.100710843-010-0072-8

Kontinen, T., & Ojala, A. (2012). Social capital in the international operations of family SMEs. *Journal of Small Business and Enterprise Development, 19*(1), 39–55. doi:10.1108/14626001211196398

Kraus, S., Mensching, H., Calabrò, A., Cheng, C. F., & Filser, M. (2016). Family firm internationalization: A configurational approach. *Journal of Business Research, 69*(11), 5473–5478. doi:10.1016/j.jbusres.2016.04.158

Kuivalainen, O., Sundqvist, S., Saarenketo, S., McNaughton, R. B., D'Angelo, A., Buck, T., Majocchi, A., & Zucchella, A. (2013). Geographical pathways for SME internationalization: Insights from an Italian sample. *International Marketing Review, 30*(2), 80–105. doi:10.1108/02651331311314538

Kunday, Ö., & Şengüler, E. P. (2015). A Study on Factors Affecting the Internationalization Process of Small and Medium Enterprises (SMEs). *Procedia: Social and Behavioral Sciences, 195*, 972–981. doi:10.1016/j.sbspro.2015.06.363

Kuratko, D. F., Morris, M. H., & Covin, J. G. (2015). Corporate Entrepreneurship. Wiley Encyclopedia of Management, 1–5.

La Porta, R., Lopez-de-Silanes, F., & Shleifer, A. (1999). Corporate ownership around the world. *The Journal of Finance, 54*(2), 471–517. doi:10.1111/0022-1082.00115

Lahiri, S., Mukherjee, D., & Peng, M. W. (2020). Behind the internationalization of family SMEs: A strategy tripod synthesis. *Global Strategy Journal, 10*(4), 813–838. doi:10.1002/gsj.1376

Lim, E. N. K., Lubatkin, M. H., & Wiseman, R. M. (2010). A family firm variant of the behavioral agency theory. *Strategic Entrepreneurship Journal, 4*(3), 197–211. doi:10.1002ej.91

Lubatkin, M. H., Simsek, Z., Ling, Y., & Veiga, J. F. (2006). Ambidexterity and performance in small- to medium-sized firms: The pivotal role of top management team behavioral integration. *Journal of Management, 32*(5), 646–672. doi:10.1177/0149206306290712

Majocchi, A., D'Angelo, A., Forlani, E., & Buck, T. (2018). Bifurcation bias and exporting: Can foreign work experience be an answer? Insight from European family SMEs. *Journal of World Business, 53*(2), 237–247. doi:10.1016/j.jwb.2017.11.005

McDougall, P. P., & Oviatt, B. M. (1996). New venture internationalization, strategic change, and performance: A follow-up study. *Journal of Business Venturing, 11*(1), 23–40. doi:10.1016/0883-9026(95)00081-X

Merino, F., Monreal-Pérez, J., & Sánchez-Marín, G. (2015). Family SMEs' Internationalization: Disentangling the Influence of Familiness on Spanish Firms' Export Activity. *Journal of Small Business Management, 53*(4), 1164–1184. doi:10.1111/jsbm.12111

Miller, D. (1983). The Correlates of Entrepreneurship in Three Types of Firms. *Management Science, 29*(7), 770–791. doi:10.1287/mnsc.29.7.770

Miller, D., & Le Breton-Miller, I. (2014). Deconstructing socioemotional wealth. *Entrepreneurship Theory and Practice, 38*(4), 713–720. doi:10.1111/etap.12111

Minichilli, A., Corbetta, G., & MacMillan, I. C. (2010). Top management teams in family-controlled companies: "Familiness", "faultlines", and their impact on financial performance. *Journal of Management Studies, 47*(2), 205–222. doi:10.1111/j.1467-6486.2009.00888.x

Mitter, C., & Emprechtinger, S. (2016). The role of stewardship in the internationalisation of family firms. *International Journal of Entrepreneurial Venturing, 8*(4), 400. doi:10.1504/IJEV.2016.082220

Mort, G. S., & Weerawardena, J. (2006). Networking capability and international entrepreneurship: How networks function in Australian born global firms. *International Marketing Review, 23*(5), 549–572. doi:10.1108/02651330610703445

Nieto, M. J., & Fernandez, Z. (2012). Impact of Ownership on the international involvement of SMEs. *International Business, 37*(3), 340–351.

Olejnik, E., & Swoboda, B. (2012). SMEs' internationalisation patterns: Descriptives, dynamics and determinants. *International Marketing Review, 29*(5), 466–495. doi:10.1108/02651331211260340

Ortiz, R. F., Ortiz, J. A., & Ramírez, A. M. (2012). How Does Management Perceive Exporting? An Empirical Study of SMEs. *The Engineering Economist, 23*(2).

Peng, M. W., Wang, D. Y. L., & Jiang, Y. (2008). An institution-based view of international business strategy: A focus on emerging economies. *Journal of International Business Studies, 39*(5), 920–936. doi:10.1057/palgrave.jibs.8400377

Petrů, N., Tomášková, A., & Krošláková, M. (2019). Diversification of export territories of family businesses as a tool of their further development. *Problems and Perspectives in Management, 17*(3), 306–322. doi:10.21511/ppm.17(3).2019.25

Pukall, T. J., & Calabrò, A. (2014). The Internationalization of Family Firms: A Critical Review and Integrative Model. *Family Business Review, 27*(2), 103–125. doi:10.1177/0894486513491423

Rasheed, H. S. (2009). Contrasting E-commerce business models: Performance implications for small enterprises. *Journal of Developmental Entrepreneurship, 14*(1), 89–101. doi:10.1142/S1084946709001168

Ray, S., Mondal, A., & Ramachandran, K. (2018). How does family involvement affect a firm's internationalization? An investigation of Indian family firms. *Global Strategy Journal, 8*(1), 73–105. doi:10.1002/gsj.1196

Rodrigues, S. B., & Child, J. (2012). Building social capital for internationalization. *Revista de Administração Contemporânea, 16*(1), 23–38. doi:10.1590/S1415-65552012000100003

Saarenketo, S., Puumalainen, K., Kuivalainen, O., & Kyläheiko, K. (2004). Dynamic knowledge-related learning processes in internationalizing high-tech SMEs. *International Journal of Production Economics, 89*(3), 363–378. doi:10.1016/S0925-5273(03)00185-3

Scholes, L., Mustafa, M., & Chen, S. (2016). Internationalization of Small Family Firms: The Influence of Family from a Socioemotional Wealth Perspective. *Thunderbird International Business Review, 58*(2), 131–146. doi:10.1002/tie.21729

Sciascia, S., Mazzola, P., Astrachan, J. H., & Pieper, T. M. (2012). The role of family ownership in international entrepreneurship: Exploring nonlinear effects. *Small Business Economics, 38*(1), 15–31. doi:10.100711187-010-9264-9

Segaro, E. (2010). Internationalization of family SMEs: The impact of ownership, governance, and top management team. *5th International Institute of Statistics and Management Engineering Symposium 2012: Data-Driven Management Science under Developing, IISMES 2012*, 29–32.

Segaro, E. L., Larimo, J., & Jones, M. V. (2014). Internationalisation of family small and medium sized enterprises: The role of stewardship orientation, family commitment culture and top management team. *International Business Review, 23*(2), 381–395. doi:10.1016/j.ibusrev.2013.06.004

Sharma, P., Chrisman, J. J., & Chua, J. H. (1999). Defining the Family Business by Behavior. *Entrepreneurship Theory and Practice*, *23*(4), 19–39. doi:10.1177/104225879902300402

Sharma, V. M., & Erramilli, M. K. (2004). Resource-Based Explanation of Entry Mode Choice. *Journal of Marketing Theory and Practice*, *12*(1), 1–18. doi:10.1080/10696679.2004.11658509

Shleifer, A., & Vishny, R. W. (1997). A survey of corporate governance. *The Journal of Finance*, *52*(2), 737–783. doi:10.1111/j.1540-6261.1997.tb04820.x

Sirmon, D. G., & Hitt, M. A. (2003). Managing Resources: Linking Unique Resources, Management, and Wealth Creation in Family Firms. *Entrepreneurship Theory and Practice*, *27*(4), 339–358. doi:10.1111/1540-8520.t01-1-00013

Tanev, S. (2012). Global from the Start: The Characteristics of Born-Global Firms in the Technology Sector. *Technology Innovation Management Review*, *2*(3), 5–8. doi:10.22215/timreview/532

Tranfield, D., & Denyer, D. (2009). Producing a systematic review. The Sage Handbook of Organizational Research Methods, 672–688.

Tranfield, D., Denyer, D., & Smart, P. (2003). Towards a Methodology for Developing Evidence-Informed Management Knowledge by Means of Systematic Review. *British Journal of Management*, *14*(3), 207–222. doi:10.1111/1467-8551.00375

UNCTAD. (2021). *How COVID-19 triggered the digital and e-commerce turning point*. UNCTAD.

Westhead, P. (2008). International opportunity exploitation behaviour reported by "types" of firms relating to exporting experience. *Journal of Small Business and Enterprise Development*, *15*(3), 431–456. doi:10.1108/14626000810892274

Wright, M., Westhead, P., & Ucbasaran, D. (2007). Internationalization of small and medium-sized enterprises (SMEs) and international entrepreneurship: A critique and policy implications. *Regional Studies*, *41*(7), 1013–1030. doi:10.1080/00343400601120288

Yang, X., Li, J., Stanley, L. J., Kellermanns, F. W., & Li, X. (2020). How family firm characteristics affect internationalization of Chinese family SMEs. *Asia Pacific Journal of Management*, *37*(2), 417–448. doi:10.100710490-018-9579-7

Zahra, S. A. (2003). International expansion of U.S. manufacturing family businesses: The effect of ownership and involvement. *Journal of Business Venturing*, *18*(4), 495–512. doi:10.1016/S0883-9026(03)00057-0

Zahra, S. A. (2005). Entrepreneurial risk taking in family firms. *Family Business Review*, *18*(1), 23–40. doi:10.1111/j.1741-6248.2005.00028.x

Zapletalová, Š. (2017). International management of Czech family enterprises: Decisions on international entrepreneurial activities. *Central European Business Review*, *6*(3), 51–61. doi:10.18267/j.cebr.186

Zucchella, A., Palamara, G., & Denicolai, S. (2007). The drivers of the early internationalization of the firm. *Journal of World Business*, *42*(3), 268–280. doi:10.1016/j.jwb.2007.04.008

Chapter 10
The Impact of COVID-19:
A Major Crisis or Just Another One?

Marcelo Amaral Dionisio
https://orcid.org/0000-0001-6346-2307
Coppead Business School, Brazil

EXECUTIVE SUMMARY

The COVID-19 pandemic has had a devastating and immediate effect on all economies, impacting in the lifestyles and livelihoods of people around the world. There are strong concerns about how the crisis will affect SMEs that represent over 90% of all firms worldwide. In emerging countries, SMEs already operate in challenging contexts characterized by institutional voids and scarce resource environments where entrepreneurs need to continuously develop strategies to survive. The purpose of this study is to examine the role of resources in a single case of a Brazilian SME and its strategies to survive the impact of the COVID-19 crisis. The study applies the resource-based view (RBV) to understand how the type and nature of resources influence the activities pursued by this SME and relate the crisis with their usual challenges. Findings highlight the important role of different key resources in the survival, growth, and sustainability of SMEs, along with the need of institutional conditions to support and foster entrepreneurship.

1. INTRODUCTION

The COVID-19 pandemic has had a devastating and immediate effect on all economies, impacting in the lifestyles, relationships and livelihoods of people all around the world, with a sudden and violent impact that has resulted in widespread illness, death, and the rapid contraction of global economies due to lockdown measures and health protocols that interrupted supply chains and kept business closed. There are strong concerns about how the COVID-19 crisis will affect SMEs that represent over 90% of all firms worldwide, making them the backbone of the world's economy in both the formal and the informal business sectors (Alvarez, Urbano, Coduras, & Ruiz-Navarro, 2011; Eggers, 2020; Weaven et al., 2021a). As SMEs already operate in challenging contexts in emerging countries, characterized by

DOI: 10.4018/978-1-7998-7657-1.ch010

institutional voids and scarce resource environments where entrepreneurs need to continuously develop strategies to survive (Caballero-Morales, 2021; Mair & Marti, 2009; Rocha & Andreassi, 2020; The World Bank Group, 2020), the purpose of this study is to examine the role of resources in a Brazilian SME and its strategies to survive in such challeging environment, comparing it with the impacts of the COVID-19 crisis.

To successfully survive in such markets and their challenging situations, SMEs must leverage their resource-base (RBV) by combining different types of social, human and financial resources in order to create social and economic value (Zahra et al., 2009). This requires crucial managerial capabilities and creativity to successfully attract resources and accomplish their mission (Bacq & Eddleston, 2018; Desa & Basu, 2013; Zahra et al., 2009), so our study attempts to address the following research questions: *1) What is the influence of key SMEs' resources on the business survival in challenging environments?, and 2) How strong was the impact of COVID-19 crisis compared to the existing challenges?*

By providing answers to these research questions, the present study seeks to examine which resources and capabilities are relevant to the strategic process of SMEs, applying the resource-based view (RBV) to explain how the type and nature of resources are pertinent to explain the activities and strategies pursued by an SME. This is relevant, specially considering that in emerging economies from Latin America, these kind of businesses are largely family-owned, commonly dealing with a large economic burden and uncertainty, in a scenario where is crucial to gather most of the knowledge regarding business management, strategic planning and innovation, to formulate alternatives to reinforce their business models for different markets and restrictions (Caballero-Morales, 2021). The methodological approach focus on a single case study of a Brazilian SME, a beauty salon, one of the segments most severely impacted by the COVID-19 crisis, where a study by Sebrae found out that 62% of activities related to beauty have been temporarily closed, and sales have decreased by an average of 50% (Ionescu-Somers & Tarnawa, 2020; Sebrae, 2021). We followed a qualitative approach and conducted several in-depth interviews with the founder and key manager of the SME, gathering information that covers the whole story of the business that was opened in 2006.

The study findings provide relevant insights regarding the role of key resources-based factors in SME's performance, contributing to enlighten the role of these resources *vis-a-vis* institutional voids and crisis, leading to more effective processes of the development of strategies in SMEs.

2.THEORETICAL FRAMEWORK

2.1 A brief Summary of COVID-19 Crisis in Brazil

On February 26th, 2020 the first COVID-19 case was confirmed in Brazil. In the beginning of March the first internal transmission was registered and on March 11th, the World Health Organization declared the coronavirus pandemic, estimating that the numbers of infected people, deaths and countries affected should increase in the following weeks. By this time there were 52 confirmed cases along with 907 suspected cases in 8 states (out of 27). On March 27th the first Covid fatality was registered and by April all states registered cases (Sanar_Saúde, 2020).

With the growth of cases, states began to declare "state of emergency" and to implement measures to contain the spread of the virus such as various types of closing non-essential activities, use of WHO's protocol (mask, social distancing, etc.), along with restrictions on the entry of foreigners. In the first six months of the pandemic, the federal government spent aproximately US$ 1 Bi in various measures to support states and on April started to distribute an individual aid of US$ 840 divided in 9 stallments, that cost a total of US$ 60 billion and reached almost 68 million people (Sanar_Saúde, 2020; Trisotto, 2021). Nevertheless a highly politized debate, a lack of leadership from the federal government leading to high levels of instability, worsened by the change of four Health Ministers during the first year of pandemic, placed Brazil in the world top list of both cases and casualties, reaching on May 2021, 16 MM cases and 461k fatalities (total population of 210 MM people). On January 17th, 2021 the country started the vaccination and as of 28 May 2021, a total of 60.017.445 vaccine doses have been administered (Https://covid19.who.int/, 2021; Sanar_Saúde, 2020).

The coronavirus pandemic changed the functioning of 5.3 million SMEs in Brazil, an equivalent of 31% of the total. Another 10.1 million, or 58.9%, temporarily stopped activities, according to a survey carried out by Sebrae. The survey also revealed that the financial situation of most companies (73.4%) was already bad before the Covid-19 crisis, and as personnel costs appear among the main expenses of most companies (57.1%), SME's had to make layoffs to maintain business. On average, they laid off three employees (SMEs have from 10 to 49 employees) after the crisis began (Sebrae, 2020).

2.2 Overview of Entrepreneurship and SMEs in Brazil

The entrepreneurial activity is one of the main factors responsible for the increase of the Brazilian income level in the last years. There are 6.4 million SMEs, where 99% are micro and small companies, accounting for 52% of formal jobs in the private sector in a total of 16.1 million positions (Rocha & Andreassi, 2020; Sebrae, 2021), The Global Entrepreneurship Monitor (GEM), the world's largest study of entrepreneurship, defines an entrepreneur as someone who takes the decision to start a business influenced by a host of personal factors such as individual ambitions and personal objectives, along with the ability to spot opportunities (GEM, 2021), at the same time that entrepreneurial ecosystem is defined as a group of variables that affect entrepreneurial activities' development. Those variables are public policy and leadership, financial resources, culture, human capital, and a variety of institutional support and infrastructure conditions (Isenberg, 2011; Rocha & Andreassi, 2020). In this sense although entrepreneurs in Brazil share the same characteristics and motivations as their counterparts in other markets, and entrepreneurship strongly impacts the economy, the Brazilian ecosystem presents challenges that makes entrepreneurship a lot harder than in any other countries.

Brazil does very well on a few Entrepreneurial Framework Conditions (EFCs) compared to both its Latin American and middle-income peers, and the business mortality rate of SMEs is aligned with more developed markets at 30% closing before completing two years in the market (Afonso, 2019; GEM, 2021; Ionescu-Somers & Tarnawa, 2020; McIntyre, 2020). But concerning the decision of starting a business, more than a vision of a new product or service, in Brazil this decision is often taken out of necessity, most of the time, because of the high levels of unemployment, as according to the last GEM report Brazil is ranked 9/43 on the entrepreneurial motivation - "To earn a living because jobs are scarce" (Afonso, 2019; GEM, 2021). Concerning the entrepreneurial ecosystem, this is where Brazil offers the greatest challenges. According to GEM, Brazil's score on taxes and bureaucracy is quite low (1.9), being one of the lowest of all surveyed countries. This is one of the reasons why the World Bank puts it in a lower tier in its Doing Business report, despite the huge domestic opportunity the country offers. In 2020's report, Brazil ranks 124, lower than all of the other BRICS countries (Russia, India, China and South

Africa), and below Colombia, Mexico, Peru, Chile and Uruguay in Latin America (GEM, 2021; The World Bank Group, 2020).

A survey conducted by Endeavor with more than 1,000 entrepreneurs identified the top five challenges for entrepreneurship in Brazil as being: human capital, access to capital, regularory framework, innovation and market conditions. It is a scenario where it is difficult to find qualified personel, expensive to hire due to and old and paternalistic legislation, capital is scarce and expensive, taxes are high and complicated, there is low availability of capital to invest and innovate in a market where is expensive, difficult and unstable, not allowing entrepreneurs to invest in long term strategies (Endeavor Brasil, 2016; Rocha & Andreassi, 2020).

2.3 A Resource-Based View (RBV) of SMEs

The resource-based view (RBV) focuses on the internal management of a company and highlights organizational resources and capabilities that firms can use to create and maintain a competitive advantage (Barney, 2001; Porter, 1979; Weaven et al., 2021b). This theoretical framework is considered ''perhaps the most influential framework for understanding strategic management'' (Barney, Jay, 2001; p.625). RBV explains how firms maintain their competitive advantage through resources and capabilities that can be viewed as tangible or intangible assets, including a firm's management skills, and its organisational processes and routines (Barney, Wright, & Ketchen, 2001). Given their diversity, not all firm resources hold the potential to sustain competitive advantages, and to do so, they must focus on four attributes: 1) it must be valuable; 2) rare; 3) imperfectly imitable; and 4) able to be exploited by a firm's organisational processes. Based on the resource-based view, a firm is considered to have a sustainable competitive advantage when it is creating more economic value than the marginal firm in its industry and when other firms are unable to duplicate the benefits of this strategy, in the case of SMEs one must consider that individual characteristics of SME owners play a pivotal role in firm growth and sustainability (Barney & Clark, 2007; Weaven et al., 2021b).

There are previous examples of adopting a resource-based view to understand SME survival and successful business continuity in times of economic uncertainty (Weaven et al., 2021b), so this study contributes to the literature on SMEs, crisis management and RBV, to both researchers and practitioner communities.

2.4 Conceptual Propositions

This study utilises the RBV approach focusing on four resources: human capital, management know-how, industry-specific know-how and capability of the founder to obtain financial resources in accordance with Westhead, Wright, & Ucbasaran (2001).

2.4.1 Human Capital

According to Westhead et al. (2001), entrepreneurs with more diverse levels of human capital are purported to have the ability to develop relevant skills, experiences, and competencies, generally regarded as key factors influencing business survival and development. According to Estrin, Mickiewicz, & Stephan (2016) human capital has positive effects on both entrepreneurial entry and performance because it enables individuals to integrate new knowledge and adapt to new situations more easily, enhancing the individual's ability to discover and exploit opportunities. This human capital refers to experience and skills associated with the necessity for the entrepreneur to identify business opportunities, to bear the risks involved in new venture creation, and to identify and organise the resources necessary for success, without considering the effect of formal education, that some studies find no relationship with business success.

2.4.2 Management and Experiential Know-How

Management know-how may assist entrepreneurs to undertake more promising competitive strategies, and identify better market opportunities (Westhead et al., 2001). Management know-how, is a form of capital representing the noneconomic knowledge that has a direct impact on individual economic behavior, that can be accumulated by founders based on their backgrounds and former professional experience, to be better prepared to face market opportunities. Knowledge based on personal experience is considered one of the most important predictors of entrepreneurial success, allowing the entrepreneur to be innovative and trigger new ideas, that emerge from their environment (Staniewski, 2016).

2.4.3 Industry-Specific Know-How

Experience in a particular industry provides the founder of businesses specific know-how with customers, suppliers, or stakeholders in general (Westhead et al., 2001). The knowledge of a competitive environment increases the possibility that organisations located in particular industries adopt generic business models that are similar in the way they configure components such as innovation, core competitive strengths, key network connections, among others (Child et al., 2017).

2.4.4 Ability to Acquire Financial Capital

Many SMEs struggle to achieve organizational sustainability. In such a competitive enviroment, the acquisition of resources and the development of capabilities to achieve social goals allow SMEs to pursue a broader range of activities and projects (Bacq & Eddleston, 2018; Westhead et al., 2001). A founder's ability to obtain financial resources can work as a buffer against random crisis while an over-reliance on personal savings can reduce the survival chance of a new venture. Additionally, the availability of capital allows entrepreneurs to overcome problems and pursue a broader range of activities and more ambitious projects, to invest in existing markets as well as enter new markets for the first time (Westhead et al., 2001).

Considering the above discussion, the following propositions are put forward:

P1: Founders with high levels of human capital are more prone to adapt to new situations, discovering and exploiting opportunities.

P2: Founders who hold high management know-how tend to be more creative and better define strategies for long-term survival.

P3: Founders evidencing high industry-specific know-how are more likely to overcome crisis and survive in the long term.

P4: Higher ability to acquire financial capital is more likely to lead SMEs to grow and succeed.

3. RESEARCH METHOD AND CASE STUDY

The study reports the findings of a Brazilian SME, a beauty salon opened in 2006, that has survived through not only a challenging institutional environment, but through a series of economic crisis. The rationale for studying a single case, in which data from one instance is enough to achieve the research objective, is based on the idea that it is a good alternative research strategy and carries more weight than multiple cases (Dul & Hak, 2008; Gerring, 2006).

The research is based on semi-structured interviews with the founder and manager of the SME. Interviews were registered and transcribed. In total, there were 3 interviews with an average of one hour each, a visit to the store and a brief talk with employees. Next a brief story and main facts about the case.

3.2 Case Study: Sttylo Beauty Sallon

The first Sttylo was opened in 2006 as a family business. A joint decision from former beauty professionals to join resources and start their own business, supplying all sorts of beauty services: unissex haircare, manicure, pedicure, facial treatments, etc., which proved successful as the initiative became a hit from the start. Gilmara was the leader and manager of the business, despite her lack of formal business background. The remaining partners split their skills working on the operational side of the venture. The capital to setup the business was fully based on personal savings from each of the partner families (a total of three families of 2 sisters and one cousin). Despite the financial sacrifices to startup the business the initial years of operation were fully focused on work, with total commitment and alignment among the partners.

The success of the venture started to take its toll in the first renewal of the rent contract of the premises. A lack of a clear regulation allowed the owner to increase rent beyond official indexes and to also charge a renovation fee, that is not legal, but was accepted due to the success they were facing, along with the lack of experience to deal with this kind of situations. In 2016 with the second contract renewal (every five years), Gilmara started to aim at another store to avoid another abusive rent increase, considering that they would be able to keep their clientele. In 2017 a next door store became vacant, what led them to immediatelly rent it, initially to move the business to a cheaper point of sale. Instead the family decided to keep both stores open in order to grow the business, what caused the first rupture in the partnership. In 2018, because of the existing disagreement among partners and difficulties with the economic crisis that reduced the costumers along with the increased costs of two points of sale that reduced margins, Gilmara decided to open a third store, in the same mall. This decision was not taken well by the rest of the family, but she opened it nonetheless, on her own. After one year, her new store became also a success, while the existing business missed her leadership and managemnt and turned to a loss, needing to incur in bank credit to keep functioning. Out of guilt, Gilmara covered some of their losses for one year but the personal pressure was too much and in 2019 she ended her partnership with her family. She left the partnership without a single dime.

Once again Gilmara used her savings to invest and maintain her new venture. She felt the burden of managing a new business on her own and suffered some drawbacks imposed by the environment of heavy taxes and bureaucracy. She also lost three professionals, which are key for the success of this kind of business, to her family's store, that did not accepted her success. Nevertheless she was one more time able to pull it out and succeed in her new venture.

In 2020 she had to face the COVID-19 crisis, that initially made her close her business for 4 months. Despite the initial shock with the new reality, her experience from the last years gave her some resolve and allowed her to successfully drive through this another crisis. She came up with two creative initiatives to keep her revenues flowing, she right away started to answer in-house calls and started to sell vouchers for future use. She also sold whatever personal belongings she could (car, furniture, computers, etc.) for cash and bought it back on credit. This revenue was used to refurbish her salon following sanitary protocols, so when she re-opened the premises, her salon was ahead of the competition what gave her a competitve advantage and renewed her clientele, increased by word of mouth, a recent implemented social media communication (Facebook, WhatsApp and Instagram) and full commitment of her employees, that she was able to keep during this crisis. Even though the crisis is not yet finished and she still not back to her revenues previous covid, her business is stable, with positive perspectives for the remaning of 2021. For the moment she is not planning any expansion, but she used this past months to learn new technics and is planning to offer higher added value services with the support of a closed tight team.

5. FINDINGS AND DISCUSSION

This case evidences the hardship faced by entrepreneurs, in a path filled with challenges and personal sacrifices. Consistent with previous research, our results confirm that the individual characteristics of SME owners play a crucial role in firm growth and sustainability, and that to survive an economic downturn the most important characteristic of an SME owner is the positive attitude they brought to bear on problems within their business (Weaven et al., 2021a). In line with Westhead et al. (2001) four resources are examined: general human capital, management know-how, specific industry know-how and the ability to acquire financial capital. Our main objective was to analyze each resource aiming to identify their influence on the business survival in challenging environments, and compare these impacts with the effect of the current COVID-19 crisis. We focused on the role of the founder and leader of the business to establish how high levels of human capital influence in the adaptation to new situations and discovery of opportunities, how management and industry-specific know-how affect the likelihood of creativity, better strategies and survival in the long term, and finally to establish the impact of a higher ability to acquire financial capital to lead to SME's growth and success.

The analysis of each resource provided valuable insights of the management, challenges and performance faced by a SME in a challenging environment, reinforcing the role of RBV in the evaluation of businesses' strategies. Considering each resource in our analysis, we observed that human capital can be considered a key element in the success of SMEs, where the role of the founder was crucial for the accomplishment of the organisation's implementation, success and growth, despite the lack of formal education and business expertise, aligned with Barney & Clark (2007), who claim that the unique circumstances of a firm's founding, under which a new management team takes over a firm, is an important determinant of a firm's long-term performance. In our case we observed that the lack of formal management know-how was not determinant for the development of the business, supporting the idea that this resource can represent a noneconomic knowledge that has a direct impact on individual economic behavior, and can be accumulated by practical experience, what in Brazil is valued as business acumen (Westhead et al., 2001). On the other side, industry know-how of the founders were essential to their success. Findings show that in most cases founders used all their expertise, skills and network for the success of their projects. In our case, this expertise was decisive for the identification of opportunities based on a deep knowledge of the market and the needs of their costumers, in addition to continuous development of specific skills that allowed them to improve their services collaborating for the growth of their business. Gilmara, the founder, said "we trusted our instincts and joined our efforts to overcome the management challenges only to have more funds to invest in our personal development, taking courses and learning new techniques to improve our services and thus increase our revenues". The last resource - the ability to acquire financial capital – showed us that here is where the institutional environment promotes a huge impact. According to GEM, Brazil has low rates on access to finance and government tax, policy and bureaucracy, especially compared to other GEM economies, (GEM, 2021), and previous GEM studies already indicated that the lack of access to financial resources is considered as the main limiting to the opening and maintenance of new businesses by 58.6% of entrepreneurs and that among all investments made by Brazilian investors, 75.2% were directed to close relatives and more than 90% of all investment was directed by family members (Souza, 2016). This situation is clearly reflected in the way our case started and expanded their business, always concentrating in family savings or the dispose of personal assets to avoid banking capital, always limited and expensive.

6. CONCLUSION, IMPLICATIONS FOR THEORY AND PRACTICE aND FURTHER RESEARCH

This study contributes to enhancing our understanding of the role of different resources in the creation, growth, and sustainability of SMEs. The findings from our case study confirm the relevance of the four considered resources, namely human capital, management know-how, industry know-how and capability to obtain financial resources for the achievement of entrepreneurial success.

We observe that although Brazilian entrepreneurs face the same motivations, challenges and hardships that entrepreneurs face in other markets, a lack of institutional support creates a huge impact on the continuation of business, to an extent that an impactful crisis like the Covid-19 becomes just another step on the way of local entrepreneurs. Although it is positive to identify that a challenging environment enhances the skills of surviving entrepreneurs, the personal cost is gigantic, in our case, leading to a family rupture, a failed marriage and a constant sense of instability that prevent the continuity of growing plans or the search for new investors or new opportunities. Nevertheless the whole experience demonstrated another strong characteristic of entrepreneurs – optimism (Shane & Venkataraman, 2000). Despite the hardship, Gilmara declared that after all her challenges at the moment she feels more independent and pretty confident about the future. She claims that the support and gratitude from her employees is a strong motivator for her and that she is ready to consolidate her business, now run by herself.

This knowledge may provide practitioners with additional insights into the key resource-based factors associated with entrepreneurial decisions. This study reinforces the importance of a supportive environment to provide stability that allows business growth. Further, the RBV demonstrated its theoretical relevance to examine the processes through which key resources influence the overall success of SMEs.

We recognise that the use of a single case limits possible generalisations, therefore, we encourage future research using multiple cases and more quantitative studies to further confirm our results.

REFERENCES

Afonso, C. (2019). *Os desafios do empreendedorismo no Brasil*. Retrieved from http://www.negociosem-movimento.com.br/artigos/os-desafios-do-empreendedorismo-no-brasil/

Alvarez, C., Urbano, D., Coduras, A., & Ruiz-Navarro, J. (2011). Environmental conditions and entrepreneurial activity: A regional comparison in Spain. *Journal of Small Business and Enterprise Development, 18*(1), 120–140. doi:10.1108/14626001111106460

Bacq, S., & Eddleston, K. A. (2018). A Resource-Based View of Social Entrepreneurship: How Stewardship Culture Benefits Scale of Social Impact. *Journal of Business Ethics, 152*(3), 589–611. doi:10.100710551-016-3317-1

Barney, J. B. (2001). Resource-based theories of competitive advantage : A ten- year retrospective on the resource-based view. *Journal of Management, 27*(6), 643–650. doi:10.1177/014920630102700602

Barney, J. B., & Clark, D. N. (2007). Resource-Based Theory: Creating and Sustaining Competitive Advantage. Oxford University Press. doi:10.1362/026725708X382046

Barney, J. B., Wright, M., & Ketchen, D. (2001). the Resource-Based View of the Firm : Ten Years After. *Journal of Management, 16*(3), 171–174.

Caballero-Morales, S. O. (2021). Innovation as recovery strategy for SMEs in emerging economies during the COVID-19 pandemic. *Research in International Business and Finance, 57*(February), 101396. doi:10.1016/j.ribaf.2021.101396 PMID:33558782

Desa, G., & Basu, S. (2013). Optimization or bricolage? Overcoming resource constraints in global social entrepreneurship. *Strategic Entrepreneurship Journal, 8*(6), 4517–4524. doi:10.1002ej.1150

Dul, J., & Hak, T. (2008). *Case Study Methodology in Business Research*. Academic Press.

Eggers, F. (2020). Masters of disasters? Challenges and opportunities for SMEs in times of crisis. *Journal of Business Research, 116*(May), 199–208. doi:10.1016/j.jbusres.2020.05.025 PMID:32501306

Endeavor Brasil. (2016). *Desafios dos empreendedores brasileiros*. Author.

Estrin, S., Mickiewicz, T., & Stephan, U. (2016). Human capital in social and commercial entrepreneurship. *Journal of Business Venturing, 31*(4), 449–467. doi:10.1016/j.jbusvent.2016.05.003

GEM. (2021). *GEM 2020/2021 Global Report*. GEM.

Gerring, J. (2006). *Case Study Research* (Vol. 53). Cambridge University Press. doi:10.1017/CBO9780511803123

Https://covid19.who.int/. (2021). *WHO Coronavirus (COVID-19) Dashboard*. Author.

Ionescu-Somers, A., & Tarnawa, A. (2020). *Diagnosing COVID-19 Impacts on Entrepreneurship Exploring policy remedies for recovery. Global Monitor*. Retrieved from https://www.gemconsortium.org/reports/covid-impact-report

Isenberg, D. J. (2011). The Entrepreneurship Ecosystem Strategy as a New Paradigm for Economic Policy: Principles for Cultivating Entrepreneurships. *The Babsos Entrepreneurship Ecosystem Project, 1*(781), 1–13. Retrieved from http://www.wheda.com/uploadedFiles/Website/About_Wheda/Babson Entrepreneurship Ecosystem Project.pdf

Mair, J., & Marti, I. (2009). Entrepreneurship in and around institutional voids: A case study from Bangladesh. *Journal of Business Venturing, 24*(5), 419–435. doi:10.1016/j.jbusvent.2008.04.006

McIntyre, G. (2020). *What Is the Small Business Failure Rate?* Retrieved from https://www.fundera.com/blog/what-percentage-of-small-businesses-fail

Porter, M. E. (1979). How Competitive Advantage forces shape strategy. *Harvard Business Review.*

Rocha, B. G., & Andreassi, T. (2020). Brazilian and American Entrepreneurial Experience: Cultural and Financial Aspects From Brazilian Entrepreneurs' Point of View. *Iberoamerican Journal of Entrepreneurship and Small Business, 9*(3), 323–343. Retrieved from http://10.0.55.131/regepe.v9i3.1403%0Ahttp://search.ebscohost.com/login.aspx?direct=true&db=buh&AN=144308353&site=ehost-live

Sanar_Saúde. (2020). *Linha do tempo do Coronavírus no Brasil.* Author.

Sebrae. (2020). *O impacto da pandemia de coronavírus nos pequenos negócios.* Author.

Sebrae. (2021). *Resumo Setorial* (Vol. 2021). Retrieved from https://www.sebrae.com.br/sites/PortalSebrae/artigos/o-impacto-da-pandemia-de-coronavirus-nos-pequenos-negocios,192da538c1be1710VgnVCM1000004c00210aRCRD#

Shane, S., & Venkataraman, S. (2000). The promise of entrepreneurship as a field of research. *Academy of Management Review, 25*(1), 217–226. https://doi.org/10.1007/978-3-540-48543-8_8

Souza. (2016). *Empreendedorismo no Brasil. Global Entrepreneurship Monitor* (Vol. 21). doi:10.3916/c30-2008-01-013

Staniewski, M. W. (2016). The contribution of business experience and knowledge to successful entrepreneurship. *Journal of Business Research, 69*(11), 5147–5152. https://doi.org/10.1016/j.jbusres.2016.04.095

The World Bank Group. (2020). *Doing Business 2020. World Bank.* doi:https://doi.org/10.1596/978-1-4648-1440-2

Trisotto, F. (2021). *Mesmo com novo auxílio emergencial, renda total do brasileiro deve cair R$ 157 bilhões em 2021, diz estudo.* O Globo.

Weaven, S., Quach, S., Thaichon, P., Frazer, L., Billot, K., & Grace, D. (2021a). Surviving an economic downturn: Dynamic capabilities of SMEs. *Journal of Business Research, 128*(February), 109–123. https://doi.org/10.1016/j.jbusres.2021.02.009

Weaven, S., Quach, S., Thaichon, P., Frazer, L., Billot, K., & Grace, D. (2021b). Surviving an economic downturn: Dynamic capabilities of SMEs. *Journal of Business Research, 128*(February), 109–123. https://doi.org/10.1016/j.jbusres.2021.02.009

Westhead, P., Wright, M., & Ucbasaran, D. (2001). The internationalization of new and small firms: A resource-based view. *Journal of Business Venturing*, *16*(4), 333–358. https://doi.org/10.1016/S0883-9026(99)00063-4

Zahra, S. A., Gedajlovic, E., Neubaum, D. O., & Shulman, J. M. (2009). A typology of social entrepreneurs: Motives, search processes and ethical challenges. *Journal of Business Venturing*, *24*(5), 519–532. https://doi.org/10.1016/j.jbusvent.2008.04.007

Chapter 11
Suggestions for SMEs as They Emerge From Crisis Periods

Engin Meriç
https://orcid.org/0000-0002-0965-3089
Trakya University, Turkey

EXECUTIVE SUMMARY

Existing financial problems of SMEs, which have an important place in the economies of countries, deepen even more in times of crisis, affecting businesses negatively and leading them to failure. In the crisis conditions, the strategies that SMEs have implemented in order to maintain their balance in their economic activities and to be successful are of critical importance. For this purpose, a method has been proposed for SMEs to determine the exit method from the crisis in the first crisis phase, which they will notice before entering the chronic crisis phase. In the proposed method; A financial check-up was planned to include 1-Current Assets, 3-Short-Term Liabilities, 5-Equity and production and sales strategies. In addition, as a result of the application of this proposed method periodically, SMEs' control of finance and cash flow will contribute significantly to both their protection from economic problems and their internal control systems.

INTRODUCTION

In today's competitive conditions, rapid developments in environmental factors cause businesses to face situations that we can call crisis. Crises can be caused by both national and international reasons, as well as by industry or businesses themselves. Regardless of their effects, all crises can significantly affect the economies and social structures of countries. The failure of a firm in times of economic crisis includes a process ranging from the firm's failure to fulfill its current obligations for temporary reasons to its bankruptcy.

SMEs may experience great difficulties due to the increasing demand every day and the economic crises that countries are in. In this context, how the crisis is handled in SMEs, how the employees cope with this situation, what measures are taken, what strategies are applied in the economic crisis and crisis periods are of great importance in terms of functioning. SMEs working within the system and program can overcome crisis periods with less losses. On the other hand, SMEs working outside the system and

DOI: 10.4018/978-1-7998-7657-1.ch011

program may lose their continuity from time to time by being affected by all kinds of crisis. Since SME-level businesses in Turkey and other countries are family businesses, the effects of the economic crisis can cause irreparable damage to both the business and the family.

As it is known, while SMEs constitute an important part of enterprises and employment in all developed and developing countries, they also have an important place in terms of production, export and added value. In this context, the contributions of SMEs in the national economies cannot be ignored. SMEs, which have a very important place in the economy of our country and also contribute in terms of social stability, should be supported in times of economic crisis. For this purpose, a method has been proposed to SMEs to get out of the crisis in the first crisis phase, which they will realize before entering the chronic crisis phase. Evaluating the data obtained from the method applied, it is aimed to have a command of the financial and cash flow related to exit from the economic crisis, to protect themselves from economic problems and to contribute significantly to internal control systems.

LITERATURE REVIEW

Researches on the effects of economic crises that have serious consequences for businesses are given below.

Boer (1999) mentioned the necessity of reducing the cash deficit, which is defined as the difference between cash inflows and cash outflows, especially in times of crisis, and also suggested that measures should be taken to reduce and slow down cash outflows in order to increase stock turnover and increase and accelerate cash inflows. Payne (2002), Wallis (2002) and Sullivan (2003) emphasized the importance of cash and the management of working capital in crisis periods. In addition, it has been revealed that the resource costs of SMEs, whose cash and financial structures are affected more in crisis periods, increase more than when comrared to larger enterprises (Arslan, 2003). According to the findings of Aşıkoğlu & Ögel (2006), which they obtained from their study on the effects of the 2001 financial crisis on manufacturing companies, the short-term debts of enterprises increase in crisis periods and the share of equity in total resources decreases. It was also due to the increase in receivables and stock turnover rates in the crisis year and the following year compared to the pre-crisis period, and the decrease in liquidity ratios, equity and total profitability during crisis periods. Apak et. al. (2012) in their research to evaluate the perspectives of SMEs on accounting measures that should be taken in times of crisis, they concluded that SMEs attach importance to cost-saving, cash flow and strategic measures. The result of the study also shows that the implementation of policies that accelerate cash flow rather than cost-reducing techniques and expansion investments during crisis periods plays the most important role.

In times of crisis, there are decreases in sales volume and contractions in production due to demand shrinkage. Many countries are trying to reduce the devastating effect of the crisis on businesses by taking measures to increase demand. An international study conducted by the OECD emphasizes that the financial crises reduce the demand for the goods and services produced by enterprises (especially SMEs), limit their credit opportunities, leading to worsening of cash flows. According to the results of the research, public authorities take measures that increase the sales of SMEs, prevent the dissolution of working capital, increase liquidity access opportunities and help ensure investment continuity (OECD, 2009).

Gençtürk et. al. (2011) in order to determine in which direction the financial structures of the enterprises were affected by the crises experienced, it was tried to determine in which direction the financial structures of the enterprises and accordingly the financing decisions were affected by the global crisis of April 1994, November 2000, February 2001 and 2008. As a result of the research, it was determined that the borrowing tendencies of the enterprises increased during the crisis periods, but this tendency was realized in the form of long-term borrowing. Iatridis & Dimitras (2013) investigated the effects of economic crises on companies. Within the scope of the research, public limited companies in Portugal, Ireland, Italy, Greece and Spain were examined. Findings from the study showed that publicly traded companies in Portugal, Italy and Greece tend to be more involved in earnings management in their efforts to increase their low profitability and liquidity, to meet their high borrowing and growth. In addition, the study highlighted that Ireland showed less evidence of earnings manipulation, while for Spain the findings were somewhat contradictory.

CONCEPTUAL FRAMEWORK

Crisis is a period that threatens the long and short-term goals of businesses, requires urgent intervention and consequently limits the decision-making time for response, and most importantly, it is a period which leads to indecision that interferes in decision-making combinations (Irvine, 1987).

In this sense, the crisis means "worsening at a particular moment or critical time"; "the situation reaching a critical stage" (Fink, 1986), "changes that require rapid adaptation" (Saracoğlu, 1995); "the great discord between the expectations of an organization and the realizations around it" (Kernisky, 1997) it can be defined as.

Economic crisis, on the other hand, is defined as macroeconomic crises that occur unexpectedly in a country or with insufficient or wrong managerial choices in a certain period (Apak, 2009). In short, the economic crisis is a difficult period that includes a sudden turning point in a certain period, an unstable and dangerous formation in the field of economy and politics (Önder, 2012).

The purpose of businesses should be to take advantage of crises and use them as a stepping stone. At this point, the crisis should be seen as a bridge that will make the business successful. The factors that distinguish crisis situations from normal situations are as follows (Rosier, 1991):

- The most important feature that distinguishes the crisis from ordinary situations is the urgent necessity to intervene.
- Another characteristic of the crisis is that the management of the enterprise is insufficient in determining the targets to be achieved and the activities to be carried out with limited resources.
- In addition, changes or developments must threaten the existence of the business.
- Whether the changes and developments that take place affect the continuity of the business positively or negatively, they will render the crisis prevention tools inadequate as they require the basic values and objectives of the business to change.

In the light of the definitions and explanations above, the characteristics of the crisis situation can be summarized as the sudden development depending on the internal and external conjuncture, which can put the lives of individuals, businesses, society and societies at global level in difficult position, and cause instability and negative expectations for future in decision-making units by creating depression, and turmoil. (Daştan, 2009).

Shrivastava and Mitroff state that the crisis in businesses threatens important goals, business survival and profitability of the business (Shrivastava & Mitroff, 1987).

Factors Causing Crisis in Business

Failure of the business to adapt to changing environmental conditions can cut its ties with the environment and this can endanger the life of the business. This incompatibility between the business and its environment, which may arise from the general and close conditions of the business or the structural characteristics of the business, is a harbinger of possible crises. Therefore, the factors causing the crisis can be divided into two as internal and external factors (Çetin, 2009).

Non-Business Factors

Environmental factors play the most important role in the organization's going into crisis. Dynamic and constantly changing environment can reduce the accuracy of managerial decisions by affecting the degree of complexity and uncertainty faced by the organization and cause the organization to be dragged into a crisis situation (Demirtaş, 2000; Can, 2002). External or environmental factors that cause a crisis in the organization can be listed as the general structure of the world and the country, the social, political, economic, security situation and problems of the country, technological developments and changes, natural disasters, international threats and dangers (Peker & Aytürk, 2000).

Internal Factors

There are many internal factors that lead businesses to failure and ultimately to crisis. The most important of these can be listed as follows (Akgüç, 1998):

- Gathering all aspects of the business, down to the details, in one hand.
- Choosing the wrong location fort he establishment of business.
- Making sudden decisions without making any feasibility study.
- Underestimation of the business or overestimation of the growth rate.
- Inadequate financial planning, lack of balance between financing requirements and resources, inconsistency between the conditions of resources and the conditions of the use of economic assets in investments,
- Inability to create an optimal capital structure due to insufficient equity capital.
- The goals and objectives of the business are not determined in advance and the plans are not revised.
- Not being in ahead of the developments in the world, in the country and in the industry or at least not being able to follow these developments.
- Failure to establish businesses at optimum capacity.
- Insufficient efficiency and effectiveness.
- Future predictions are not accurate.
- Inadequate coordination in management activities.
- Failure to apply modern management techniques.
- Lack of knowledgeable and skilled managers.

Phases of the Crisis

A crisis can occur in four different ways. The phases of consist of; first crisis phase, had (peak) crisis phase, chronic crisis phase and the return to normal phase (Çetin, 2009).

First Crisis Phase: This phase is the warning phase and in most cases it is the turning point. If the turning point, which is the first stage of the crisis, is missed in the beginning since it is not noticed, the hadd crisis will occur. Symptoms of the crisis should be seen in the first crisis phase and measures should be taken according to these symptoms. Crisis management may be easier if the symptoms of the first phase of the crisis are noticed on time.

The Had Crisis Phase: This phase is, in many ways, the phase in which no return is possible. Once the symptoms are over and the crisis is in the first phase, it is no longer possible to recover those who have been lost. After this stage, how much damage there will be depends on the management.

Chronic Crisis Phase: It is the period in which the negativities caused by the crisis are tried to be corrected and eliminated. This phase is also the recovery period.

The Phase of Return to Normal: In this last phase, the results of taking the crisis under control are seen.

While managers are generally concerned with the extreme and chronic phases of the crisis, they can think about how quickly they will be caught in this period and how they will not be caught again. But when the first phase of the crisis begins, managers must establish direct and appropriate control mechanisms for a solution.

SMEs, which make up 73.5% of employment in Turkey (compared to 63% in the OECD region), realize more than half of added value and exports (OECD, 2016). In addition, it constitutes 99.8% of total enterprises, 75.8% of employment in terms of number of employees, 54.5% of added value and 53.2% of investments (Ministry of Science, Industry and Technology, 2020).

In this context, SMEs, which are very important for the economies of the country, are the organizations most affected by the economic crises. In the study, about the exit from the crisis period in SMEs (Small and Medium Sized) operating in the production sector;

```
10- LIQUID ASSETS
11- SECURITIES
12- TRADE RECEIVABLE
13- OTHER COMMERCIAL RECEIVABLES
15- INVENTORIES
19- OTHER CURRENT ASSETS
30- FINANCIAL LIABILITIES
32- TRADE PAYABLES
33- OTHER PAYABLES
34- ADVANCES RECEİVED
36- TAXES AND OTHER LIABILITIES
39- OTHER SHORT - TERM EXTERNAL RESOURCES
50- PAID-UP CAPITAL
```

the accounting records related to the data are examined and given in Table 1-3.

In addition, the headings that will include financial and technical analysis related to the business in this study are listed below.

- Production Method
- Average Sales Profit Determination (%)
- Average Collection of Receivables (Checques Received + Customers Open Account + Notes Receivable)
- Average Maturity of Commercial Debt Payments (Cheques Given and Payment Orders + Payables Open to Suppliers + Debt Notes)
- Product Stock Turnover Detection
- Detection of Average Availability Time
- Detection of Out of Sale Product
- Detection of Decreasing Sales Speed
- Loan Usage Cost Determination

METHOD

It is extremely important for businesses to know their financial and cash flow situations completely. The fact that businesses have a command on their daily, weekly, monthly and quarterly cash flows will enable them not to be affected by crises and to make a purchase under better conditions. In a sense, this can be considered as a better cost. For a healthy financial check-up, an accurate registration method and financial check-up tables suitable for analysis are important.

In this respect, a detailed due diligence has been made on Current Assets, Short-Term Liabilities and Capital accounts over month-end trial balance data and other accounting records by adhering to the uniform chart of accounts in the application example.

FINDINGS

8 types of lighting fixtures are produced in the SMEs which are subjected to the study. While 80% of the production is carried out within the enterprise, 20% is produced in another production facility with a monthly labor cost of 8.000,00 $.

After these explanations, Current Assets and Short-Term Liabilities and Equity as of 30.04.2020 for the financial and cash flow due diligence of the enterprise are given in Table 1-3.

Table 1. First Crisis Phase Detection Table (Current Assets)

1 CURRENT ASSETS		
ACCOUNT CODE	**EXPLANATION**	**FIRST CRISIS PHASE DETECTION ($)**
10.	**LIQUID ASSETS**	**28.350,00**
.100	Cash and Cash Equivalents	800,00
.101	Cheques Received	62.100,00
.102	Cash in Banks	4.900,00
.103	Cheques Issued and Payment Orders (-)	39.450,00
.108	Other Liquid Assets	-
11.	**SECURITIES**	**3.000,00**
.110	Common Stocks	1.000,00
.111	Private Sector Bonds, Notes and Shares	-
.112	Public Sector Bonds, Notes And Shares	2.000,00
12.	**TRADE RECEIVABLE**	**20.100,00**
.120	Customers	11.100,00
.121	Notes Receivable	7.800,00
.126	Deposits and Guarantees Given	1.200,00
.127	Other Trade Receivables	-
.128	Doubtful Trade Receivables	-
13.	**OTHER COMMERCIAL RECEIVABLES**	**3.200,00**
.131	Due from Shareholders	1.500,00
.132	Due from Participations	-
.133	Due from Subsidiaries	-
.135	Due from Personnel	600,00
.136	Other Receivables	1.100,00
.138	Other Doubtful Receivables	-
15.	**INVENTORIES**	**153.520,00**
.150	Raw Materials and Supplies	24.300,00
.151	Semi-finished Goods in Production	8.100,00
.152	Finished Goods	117.370,00
.153	Trade Goods	650,00
.157	Other Inventories	-
.159	Advances Given to Suppliers	3.100,00
19.	**OTHER CURRENT ASSETS**	**11.300,00**
.190	Deferred VAT	-
.191	Deductible VAT	1.600,00
.192	Other VAT	-
.193	Prepaid Taxes and Funds	-
.195	Work Advance	6.500,00
.196	Advance Given To Personnel	3.200,00
1- TOTAL OF CURRENT ASSETS		**219.470,00**

Table 2. First Crisis Phase Detection Table (Short Term External Resources)

3 SHORT TERM EXTERNAL RESOURCES		
ACCOUNT CODE	**EXPLANATION**	**FIRST CRISIS PHASE DETECTION ($)**
30.	**FINANCIAL LIABILITIES**	**293.300,00**
.300	Bank Loans	190.000,00
.301	Leasing Payables	82.000,00
.303	Principal Installments and Interests of Long-Term Loans	16.800,00
.309	Other Financial Liabilities	4.500,00
32.	**TRADE PAYABLES**	**9.200,00**
.320	Suppliers	4.500,00
.321	Notes Payable	2.100,00
.326	Deposits and Guarantees Taken	-
.329	Other Trade Payables	2.600,00
33.	**OTHER PAYABLES**	**67.265,00**
.331	Due to Shareholders	26.500,00
.332	Due to Participations	-
.333	Due to Subsidiaries	-
.335	Due to Personnel	28.140,00
.336	Other Liabilities	12.625,00
34.	**ADVANCES TAKEN**	**800,00**
.340	Advances Received	800,00
.349	Other Advances Received	-
36.	**TAXES AND OTHER LIABILITIES**	**18.205,00**
.360	Taxes And Funds Payables	9.210,00
.361	Social Security Premiums Payable	6.540,00
.368	Overdue, Deferred or Restructed Taxes and Other Liabilities	1.805,00
.369	Other Liabilities Payable	650,00
39.	**OTHER SHORT - TERM EXTERNAL RESOURCES**	**1.950,00**
.391	Calculated VAT	1.950,00
.392	Other VAT	-
.393	Head Office and Branch Current Accounts	-
.399	Other Short Term Liabilities	-
3- TOTAL OF SHORT TERM EXTERNAL RESOURCES		**390.720,00**
TOTAL OF CURRENT ASSETS (-) TOTAL OF SHORT TERM EXTERNAL RESOURCES		**(171.250,00)**

Table 3. First Crisis Phase Detection Table (Equity)

5 EQUITY		
ACCOUNT CODE	**EXPLANATION**	**FIRST CRISIS PHASE DETECTION ($)**
50.	**PAID-UP CAPITAL**	**100.000,00**
.500	Capital	100.000,00

As of 30.04.2020, the ready values of the enterprise were around 28.350,00 $ the total Current Assets were calculated as 219.470,00 $ and the total Foreign Resources were calculated as 390.720,00 $ This financial structure for the enterprise during the crisis period means that cash and cash equivalents are low and receivables and stocks are high. In addition, the fact that a very high part of the foreign resources are in the form of bank loan debt and that since the due dates are determined well in advance makes it necessary for the enterprise to take urgent measures for the exit from the crisis.

After this point, the following analyzes have been made by making use of financial records that have a direct impact on finance and cash flow in order to make healthier suggestions and goals regarding the exit of the business from the crisis.

Production Method

It has been observed that the enterprise carries out its production by mass production method and produces 80% of its production within its own structure and 20% of it is realized in another production facility outside the enterprise by paying a monthly labor cost of $ 8,000.00.

Especially during this crisis period, continuing contract manufacturing in the enterprise, which has such an idle stock, will increase the stock load and will put a financial burden to the business, and the cost increase will decrease the profitability.

% of Average Sales Profit

During the financial check-up as of April 30, 2020, the net profit (loss) of the business for the period January-April 4 months was calculated as a loss of 11.600,00 $.

In addition, it has been observed that some products are not saleable at these sales prices due to the high costs. In this respect, it would be appropriate to reduce costs and sell the business with a gross 20% profit margin.

Average Collection Maturity of Receivables

The business receivables from buyers with deferred checks, bills and open accounts in return for the products it sells;

- Total Check Due 62.100,00 $
- Open Account Receivables Total 11.100,00 $
- Total of the Notes Receivable being 7.800,00 $

The total is 81.000,00 $

In a detailed study based on checks and notes with different due dates and on the birth dates of open account receivables, the average due date of a total of $ 81.000,00 receivables was calculated as 168 days. In other words, 5 months and 18 days is an extremely long time.

It can be considered as a situation that can create much more negative consequences, especially for a business that uses a loan.

Average Loan Payment Maturity

Post-dated checks, bills of exchange and open account debts related to the supply of all materials required for production;

- Total amount of checks given with different due dates 39.450,00 $
- Open Account Debt to Sellers 4.500,00 $
- The Amount of Notes Given on Different Dates is 2.100,00 $

The total is 46.050,00 $

It is seen that the average due date of this debt is 85 days in calculations. In other words, it means an average debt payment term of 2 months and 25 days.

While the business could not limit the collection period, it has lost its control in debt payments. This can be considered as one of the tightness in finance.

Stock Turnover Detection

For the 4-month period of the company between 01.01.2020-30.04.2020;

Inventory turnover = 373.450,00 $ / ((187.521,00 + 117.370,00) / 2)

Inventory turnover = 373.450,00 $ / 152.445,50 $

Inventory turnover is calculated as 2.45.

The ARM-2142001 coded product, which has a low turnover and has lost sales with the product with code ARM-142 316, which is out of sale, was seen as the most important reason for the low inventory turnover rate.

Detection of Time Out of Stock

The time to stay in stock for the 4-month period between 01.01.2020-30.04.2020;

It was calculated as 360/12 months * 4 months / 2.45 Turnover Speed = 49 days. The stock period resulting from the stock turnover can be considered high for an SME with financial difficulties.

Detection of Out of Sale Items

Between the dates of 01.01.2020-30.04.2020 there was no transaction in the stock movements of the ARM-142 316 coded lighting fixture product, which is in the production range. It has been observed that 240 products in stock * 80.00 $ = 19.200,00 $ are out of stock for 4 months. For a business in crisis, the stock load of a product whose sale has stopped completely is not an acceptable situation.

Detection of Products with Decreasing Sales Speed

It has been determined that 542 pieces of lighting fixture with the code ARM-Z.142001, which is also in the product range, were produced between 01.01.2020-30.04.220, and only 140 sales were done and this number of sales was omitted from the stocks.

The inventory cost of this product is 85.00 $ and in this case 542 pieces - 140 pieces * 85,00 $ = 34.170,00$ can be considered as idle stock.

Cost Determination of Loan Usage

For the bank loan of 190.000,00 $ used by the company, an annual interest burden of 8.40% was calculated as 15.960,00 $ while an interest burden of 4.264,00 $ was calculated with an interest rate of 82.000,00 $ * 5.20% for the leasing debt.

For the long-term loan payment of 16.800,00$ interest borrowing is 7% and the calculated interest burden is calculated as 1.176,00 $. In this case, the annual loan interest burden to be paid to banks by the enterprise is 21.400,00 $ and it can be considered as a high expense burden for a non-profitable business, especially in such a crisis period.

According to the results of the evaluation and analysis made on the check-up results:

It has been determined that the management of the company could not collect its receivables on time due to the deficiencies in the record order and management weakness, and also did not use the due date in favor of the enterprise in the commercial debt payments. In addition, the business faced an extremely high idle stock due to the products that have stopped selling or becauseof the decreasing sales rate.

As a result the company not only could not manage its stocks but also made the mistake of contarct manufacturing its products. The financial structure of the business is not suitable for mass production and it will be more appropriate to make order-based production. All these problems were tried to be overcome with the use of loans, but it was found that it was difficult to meet this loan interest rate with this profit margin. The recommendations to be applied to the business regarding the exit from the crisis for a period of 4 months as well as the targets and achievements regarding these problems are given below.

The implementation recommendations for getting out of the crisis are given in Table 4 with the targeted gains.

Table 4. Crisis Exit Suggestion - Target Achievements Table

RECOMMENDATIONS	TARGETED ACHIEVEMENTS
Reducing the average collection term for receivables to 90 days	With this application, it is aimed to contribute to the relief of cash flow of 30.000,00 $ in the 4-month period during the exit from the crisis.
Increasing the stock turnover within a period of 4 months	As a result of this practice, it is aimed to keep the company's finished product stocks at 70.000,00 $ while a relaxation of 50.000,00 $ in financial cash flow is targeted.
Increasing the due date of debt to 120 days	With debt payments spread over 120 days, a contribution of 20.000,00 $ to the cash flow of the business is targeted.
A capital increase of 50.000,00 $ in a 4-month period	With the capital sale to be performed in the 4-month period, it is aimed to decrease the bank loans by 50.000,00 $. Therefore, savings in interest expenses will be achieved.
Transition from mass production to order-based production	It is aimed to get rid of the idle stock and thus to relax the financial cash flow.
Suspension of contract manufacturing	It has been determined that the enterprise working with idle stock does not need this production as a contract. It is also aimed to save 9.000,00 $ * 4 months = 36.000,00 $.
Determining the % of sales profit	As a result of cost studies and determining saleable prices, the gross profit percentage is targeted as 20%.
Sales of out-of-stock products	The sale of the product with stock code ARM-142316, which is out of sale, at cost price is important in terms of cash flow.
Making the sales of the product with slowing sales attractive	It would be appropriate to sell the product with inventory code ARM-Z.142001 with a reduced sales rate with a 10% profit margin on cost.
Focusing on expense savings	It is aimed to take a saving measure of 10.000,00 $ in energy expenses, maintenance-repair expenses and general expenses for a 4-month period.

In the light of the data obtained as a result of all these studies, an implementation process was experienced for the exit from the crisis for a period of 4 months, from May to August. At the point reached regarding this process, the comparison of the detection of the first crisis phase and the phase of return to normal was made by evaluating the trial balance data of August 2020. (see Tables 5-7)

Table 5. Crisis Phases Comparison Chart (Current Assets)

1 CURRENT ASSETS				
ACCOUNT CODE	**EXPLANATION**	**FIRST CRISIS PHASE DETECTION ($) (30.04.2020)**	**DETERMINATION OF RETURN TO NORMAL PHASE ($) (31.08.2020)**	**DIFFERENCE ($)**
10.	**LIQUID ASSETS**	**28.350,00**	**50.342,00**	**21.992,00**
.100	Cash and Cash Equivalents	800,00	450,00	-350,00
.101	Cheques Received	62.100,00	82.000,00	19.900,00
.102	Cash in Banks	4.900,00	11.420,00	6.520,00
.103	Cheques Issued and Payment Orders (-)	39.450,00	43.528,00	4.078,00
.108	Other Liquid Assets	-	-	-
11.	**SECURITIES**	**3.000,00**	**3.000,00**	**-**
.110	Common Stocks	1.000,00	1.000,00	-
.111	Private Sector Bonds, Notes and Shares	-	-	-
.112	Public Sector Bonds, Notes And Shares	2.000,00	2.000,00	-
12.	**TRADE RECEIVABLE**	**20.100,00**	**15.995,00**	**-4.105,00**
.120	Customers	11.100,00	13.645,00	2.545,00
.121	Notes Receivable	7.800,00	1.150,00	-6.650,00
.126	Deposits and Guarantees Given	1.200,00	1.200,00	-
.127	Other Trade Receivables	-	-	-
.128	Doubtful Trade Receivables	-	-	-
13.	**OTHER COMMERCIAL RECEIVABLES**	**3.200,00**	**740,00**	**-2.460,00**
.131	Due from Shareholders	1.500,00	-	-1.500,00
.132	Due from Participations	-	-	-
.133	Due from Subsidiaries	-	-	-
.135	Due from Personnel	600,00	-	-600,00
.136	Other Receivables	1.100,00	740,00	-360,00
.138	Other Doubtful Receivables	-	-	
15.	**INVENTORIES**	**153.520,00**	**127.877,00**	**-25.643,00**
.150	Raw Materials and Supplies	24.300,00	38.642,00	14.342,00
.151	Semi-finished Goods in Production	8.100,00	4.610,00	-3.490,00
.152	Finished Goods	117.370,00	84.625,00	-32.745,00
.153	Trade Goods	650,00	-	-650,00
.157	Other Inventories	-	-	-
.159	Advances Given to Suppliers	3.100,00	-	-3.100,00
19.	**OTHER CURRENT ASSETS**	**11.300,00**	**6.722,00**	**-4.578,00**
.190	Deferred VAT	-	1.182,00	1.182,00
.191	Deductible VAT	1.600,00	-	-1.600,00
.192	Other VAT	-	-	-
.193	Prepaid Taxes and Funds	-	-	-
.195	Work Advance	6.500,00	2.600,00	-3.900,00
.196	Advance Given To Personnel	3.200,00	2.940,00	-260,00
1- TOTAL OF CURRENT ASSETS		**219.470,00**	**204.676,00**	**-14.794,00**

Table 6. Crisis Stages Comparison Table (Short Term External Resources)

3 SHORT TERM EXTERNAL RESOURCES				
ACCOUNT CODE	EXPLANATION	FIRST CRISIS PHASE DETECTION ($) (30.04.2020)	DETERMINATION OF RETURN TO NORMAL PHASE ($) (31.08.2020)	DIFFERENCE ($)
30.	**FINANCIAL LIABILITIES**	**293.300,00**	**218.550,00**	**-74.750,00**
.300	Bank Loans	190.000,00	145.000,00	-45.000,00
.301	Leasing Payables	82.000,00	55.000,00	-27.000,00
.303	Principal Installments and Interests of Long-Term Loans	16.800,00	16.800,00	-
.309	Other Financial Liabilities	4.500,00	1.750,00	-2.750,00
32.	**TRADE PAYABLES**	**9.200,00**	**9.645,00**	**445,00**
.320	Suppliers	4.500,00	6.245,00	1.745,00
.321	Notes Payable	2.100,00	-	.-2.100,00
.326	Deposits and Guarantees Taken	-	-	-
.329	Other Trade Payables	2.600,00	3.400,00	800,00
33.	**OTHER PAYABLES**	**67.265,00**	**56.573,00**	**-10.692,00**
.331	Due to Shareholders	26.500,00	26.500,00	-
.332	Due to Participations	-	-	-
.333	Due to Subsidiaries	-	-	-
.335	Due to Personnel	28.140,00	16.428,00	-11.712,00
.336	Other Liabilities	12.625,00	13.645,00	1,020,00
34.	**ADVANCES TAKEN**	**800,00**	**-**	**-800,00**
.340	Advances Received	800,00	-	-800,00
.349	Other Advances Received	-	-	-
36.	**TAXES AND OTHER LIABILITIES**	**18.205,00**	**13.734,00**	**-4.471,00**
.360	Taxes and Funds Payables	9.210,00	8.460,00	-750,00
.361	Social Security Premiums Payable	6.540,00	5.274,00	-1.266,00
.368	Overdue, Deferred or Restructed Taxes and Other Libilities	1.805,00	-	-1.805,00
.369	Other Liabilities Payable	650,00	-	-650,00
39.	**OTHER SHORT-TERM EXTERNAL RESOURCES**	**1.950,00**	**2.711,00**	**761,00**
.391	Calculated VAT	1.950,00	2.711,00	761,00
.392	Other VAT	-	-	-
.393	Head Office and Branch Current Accounts	-	-	-
.399	Other Short Term Liabilities	-	-	-
3- TOTAL OF SHORT TERM EXTERNAL RESOURCES		**390.720,00**	**301.213,00**	**-89.507,00**

Table 7. Crisis Stages Comparison Chart (Equity)

5 EQUITY				
ACCOUNT CODE	EXPLANATION	FIRST CRISIS PHASE DETECTION ($) (30.04.2020)	DETERMINATION OF RETURN TO NORMAL PHASE ($) (31.08.2020)	DIFFERENCE ($)
50.	**PAID-UP CAPITAL**	**100.000,00**	**110.000,00**	**10.000,00**
.500	Capital	100.000,00	110.000,00	10.000,00

The data regarding the finance and cash flow of the enterprise between 30.04.2020 and 31.08.2020 are given in Figure 1.

Figure 1. Finance and Cash Flows Between 30.04.2020-31.08.2020

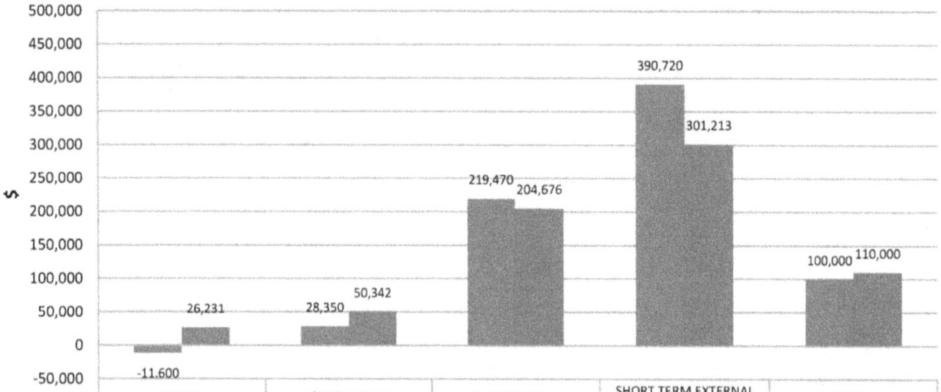

	PROFIT	LİQUİD ASSETS	CURRENT ASSETS	SHORT TERM EXTERNAL RESOURCES	EQUITY
30.4.2020	-11,600	28,350	219,470	390,720	100,000
31.8.2020	26,231	50,342	204,676	301,213	110,000

As it can be seen on the chart, the financial data of the enterprise obtained at the end of a 4-month period have been compared. According to the results of the comparison, there is an increase in the ready values and profits of the company.

As a result of the success achieved, even if the proposals for exit from the crisis and the realization of the targets are not 100%, the company became a business that made a profit of $ 26,231.00 in the second quarter, while it lost $ 11,600.00 in the first quarter.

In addition, it increased its cash and cash equivalents by $ 21.992.00, while reducing its short-term liabilities by $ 89.507.00. This gave the business a total of $111,499.00 in financial and cash flow relief. Resources related to this finance and cash flow relief;

- From Current Asset 36.768,00 $
  (Securities, trade receivables, other receivables, stocks and other current assets)
- From capital increase 10.000,00 $
- From the suspension of contract manufacturing 36.000,00 $
  4 months * 9.000,00 $
- Energy and Overhead Savings 2.500,00 $
- From profit 26.231,00 $_

  Total 111.499,00 $

These data indicate that the enterprise has successfully completed the first crisis phase and that the measures taken have yielded good results.

After this stage, it can be predicted that the enterprise will completely recover from the crisis and enter the growth phase as a result of the continuation of these measures for the second 4-month period as the crisis return to normal phase.

DISCUSSION

In times of crisis, the decrease in sales, combined with the decrease in inventory and receivable turnover, leads to decreases in liquidity related to working capital. In this case, failure to pay debts on time leads to bankruptcy or financial difficulties. The responses of enterprises (especially SMEs) to these problems caused by the crisis can be summarized as follows: (i) in order to cope with the problems of profitability, they adjust their production costs according to less product demand and services by reducing their costs, (ii) they delay cash outflows for liquidity, search for additional resources, including reducing or stopping their share allocations, (iii) delaying their investment and expansion plans (OECD, 2009).

By evaluating the data obtained from the applied method, the accounting uniform chart of accounts was adhered to during the implementation of the roadmap determined for exiting the economic crisis. In addition, as a result of the application of this proposed method in quarterly periods, SMEs' dominance of finance and cash flow will significantly contribute both to their protection in economic crisis environments and to internal control systems. In addition, as a result of the application of the method suggested by the business management, it will be helpful and guiding in seeing the targeted financial values and making favorable correction decisions.

Güler & Yılmaz (2009) stated that since SMEs do not have a professional management style, they also have an insufficient structure in determining targets and developing strategies, and this situation results in the products and services produced in SMEs not being sold. They stated that as a result of this, stocks will increase and there will be a cash shortage as a consequence of the inability to convert products and services into cash.

The results obtained from the study will contribute to the company management to make comparison and take favorable measures for the specified periods. Moreover, while providing financial control in the enterprise it will be ensured to be seen clearly the financial status of the enterprise. In addition, the financial structure was strengthened with the specified target, suggestions and achievements. The findings obtained at the end of the study confirm that the method applied is an effective method for finance and cash flow in the enterprise.

Uçkun (2009) stated that banks are reluctant to provide short-term financing to SMEs, while different banks have short-term business loans for SMEs. However, in these loans, SMEs also have problems with payment terms, limits and interest rates, and that banks stop giving loans and recall the allocated loans as the first thing in crisis periods, and in this case, SMEs face a situation outside of their cash flow plans.

With the method suggested in the study carried out, it was observed that in crisis periods, after the targets determined as a result of the check-up investigations made about the enterprise in the first crisis phase, the financial data obtained in the phase of returning to normal from the crisis increased the ready values of the company, and managed to reduce the short-term foreign resources by reducing them. The findings obtained at the end of the study showed that the method applied is an effective method for finance and cash flow in the enterprise.

CONCLUSION

The most important problems caused by the economic crises to SMEs are the decrease in demand and consequently the decrease in production and thus the increase in fixed expenses and production costs per product and the increase in financing costs in these periods. For the solution of these problems caused by the crises, SMEs are required to make detailed financial analyzes and make decisions for determining and reducing unnecessary activity and non-activity expenses. In this context, it is important to show the necessary sensitivity in making these decisions.

Especially SMEs in developing countries experience great financial difficulties. It is seen that the financial opportunities provided by the banking sector for SMEs are not suitable for the use of SMEs, and they are not sufficient for their development and survival. SMEs in developing countries need to use their existing resources efficiently and financial resources with which they can solve their problems.

In recent years, financial instability has become the most prominent feature of all economies in the world. Periodic financial crises have had permanent effects on the economies of developing countries. As in developing countries, the enterprises faced difficult situations due to the economic crises experienced from time to time in Turkey, and especially the small enterprises with the characteristics of SMEs were much more pronounced to be affected by these processes. In this context, taking into account the importance of SMEs for the economy, permanent policies that will strengthen SMEs are needed. In this context, it is necessary to support SMEs in terms of financing resources, to take continuous measures in terms of their survival and to minimize the existing problems in practice.

Within the framework of this method proposed to SMEs regarding the exit from the crisis, suggestions and targets were set in line with the specifications made on 30.04. The financial data obtained on 31.08.2020 and the period of returning from the crisis to normal at the end of a 4-month period, after the company made maximum effort to comply with the suggestions and goals and to make effort, were compared with the data of the first crisis phase. According to the results of the comparison, the company increased its cash values by 21.992,00 $ from 28.350,00 $ to 50.312,00 $. It has managed to reduce its short-term foreign resources from 390.720,00 $ to 89.507,00 $ to 301.213,00 $.

In addition, the company made a loss of 11.620,00 $ on 30.04.2020 and a profit of 26.231,00 $ on 31.08.2020. It can be seen that this method suggested for exit from the crisis made a positive contribution to the exit of the business from the crisis. The application of the method in periodic periods of 4 months will contribute to SMEs in protection from the crisis as well as in their continuity.

REFERENCES

Akgüç, Ö. (1998). *Finansal yönetim*. Muhasebe Enstitüsü Yayınları.

Apak, S. (2009). 1929 ve 2008 Krizlerinin Karşılaştırılması: Dünya ve Türkiye Örneği. *Muhasebe ve Finansman Dergisi*, (41), 6–16.

Apak, S., Erol, M., & Atmaca, M. (2012). Accounting measures to be taken for the enterprises in difficulty during times of economic crisis: A study on small and medium-sized enterprises (SMEs). *African Journal of Business Management*, *6*(23), 6832–6844.

Arslan, Ö. (2003). Küçük ve orta ölçekli işletmelerde çalışma sermayesi ve bazı finansal yönetim uygulamaları. *Cumhuriyet Üniversitesi İktisadi ve İdari Bilimler Dergisi*, *4*(1), 121–135.

Aşıkoğlu, R., & Ögel, S. (2006). 2001 krizinin İMKB'de hisse senetleri işlem gören imalat işletmelerinin finansal yapısı üzerindeki etkileri. *Afyon Kocatepe Üniversitesi İ.İ.B.F. Dergisi*, *8*(2), 1–18.

Boer, G. (1999). Managing the cash gap. *Journal of Accountancy*, *188*(4), 27–32.

Can, H. (2002). *Organizasyon ve yönetim*. Siyasal Kitabevi.

Çetin, H. (2009). *Kriz yönetimi ve işletmeler açısından alınacak önlemler. In 6.uluslararası Türk Dünyası Sosyal Bilimler Kongresi*. Avcı Ofset Basımevi.

Daştan, A. (2009). Ekomomik kriz dönemlerinde muhasebe bilgi sisteminin işletmelerdeki rolü ve kriz yönetimine katkısı. *Muhasebe ve Finansman Dergisi, 28*, 57–72.

Demirtaş, H. (2000). Kriz yönetimi. *Kuram ve Uygulamada Eğitim Yönetimi, 23*, 353–373.

Fink, S. (1986). *Crisis management: Planning for the inevitable*. American Management Association.

Gençtürk, M., Dalğar, H., & Yılmaz, T. (2011). Finansal krizlerin işletmelerin finansman kararlarına etkileri, İMKB'de işlem gören işletmeler üzerinde bir araştırma. *Cumhuriyet Üniversitesi İktisadi ve İdari Bilimler Fakültesi Dergisi, 12*(1), 187–207.

Güler, E., & Yılmaz, B. (2009). Ekonomik kriz, KOBİ'lere yansıması ve bir çıkış yolu olarak barter. *Sosyal Ekonomik Araştırmalar Dergisi, 9*(18), 87–104.

Iatridis, G., & Dimitras, A. I. (2013). Financial crisis and accounting quality: Evidence from five European countries. *Advances in Accounting, Incorporating. Advances in International Accounting, 29*(1), 154–160. doi:10.1016/j.adiac.2013.03.001

Irvine, R. B. (1987). What's a crisis, anyway? *Midyear*, (Special), 30–39.

Kernisky, D. A. (1997). Proactive crisis management and ethical discourse: Dow chemical's issues management bulletins 1979-1990. *Journal of Business Ethics, 16*(8), 843–853. doi:10.1023/A:1017901501108

OECD. (2009). *The Impact of the Global Crisis on SME and Entrepreneurship Financing and Policy Responses*. Centre for Entrepreneurship, SMEs and Local Development. https://www.oecd.org/cfe/smes/theimpactoftheglobalcrisisonsmeandentrepreneurshipfinancingandpolicyresponses.htm

OECD. (2016). *Improving the framework conditions for small and medium-sized enterprises*. Better Policies Series. https://www.oecd.org/policy-briefs/turkey-improving-the-framework-conditions-for-SMEs.pdf

Önder, İ. (2012). *İktisat üzerine düşünceler*. Yordam Kitap.

Payne, S. (2002). Working capital optimisation can yield real gains. *Financial Executives, 18*(6), 40–46.

Peker, Ö., & Aytürk, N. (2000). *Etkili yönetim becerileri öğrenilebilir ve geliştirilebilir*. Yargı Yayınevi.

Rosier, B. (1991). *İktisadi kriz kavramları*. İletişim Yayınları.

Saracoğlu, R. (1995). İstikrar programı üzerine düşünceler, Türkiye için yeni bir orta vadeli istikrar programına doğru. TUSIAD Yayın No:6-180, İstanbul.

Shrivastava, P., & Mitroff, I. I. (1987). Strategic management of corporate crisis. *The Columbia Journal of World Business*, (Spring), 5–17.

Sullivan, M. (2003). Retailers break new ground with open account trade programs. *AFP Exchange, 23*(2), 30–33.

TC Bilim Sanayi ve Teknoloji Bakanlığı. (2020). *KOBİ'ler ve girişimciler'in Türk ekonomisindeki yeri ve önemi.* https://anahtar.sanayi.gov.tr/tr/news/kobiler-ve-girisimcilerinturk-ekonomisindeki-yeri-ve-onemi/261

Uçkun, N. (2009). KOBİ'lerin finansal sorunlarına melek sermaye çözüm olabilir mi? *Muhasebe Finansman Dergisi, 41*, 121–130.

Wallis, L. P. (2002). Managing your receivable in today's economy. *Strategic Finance, 84*(2), 42–45.

KEY TERMS AND DEFINITIONS

Accounting Internal Control: These are all methods and procedures for businesses to achieve the goals they have set, to make accurate and complete accounting transactions such as income, expense, receivables, and debt to detect and prevent mistakes and frauds, to prepare financial statements in a reliable and analytical manner in accordance with their purpose.

Cash Flow: These are the changes that occur in the cash status of the business between two specific periods.

Competitive Advantage: Conditions that enable a business to produce a good or service of equal value at a lower price or more desirable than its competitors.

Economic Crisis: Economic crises that occur in a certain period or unexpectedly due to inadequate or wrong management.

Financial Check-Up: Identifying financial problems that are noticed and overlooked or unrecognized by evaluating the data through financial statements and having information about various financing alternatives.

Idle Stock: It is the situation that there is no demand for the products in stock for a certain period of time.

Short-Term External Resources: It covers the foreign resources that the enterprise will pay within one year or until the end of the operating period.

Small and Medium-Sized Enterprises (SMEs): Compared to large-scale enterprises, they are enterprises with smaller employee numbers, turnover or balance sheets and defined borders.

Compilation of References

Abdullah, M. A. (2002). An overview of the macroeconomic contribution of small and medium enterprises in Malaysia. In C. Harvie & B.-C. Lee (Eds.), *The role of SMEs in national economies in East Asia*. Edward Elgar.

Acs, Z. J., & Audretsch, D. B. (2003). Innovation and Technological Change. In Z. J. Acs & D. B. Audretsch (Eds.), *Handbook of Entrepreneurship Research* (pp. 55–79). Kluwer Academic Publishers. doi:10.1007/b105789

ADB. (2009). *Key indicators for Asia and the Pacific 2009*. Asian Development Bank.

ADB. (2020). *The Economic Impact of the COVID-19 Outbreak on Developing Asia. ADB Briefs, No.128, 6 March*. Asian Development Bank.

Afifiyah, S. (2020). *Jenis Usaha yang Justru Melejit Saat Wabah Covid-19*. Available online: https://www.tagar.id/jenis-usaha-yang-justru-melejit-saat-wabah-covid19

Afonso, C. (2019). *Os desafios do empreendedorismo no Brasil*. Retrieved from http://www.negociosemmovimento.com.br/artigos/os-desafios-do-empreendedorismo-no-brasil/

Ahmadi, H., & O'Cass, A. (2015). The role of entrepreneurial marketing in new technology ventures first product commercialisation. *Journal of Strategic Marketing*, *24*(1), 47–60. doi:10.1080/0965254X.2015.1035039

Ajzen, I. (1991). The theory of planned behavior. *Organizational Behavior and Human Decision Processes*, *50*(2), 1–63. doi:10.1016/0749-5978(91)90020-T

AKATIGA and the Asia Foundation. (1999). The impact of economic crisis on Indonesian small and medium enterprises. Study prepared for the United States Agency for International Development, Jakarta.

Akgüç, Ö. (1998). *Finansal yönetim*. Muhasebe Enstitüsü Yayınları.

Akpan, I. J., Udoh, E. A. P., & Adebisi, B. (2020). Small business awareness and adoption of state-of-the-art technologies in emerging and developing markets, and lessons from the COVID-19 pandemic. *Journal of Small Business and Entrepreneurship*, 1–18. Advance online publication. doi:10.1080/08276331.2020.1820185

Aladejebi, O. (2020). Managing small businesses in Nigeria during covid-19 crisis: Impact and survival strategies. *IOSR Journal of Business and Management, 22*(8), 24-34.

Alauddin, M., & Chowdhury, M. M. (2015). Small and medium enterprise in Bangladesh-Prospects and Challenges. *Global Journal of Management and Business Research. C Finance*, *15*(7), 1–10.

Alayo, M., Maseda, A., Iturralde, T., & Arzubiaga, U. (2019). Internationalization and entrepreneurial orientation of family SMEs: The influence of the family character. *International Business Review*, *28*(1), 48–59. doi:10.1016/j.ibusrev.2018.06.003

Alberti, F. G., Ferrario, S., & Pizzurno, E. (2018). Resilience: Resources and strategies of SMEs in a new theoretical framework. *International Journal of Learning and Intellectual Capital, 15*(2), 165–188. doi:10.1504/IJLIC.2018.091969

Ali, M., & Hollis, L. (2014). Developing Talent 1. *Strategic HR Review, 4*(2), 1–5.

Alonso, A. D., Bressan, A., Kok, S. K., Sakellarios, N., Koresis, A., O'Shea, M., . . . Santoni, L. J. (2021). Facing and responding to the COVID-19 threat–an empirical examination of MSMEs. European Business Review. ahead-of-print. doi:10.1108/EBR-09-2020-0231

Alvarado, A. A. (2020). Perdurability, families, and internationalization processes: Approaches from business history in latin america. *Journal of Evolutionary Studies in Business, 5*(2), 1–32. doi:10.1344/jesb2020.2.j075

Alvarez, C., Urbano, D., Coduras, A., & Ruiz-Navarro, J. (2011). Environmental conditions and entrepreneurial activity: A regional comparison in Spain. *Journal of Small Business and Enterprise Development, 18*(1), 120–140. doi:10.1108/14626001111106460

Alves, J. C., Lok, T. C., Luo, Y., & Hao, W. (2020). Crisis challenges of small firms in Macao during the COVID-19 pandemic. *Frontiers of Business Research in China, 14*(1), 1–23. doi:10.118611782-020-00094-2

Alziari, L. (2017). A chief HR officer's perspective on talent management. *Journal of Organizational Effectiveness: People and Performance, 4*(4). doi:10.1108/JOEPP-05-2017-0047

Amankwah-Amoah, J., Khan, Z., & Wood, G. (2020). COVID-19 and business failures: the paradoxes of experience, scale and scope for theory and practice. *European Management Journal.*

Anand, R. (2013). Internationalisation of the small and medium family firm in Japan. *International Journal of Business and Globalisation, 11*(2), 117–135. doi:10.1504/IJBG.2013.055598

Andalib, T. (2020). A conceptual model to resolve frustration of employees in the SMEs of Bangladesh. *Indian Journal of Science and Technology, 13*(09), 1015–1026. doi:10.17485/ijst/2020/v013i09/147200

Andalib, T., & Halim, H. (2019). Convergence of Conceptual Innovation Model to Reduce Challenges Faced by the Small and Medium Sized Enterprises' (SMEs) in Bangladesh. *Journal of Open Innovation, 5*(3), 63. doi:10.3390/joitmc5030063

Anderson, R. C., & Reeb, D. M. (2003). Founding-Family Ownership and Firm Performance: Evidence from the S&P 500. *Journal of Finance, JSTOR, 58*(3), 1301–1328. doi:10.1111/1540-6261.00567

Andrei, J., Chivu, L., Gheorghe, I., Grubor, A., Sedlarski, T., Sima, V., Subić, J., & Vasic, M. (2021). Small and medium-sized enterprises, business demography and european socio-economic model: Does the paradigm really converge*? Journal of Risk and Financial Management, 14*(2), 64. doi:10.3390/jrfm14020064

Anwar, K. (2020). *10.238 UMKM di Kota Serang Terdampak Wabah COVID-19*. Available online: https://banten.idntimes.com/business/economy/khaerul-anwar-2/10238-umkm-di-kota-serang-terdampak-wabah-covid

Apak, S. (2009). 1929 ve 2008 Krizlerinin Karşılaştırılması: Dünya ve Türkiye Örneği. *Muhasebe ve Finansman Dergisi*, (41), 6–16.

Apak, S., Erol, M., & Atmaca, M. (2012). Accounting measures to be taken for the enterprises in difficulty during times of economic crisis: A study on small and medium-sized enterprises (SMEs). *African Journal of Business Management, 6*(23), 6832–6844.

Aragon-Sanchez, A., Baixauli-Soler, S., & Carrasco-Hernandez, A. J. (2017). A missing link: The behavioral mediators between resources and entrepreneurial intentions. *International Journal of Entrepreneurial Behaviour & Research, 23*(5), 752–768. doi:10.1108/IJEBR-06-2016-0172

Armitage, C. J., & Conner, M. (2001). Efficacy of the theory of planned behavior: A meta-analytic review. *British Journal of Social Psychology*, *40*(4), 471–499. doi:10.1348/014466601164939 PMID:11795063

Arregle, J. L., Naldi, L., Nordqvist, M., & Hitt, M. A. (2012). Internationalization of Family-Controlled Firms: A Study of the Effects of External Involvement in Governance. *Entrepreneurship Theory and Practice*, *36*(6), 1115–1143. doi:10.1111/j.1540-6520.2012.00541.x

Arregle, J., Hitt, M. A., Sirmon, D. G., & Very, P. (2007). The development of organizational social capital: Attributes of family firms. *Journal of Management Studies*, *44*(1), 73–95. doi:10.1111/j.1467-6486.2007.00665.x

Arslan, Ö. (2003). Küçük ve orta ölçekli işletmelerde çalışma sermayesi ve bazı finansal yönetim uygulamaları. *Cumhuriyet Üniversitesi İktisadi ve İdari Bilimler Dergisi*, *4*(1), 121–135.

Asian Development Bank. (2012). *The Informal Sector and Informal Employment in Bangladesh*. Asian Development Bank and Bangladesh Bureau of Statistics. https://www.adb.org/sites/default/files/publication/30084/informal-sector-informal-employment-bangladesh.pdf

Asia-Pacific Economic Cooperation. (2002). *Profile of SMEs and SME Issues in APEC 1990-2000*. https://www.apec.org/Publications/2003/12/Profile-of-Small-and-Medium-Enterprises-SMEs-and-SME-Issues-in-APEC-19902000-Published-in-2003

Asikhia, O. (2010). Customer orientation and firm performance among Nigerian small and medium scale businesses. *International Journal of Marketing Studies*, *2*(1), 197–212. doi:10.5539/ijms.v2n1p197

Aşıkoğlu, R., & Ögel, S. (2006). 2001 krizinin İMKB'de hisse senetleri işlem gören imalat işletmelerinin finansal yapısı üzerindeki etkileri. *Afyon Kocatepe Üniversitesi İ.İ.B.F. Dergisi*, *8*(2), 1–18.

Audu, I. M., & Bristone, W. T. (2020). The Socio-Economic Effects of Boko Haram Insurgency in Hong Local Government Area of Adamawa State, Nigeria. *International Journal of Academic Research*, *2*(1), 40–63.

Australian Bureau of Statistics. (2020). *Australian Industry*. https://www.abs.gov.au/statistics/industry/industry-overview/australian-industry/2018-19

Awotoye, Y., & Singh, R. P. (2017). Entrepreneurial Resilience, High Impact Challenges, and Firm Performance. *Journal of Management Policy and Practice*, *18*(2).

Ayala, J. C., & Manzano, G. (2014). The resilience of the entrepreneur. Influence on the success of the business. A longitudinal analysis. *Journal of Economic Psychology*, *42*, 126–135. doi:10.1016/j.joep.2014.02.004

Azar, G., & Ciabuschi, F. (2017). Organizational innovation, technological innovation, and export performance: The effects of innovation radicalness and extensiveness. *International Business Review*, *26*(2), 324–336. doi:10.1016/j.ibusrev.2016.09.002

Azhar, A., Javaid, A., Rehman, M., & Hyder, A. (2010). Entrepreneurial intentions among business students in Pakistan. *Journal of Business Systems, Governance and Ethics*, *5*(2), 13–21. doi:10.15209/jbsge.v5i2.181

Azizi, M., & Sudhartio, L. (2020). The influence of entrepreneurial and marketing orientation to strategic learning capability and SME performance automotive industry in Indonesia - a conceptual framework. *Contemporary Research on Business and Management*, 118-122.

Babor, T. F., & Robaina, K. (2013). Public health, academic medicine, and the alcohol industry's corporate social responsibility activities. *American Journal of Public Health*, *103*(2), 206–214. doi:10.2105/AJPH.2012.300847 PMID:23237151

Bacq, S., & Eddleston, K. A. (2018). A Resource-Based View of Social Entrepreneurship: How Stewardship Culture Benefits Scale of Social Impact. *Journal of Business Ethics, 152*(3), 589–611. doi:10.100710551-016-3317-1

Baird, I., & Thomas, H. (1985). Toward a contingency model of strategic risk-taking. *Academy of Management Review, 10*(2), 230–243. doi:10.5465/amr.1985.4278108

Bakiewicz, A. (2004). Small and medium enterprises in Thailand. Following the leader. *Asia & Pacific Studies, 2*, 131–151.

Baldwin, R., & Tomiura, E. (2020). Thinking ahead about the trade impact of COVID-19. In R. Baldwin & B. W. di Mauro (Eds.), *Economics in the Time of COVID-19* (pp. 59–72). CEPR Press.

Bangladesh Bank. (2010). *SME Credit Policies & Programs.* https://bb.org.bd/sme/smepolicye.pdf

Bangladesh Bureau of Statistics. (2015). Economic Census 2013. Statistics and Informatics Division, Ministry of Planning. Dhaka: Government of the People's Republic of Bangladesh.

Bank Negara Malaysia. (2008). *SME Annual Report 2007.* https://www.bnm.gov.my/-/sme-annual-report-2007

Baporikar, N. (2018b). Entrepreneurship Development and Project Management (Text & Cases). Himalaya Publishing House.

Baporikar, N. (2014). Innovation Strategies in SME: Global Perspective. In C. Machado & P. Melo (Eds.), *Effective Human Resources Management in Small and Medium Enterprises: Global Perspectives* (pp. 315–341). Business Science Reference. doi:10.4018/978-1-4666-4731-2.ch016

Baporikar, N. (2014). Strategic Management Overview and SME in Globalized World. In K. Todorov & D. Smallbone (Eds.), *Handbook of Research on Strategic Management in Small and Medium Enterprises* (pp. 22–39). Business Science Reference. doi:10.4018/978-1-4666-5962-9.ch002

Baporikar, N. (2015). Role of Entrepreneurship in Networked Indian Economy. In P. Ordóñez de Pablos (Ed.), *Technological Solutions for Sustainable Business Practice in Asia* (pp. 36–59). Business Science Reference. doi:10.4018/978-1-4666-8462-1.ch003

Baporikar, N. (2017a). Global Perspective on Talent Management: The South African Experience. In M. Mupepi (Ed.), *Effective Talent Management Strategies for Organizational Success* (pp. 283–300). IGI Global. doi:10.4018/978-1-5225-1961-4.ch018

Baporikar, N. (2017b). Sustainable Framework to Attract, Develop, and Retain Global Talent. In K. Tamzini, T. Ayed, A. Boulanouar, & Z. Boulanouar (Eds.), *Driving Multinational Enterprises Through Effective Global Talent Management* (pp. 50–74). IGI Global. doi:10.4018/978-1-5225-2557-8.ch003

Baporikar, N. (2018a). Innovation and Sustainability in SMEs. In R. Perez-Uribe, C. Salcedo-Perez, & D. Ocampo-Guzman (Eds.), *Handbook of Research on Intrapreneurship and Organizational Sustainability in SMEs* (pp. 163–181). IGI Global. doi:10.4018/978-1-5225-3543-0.ch008

Baporikar, N. (2018c). *Knowledge Integration Strategies for Entrepreneurship and Sustainability.* IGI Global. doi:10.4018/978-1-5225-5115-7

Baporikar, N. (2019). Factors Creating Competitive Advantage for Family-Owned Business. In J. M. Saiz-Alvarez (Ed.), *Handbook of Research on Digital Marketing Innovations in Social Entrepreneurship and Solidarity Economics* (pp. 47–62). IGI Global. doi:10.4018/978-1-5225-8939-6.ch003

Baporikar, N. (2020a). Role and Room for Knowledge Management in Small and Medium Enterprises. In E. C. Idemudia (Ed.), *Handbook of Research on Social and Organizational Dynamics in the Digital Era* (pp. 115–134). IGI Global. doi:10.4018/978-1-5225-8933-4.ch006

Baporikar, N. (2020b). *Handbook of Research on Entrepreneurship Development and Opportunities in Circular Economy*. IGI Global. doi:10.4018/978-1-7998-5116-5

Baporikar, N. (2021). *Handbook of Research on Sustaining SMEs and Entrepreneurial Innovation in the Post-COVID-19 Era*. IGI Global. doi:10.4018/978-1-7998-6632-9

Barbhuiya, M. R., & Chatterjee, D. (2020). Vulnerability and resilience of the tourism sector in India: Effects of natural disasters and internal conflict. *Tourism Management Perspectives*, *33*, 100616. doi:10.1016/j.tmp.2019.100616

Barney, J. B., & Clark, D. N. (2007). Resource-Based Theory: Creating and Sustaining Competitive Advantage. Oxford University Press. doi:10.1362/026725708X382046

Barney, J. (2001). Is the resource-based "view" a useful perspective for strategic management research? *Academy of Management Review*, *26*(1), 41–56.

Barney, J. B. (2001). Resource-based theories of competitive advantage : A ten- year retrospective on the resource-based view. *Journal of Management*, *27*(6), 643–650. doi:10.1177/014920630102700602

Barney, J. B., Wright, M., & Ketchen, D. (2001). the Resource-Based View of the Firm : Ten Years After. *Journal of Management*, *16*(3), 171–174.

Baronchelli, G., Bettinelli, C., Del Bosco, B., & Loane, S. (2016). The impact of family involvement on the investments of Italian small-medium enterprises in psychically distant countries. *International Business Review*, *25*(4), 960–970. doi:10.1016/j.ibusrev.2016.01.011

Bartik, A. W., Bertrand, M., Cullen, Z., Glaeser, E. L., Luca, M., & Stanton, C. (2020). The impact of COVID-19 on small business outcomes and expectations. *Proceedings of the National Academy of Sciences of the United States of America*, *117*(30), 17656–17666. doi:10.1073/pnas.2006991117 PMID:32651281

Basco, R. (2015). Family business and regional development-A theoretical model of regional familiness. *Journal of Family Business Strategy*, *6*(4), 259–271. doi:10.1016/j.jfbs.2015.04.004

Basly, S. (2007). The internationalization of family sme an organizational learning and knowledge development perspective. *Baltic Journal of Management*, *2*(2), 154–180. doi:10.1108/17465260710750973

Basly, S., & Saunier, P. L. (2020). Familiness, socio-emotional goals and the internationalization of French family SMEs. *Journal of International Entrepreneurship*, *18*(3), 270–311. doi:10.100710843-019-00265-0

Battisti, M., & Deakins, D. (2012). Perspectives from New Zealand small firms: crisis management and the impact of the Canterbury earthquakes. In New Zealand Centre for Small & Medium Enterprise Research (Ed.), BusinesSMEasure. Massey University.

Beglaryan, M., & Shakhmuradyan, G. (2020). The impact of COVID-19 on small and medium-sized enterprises in Armenia: Evidence from a labor force survey. *Small Business International Review*, *4*(2), e298. doi:10.26784bir.v4i2.298

Bell, J., McNaughton, R., Young, S., & Crick, D. (2003). Towards an Integrative Model of Small Firm Internationalisation. *Journal of International Entrepreneurship*, *1*(4), 339–362. doi:10.1023/A:1025629424041

Bello, W. (1999). The Asian financial crisis: Causes, dynamics, prospects. *Journal of the Asia Pacific Economy*, *4*(1), 33–55.

Berger, A., & Udell, G. (1998). The economics of small business finance: The roles of private equity and debt markets in the financial growth cycle. *Journal of Banking & Finance*, *22*(6-8), 613–673. doi:10.1016/S0378-4266(98)00038-7

Bernard, M. J., & Barbosa, S. D. (2016). Resilience and entrepreneurship: A dynamic and biographical approach to the entrepreneurial act. *Management*, *19*(2), 89–123.

Berry, A., & Rodriguez, E. (2001). *Dynamics of small and medium enterprises in a slow-growth economy: The Philippines in the 1990s* (Stock No. 37181). The International Bank for Reconstruction and Development/The World Bank.

Berry, A., Rodriguez, E., & Sandee, H. (2001). Small and medium enterprise dynamics in Indonesia. *Bulletin of Indonesian Economic Studies*, *37*(3), 363–384.

Bettiol, M., Di Maria, E., & Grandinetti, R. (2011). Market extension and knowledge management strategies of knowledge-intensive business services. *Knowledge Management Research and Practice*, *9*(4), 305–314. doi:10.1057/kmrp.2011.35

Bhamra, R., Dani, S., & Burnard, K. (2011). Resilience: The concept, a literature review and future directions. *International Journal of Production Research*, *49*(18), 5375–5393. doi:10.1080/00207543.2011.563826

Bhatnagar, J. (2008). Managing capabilities for talent engagement and pipeline development. *Industrial and Commercial Training*, *40*(1), 19–28. doi:10.1108/00197850810841602

Bika, Z., & Kalantaridis, C. (2019). Organizational-Social-Capital, Time and International Family SMEs: An Empirical Study from the East of England. European Management Review, Boellis, A., Mariotti, S., Minichilli, A., & Piscitello, L. (2016). Family involvement and firms' establishment mode choice in foreign markets. *Journal of International Business Studies*, *47*(8), 929–950.

Bird, B. J. (1989). *Entrepreneurial behavior*. Scott, Foresman.

Bishop, J. (2020, June). Economic effects of the Spanish Flu. *Reserve Bank of Australia,* 8–17. https://www.rba.gov.au/publications/bulletin/2020/jun/economic-effects-of-the-spanish-flu.html

Bjorklund, T. A., Mikkonen, M., Mattila, P., & Van-Der-Marel, F. (2020). Expanding entrepreneurial solution spaces in times of crisis: Business model experimentation amongst packaged food and beverage ventures. *Journal of Business Venturing Insights*, *14*, e00197. doi:10.1016/j.jbvi.2020.e00197

Blundell, J., & Machin, S. (2020). *Self-employment in the Covid-19 crisis: CEP COVID-19 analysis*. Retrieved May 15, 2021, from https://cep.lse.ac.uk/pubs/download/cepcovid-19-003.pdf

Bodenhorn, H. (2020). Business in a time of Spanish influenza. *National Bureau of Economic Research, N11*(July). https://www.nber.org/system/files/working_papers/w27495/w27495.pdf

Boer, G. (1999). Managing the cash gap. *Journal of Accountancy*, *188*(4), 27–32.

Boettke, P., Chamlee-Wright, E., Gordon, P., Ikeda, S., Leeson, P. T., & Sobel, R. (2007). The political, economic, and social aspects of Katrina. *Southern Economic Journal*, *74*(2), 363–376.

Bonanno, G. A. (2004). Loss, trauma, and human resilience. *The American Psychologist*, *59*(1), 20–28. doi:10.1037/0003-066X.59.1.20 PMID:14736317

Bonanno, G. A. (2005). Clarifying and extending the construct of adult resilience. *The American Psychologist*, *60*(3), 265–267. doi:10.1037/0003-066X.60.3.265b PMID:15796689

Bonanno, G. A. (2012). Uses and abuses of the resilience construct: Loss, trauma, and health-related adversities. *Social Science & Medicine*, *74*(5), 753–756. doi:10.1016/j.socscimed.2011.11.022 PMID:22300714

Bose, T. (2016). Critical success factors of SME internationalization. *Journal of Small Business Strategy, 26*(2), 87–109. https://libjournals.mtsu.edu/index.php/jsbs/article/view/614

Bosher, L., Dainty, A., Carillo, P., Glass, J., & Price, A. (2007). Integrating disaster risk management into construction: A UK perspective. *Building Research and Information, 35*(2), 163–177. doi:10.1080/09613210600979848

Bosri, R. (2016). SME financing practices in Bangladesh: Scenario and challenges evaluation. *World Journal of Social Sciences, 6*(2), 39–50.

Branicki, L., Sullivan-Taylor, B., & Livschitz, S. (2018). How entrepreneurial resilience generates resilient SMEs. *International Journal of Entrepreneurial Behaviour & Research, 24*(7), 1244–1263. doi:10.1108/IJEBR-11-2016-0396

Braun, V., & Clarke, V. (2012). Thematic analysis. In H. Cooper (Ed.), *APA handbook of research methods in psychology: research design: quantitative, qualitative, neuropsychological and biological* (Vol. 2, pp. 57–71). American Psychological Association. doi:10.1037/13620-004

Brettel, M., Bendig, D., Keller, M., Friederichsen, N., & Rosenberg, M. (2014). Effectuation in Manufacturing: How Entrepreneurial Decision-making Techniques can be used to Deal with Uncertainty in Manufacturing. *Procedia CIRP, 17*, 611–616. doi:10.1016/j.procir.2014.03.119

Briguglio, L. (2004). *Economic vulnerability and resilience: concepts and measurements*. University of Malta. Islands and Small States Institute & The Commonwealth Secretariat.

Briguglio, L. (2014). *A vulnerability and resilience framework for small states*. Working Paper, University of Malta, 1-02.

Briguglio, L., Cordina, G., Farrugia, N., & Vella, S. (2009). Economic vulnerability and resilience: Concepts and measurements. *Oxford Development Studies, 37*(3), 229–247. doi:10.1080/13600810903089893

Brown & Rocha. (2020). Entrepreneurial uncertainty during the Covid-19 crisis: Mapping temporal dynamics of entrepreneurial finance. *Journal of Business Venturing Insights*. Retrieved from: https://www.ncbi.nlm.nih.gov/pmc/articles/PMC7283071/

Brown, R., & Rocha, A. (2020). Entrepreneurial uncertainty during the Covid-19 crisis: Mapping the temporal dynamics of entrepreneurial finance. *Journal of Business Venturing Insights, 14*, e00174. doi:10.1016/j.jbvi.2020.e00174

Buckle, P., Mars, G., & Smale, S. (2000). New approaches to assessing vulnerability and resilience. *Australian Journal of Emergency Management, 15*(2), 8–14.

Bullough, A., & Renko, M. (2013). Entrepreneurial resilience during challenging times. *Business Horizons, 57*(3), 343–350. doi:10.1016/j.bushor.2013.01.001

Bullough, A., Renko, M., & Myatt, T. (2014). Danger zone entrepreneurs: The importance of resilience and self-efficacy for entrepreneurial intentions. *Entrepreneurship Theory and Practice, 38*(3), 473–499. doi:10.1111/etap.12006

Bureau of Economic Research. (2016). *The small, medium, and micro-enterprise sector of South Africa*. University of Stellenbosch. Retrieved May 10, 2021, from http://www.seda.org.za/

Burger, A., Damijan, J. P., Kostevc, Č., & Rojec, M. (2017). Determinants of firm performance and growth during economic recession: The case of Central and Eastern European countries. *Economic Systems, 41*(4), 569–590. doi:10.1016/j.ecosys.2017.05.003

Burgueño-Salas, E. (2020). Volumen de producción mensual de fertilizantes fosfatados en México de enero de 2019 a julio de 2020 (en toneladas métricas). *Statista*. Retrieve on the 2 of July 2021 from https://es.statista.com/estadisticas/594554/volumen-de-produccion-de-fertilizantes-superfosfatados-en-mexico/

Burhan, F. A. (2020). *Bisnis Anjlok akibat Pandemi Corona, UMKM Bisa Ubah Strategi Usaha*. Available online: https://katadata.co.id/berita/2020/04/15/bisnis-anjlok-akibat-pandemi-corona-umkm-bisa-ubah-strategi-usaha

Burns, P., & Dewhurst, J. (2016). *Small Business and Entrepreneurship* (4th ed.). Palgrave. doi:10.1007/978-1-137-43034-2

Busenitz, L. W. (1999). Entrepreneurial Risk and Strategic Decision Making: It's a Matter of Perspective. *The Journal of Applied Behavioral Science*. Retrieved from https://shareok.org/bitstream/handle/11244/24846/10.1177.0021886399353005.pdf?sequence=1

Bužavaitė, M., Ščeulovs, D., & Korsakienė, R. (2019). Theoretical approach to the internationalization of SMEs: Future research prospects based on bibliometric analysis. *Entrepreneurship and Sustainability Issues*, *6*(3), 1497–1511. doi:10.9770/jesi.2019.6.3(31)

Caballero-Morales, S. O. (2021). Innovation as recovery strategy for SMEs in emerging economies during the COVID-19 pandemic. *Research in International Business and Finance*, *57*(February), 101396. doi:10.1016/j.ribaf.2021.101396 PMID:33558782

Calabrò, A., & Mussolino, D. (2012). How Do Boards of Directors Contribute to Family SME Export Intensity? The Role of Formal and Informal Governance Mechanisms. SSRN *Electronic Journal*.

Calabrò, A., Brogi, M., & Torchia, M. (2016). What Does Really Matter in the Internationalization of Small and Medium-Sized Family Businesses? *Journal of Small Business Management*, *54*(2), 679–696. doi:10.1111/jsbm.12165

Calabrò, A., Torchia, M., Pukall, T., & Mussolino, D. (2013). The influence of ownership structure and board strategic involvement on international sales: The moderating effect of family involvement. *International Business Review*, *22*(3), 509–523. doi:10.1016/j.ibusrev.2012.07.002

Calabrò, A., Vecchiarini, M., Gast, J., Campopiano, G., De Massis, A., & Kraus, S. (2019). Innovation in Family Firms: A Systematic Literature Review and Guidance for Future Research. *International Journal of Management Reviews*, *21*(3), 317–355. doi:10.1111/ijmr.12192

Caligirui, P., De Cierei, H., Minbaeva, D., Verbeke, A., & Zimmermann, A. (2020). International HRM insights for navigating the COVID-19 pandemic: Implications for future research and practice. *Journal of International Business Studies*, *51*(5), 697–713. Advance online publication. doi:10.105741267-020-00335-9 PMID:32836500

Callaway, S. (2004). Elements of infrastructure: Factors driving international entrepreneurship. *New England Journal of Entrepreneurship*, *7*(1), 27–37. doi:10.1108/NEJE-07-01-2004-B004

Canabal, A., & White, G. O. III. (2008). Entry mode research: Past and future. *International Business Review*, *17*(3), 267–284. doi:10.1016/j.ibusrev.2008.01.003

Can, H. (2002). *Organizasyon ve yönetim*. Siyasal Kitabevi.

Cantú, P. (2008). *Desarrollo sustentable: conceptos y reflexiones*. Universidad Autónoma de Nuevo León. Colección: Tendencias Científicas.

Cappelli, P. (2008). Talent management for the twenty-first century. *Harvard Business Review*, *86*(3), 74–82. doi:10.100710551-010-0541-y PMID:18411966

Caralli, R. A., Allen, J. H., & White, D. W. (2010). *CERT resilience management model: A maturity model for managing operational resilience*. Addison-Wesley Professional.

Carney, M., Duran, P., van Essen, M., & Shapiro, D. (2017). Family firms, internationalization, and national competitiveness: Does family firm prevalence matter? *Journal of Family Business Strategy*, *8*(3), 123–136. doi:10.1016/j.jfbs.2017.06.001

Carree, M. A., & Thurik, A. R. (2010). The impact of entrepreneurship on economic growth. In J. Zoltan & D. Audretsch (Eds.), *Handbook of entrepreneurship research* (pp. 557–594). Springer. doi:10.1007/978-1-4419-1191-9_20

Carter, M. R., & Barrett, C. B. (2006). The economics of poverty traps and persistent poverty: An asset-based approach. *The Journal of Development Studies*, *42*(2), 178–199. doi:10.1080/00220380500405261

Casillas, J. C., & Acedo, F. J. (2005). Internationalisation of Spanish family SMEs: An analysis of family involvement. *International Journal of Globalisation and Small Business*, *1*(2), 134–151. doi:10.1504/IJGSB.2005.008010

Castro, A. (1998). *Hacia el desarrollo sostenible y la ecoeficiencia: integración de las normas ISO 9000, ISO 14000 e ISO 18000 diseño de un sistema de gestión ambiental certificable. (Tesis de maestría inédita).* Obtenido de Facultad Regional de Buenos Aires: http://posgrado.frba.utn.edu.ar/investigacion/tesis/MIA-1998-Castro.pdf

Centeno, M. A., Nag, M., Patterson, T. S., Shaver, A., & Windawi, A. J. (2014). The emerge of global systemic risk. *Annual Review of Sociology*, *41*(1), 65–85. doi:10.1146/annurev-soc-073014-112317

Center for Disease Control and Prevention (CDCP). (2020). Influenza (Flu) 1918 Pandemic (H1N1 virus). *1918 Pandemic Webpage, 2019*, 1918–1920. https://www.cdc.gov/flu/pandemic-resources/1918-pandemic-h1n1.html#:~:text=It is estimated that about,occurring in the United States.

Cerrato, D., & Piva, M. (2012). The internationalization of small and medium-sized enterprises: The effect of family management, human capital and foreign ownership. *The Journal of Management and Governance*, *16*(4), 617–644. doi:10.100710997-010-9166-x

Çetin, H. (2009). *Kriz yönetimi ve işletmeler açısından alınacak önlemler. In 6.uluslararası Türk Dünyası Sosyal Bilimler Kongresi*. Avcı Ofset Basımevi.

Chakraborty, P. (2012). *The Great Trade Collapse and Indian Firms* (Unpublished PhD dissertation). Graduate Institute of International and Development Studies.

Chantrasawang, N. (1999). *Current issues of SMEs in Thailand: Its linkages with FDI and the impact of the financial crisis*. Paper presented at the International Conference on Small and Medium Enterprises At New Crossroads: Challenges and Prospects, Penang, Malaysia.

Chesbrough, H. (2020). To recover faster from Covid-19, open up: Managerial implications from an open innovation perspective. *Industrial Marketing Management*, *88*, 410–413. j.indmarman.2020.04.010 doi:10.1016/

Chibueze, O. O., Mairami, F. F., Ugwu, D. O., Agwu, A. N., & Lawal, H. B. (2020). *Implications of COVID-19 on Nigeria's Economy*. Connected Development.

Chitranshi, J. (2015). Talent Management. In S. Kalia, B. Bhalla, L. Das, & N. Awasthy (Eds.), *Promoting Socio-Economic Development through Business Integration* (pp. 124–134). IGI Global. doi:10.4018/978-1-4666-8259-7.ch009

Chong, P. L., Onga, T. S., Abdullah, A., & Choo, W. C. (2019). Internationalisation and innovation on balanced scorecard (BSC) among Malaysian small and medium enterprises (SMEs). *Management Science Letters*, *9*(10), 1617–1632. doi:10.5267/j.msl.2019.5.025

Chowdhury, M., Alam, Z., & Arif, M. (2013). Success factors of entrepreneurs of small and medium sized enterprises: Evidence from Bangladesh. *Business and Economic Review*, *3*(2), 38. doi:10.5296/ber.v3i2.4127

Christensen, C., & Bower, J. (1996). Customer power, strategic investment, and the failure of leading firms. *Strategic Management Journal*, *17*(3), 197–218. doi:10.1002/(SICI)1097-0266(199603)17:3<197::AID-SMJ804>3.0.CO;2-U

Chumphong, O., Srimai, S., & Potipiroon, W. (2020). The Resource-Based View, Dynamic Capabilities and SME Performance for SMEs to Become Smart Enterprises. *ABAC ODI Journal Vision, 7*(2), 129–146.

Ciremaitoday. (2020). *Kisah Perajin Batik Perempuan di Cirebon, Bangkit Ditengah Pandemi COVID-19.* Available online: https://kumparan.com/ciremaitoday/kisah-perajin-batik-perempuan-di-cirebon-bangkit-ditengah pandemi-covid-19-1tGcuTSTNoV/full

Claessens, S., Tong, H., & Shang-Jin, W. (2011). *From the Financial Crisis to the Real economy: Using Firm-level Data to Identify Transmission Channels.* NBER Working Paper No.17360. Washington, DC: National Bureau of Economic Research.

Claver, E., Rienda, L., & Quer, D. (2007). The internationalisation process in family firms: Choice of market entry strategies. *Journal of General Management, 33*(1), 1–14. doi:10.1177/030630700703300101

Claver, E., Rienda, L., & Quer, D. (2008). Family firms' risk perception: Empirical evidence on the internationalization process. *Journal of Small Business and Enterprise Development, 15*(3), 457–471. doi:10.1108/14626000810892283

Claver, E., Rienda, L., & Quer, D. (2009). Family Firms' International Commitment: The Influence of Family-Related Factors. *Family Business Review, 22*(2), 125–135. doi:10.1177/0894486508330054

Coleman, J. S. (2009). Social capital in the creation of human capital. *Knowledge and Social Capital,* 17–42.

Colombo, M. G., D'Adda, D., & Quas, A. (2019). The geography of venture capital and entrepreneurial ventures' demand for external equity. *Research Policy, 48*(5), 1150–1170. doi:10.1016/j.respol.2018.12.004

Compagno, C., Pittino, D., & Visintin, F. (2005). Corporate governance and advanced forms of internationalisation in Italian SMEs. *International Journal of Globalisation and Small Business, 1*(2), 168–182. doi:10.1504/IJGSB.2005.008012

Consejo Mundial Empresarial para el Desarrollo Sostenible. (1991). Ecoeficiencia y sustentabilidad. *Ciencia UANL, 35,* 15–28.

Cook, L., & Barrett, C. (2020). *How Covid-19 is escalating problem debt.* https://www.ft.com/content/4062105a-afaf-4b28-bde6-ba71d5767ec0

Cordina, G. (2004a). Economic Vulnerability, Resilience and Capital Formation. In L. Briguglio & E. J. Kisanga (Eds.), Economic Vulnerability and Resilience of Small States. Malta: Islands and Small States Institute and London: Commonwealth Secretariat.

Cordina, G. (2004b). 'Economic Vulnerability and Economic Growth: Some Results from a Neo-Classical Growth Modelling Approach'. *Journal of Economic Development, 29*(2), 21–39.

Covin, J. G., & Slevin, D. P. (1989). Strategic management of small firms in hostile and benign environments. *Strategic Management Journal, 10*(1), 75–87. doi:10.1002mj.4250100107

Creswell, J. W. (2014). *Research design: Qualitative, quantitative, and mixed-method approaches* (4th ed.). Sage.

Crick, J. M. (2018). The facets, antecedents and consequences of coopetition. *Qualitative Market Research, 21*(2), 253–272. doi:10.1108/QMR-11-2016-0109

Cumming, D., & Dai, N. (2010). Local bias in venture capital investments. *Journal of Empirical Finance, 17*(3), 362–380. doi:10.1016/j.jempfin.2009.11.001

D'Angelo, A., Majocchi, A., & Buck, T. (2016). External managers, family ownership and the scope of SME internationalization. *Journal of World Business, 51*(4), 534–547. doi:10.1016/j.jwb.2016.01.004

Dai, R., Feng, H., Hu, J., Jin, Q., Li, H., Wang, R., Wang, R., Xu, L., & Zhang, X. (2020). The Impact of COVID-19 on Small and Medium-sized enterprises: Evidence from two-wave phone surveys in China. *Center for Global Development*. https://www.cgdev.org/publication/impact-covid-19-small-and-medium-sized-enterprises-evidence-two-wave-phone-surveys-china%0ACenter

Dalal, R., & Akdere, M. (2018). Talent development: Status quo and future directions. *Industrial and Commercial Training, 50*(6), 342–355. doi:10.1108/ICT-03-2018-0033

Dana, L. P., & Dana, T. E. (2005). Expanding the scope of methodologies used in entrepreneurship research. *International Journal of Entrepreneurship and Small Business, 2*(1), 79–88.

Dangayach, G., & Deshmukh, S. (2005). Advanced manufacturing technology implementation. *Journal of Manufacturing Technology Management, 16*(5), 483–496. doi:10.1108/17410380510600473

Daspit, J. J., Chrisman, J. J., Ashton, T., & Evangelopoulos, N. (2021). Family Firm Heterogeneity: A Definition, Common Themes, Scholarly Progress, and Directions Forward. *Family Business Review*. Advance online publication. doi:10.1177/08944865211008350

Daştan, A. (2009). Ekomomik kriz dönemlerinde muhasebe bilgi sisteminin işletmelerdeki rolü ve kriz yönetimine katkısı. *Muhasebe ve Finansman Dergisi, 28*, 57–72.

Davidkov, T. P., & Yordanova, D. I. (2016). Exploring the Bulgarian family SMEs' reluctance to internationalise. *International Journal of Business and Globalisation, 17*(1), 123–148. doi:10.1504/IJBG.2016.077570

Davidson, R. J. (2000). Affective style, psychopathology and resilience: Brain mechanisms and plasticity. *The American Psychologist, 55*(11), 1196–1214. doi:10.1037/0003-066X.55.11.1196 PMID:11280935

Davis, T. J. (2020, June 1). Their stores were burned, ran sacked and looted. What's next for Minneapolis-area small business owners? *USA Today*. Retrieved from https://eu.usatoday.com/story/news/nation/2020/06/01/george-floyd-protests-riots-minneapolis-small-businesses/5300736002/

De Clercq, D., & Sapienza, H. J. (2006). Effects of relational capital and commitment on venture capitalists' perception of portfolio company performance. *Journal of Business Venturing, 21*(3), 326–347. doi:10.1016/j.jbusvent.2005.04.007

De Massis, A., Frattini, F., Majocchi, A., & Piscitello, L. (2018a). Family firms in the global economy: Toward a deeper understanding of internationalization determinants, processes, and outcomes. *Global Strategy Journal, 8*(1), 3–21. doi:10.1002/gsj.1199

De Vries, M. F. R. K. (1977). The entrepreneurial personality: A person at the crossroads. *Journal of Management Studies, 14*(1), 34–57. doi:10.1111/j.1467-6486.1977.tb00616.x

Deakins, D., & Freel, M. (1998). Entrepreneurial learning and the growth process in SMEs. *The Learning Organization, 5*(3), 144–155. doi:10.1108/09696479810223428

Demirtaş, H. (2000). Kriz yönetimi. *Kuram ve Uygulamada Eğitim Yönetimi, 23*, 353–373.

Denicolai, S., Hagen, B., & Pisoni, A. (2015). Be international or be innovative? Be both? The role of the entrepreneurial profile. *Journal of International Entrepreneurship, 13*(4), 390–417. doi:10.100710843-015-0143-y

Department of Statistics Malaysia. (2021). *Malaysian Economic Statistics Review*. https://www.dosm.gov.my/v1/index.php?r=column/cthemeByCat&cat=481&bul_id=U05RQmY4cU1MK1FQdDRMSmNURlVrdz09&menu_id=azJjRWpYL0VBYU90TVhpclByWjdMQT09

Desa, G., & Basu, S. (2013). Optimization or bricolage? Overcoming resource constraints in global social entrepreneurship. *Strategic Entrepreneurship Journal*, *8*(6), 4517–4524. doi:10.1002ej.1150

DGHS Press Release. (2021, April 12). *COVID-19 Press Bulletin.* https://corona.gov.bd/

Dhaka Tribune. (2020, October 31). *No mask, no service.* https://www.dhakatribune.com/bangladesh/government-affairs/2020/10/31/no-mask-no-entry

Dhaka Tribune. (2021). *Survey: New poor in Bangladesh stands at 24.5 million.* Author.

Dibrell, C., Davis, P. S., & Craig, J. (2008). Fueling innovation through information technology in SMEs. *Journal of Small Business Management*, *46*(2), 203–218. doi:10.1111/j.1540-627X.2008.00240.x

Dieguez, T. (2020). Cultural Approach to Mitigate COVID-19's Impact: Comparative Perspective. In N. Baporikar (Ed.), *Handbook of Research on Strategies and Interventions to Mitigate COVID-19 Impact on SMEs*. IGI Global.

Dierman, van, P., Tambunan, T., Tambunan, M., & Wie, T. K. (1998). *The IMF 50-point program: Evaluating the likely impact on SMEs.* Draft report for the Asia Foundation.

Dietrich, F., Palm, D., & Louw, L. (2020). Smart contract based framework to increase transparency of manufacturing networks. *Procedia CIRP*, *91*, 278–283. doi:10.1016/j.procir.2020.02.177

Dionne, S. D., Yammarino, F. J., Atwater, L. E., & Spangler, W. D. (2004). Transformational leadership and team performance. *Journal of Organizational Change Management*, *17*(2), 177–193. doi:10.1108/09534810410530601

Do Paço, F., Arminda, M., Ferreira, J. M., Raposo, M., Gouveia, R., & Dinis, A. (2011). Behaviours and entrepreneurial intention: Empirical findings about secondary students. *Journal of International Entrepreneurship*, *9*(1), 20–38. doi:10.100710843-010-0071-9

Dobni, C. B. (2010). The relationship between an innovation orientation and competitive strategy. *International Journal of Innovation Management*, *14*(02), 331–357. doi:10.1142/S1363919610002660

Doern, R. (2017). Strategies for resilience in entrepreneurship: Building resources for small business survival after a crisis. In T. Vorley & N. Williams (Eds.), *Creating resilient economies: Entrepreneurship, growth and development in uncertain times*. Edward Elgar. doi:10.4337/9781785367649.00008

Doern, R., Williams, N., & Vorley, T. (2019). Special issue on entrepreneurship and crises: Business as usual? An introduction and review of the literature. *Entrepreneurship and Regional Development*, *31*(5–6), 400–412. doi:10.1080/08985626.2018.1541590

Doh, J. P., Smith, R. R., Stumpf, S. A., & Tymon, W. G. Jr. (2011). Pride and professionals: Retaining talent in emerging economies. *The Journal of Business Strategy*, *32*(5), 35–42. doi:10.1108/02756661111165453

Douglas, E. J., & Shepherd, D. A. (2002). Self-Employment as a Career Choice: Attitudes, Entrepreneurial Intentions, and Utility Maximization. *Entrepreneurship Theory and Practice*, *26*(3), 81–90. doi:10.1177/104225870202600305

Dowling & Stephen. (2020). *Coronavirus: What can we learn from the Spanish flu?* https://www.bbc.com/future/article/20200302-coronavirus-what-can-we-learn-from-the-spanish-flu

Drucker, P. F. (1994). *Innovation and Entrepreneurship: Practice and Principles*. Heinemann.

Duchek, S. (2018). Entrepreneurial resilience: A biographical analysis of successful entrepreneurs. *The International Entrepreneurship and Management Journal*, *14*(2), 429–455. doi:10.100711365-017-0467-2

Dul, J., & Hak, T. (2008). *Case Study Methodology in Business Research*. Academic Press.

Dzingirai, M. (2020). Demographic determinants of youth entrepreneurial success. *International Journal of Sustainable Entrepreneurship and Corporate Social Responsibility*, *5*(2), 1–16. doi:10.4018/IJSECSR.2020070101

Dzingirai, M., Chagwesha, M., & Mudzurandende, F. (2021). Challenges and opportunities from covid-19 vis-à-vis informal cross-border women entrepreneurs scenario in Zimbabwe. In N. Baporikar (Ed.), *Handbook of research on sustaining SMEs and entrepreneurial innovation in the post-COVID-19 Era* (pp. 40–59). IGI Global. doi:10.4018/978-1-7998-6632-9.ch003

Ebeke, C., Jovanovic, N., Valderrama, L., & Zhou, J. (2021). Corporate Liquidity and Solvency in Europe during COVID-19. *IMF Working Papers, 21*(278).

Eberhard, M., & Craig, J. (2013). The evolving role of organisational and personal networks in international market venturing. *Journal of World Business*, *48*(3), 385–397. doi:10.1016/j.jwb.2012.07.022

Economic Planning Unit Malaysia (EPU). (2021). *Malaysia Digital Economy Blueprint*. EPU.

Eddleston, K. A., Sarathy, R., & Banalieva, E. R. (2019). When a high-quality niche strategy is not enough to spur family-firm internationalization: The role of external and internal contexts. *Journal of International Business Studies*, *50*(5), 783–808. doi:10.105741267-018-0199-8

Editorial. (2006). Resilience, vulnerability, and adaptation: A crosscutting theme of the International Human Dimensions Programme on Global Environmental Change. *Global Environmental Change, 16*(3), 237–239.

Eduardsen, J. S. (2021). COVID-19, Global Value Chains, Risk and Resilience. In A. Marinov & S. T. Marinova (Eds.), *COVID-19 and International Business: Change of Era*. Taylor & Francis Group.

Eggers, F. (2020). Masters of disasters? Challenges and opportunities for SMEs in times of crisis. *Journal of Business Research*, *116*(May), 199–208. doi:10.1016/j.jbusres.2020.05.025 PMID:32501306

Eibe Sørensen, H. (2009). Why competitors matter for market orientation. *European Journal of Marketing*, *43*(5/6), 735–761. doi:10.1108/03090560910947025

Eisenhardt, K. M. (1989). Building Theories from Case Study Research. *Academy of Management Review*, *14*(4), 532–550. doi:10.5465/amr.1989.4308385

Eisenhardt, K. M., & Graebner, M. E. (2007). Theory Building from Cases: Opportunities and Challenges. *Academy of Management Journal*, *50*(1), 25–32. doi:10.5465/amj.2007.24160888

Ellis, P. D. (2006). Market orientation and performance: A meta-analysis and cross-national comparisons. *Journal of Management Studies*, *43*(5), 1089–1107. doi:10.1111/j.1467-6486.2006.00630.x

Emergency Management Australia. (1998). *Australian Emergency Management Glossary*. Author.

Endeavor Brasil. (2016). *Desafios dos empreendedores brasileiros*. Author.

Eniola, A. A., & Entebang, H. (2015). Government policy and performance of small and medium business management. *International Journal of Academic Research in Business & Social Sciences*, *5*(2), 237–248. doi:10.6007/IJARBSS/v5-i2/1481

Espiner, S., & Becken, S. (2014). Tourist towns on the edge: Conceptualising vulnerability and resilience in a protected area tourism system. *Journal of Sustainable Tourism*, *22*(4), 646–665. doi:10.1080/09669582.2013.855222

Estrin, S., Mickiewicz, T., & Stephan, U. (2016). Human capital in social and commercial entrepreneurship. *Journal of Business Venturing*, *31*(4), 449–467. doi:10.1016/j.jbusvent.2016.05.003

Etikan, I., & Bala, K. (2017). Sampling and sampling methods. *Biometrics and Biostatistics International Journal, 5*(6), 215–217. doi:10.15406/bbij.2017.05.00149

Etikan, I., Musa, S. A., & Alkassim, R. S. (2016). Comparison of convenience sampling and purposive sampling. *American Journal of Theoretical and Applied Statistics, 5*(1), 1–4. doi:10.11648/j.ajtas.20160501.11

European Investment Bank. (2020). *Does this change everything? Small business gets sick.* https://www.eib.org/en/stories/smes-coronavirus

Evans, D. S., & Leighton, L. S. (1989). Some empirical aspects of entrepreneurship. *The American Economic Review, 79*, 519–535.

Fairlie, R. W. (2020). *The Impact of COVID-19 on Small Business Owners: Continued Losses the Partial Rebound in May 2020.* National Bureau of Economic Research Working Paper 27462.

Falahat, M., Ramayah, T., Soto-Acosta, P., & Lee, Y. Y. (2020). SMEs internationalization: The role of product innovation, market intelligence, pricing and marketing communication capabilities as drivers of SMEs' international performance. *Technological Forecasting and Social Change, 152*(June), 119908. doi:10.1016/j.techfore.2020.119908

Falkner, E. M., & Hiebl, M. R. W. (2015). Risk management in SMEs: A systematic review of available evidence. *The Journal of Risk Finance, 16*(2), 122–144. doi:10.1108/JRF-06-2014-0079

Farhana, K. M., & Mannan, K. A. (2020). Knowledge and perception towards Novel Coronavirus (COVID 19) in Bangladesh. *International Research Journal of Business and Social Science, 6*(2), 76–87. doi:10.2139srn.3578477

Fatoki, O. (2018). The Impact of Entrepreneurial Resilience on the Success of Small and Medium Enterprises in South Africa. *Sustainability, 10*(7), 2527. doi:10.3390u10072527

Ferguson, N. (2020). Historian Niall Ferguson on what the pandemic means for the global economy, geopolitics – and parties. *World Economic Forum.* Retrieved from https://www.weforum.org/agenda/2020/05/niall-ferguson-economy-pandemic-coronavirus-covid/

Fernández-Olmos, M., Gargallo-Castel, A., & Giner-Bagües, E. (2016). Internationalisation and performance in Spanish family SMES: The W-curve. *BRQ Business Research Quarterly, 19*(2), 122–136. doi:10.1016/j.brq.2015.07.001

Fernandez, Z., & Nieto, M. J. (2005). Internationalization Strategy of Small and Medium-Sized Family Businesses. *Family Business Review, 18*(1), 77–89. doi:10.1111/j.1741-6248.2005.00031.x

Fernando, I. (2021). Assessing the Competitiveness of Sri Lanka's Tourism in the COVID Period by Porter's Diamond Model. In N. Baporikar (Ed.), *Handbook of Research on Strategies and Interventions to Mitigate COVID-19 Impact on SMEs*. IGI Global. doi:10.4018/978-1-7998-7436-2.ch001

Fernet, C., Torrès, O., Austin, S., & St-Pierre, J. (2016). The psychological costs of owning and managing an SME: Linking job stressors, occupational loneliness, entrepreneurial orientation, and burnout. *Burnout Research, 3*(2), 45–53. doi:10.1016/j.burn.2016.03.002

Festing, M., Harsch, K., Schäfer, L., & Scullion, H. (2017). Talent management in small and medium-sized enterprises. In The Oxford handbook of talent management. OUP.

Fillis, I. (2001). Small firm internationalisation: An investigative survey and future research directions. *Management Decision, 39*(9), 767–783. doi:10.1108/00251740110408683

Filser, M., Eggers, F., Kraus, S., & Málovics, É. (2014). The effect of financial resource availability on entrepreneurial orientation, customer orientation and firm performance in an international context: An empirical analysis from Austria and Hungary. *Journal for East European Management Studies, 19*(1), 7–30. doi:10.5771/0949-6181-2014-1-7

Fink, S. (1986). *Crisis management: Planning for the inevitable*. American Management Association.

FIRA (2020). *Reporte trimestral de fertilizantes, Dirección de Investigación y Evaluación Económica del Fideicomisos Instituidos en relación con la Agricultura*. FIRA, Diciembre 2020.

Friede, G., Busch, T., & Bassen, A. (2015). ESG and financial performance: Aggregated evidence from more than 2000 empirical studies. *Journal of Sustainable Finance and Investment, 5*(4), 210–233. doi:10.1080/20430795.2015.1118917

Fuchs, S., & Thaler, T. (Eds.). (2018). *Vulnerability and resilience to natural hazards*. Cambridge University Press. doi:10.1017/9781316651148

Gallardo-gallardo, E., Dries, N., & González-cruz, T. F. (2013). Human Resource Management Review What is the meaning of "talent" in the world of work? *Human Resource Management Review, 23*(4), 290–300. doi:10.1016/j.hrmr.2013.05.002

Gallegos-Cedillo, G. (2021). Working paper *Agronegocios FIRA*.

Gallo, M. A., & Sveen, J. (1991). Internationalizing the Family Business: Facilitating and Restraining Factors. *Family Business Review, 4*(2), 181–190. doi:10.1111/j.1741-6248.1991.00181.x

Game, R., & Apfelthaler, G. (2016). Attitude and its role in SME internationalisation: Why do firms commit to advanced foreign market entry modes? *European Journal of International Management, 10*(2), 221–248. doi:10.1504/EJIM.2016.074473

Garrett, T. A. (2007). Economic effects of the 1918 influenza pandemic: Implications for a modern-day pandemic. *Federal Reserve Bank of St. Louis*. www.stlouisfed.org/community/other_pubs.html.%0Ahttp://199.169.201.166/community_development/assets/pdf/pandemic_flu_report.pdf

GEM. (2021). *GEM 2020/2021 Global Report*. GEM.

Gençtürk, M., Dalğar, H., & Yılmaz, T. (2011). Finansal krizlerin işletmelerin finansman kararlarına etkileri, İMKB'de işlem gören işletmeler üzerinde bir araştırma. *Cumhuriyet Üniversitesi İktisadi ve İdari Bilimler Fakültesi Dergisi, 12*(1), 187–207.

George, G., Wiklund, J., & Zahra, S. A. (2005). Ownership and the internationalization of small firms. *Journal of Management, 31*(2), 210–233. doi:10.1177/0149206304271760

Georgiadou, A., Mouzakitis, S., & Askounis, D. (2021). Working from home during COVID-19 crisis: A cyber security culture assessment survey. *Security Journal*. Advance online publication. doi:10.105741284-021-00286-2

Gerring, J. (2006). *Case Study Research* (Vol. 53). Cambridge University Press. doi:10.1017/CBO9780511803123

Ghobakhloo, M. (2018). The future of manufacturing industry: A strategic roadmap toward Industry 4.0. *Journal of Manufacturing Technology Management, 29*(6), 910–936. doi:10.1108/JMTM-02-2018-0057

Ghosh, S. (2020). Examining the Covid-19 relief package for MSMEs. *Economic and Political Weekly, 55*(22), 10–68.

Gilmore, T. N., & Kazanjian, R. K. (1989). Clarifying decision making in high-growth ventures: The use of responsibility charting. *Journal of Business Venturing, 4*(1), 69–83. doi:10.1016/0883-9026(89)90034-7

Giones, F., Brem, A., Pollack, J. M., Michaelis, T. L., Klyver, K., & Brinckmann, J. (2020). Revising entrepreneurial action in response to exogenous shocks: Considering the COVID-19 pandemic. *Journal of Business Venturing Insights, 14*, e00186. doi:10.1016/j.jbvi.2020.e00186

Glasser, B. G., & Strauss, A. L. (2017). *The discovery of grounded theory: Strategies for qualitative research*. Routledge. doi:10.4324/9780203793206

Gomezelj Omerzel, D., & Antončič, B. (2008). Critical entrepreneur knowledge dimensions for the SME performance. *Industrial Management & Data Systems, 108*(9), 1182–1199. doi:10.1108/02635570810914883

Gomez-Mejia, L. R., Cruz, C., Berrone, P., & de Castro, J. (2011). The Bind that ties: Socioemotional wealth preservation in family firms. *The Academy of Management Annals, 5*(1), 653–707. doi:10.5465/19416520.2011.593320

Gómez-Mejía, L. R., Haynes, K. T., Núñez-Nickel, M., Jacobson, K. J. L., & Moyano-Fuentes, J. (2007). Socioemotional Wealth and Business Risks in Family-controlled Firms: Evidence from Spanish Olive Oil Mills. *Administrative Science Quarterly, 52*(1), 106–137. doi:10.2189/asqu.52.1.106

Gomez-Mejia, L. R., Makri, M., & Kintana, M. L. (2010). Diversification decisions in family-controlled firms. *Journal of Management Studies, 47*(2), 223–252. doi:10.1111/j.1467-6486.2009.00889.x

Gough, D., Thomas, J., & Oliver, S. (2012). Clarifying differences between review designs and methods. *Systematic Reviews, 1*(1), 28. doi:10.1186/2046-4053-1-28 PMID:22681772

Government of Canada. (2020). *Key Small Business Statistics – 2020*. http://www.ic.gc.ca/eic/site/061.nsf/eng/h_03126.html#definition

Grandon, E. E., & Pearson, J. M. (2004). Electronic commerce adoption: An empirical study of small and medium US businesses. *Information & Management, 42*(1), 197–216. doi:10.1016/j.im.2003.12.010

Graves, C., & Shan, Y. G. (2014). An Empirical Analysis of the Effect of Internationalization on the Performance of Unlisted Family and Nonfamily Firms in Australia. *Family Business Review, 27*(2), 142–160. doi:10.1177/0894486513491588

Graves, C., & Thomas, J. (2006). Internationalization of Australian family businesses: A managerial capabilities perspective. *Family Business Review, 19*(3), 207–224. doi:10.1111/j.1741-6248.2006.00066.x

Graves, C., & Thomas, J. (2008). Determinants of the internationalization pathways of family firms: An examination of family influence. *Family Business Review, 21*(2), 151–167. doi:10.1111/j.1741-6248.2008.00119.x

Gregurec, I., Tomičić Furjan, M., & Tomičić-Pupek, K. (2021). The impact of COVID-19 on sustainable business models in SMEs. *Sustainability, 13*(3), 1098. doi:10.3390u13031098

Griffith-Jones, S., & Ocampo, J. A. (2009). *The financial crisis and its impacts on developing countries*. Working Paper No. 53. Brasilia: International Policy Center for Inclusive Growth.

Güler, E., & Yılmaz, B. (2009). Ekonomik kriz, KOBİ'lere yansıması ve bir çıkış yolu olarak barter. *Sosyal Ekonomik Araştırmalar Dergisi, 9*(18), 87–104.

Gunasekaran, A., Subramanian, N., & Rahman, S. (2015). Supply claim resilience: Role of complexities and strategies. *International Journal of Production Research, 53*(22), 6809–6819. doi:10.1080/00207543.2015.1093667

Guo, H., Yang, Z., Huang, R., & Guo, A. (2020). The digitalization and public crisis responses of small and medium enterprises: Implications from a COVID-19 survey. *Frontiers of Business Research in China, 14*(1), 1–25. doi:10.118611782-020-00087-1

Gürbüz, G., & Aykol, S. (2009). Entrepreneurial management, entrepreneurial orientation and Turkish small firm growth. *Management Research News, 32*(4), 321–336. doi:10.1108/01409170910944281

Hambrick, D. C., & Crozier, L. (1985). Stumblers and stars in the management of rapid growth. *Journal of Business Venturing, 1*(1), 31–45. doi:10.1016/0883-9026(85)90005-9

Harsch, K., & Festing, M. (2020). Dynamic talent management capabilities and organizational agility—A qualitative exploration. *Human Resource Management, 59*(1), 43–61. doi:10.1002/hrm.21972

Hartono, D. (2011). Assessing policy effectiveness during the crisis: The case of Indonesia. Geneva: International Labour Organization (International Institute for Labour Studies).

Hasan, A. (2020, August 23). *The growth of e-commerce during the pandemic in Bangladesh.* New Age.

Hashim, N. B., Raza, S., & Minai, M. S. (2018). Relationship between entrepreneurial competencies and small firm performance: Are dynamic capabilities the missing link? *Academy of Strategic Management Journal, 17*(2), 1–2.

Hatton, T., Seville, E., & Vargo, J. (2012). *Improving the resilience of SMEs: policy and practice in New Zealand.* Christchurch, New Zealand: Asia Pacific Economic Co-operation (APEC). https://www.resorgs.org.nz/wp-content/uploads/2019/04/apec-sme-resilience-policy-final-report.pdf

Hedner, T., Albouzeedan, A., & Klofsten, M. (2017). Entrepreneurial resilience. *Annals of Innovation amp; Entrepreneurship, 2.* https://www.tandfonline.com/doi/full/10.3402/aie.v2i1.6002

Hegarty, C., Gallagher, P., Cunningham, I., & Stephens, S. (2020). *Šebestová, J. (e.d) Developing Entrepreneurial Competencies for Start-Ups and Small Business.* IGI Global. Retrieved from https://www.igi-global.com/gateway/book/237831

Heider, F. (1958). *The psychology of interpersonal relations.* Wiley. doi:10.1037/10628-000

Hennart, J. F., Majocchi, A., & Forlani, E. (2019). The myth of the stay-at-home family firm: How family-managed SMEs can overcome their internationalization limitations. *Journal of International Business Studies, 50*(5), 758–782. doi:10.105741267-017-0091-y

Herciu, M. (2017). Financing small businesses: From venture capital to crowdfunding. *Studies in Business and Economics, 12*(2), 63–69. doi:10.1515be-2017-0022

Hermansah. (2020). *Simak strategi bertahan bagi UKM hadapi krisis akibat Covid-19 Pastikan bisnis Anda tetap berjalan dan mampu bertahan pada saat kondisi pandemi saat ini.* Available online: https:// www.alinea.id/bisnis/strategi-bertahan-bagi-ukm-hadapi-krisis-akibat-covid-19-b1ZLs9tpp

Hignett, T. P. (1985). Compound Fertilizers. In T. P. Hignett (Ed.), *Fertilizer Manual. Developments in Plant and Soil Sciences, (15).* Springer. doi:10.1007/978-94-017-1538-6_19

Hill, H. (1999). Indonesia in crisis. Unpublished draft postscript for the second edition of The Indonesian Economy since 1966. Cambridge University Press.

Hill, H. (2001a). Small and medium enterprises. *Indonesia Asian Survey, 41*(2), 248–270.

Hill, H. (2001b). Small and medium enterprises in Indonesia: Old policy challenges for a new administration. *Asian Survey, 41*(2), 248–270.

Hisrich, R. D., & Peters, M. P. (1998). Entrepreneurship (4th ed.). Irwin/McGraw-Hill.

Hitt, M. A., Ireland, R. S., Camp, S. M., & Sexton, D. L. (2001). Strategic entrepreneurship: Entrepreneurial strategies for wealth creation. *Strategic Management Journal, 22*(6-7), 479–491. doi:10.1002mj.196

Holland, D. V., & Shepherd, D. A. (2013). Deciding to persist: Adversity, values and entrepreneurs' decision policies. *Entrepreneurship Theory and Practice, 37*(2), 331–358. doi:10.1111/j.1540-6520.2011.00468.x

Holmes, T. J., & Schmitz, J. A. Jr. (1990). A theory of entrepreneurship and its application to the study of business transfers. *Journal of Political Economy, 98*(2), 265–294. doi:10.1086/261678

Hoque, A.S.M.M., & Awang, Z.B. (2019). Does gender difference play moderating role in the relationship between entrepreneurial marketing and Bangladeshi SME performance? *Accounting*, 35–52.

Howell, S., Lerner, J., Nanda, R., & Townsend, R. (2020). *Financial Distancing: How Venture Capital Follows the Economy Down and Curtails Innovation.* Harvard Business School Working Paper, 20–115. Retrieved from https://www.nber.org/system/files/working_papers/w27150/w27150.pdf

Https://covid19.who.int/. (2021). *WHO Coronavirus (COVID-19) Dashboard.* Author.

Hu, M. K., & Kee, D. M. H. (2021a). SMEs and business sustainability: Achieving sustainable business growth in the new normal. Handbook of Research on Sustaining SMEs and Entrepreneurial Innovation in the Post-COVID-19 Era, 331–351. doi:10.4018/978-1-7998-6632-9.ch016

Hu, M. K., & Kee, D. M. H. (2021b). Strategic measures and tactical interventions for COVID-19 impact relief on SMEs. Handbook of Research on Strategies and Interventions to Mitigate COVID-19 Impact on SMEs, 522–541. doi:10.4018/978-1-7998-7436-2.ch026

Hu, E. (2017). *SME Challenges and Solutions* (1st ed.). MPH Group Publishing. https://www.mphonline.com/en/productdetails/books/business-and-management/9789674152208

Huggins, R., & Thompson, P. (2015). Local entrepreneurial resilience and culture: The role of social values in fostering economic recovery. *Cambridge Journal of Regions, Economy and Society, 8*(2), 326. doi:10.1093/cjres/rsu035

Humphrey, J. (2009). *Are exporters in Africa facing reduced availability of trade finance* (Unpublished research Paper). Institute of Development Studies.

Huse, M. (2000). Boards of directors in smes: A review and research agenda. *Entrepreneurship and Regional Development, 12*(4), 271–290. doi:10.1080/08985620050177912

Hussain, S., Khattak, J., Rizwan, A., & Latif, M. A. (2013). ANSOFF matrix, environment, and growth-an interactive triangle. *Management and Administrative Sciences Review, 2*(2), 196–206.

Huyghebaert, N., & Van de Gucht, L. M. (2004). Incumbent strategic behavior in financial markets and the exit of entrepreneurial start-ups. *Strategic Management Journal, 25*(7), 669–688. doi:10.1002mj.415

Iatridis, G., & Dimitras, A. I. (2013). Financial crisis and accounting quality: Evidence from five European countries. *Advances in Accounting, Incorporating. Advances in International Accounting, 29*(1), 154–160. doi:10.1016/j.adiac.2013.03.001

Idris, B., & Saridakis, G. (2018). Local formal interpersonal networks and SMEs internationalisation: Empirical evidence from the UK. *International Business Review, 27*(3), 610–624. doi:10.1016/j.ibusrev.2017.10.010

Iles, P. (2013). Human Resource Management Review Commentary on "The meaning of 'talent' in the world of work". *Human Resource Management Review, 23*(4), 301–304. doi:10.1016/j.hrmr.2013.08.002

ILO. (2020a). *COVID-19 and the world of work: Impact and policy responses. ILO Monitor* (1st ed.). International Labour Organization.

ILO. (2020b). *COVID-19 and the world of work: Updated estimates and analysis. ILO Monitor* (2nd ed.). International Labour Organization.

ILO. (2020c). *COVID-19: Protecting workers in the workplace.* Geneva: International Labour Organization. Available online: https://www.ilo.org/global/about-the-ilo/newsroom/news/WCMS_738742/lang–en/index.htm

ILO. (2020d). MSME Day 2020: the COVID -19 pandemic and its impact on small business. Geneva: International Labor Office. Available online: file:///D:/FILE%20FEB%202018/FILE%2001%20FEB%202018/DIKTI/BKD/

IMF. (2020). *A Crisis Like No Other.* International Monetary Fund Annual Report. Retrieved from: https://www.imf.org/external/pubs/ft/ar/2020/eng/spotlight/covid-19/

IMF. (2020). *World economic outlook update, June 2020: A crisis like no other, an uncertain recovery.* Retrieved May 16, 2021, from https://www.imf.org/en/Publications/WEO/Issues/2020/06/24/WEOUpdateJune2020?utm_medium=emailandutm_source=govdelivery

Ingirige, M. J. B., Proverbs, D., & Joness, K. G. (2008). *Investigating SME Resilience and Their Adaptive Capacities to Extreme Weather Events: A Literature Review and Synthesis.* University of Salford. Retrieved from http://usir.salford.ac.uk/18262/1/SMEs.pdf

Ingram, T. (2016). Relationships between Talent Management and Organizational Performance : The Role of Climate for Creativity. *Entrepreneurial Business and Economics Review*, *4*(3), 195–205. doi:10.15678/EBER.2016.040315

Insee. (2019). *Small and medium enterprises / SME.* https://www.insee.fr/en/metadonnees/definition/c1962

Ionescu-Somers, A., & Tarnawa, A. (2020). *Diagnosing COVID-19 Impacts on Entrepreneurship Exploring policy remedies for recovery. Global Monitor.* Retrieved from https://www.gemconsortium.org/reports/covid-impact-report

Irawan, A. (2020). Challenges and opportunities for small and medium enterprises in Eastern Indonesia in facing the COVID-19 pandemic and the new normal Era. *TIJAB*, *4*(2), 79. doi:10.20473/tijab.V4.I2.2020.79-89

Irvine, R. B. (1987). What's a crisis, anyway? *Midyear*, (Special), 30–39.

Isenberg, D. J. (2011). The Entrepreneurship Ecosystem Strategy as a New Paradigm for Economic Policy: Principles for Cultivating Entrepreneurships. *The Babsos Entrepreneurship Ecosystem Project*, *1*(781), 1–13. Retrieved from http://www.wheda.com/uploadedFiles/Website/About_Wheda/Babson Entrepreneurship Ecosystem Project.pdf

Islam, M. Z. (2020, April 28). *Online grocers fail to seize the day during biggest opening yet.* The Daily Star.

Islam, K., & Miajee, M. R. K. (2018). Small and Medium Enterprises (SMEs) financing in Bangladesh: A review of literature. *International Journal of Small and Medium Enterprises*, *1*(1), 11–15. doi:10.46281/ijsmes.v1i1.62

ITC. (2020). *COVID-19: The great lockdown and its impact on small business.* International Trade Centre.

ITC. (2020). *SME competitiveness outlook 2020: COVID-19: the great lockdown and its impact on small business.* ITC. Retrieved May 18, 2021, from http://www.intracen.org

Iwu, C., & Benedict, H. (2013). Economic recession and investment on human resource information systems (HRIS): Perspectives on some South African firms. *Journal of Management Development*, *32*(4), 404–418. doi:10.1108/02621711311326383

Jaklič, A., & Burger, A. (2020). Complex Internationalisation Strategies During Crises: The Case of Slovenian Exporters During the Great Recession and COVID-19 Pandemic 1. *Teorija in Praksa*, *57*(4), 1018–1041.

Jellinek, L., & Rustanto, B. (1999). Survival strategies of the Javanese during the economic crisis. Consultancy Report to the World Bank.

Jeong, S. W. (2016). Types of foreign networks and internationalization performance of Korean SMEs. *Multinational Business Review*, *24*(1), 47–61. doi:10.1108/MBR-08-2015-0039

Jha, S. K., & Kumar, A. (2020). Revitalizing MSME Sector in India: Challenges and the Road Ahead. *Journal of Politics & Governance*, *8*(5), 4–10. doi:10.47914/jpg.2020.v08i10.001

Johanson, J., & Vahlne, J.-E. (1977). The internationalization process of the firm - a model of knowledge development and increasing foreign market commitments. *Journal of International Business Studies*, *8*(1), 23–32. doi:10.1057/palgrave.jibs.8490676

Jones, R., & Rowley, J. (2009). Presentation of a generic "EMICO" framework for research exploration of entrepreneurial marketing in SMEs. *Journal of Research in Marketing and Entrepreneurship*, *11*(1), 5–21. doi:10.1108/14715200911014112

Jordan, D., Tumpey, T., & Jester, B. (2019). The deadliest flu: The complete story of the discovery and reconstruction of the 1918 pandemic virus. *Centers for Disease Control and Prevention (CDC), 2019*, 1–2. https://www.cdc.gov/flu/pandemic-resources/reconstruction-1918-virus.html#references

Jorge, M., Couto, M., Veloso, T., & Franco, M. (2017). When family businesses go international: Management sets the path. *The Journal of Business Strategy*, *38*(1), 31–38. doi:10.1108/JBS-01-2016-0006

Jovanovikj, B., & Georgievska, L. (2015). Transmission Channels of the Global Economic Crisis: Micro Evidence for Macedonia. *Journal of Contemporary Economic and Business Issues*, *2*(1), 5–20.

Juergensen, J., Guimón, J., & Narula, R. (2020). European SMEs amidst the COVID-19 crisis: Assessing impact and policy responses. *Economia e Politica Industriale*, *47*(3), 499–510. doi:10.100740812-020-00169-4

Kabir, S., Bloch, H., & Salim, R. A. (2018). Global financial crisis and southeast Asian trade performance: Empirical Evidence. *Review of Urban and Regional Development Studies*, *30*(2), 114–144. doi:10.1111/rurd.12080

Kader, A. W., & Pattanayak, M. (2021). *Business Pulse Survey: Impact of COVID-19 on MSMEs in Bangladesh (English)*. https://documents.worldbank.org/curated/en/172841613718788462/Business-Pulse-Survey-Impact-of-COVID-19-on-MSMEs-in-Bangladesh

Kana, G. (2021a). A necessary but painful move. *The Star Malaysia*. https://www.thestar.com.my/business/business-news/2021/05/31/a-necessary-but-painful-move

Kana, G. (2021b). Employment dilemma. *The Star Malaysia*. https://www.thestar.com.my/business/business-news/2021/05/21/labour-productivity-value-added-per-employment

Kansikas, J., Huovinen, J., & Hyrsky, K. (2014). Family firm prerequisites for international business operations: A production and marketing capabilities Approach. *World Review of Entrepreneurship, Management and Sustainable Development*, *10*(4), 435–448. doi:10.1504/WREMSD.2014.064949

Karadag, H. (2015). Financial management challenges in small and medium-sized enterprises: A strategic management approach. *EMAJ: Emerging Markets Journal*, *5*(1), 26–40. doi:10.5195/EMAJ.2015.67

Kashmiri, S., & Mahajan, V. (2014). Beating the recession blues: Exploring the link between family ownership, strategic marketing behavior and firm performance during recessions. *International Journal of Research in Marketing*, *31*(1), 78–93. doi:10.1016/j.ijresmar.2013.08.003

Kathleen, R. (1991). A Historical Comparison of Resource-Based Theory and Five Schools of Thought Within Industrial Organization Economics: Do We Have a New Theory of the Firm. *Journal of Management*, *17*(1), 121–154. doi:10.1177/014920639101700109

KB. (2020). *Daftar Usaha yang Bisa Jadi Pilihan di Tengah Pandemi Virus Corona*. KumparanBISNIS. Available online: https://kumparan.com/kumparanbisnis/daftar-usaha-yang-bisa-jadi-pilihan-di-tengah-pandemi-virus-corona-1tDiIgDLASf/full.

Kernisky, D. A. (1997). Proactive crisis management and ethical discourse: Dow chemical's issues management bulletins 1979-1990. *Journal of Business Ethics*, *16*(8), 843–853. doi:10.1023/A:1017901501108

Khalil, T. (2020, August 11). The impact of COVID-19 on small businesses. *The Daily Star*. https://www.thedailystar.net/lifestyle/news/the-impact-covid-19-small-businesses-1942713

Khor, N., & Sebastian, I. (2009). *Exports and the global crisis: Still alive, though not quite kicking yet*. ADB Economics Working Paper Series No. 190. Manila: Asian Development Bank.

Kilic, K., Ulusoy, G., Gunday, G., & Alpkan, L. (2015). Innovativeness, operations priorities and corporate performance: An analysis based on a taxonomy of innovativeness. *Journal of Engineering and Technology Management*, *35*, 115–133. doi:10.1016/j.jengtecman.2014.09.001

Kim, Han, & Oh. (2014). Historical review of market orientation: Generation, refinement, differentiation, and debates of the concept. *The Review of Business History*, *29*(1), 5–25. doi:10.22629/kabh.2014.29.1.001

Kim, J., Kim, J., Lee, S. K., & Tang, L. (2020). Effects of epidemic disease outbreaks on financial performance of restaurants: Event study method approach. *Journal of Hospitality and Tourism Management*, *43*, 32–41.

Kim, K. (2017). Factors affecting the internationalization of small and medium-sized enterprises in South Korea: Entrepreneurial Orientation, Human Capital and Technological Capabilities. *International Journal of Economics and Financial Issues*, *7*(5), 371–379.

Kitching, J., Smallbone, D., & Xheneti, M. (2009) *Have small businesses beaten the recession?* In 32nd Institute for Small Business and Entrepreneurship (ISBE) Conference: Celebrating 3 decades of excellence in education, research and practice: at the cutting edge of international entrepreneurship, Liverpool, UK.

Kleinhans, R., Resyschke, D., Van Ham, M., Mason, C., & Syrett, S. (2017). Unravelling the nexus between entrepreneurship, neighbourhoods and commuinciites – introduction. In M. V. Ham, D. Reuschke, R. Kleinhans, C. Mason, & S. Syrett (Eds.), *Entrepreneurial Neighbourhoods*. Edward Elgar Publishing. doi:10.4337/9781785367243.00008

Kolarov, K., & Georgieva, S. (2020). Management features in bulgarian smes as determinants of business internationalization. *Polish Journal of Management Studies*, *22*(1), 279–294. doi:10.17512/pjms.2020.22.1.18

Kompas. (2020a). *Industri Terimbas*. Jakarta: Kompas Newspaper.

Kompas. (2020b). *Industri Terpukul Covid-19*. Jakarta: Kompas Newspaper.

Kompas. (2020c). *Peluang Memanfaatkan Lonjakan Pengunjung Laman E-dagang*. Jakarta: Kompas Newspaper.

Kompas. (2020d). *Jumlah Korban PHK Terus Bertambah*. Jakarta: Kompas Newspaper.

Kompas. (2020e). *Stabilitas Sosial Dijaga*. Jakarta: Kompas Newspaper.

Kontinen, T., & Ojala, A. (2010a). Internationalization pathways of family SMEs: Psychic distance as a focal point. *Journal of Small Business and Enterprise Development*, *17*(3), 437–454. doi:10.1108/14626001011068725

Kontinen, T., & Ojala, A. (2010b). The internationalization of family businesses: A review of extant research. *Journal of Family Business Strategy*, *1*(2), 97–107. doi:10.1016/j.jfbs.2010.04.001

Kontinen, T., & Ojala, A. (2011a). International Opportunity Recognition among Small and Medium-Sized Family Firms. *Journal of Small Business Management*, *49*(3), 490–514. doi:10.1111/j.1540-627X.2011.00326.x

Kontinen, T., & Ojala, A. (2011b). Network ties in the international opportunity recognition of family SMEs. *International Business Review*, *20*(4), 440–453. doi:10.1016/j.ibusrev.2010.08.002

Kontinen, T., & Ojala, A. (2011c). Social capital in relation to the foreign market entry and post-entry operations of family SMEs. *Journal of International Entrepreneurship*, *9*(2), 133–151. doi:10.100710843-010-0072-8

Kontinen, T., & Ojala, A. (2012). Social capital in the international operations of family SMEs. *Journal of Small Business and Enterprise Development*, *19*(1), 39–55. doi:10.1108/14626001211196398

Korber, S., & McNaughton, R. B. (2018). *Resilience and entrepreneurship: a systematic literature review.* University of Auckland. Retrieved from https://www.researchgate.net/profile/Stefan-Korber/publication/321380097_Resilience_and_entrepreneurship_A_systematic_literature_review/links/5b63cd97aca272e3b6ac2651/Resilience-and-entrepreneurship-A-systematic-literature-review.pdf

Korber, S., & McNaughton, R. B. (2018). Resilience and entrepreneurship: A systematic literature review. *International Journal of Entrepreneurial Behaviour & Research*, *24*(7), 1129–1154. doi:10.1108/IJEBR-10-2016-0356

Kowalik, I., & Danik, L. (2019). Marketing activity of international new ventures – application of the EMICO framework. *Journal of Business and Industrial Marketing*, *34*(4), 779–791. doi:10.1108/JBIM-02-2018-0079

Kraus, S., Filser, M., Eggers, F., Hills, G. E., & Hultman, C. M. (2012). The entrepreneurial marketing domain: A citation and Co-citation analysis. *Journal of Research in Marketing and Entrepreneurship*, *14*(1), 6–26. doi:10.1108/14715201211246698

Kraus, S., Mensching, H., Calabrò, A., Cheng, C. F., & Filser, M. (2016). Family firm internationalization: A configurational approach. *Journal of Business Research*, *69*(11), 5473–5478. doi:10.1016/j.jbusres.2016.04.158

Krishnan, T. N., & Scullion, H. (2017). Human Resource Management Review Talent management and dynamic view of talent in small and medium enterprises. *Human Resource Management Review*, *27*(3), 431–441. doi:10.1016/j.hrmr.2016.10.003

Krueger, N. F. Jr, Reilly, M. D., & Carsrud, A. L. (2000). Competing models of entrepreneurial intentions. *Journal of Business Venturing*, *15*(5-6), 411–432. doi:10.1016/S0883-9026(98)00033-0

Kuckertz, A., Brändle, L., Gaudig, A., Hinderer, S., Morales Reyes, C. A., Prochotta, A., Steinbrink, K. M., & Berger, E. S. C. (2020). Startups in times of crisis – A rapid response to the COVID-19 pandemic. *Journal of Business Venturing Insights*, *13*(April), e00169. Advance online publication. doi:10.1016/j.jbvi.2020.e00169

Kuivalainen, O., Sundqvist, S., Saarenketo, S., McNaughton, R. B., D'Angelo, A., Buck, T., Majocchi, A., & Zucchella, A. (2013). Geographical pathways for SME internationalization: Insights from an Italian sample. *International Marketing Review*, *30*(2), 80–105. doi:10.1108/02651331311314538

Kukanja, M., Planinc, T., & Sikošek, M. (2020). Crisis management practices in tourism SMEs during the Covid-19 pandemic. *Organizacija*, *53*(4), 346–361. doi:10.2478/orga-2020-0023

Kumar, R. (2014). When talent management goes wrong. *Development and Learning in Organizations*, *28*(5), 24–26. doi:10.1108/DLO-06-2014-0046

Kunday, Ö., & Şengüler, E. P. (2015). A Study on Factors Affecting the Internationalization Process of Small and Medium Enterprises (SMEs). *Procedia: Social and Behavioral Sciences*, *195*, 972–981. doi:10.1016/j.sbspro.2015.06.363

Kuratko, D. F., Morris, M. H., & Covin, J. G. (2015). Corporate Entrepreneurship. Wiley Encyclopedia of Management, 1–5.

La Porta, R., Lopez-de-Silanes, F., & Shleifer, A. (1999). Corporate ownership around the world. *The Journal of Finance, 54*(2), 471–517. doi:10.1111/0022-1082.00115

Lahiri, S., Mukherjee, D., & Peng, M. W. (2020). Behind the internationalization of family SMEs: A strategy tripod synthesis. *Global Strategy Journal, 10*(4), 813–838. doi:10.1002/gsj.1376

Lamb, W., & Sherman, H. (2010). Developing high-growth businesses in rural areas: A study of four US States. *New England Journal of Entrepreneurship, 13*(2), 9–19. doi:10.1108/NEJE-13-02-2010-B001

Latham, S. (2009). Contrasting strategic response to economic recession in start-up versus established software firms. *Journal of Small Business Management, 47*(2), 180–201. doi:10.1111/j.1540-627X.2009.00267.x

Latham, S., & Braun, M. (2011). Economic recessions, strategy, and performance: A synthesis. *Journal of Strategy and Management, 4*(2), 95–115. doi:10.1108/17554251111128592

Leadbeater, B., Dodgen, D., & Solarz, A. (2005). *The resilience revolution: A paradigm shift for research and policy?* doi:10.1007/0-387-23824-7_4

Leedy, P. D., & Ormrod, J. E. (2016). *Practical research: Planning and design* (11th ed.). Pearson Education Inc.

Lee, P. P., & Tham, S. Y. (2007). Malaysia ten years after the Asian financial crisis. *Asian Survey, 47*(6), 915–929. doi:10.1525/as.2007.47.6.915

Leipold, B., & Greve, W. (2009). Resilience: A conceptual bridge between coping and development. *European Psychologist, 14*(1), 40–50. doi:10.1027/1016-9040.14.1.40

Liao, J. (2004). *Entrepreneurial failures: Key challenges and future directions. In Entrepreneurship: The way ahead.* Routledge.

Liew, K. K. (2010). Planters, Estate Health & amp ; Malaria in British Malaya (1900 – 1940). *Journal of the Malaysian Branch of the Royal Asiatic Society.*

Liew, K. K. (2007). Terribly severe though mercifully short: The episode of the 1918 influenza in British Malaya. *Modern Asian Studies, 41*(2), 221–252. doi:10.1017/S0026749X05002180

LightCastle Analytics Wing. (2020, April 25). *COVID-19: Impact on Bangladesh's SME Landscape.* https://covid-19-impact-on-bangladeshs-sme-landscape.html

Li, H., Sajjad, N., Wang, Q., Ali, A. M., Khaqan, Z., & Amina, S. (2019). *Influence of transformational leadership on employees' innovative work behavior in sustainable organizations: Test of mediation and moderation processes.* Sustainability. doi:10.3390u11061594

Lima, M. (2021). *Entrepreneurship and Innovation Education: Frameworks and Tools* (Vol. 32). ISTE Ltd. doi:10.1002/9781119804147

Lim, D. S. K., Morse, E. A., & Yu, N. (2020). The impact of the global crisis on the growth of SMEs: A resource system perspective. *International Small Business Journal: Researching Entrepreneurship, 38*(6), 492–503. doi:10.1177/0266242620950159

Lim, E. N. K., Lubatkin, M. H., & Wiseman, R. M. (2010). A family firm variant of the behavioral agency theory. *Strategic Entrepreneurship Journal, 4*(3), 197–211. doi:10.1002ej.91

Linnenluecke, M. K. (2017). Resilience in business and management research: A review of influential publications and a research agenda. *International Journal of Management Reviews, 19*(1), 4–30. doi:10.1111/ijmr.12076

Linnenluecke, M. K., Griffiths, A., & Winn, M. (2012). Extreme weather events and the critical importance of anticipatory adaptation and organizational resilience in responding to impacts. *Business Strategy and the Environment*, *21*(1), 17–32. doi:10.1002/bse.708

Lin, Z., Manser, M. E., & Picot, G. (1998), T*he Role of Self-Employment in Job Creation in Canada and the U.S. OECD-CERF-CILN International Conference on Self-Employment*, Burlington, Ontario, Canada.

Łobejko, S. (2020). Digital transformation and innovativeness of enterprises. *Optimum. Economic Studies*, *2*(2(100)), 36–46. doi:10.15290/oes.2020.02.100.03

Lubatkin, M. H., Simsek, Z., Ling, Y., & Veiga, J. F. (2006). Ambidexterity and performance in small-to medium-sized firms: The pivotal role of top management team behavioral integration. *Journal of Management*, *32*(5), 646–672. doi:10.1177/0149206306290712

Lum, B. W. (2017). Business Strategies for Small Business Survival. Walden Dissertations and Doctoral Studies. Walden University.

Luna-Arocas, R. (2012). Talent Management: A New Perspective in Human Resource Management. In Human Resource Management in the Digital Economy: Creating Synergy between Competency Models and Information (pp. 50-65). IGI Global. doi:10.4018/978-1-61350-207-5.ch003

Luo, J. (2014). Entrepreneurial marketing- How marketers can satisfy customers' needs when applying entrepreneurial marketing approaches. *International Journal of Advances in Management Science*, *3*(4), 109–112. doi:10.14355/ijams.2014.0304.02

Lutfi, M., Buntuang, P. C. D., & Kornelius, Y. (2020). The impact of social distancing policy on small and medium-sized enterprises (SMEs) in Indonesia. *Problems and Perspectives in Management*, *18*(3), 492–503. doi:10.21511/ppm.18(3).2020.40

Luthans, F., Vogelgesang, G. R., & Lester, P. B. (2006). Developing the psychological capital of resiliency. *Human Resource Development Review*, *5*(1), 25–44. doi:10.1177/1534484305285335

Lu, Y., Wu, J., Peng, J., & Lu, L. (2020). The perceived impact of the Covid-19 epidemic: Evidence from a sample of 4807 SMEs in Sichuan Province, China. *Environmental Hazards*, *19*(4), 323–340. doi:10.1080/17477891.2020.1763902

M&E Studies. (2021). *Types of Vulnerabilities in Disaster Management*. http://www.mnestudies.com/disaster-management/vulnerability-types

Maco, B., Bardos, P., Coulon, F., Erickson-Mulanax, E., Hansen, L. J., Harclerode, M., ... Wick, W. D. (2018). Resilient remediation: Addressing extreme weather and climate change, creating community value. *Remediation Journal*, *29*(1), 7–18.

Mair, J., & Marti, I. (2009). Entrepreneurship in and around institutional voids: A case study from Bangladesh. *Journal of Business Venturing*, *24*(5), 419–435. doi:10.1016/j.jbusvent.2008.04.006

Majocchi, A., D'Angelo, A., Forlani, E., & Buck, T. (2018). Bifurcation bias and exporting: Can foreign work experience be an answer? Insight from European family SMEs. *Journal of World Business*, *53*(2), 237–247. doi:10.1016/j.jwb.2017.11.005

Marrella, A., Mecella, M., Pernici, B., & Plebani, P. (2019). A design-time data-centric maturity model for assessing resilience in multi-party business processes. *Information Systems*, *86*, 62–78.

Marroquin, M. (2021, March 22). *COVID-19 continues to hurt NY's small businesses. New data show how many are hurting*. https://www.lohud.com/story/money/business/2021/03/22/covid-new-york-small-business-report-pandemic-impact-revenue/4769606001/

Martini, E., & Vespasiano, F. (2015). The Spaces of Resilience: Learning and Adaptation. *Italian Sociological Review*, *5*(1), 21–38.

Masten, A. S. (2001). Ordinary magic: Resilience processes in development. *The American Psychologist*, *56*(3), 227–238. doi:10.1037/0003-066X.56.3.227 PMID:11315249

Masten, A. S. (2009). Ordinary magic: Lessons from research on resilience in human development. *Education Canada*, *49*(3), 28–32.

Mateias, M., & Brettel, M. (2016). Effects of customer interaction orientation on customer satisfaction and firm performance: A longitudinal study. *Global Marketing Conference at Hong Kong*, 147-148.

Matsuo, M. (2006). Customer orientation, conflict, and innovativeness in Japanese sales departments. *Journal of Business Research*, *59*(2), 242–250.

May, P. J., & Koski, C. (2013). Addressing public risks: Extreme events and critical infrastructures. *The Review of Policy Research*, *30*(2), 139–159. doi:10.1111/ropr.12012

McClelland, D. C. (1961). *The achieving society*. The Free Press. doi:10.1037/14359-000

McDougall, P. P., & Oviatt, B. M. (1996). New venture internationalization, strategic change, and performance: A follow-up study. *Journal of Business Venturing*, *11*(1), 23–40. doi:10.1016/0883-9026(95)00081-X

McDougall, P., & Oviatt, B. M. (2000). International entrepreneurship: The intersection of two research paths. *Academy of Management Journal*, *43*(5), 902–906.

McIntyre, G. (2020). *What Is the Small Business Failure Rate?* Retrieved from https://www.fundera.com/blog/what-percentage-of-small-businesses-fail

Megersa, K. (2020). *Improving SMEs' Access to Finance Through Capital Markets and Innovative Financing Instruments: Some Evidence from Developing Countries. K4D Helpdesk Report 733*. Institute of Development Studies.

Meng, L., Qamruzzaman, M., & Adow, A. (2021). Technological adaption and open innovation in SMEs: A strategic assessment for women-owned SMEs sustainability in Bangladesh. *Sustainability*, *13*(5), 2942. doi:10.3390u13052942

Merino, F., Monreal-Pérez, J., & Sánchez-Marín, G. (2015). Family SMEs' Internationalization: Disentangling the Influence of Familiness on Spanish Firms' Export Activity. *Journal of Small Business Management*, *53*(4), 1164–1184. doi:10.1111/jsbm.12111

Miglo, A. (2020). Financing of entrepreneurial firms in Canada: Some patterns. *Administrative Sciences*, *10*(3), 50. doi:10.3390/admsci10030050

Miller, D. (1983). The Correlates of Entrepreneurship in Three Types of Firms. *Management Science*, *29*(7), 770–791. doi:10.1287/mnsc.29.7.770

Miller, D., & Le Breton-Miller, I. (2014). Deconstructing socioemotional wealth. *Entrepreneurship Theory and Practice*, *38*(4), 713–720. doi:10.1111/etap.12111

Milovanovic, G., Milovanovic, S., & Radisavljevic, G. (2017). Globalization: The key challenge of modern supply chains. *Ekonomika (Nis)*, *63*(1), 31–40. doi:10.5937/ekonomika1701031M

Minichilli, A., Corbetta, G., & MacMillan, I. C. (2010). Top management teams in family-controlled companies: "Familiness", "faultlines", and their impact on financial performance. *Journal of Management Studies*, *47*(2), 205–222. doi:10.1111/j.1467-6486.2009.00888.x

Ministry of Micro, Small and Medium Enterprises. (2020). *What's MSME.* https://msme.gov.in/know-about-msme

Mintzberg, H. (1987). The strategy concept I: Five P's for strategy. *California Management Review, 30*(1), 11–24.

Mishra, S. (2017). Integration of talent and mobility function: Strategy for HR to manage business. *Strategic HR Review, 16*(6), 274–278. doi:10.1108/SHR-07-2017-0043

Mitter, C., & Emprechtinger, S. (2016). The role of stewardship in the internationalisation of family firms. *International Journal of Entrepreneurial Venturing, 8*(4), 400. doi:10.1504/IJEV.2016.082220

Monllor, J., & Murphy, P. J. (2017). Natural disasters, entrepreneurship, and creation after destruction: A conceptual approach. *International Journal of Entrepreneurial Behaviour & Research, 23*(4), 618–637. doi:10.1108/IJEBR-02-2016-0050

Morgan, R. E., & Berthon, P. (2008). Market orientation, generative learning, innovation strategy and business performance inter-relationships in bioscience firms. *Journal of Management Studies, 45*(8), 1329–1353.

Morikawa, M. (2020). Productivity of working from home during the COVID-19 pandemic: Evidence from an employee survey. In *Covid Economics* (Issue 49, pp. 123–147). https://econpapers.repec.org/RePEc:eti:rpdpjp:20020

Morrish, S. C., Miles, M. P., & Deacon, J. H. (2010). Entrepreneurial marketing: Acknowledging the entrepreneur and customer-centric interrelationship. *Journal of Strategic Marketing, 18*(4), 303–316.

Mort, G. S., & Weerawardena, J. (2006). Networking capability and international entrepreneurship: How networks function in Australian born global firms. *International Marketing Review, 23*(5), 549–572. doi:10.1108/02651330610703445

Mueller, P. (2017). *Exploiting entrepreneurial opportunities: The impact of entrepreneurship on growth.* Retrieved May 20, 2021, from https://www.econstor.eu/obitstream/10419/27104/1/518488292.PDF

Mukerjee, K. (2013). Customer-oriented organizations: A framework for innovation. *The Journal of Business Strategy, 34*(3), 49–56.

Mukerjee, K., & Shaikh, A. (2019). Impact of customer orientation on word-of-mouth and cross-buying. *Marketing Intelligence & Planning, 37*(1), 97–110.

Mungal, A., & Garbharran, H. (2014). Cash management challenges of small businesses in a developing community. *Mediterranean Journal of Social Sciences, 5*(27 P1), 11. doi:10.5901/mjss.2014.v5n27p11

Musa, A. (1998). A study on access to credit for small and medium enterprises (SMEs) in Indonesia before and during the economic crisis (1997–1998). Study prepared for the Asia Foundation and the United States Agency for International Development.

Mustafa, R., & Mansor, S. A. (1999). *Malaysia's financial crisis and contraction of human resource: Policies and lessons for SMIs.* Paper presented at the APEC Human Resource Management Symposium on SMEs, Kaoshiung.

Mwangi, H. W., & Bwisa, H. (2013). The Effects of Entrepreneurial Marketing Practices on the Growth of Hair Salons. *International Journal of Academic Research in Business and Social Sciences, 3*(5), 467–480.

Natacha Golik, M., & Rita Blanco, M. (2014). Talent identification and development tools. *Management Research: Journal of the Iberoamerican Academy of Management, 12*(1), 23–39. doi:10.1108/MRJIAM-01-2013-0498

Nguanbanchong, A. (2009). *Feminized recession impact of global economic crisis on women in Southeast Asia.* Paper presented at the seminar on Gender and the Economic Crisis: Impact and Responses, Oxford, UK.

Nieto, M. J., & Fernandez, Z. (2012). Impact of Ownership on the international involvement of SMEs. *International Business, 37*(3), 340–351.

Nijs, S., Gallardo-gallardo, E., Dries, N., & Sels, L. (2014). A multidisciplinary review into the definition, operationalization, and measurement of talent. *Journal of World Business*, *49*(2), 180–191. doi:10.1016/j.jwb.2013.11.002

Nurzaman. (2020). *Dampak Wabah Covid-19 UMKM (Usaha Micro Kecil Menengah) Banyak Gulung Tikar.* Available online: https://kicaunews.com/2020/04/07/dampak-wabah-covid-19-umkm-usaha-micro-kecil-menengah-banyak-gulung-tikar/

Obrenovic, B., Du, J., Godinic, D., Tsoy, D., Khan, M., & Jakhongirov, I. (2020). Sustaining Enterprise Operations and Productivity during the COVID-19 Pandemic: "Enterprise Effectiveness and Sustainability Model. *Sustainability*, *12*(15), 5981. doi:10.3390u12155981

Odero, K. K. (2016). *Small and Medium Enterprises Support System in Zimbabwe.* Paper presented at IDS Seminar, University of Nairobi, Kenya.

OECD. (2009). *The Impact of the Global Crisis on SME and Entrepreneurship Financing and Policy Responses.* Centre for Entrepreneurship, SMEs and Local Development. https://www.oecd.org/cfe/smes/theimpactoftheglobalcrisisonsmeandentrepreneurshipfinancingandpolicyresponses.htm

OECD. (2016). *Financing SMEs and Entrepreneurs 2016: An OECD Scoreboard.* OECDnPublishing. . doi:10.1787/fin_sme_ent-2016-en

OECD. (2016). *Improving the framework conditions for small and medium-sized enterprises.* Better Policies Series. https://www.oecd.org/policy-briefs/turkey-improving-the-framework-conditions-for-SMEs.pdf

OECD. (2018), SME and Entrepreneurship Policy in Indonesia 2018. OECD Studies on SMEs and Entrepreneurship, OECD Publishing. doi:10.1787/9789264306264-en

OECD. (2019). *OECD SME and Entrepreneurship Outlook 2019 Policy Highlights.* OECD.

OECD. (2020). *Coronavirus (COVID-19): SME Policy Responses.* OECD Policy Responses to Coronavirus (COVID-19), July 15 Edition. https://www.oecd.org/coronavirus/policy-responses/coronavirus-covid-19-sme-policy-responses-04440101/

OECD. (2020). *COVID-19 in Africa: Regional Socio-Economic Implications and Policy Priorities.* OECD Publishing.

OECD. (2020). *Financing SMEs and Entrepreneurs 2020: An OECD Scoreboard.* OECD Publishing.

OECD. (2020). *Tackling the coronavirus (COVID-19) crisis together: OECD policy contributions for co-ordinated action.* OECD Website of Coronavirus Collection.

OECD. (2020a). *Coronavirus (COVID-19): SME Policy Responses.* Organisation for Economic Co-operation and Development.

OECD. (2020b). *Evaluating the initial impact of COVID-19 containment measures on economic activity.* OECD Policy Responses to Coronavirus (Covid-19). Available online: https://www.oecd.org/coronavirus/policy responses/evaluating-the-initial-impact-of-covid-19-containment- measures-on-economic-activity/

Olejnik, E., & Swoboda, B. (2012). SMEs' internationalisation patterns: Descriptives, dynamics and determinants. *International Marketing Review*, *29*(5), 466–495. doi:10.1108/02651331211260340

Olson, D. L., & Wu, D. (2020). *Enterprise Risk Management Models* (Vol. 3). Springer. doi:10.1007/978-3-662-60608-7

Önder, İ. (2012). *İktisat üzerine düşünceler.* Yordam Kitap.

Opinium Research. (2020). *Impact of coronavirus on UK SMEs.* Opinium Research.

Oppong, N. Y. (2017). Mastering Talent Management: The Uncertainties, Lack of Clarity and Misunderstandings. In M. Mupepi (Ed.), *Effective Talent Management Strategies for Organizational Success* (pp. 31–46). IGI Global. doi:10.4018/978-1-5225-1961-4.ch003

Organisation for Economic Co-operation and Development (OECD). (2020). *Coronavirus (COVID-19): SME policy responses*. Retrieved from https://www.oecd.org/coronavirus/policy-responses/coronavirus-covid19-sme-policy-responses-04440101/

Orr, J. A., King, R. J., Hawke, P., & Dalgleish, J. (2013). Can we text you? A qualitative exploration of young unemployed jobseekers' attitudes to receiving resilience-building SMS messages. *Advances in Mental Health*, *11*(3), 268–285. doi:10.5172/jamh.2013.11.3.268

Ortega-Anderezand, D., & Lai, E. (2017). The Main Factors Influencing Entrepreneurial Activities and Intentions within a Country—A Case Study of Spain. *International Journal of Innovation, Management and Technology*, *8*(1), 32–37. doi:10.18178/ijimt.2017.8.1.698

Ortiz, R. F., Ortiz, J. A., & Ramírez, A. M. (2012). How Does Management Perceive Exporting? An Empirical Study of SMEs. *The Engineering Economist*, *23*(2).

Osei-Bonsu, N. (2020). Entrepreneurial orientation and internationalization of SMEs –empirical evidence from developing markets. *Journal of Management Research*, *12*(2), 1–13.

Osuagwu, L. (2015). Market Orientation in Small Business Enterprises (SBES) in North-Eastern Nigeria: A Research Agenda. *Proceedings of 11th International Business and Social Science Research Conference.*

Our World in Data. (2021, April 12). *Coronavirus (COVID-19) Vaccinations*. https://ourworldindata.org/grapher/cumulative-covid-vaccinations?tab=chart&time=latest

Ouyang, M., Hong, L., Mao, Z. J., Yu, M. H., & Qi, F. (2009). A methodological approach to analyze vulnerability of interdependent infrastructures. *Simulation Modelling Practice and Theory*, *17*(5), 817–828.

Page, B. (2020). CBI / Ipsos MORI survey : COVID-19 provides pathway to future of carbon reduction, flexible working & local shopping. *Ipsos Mori*, 1–9. https://www.ipsos.com/ipsos-mori/en-uk/cbi-ipsos-mori-survey-covid-19

Palich, L. E., & Bagby, D. R. (1995). Using cognitive theory to explain entrepreneurial risk-taking: Challenging conventional wisdom. *Journal of Business Venturing*, *10*(6), 425–438. doi:10.1016/0883-9026(95)00082-J

Papathoma-Köhle, M., Thaler, T., & Fuchs, S. (2021). An institutional approach to vulnerability: Evidence from natural hazard management in Europe. *Environmental Research Letters*, *16*(4), 044056.

Park, B., & Ghauri, P. N. (2015). Determinants influencing CSR practices in small and medium-sized MNE subsidiaries: A stakeholder perspective. *Journal of World Business*, *50*(1), 192–204. doi:10.1016/j.jwb.2014.04.007

Pasadilla, G. O. (2010). *Financial Crisis, Trade Finance, and SMEs: Case of Central Asia*. ADBI Working Paper Series, No. 187. January. Tokyo: ADB Institute.

Paton, D., Bajek, R., Okada, N., & McIvor, D. (2010). Predicting community earthquake preparedness: A cross-cultural comparison of Japan and New Zealand. *Natural Hazards*, *54*(3), 765–781. doi:10.100711069-010-9500-2

Paul, S. K. (2013). Vulnerability concepts and its application in various fields: A review on geographical perspective. *Journal of Life and Earth Science*, *8*, 63–81.

Păunescu, C., & Mátyus, E. (2020). Resilience measures to dealing with the COVID-19 pandemic: Evidence from Romanian micro and small enterprises. *Management & Marketing. Challenges for the Knowledge Society, 15*(s1), 439–457. doi:10.2478/mmcks-2020-0026

Payne, S. (2002). Working capital optimisation can yield real gains. *Financial Executives, 18*(6), 40–46.

Pearce, J. A., & Robinson, R. B. (2019). *Formulation, implementation, and control of competitive strategy* (12th ed.). McGraw-Hill/Irwin.

Pearson, R., & Sweetman, C. (Eds.). (2011). *Gender and the Economic Crisis*. OXAM.

Peker, Ö., & Aytürk, N. (2000). *Etkili yönetim becerileri öğrenilebilir ve geliştirilebilir*. Yargı Yayınevi.

Peng, M. W., & Shekshnia, S. V. (2001). *How entrepreneurs create wealth in transition economies*. Academy of Management. Retrieved from: https://www.jstor.org/stable/4165713?origin=JSTOR-pdf&seq=1

Peng, M. (2012). *Global Strategy*. Thomsom South-Western.

Peng, M. W., Wang, D. Y. L., & Jiang, Y. (2008). An institution-based view of international business strategy: A focus on emerging economies. *Journal of International Business Studies, 39*(5), 920–936. doi:10.1057/palgrave.jibs.8400377

Petrů, N., Tomášková, A., & Krošláková, M. (2019). Diversification of export territories of family businesses as a tool of their further development. *Problems and Perspectives in Management, 17*(3), 306–322. doi:10.21511/ppm.17(3).2019.25

Pettit, R., & Singer, R. (1985). Small business finance: A research agenda. *Financial Management, 14*(3), 47. doi:10.2307/3665059

Pfeiffer, F., & Reize, F. (2000). Business Start-ups by the Unemployed - an Econometric Analysis Based on Firm Data. *Labour Economics, 7*(5), 629–663. doi:10.1016/S0927-5371(00)00016-6

Phillips-Wren, G., Pomerol, J. C., Neville, K., & Adam, F. (2020). Supporting Decision Making During a Pandemic: Influence of Stress, Analytics, Experts, and Decision Aids. In J. Leibowitz (Ed.), *The Business of Pandemic: The COVID-19 Story*. Auerbach Publishers, Incorporated. doi:10.1201/9781003094937-12

Porter, M. (1980). *Competitive Strategy*. Free Press.

Porter, M. E. (1979). How Competitive Advantage forces shape strategy. *Harvard Business Review*.

Portuguez Castro, M., Ross Scheede, C., & Gómez Zermeño, M. (2020). Entrepreneur profile and entrepreneurship skills: Expert's analysis in the Mexican entrepreneurial ecosystem. *International Conference on Technology and Entrepreneurship - Virtual (ICTE-V),* 1-6.

Portuguez-Castro, M., & Gómez-Zermeno, M. G. (2020). (Forthcoming). Being an entrepreneur post-COVID-19 – resilience in times of crisis: A systematic literature review. *Journal of Entrepreneurship in Emerging Economies*. Advance online publication. doi:10.1108/JEEE-07-2020-0246

PricewaterhouseCoopers. (2010). *Nigeria SME survey*. https://www.pwc.com/ng/en/events/nigeria-sme-survey.html

Priyambada, Suryahadi, & Sumarto. (2005). *What Happened to Child Labor in Indonesia during the Economic Crisis: The Trade-off between School and Work*. Jakarta: SMERU Research Institute.

Priyono, A., Moin, A., Aini, V. N., & Putri, O. (2020). Identifying digital transformation paths in the business model of SMEs during the COVID-19 pandemic. *Journal of Open Innovation, 6*(4), 104. doi:10.3390/joitmc6040104

Proag, V. (2014). The concept of vulnerability and resilience. *Procedia Economics and Finance, 18*, 369–376.

Psaltopoulos, D., Stathopoulou, S., & Skuras, D. (2005). The location of markets, perceived entrepreneurial risk, and start-up capital of micro rural Firms. *Small Business Economics*, *25*(2), 147–158. doi:10.100711187-003-6456-6

Pukall, T. J., & Calabrò, A. (2014). The Internationalization of Family Firms: A Critical Review and Integrative Model. *Family Business Review*, *27*(2), 103–125. doi:10.1177/0894486513491423

Rae, D., Prince, L., Bosworth, G., & Parkinson, P. (2012). Business inspiration: Small business leadership in recovery? *Industry and Higher Education*, *26*(6), 473–489. doi:10.5367/ihe.2012.0125

Rahman, R. (2020). 37,000 SMEs hit by COVID-19 crisis as government prepares aid. *The Jakarta Post*. Available online: https://www.thejakartapost.com/news/2020/04/16/37000-smes-hit-by-covid-19-crisis-as-governmentprepares-aid.html

Rahman, M., Islam, M., Esha, B., Sultana, N., & Chakravorty, S. (2018). Consumer buying behavior towards online shopping: An empirical study on Dhaka city, Bangladesh. *Cogent Business & Management*, *5*(1), 1514940. doi:10.1080/23311975.2018.1514940

Raihan, S. (2021). *Strategies to tackle pandemic induced poverty in Bangladesh*. The Daily Star.

Raimi, L. (2021). Innovative Government-Backed Policy Measures in Nigeria for Sustaining MSMEs Post Pandemic (290820-071327). In N. Baporikar (Ed.), *Handbook of Research on Strategies and Interventions to Mitigate COVID-19 Impact on SMEs*. IGI Global.

Rajani, A. V. (2019). *Chapter: 8 Fertilizer mixtures (mixed fertilizers)*. DOI., doi:10.13140/RG.2.2.23850.36801

Ramachandran, R. (2021). Leadership during COVID Crisis-Part 1. SSRN *Electronic Journal*. doi:10.2139srn.3791574

Randa, I. (2020). Corporate Social Responsibility Interventions for Namibia's Post-COVID-19 Sustainable Banking Sector. In N. Baporikar (Ed.), *Handbook of Research on Strategies and Interventions to Mitigate COVID-19 Impact on SMEs*. IGI Global.

Rank, O. N., & Strenge, M. (2018). Entrepreneurial orientation as a driver of brokerage in external networks: Exploring the effects of risk taking, proactivity, and innovativeness. *Strategic Entrepreneurship Journal*, *12*(4), 482–503.

Rank, O. N., Strenge, M., & Brennecke, J. (2013). Entrepreneurial orientation, Interfirm networks, and organisational performance. *Academy of Management Proceedings*, *1*, 11433–11433.

Rashad, N. M. (2018). The impact of entrepreneurial marketing dimensions on the organizational performance within Saudi SMEs. *Eurasian Journal of Business and Management*, *6*(3), 61–71.

Rasheed, H. S. (2009). Contrasting E-commerce business models: Performance implications for small enterprises. *Journal of Developmental Entrepreneurship*, *14*(1), 89–101. doi:10.1142/S1084946709001168

Rashid, S., & Ratten, V. (2021). Entrepreneurial ecosystems during COVID-19: The survival of small businesses using dynamic capabilities. *World Journal of Entrepreneurship, Management and Sustainable Development*, *17*(1).

Ratten, V. (2020). Coronavirus and international business: An entrepreneurial ecosystem perspective. *Thunderbird International Business Review*, *62*(5), 1–6. doi:10.1002/tie.22161

Ray, S., Mondal, A., & Ramachandran, K. (2018). How does family involvement affect a firm's internationalization? An investigation of Indian family firms. *Global Strategy Journal*, *8*(1), 73–105. doi:10.1002/gsj.1196

Régnier, P. (2005). The East Asian financial crisis in Thailand: Distress and resilience of local SMEs. In C. Harvie & B.-C. Lee (Eds.), *Sustaining growth and performance in East Asia*. Edward Elgar.

Reivich, K. J., Seligman, M. E. P., & McBride, S. (2011). Master resilience training in the U.S. army. *The American Psychologist, 66*(1), 25–34. doi:10.1037/a0021897 PMID:21219045

Reynolds, A., Fourie, H., & Erasmus, L. (2019). A Generic Balanced Scorecard for Small and Medium Manufacturing Enterprises in South Africa. *The Southern African Journal of Entrepreneurship and Small Business Management, 11*(1), 1–15. doi:10.4102ajesbm.v11i1.193

Ribera, J. (2020). Business and Management Lessons Learned from COVID-19. In J. Leibowitz (Ed.), *The Business of Pandemic: The COVID-19 Story*. Auerbach Publishers, Incorporated. doi:10.1201/9781003094937-1

Rocha, B. G., & Andreassi, T. (2020). Brazilian and American Entrepreneurial Experience: Cultural and Financial Aspects From Brazilian Entrepreneurs' Point of View. *Iberoamerican Journal of Entrepreneurship and Small Business, 9*(3), 323–343. Retrieved from http://10.0.55.131/regepe.v9i3.1403%0Ahttp://search.ebscohost.com/login.aspx?direct=true&db=buh&AN=144308353&site=ehost-live

Rodrigues, S. B., & Child, J. (2012). Building social capital for internationalization. *Revista de Administração Contemporânea, 16*(1), 23–38. doi:10.1590/S1415-65552012000100003

Rosa, A.C.M., Rosa, A. M., Neves, J.M.S. & Santos, R.O.B.D. (2021). Innovative Entrepreneur and Creativity: A Bibliometric Analysis. *Global Scientific Journals, 9*(3). Retrieved from file:///home/chronos/u-c99ce39cb0cd0fcc8b77fc8301015dd7a2e8c6d4/MyFiles/Downloads/Innovative_Entrepreneur_and_Creativity_A_Bibliometric_Analysis.pdf

Rosier, B. (1991). *İktisadi kriz kavramları*. İletişim Yayınları.

Rotolo, C. T., Church, A. H., Adler, S., Smither, J. W., Colquitt, A. L., Shull, A. C., Paul, K. B., & Foster, G. (2018). Putting an End to Bad Talent Management: A Call to Action for the Field of Industrial and Organizational Psychology. *Industrial and Organizational Psychology: Perspectives on Science and Practice, 11*(2), 176–219. doi:10.1017/iop.2018.6

Rutter, M. (2008). *Developing concepts in developmental psychopathology. Developmental psychopathology and wellness: Genetic and environmental influences*. American Psychiatric Publishing.

Saarenketo, S., Puumalainen, K., Kuivalainen, O., & Kyläheiko, K. (2004). Dynamic knowledge-related learning processes in internationalizing high-tech SMEs. *International Journal of Production Economics, 89*(3), 363–378. doi:10.1016/S0925-5273(03)00185-3

Sahoo, S., Hossain, M. N. A., & Hassan, K. S. (2020). *A boon for online commerce: How COVID-19 is transforming the industry in Bangladesh*. Next Billion. https://nextbillion.net/online-commerce-covid19-industry-bangladesh/

Salisu, I., Hashim, N., Mashi, M. S., & Aliyu, H. G. (2020). Perseverance of effort and consistency of interest for entrepreneurial career success: Does resilience matter? *Journal of Entrepreneurship in Emerging Economies, 12*(2), 279–304. doi:10.1108/JEEE-02-2019-0025

Sanar_Saúde. (2020). *Linha do tempo do Coronavírus no Brasil*. Author.

Sandee, H., Andadari, R. K., & Sulandjari, S. (2000). Small firm development during good times and bad: The Jepara furniture industry. In C. Manning & P. Dierman (Eds.), *Indonesia in transition: Social aspects of reformasi and crisis*. Indonesia Assessment Series. Research School of Pacific and Asian Studies. Australian National University Canberra and Institute of Southeast Asian Studies.

Santoso, Y. I. (2020). *Menghitung dampak Covid19 terhadap dunia usaha hingga UMKM*. Available online: https://nasional.kontan.co.id/news/menghitungdampak-covid-19-terhadap-dunia-usahahinggaumkm?page=all

Saracoğlu, R. (1995). İstikrar programı üzerine düşünceler, Türkiye için yeni bir orta vadeli istikrar programına doğru. TUSIAD Yayın No:6-180, İstanbul.

Sarkar, S., & Clegg, S. R. (2021). Resilience in a time of contagion: Lessons from small businesses during the COVID-19 pandemic. *Journal of Change Management*, 1–26.

Sarmiento, J. P., Hoberman, G., Jerath, M., & Ferreira Jordao, G. (2016). Disaster risk management and business education: The case of small and medium enterprises. *AD-Minister*, (28), 73–90.

Sato, Y. (2000). How did the crisis affect small and medium-sized enterprises? From a field study of the metal working industry in Java. *The Developing Economies*, *38*(4), 572–595.

Savrul, M., & Kılıç, C. (2011). E-commerce as an alternative strategy in recovery from the recession. *Procedia: Social and Behavioral Sciences*, *24*, 247–259.

Sawalha, I. H. (2020). A contemporary perspective on the disaster management cycle. *Foresight*, *22*(4), 469–482. Advance online publication. doi:10.1108/FS-11-2019-0097

Schaltegger, S., Lüdeke-Freund, F., & Hansen, E. G. (2016). Business models for sustainability. *Organization & Environment*, *29*(3), 264–289. Advance online publication. doi:10.1177/1086026616633272

Schindehutte, M., & Morris, M. (2010). Entrepreneurial marketing strategy: Lessons from the Red Queen. *International Journal of Entrepreneurship and Innovation Management*, *11*(1), 75–94.

Schmengler, K., & Kraus, S. (2010). Entrepreneurial marketing over the internet: An explorative qualitative empirical analysis. *International Journal of Entrepreneurial Venturing*, *2*(1), 56–71.

Schneider, R. O. (2002). Hazard mitigation and sustainable community development. *Disaster Prevention and Management*, *11*(2), 141–147. doi:10.1108/09653560210426821

Scholes, L., Mustafa, M., & Chen, S. (2016). Internationalization of Small Family Firms: The Influence of Family from a Socioemotional Wealth Perspective. *Thunderbird International Business Review*, *58*(2), 131–146. doi:10.1002/tie.21729

Schreibauer, E. C., Hippler, M., Burgess, S., Rieger, M. A., & Rind, E. (2020). Work-related psychosocial stress in small and medium-sized enterprises: An integrative review. *International Journal of Environmental Research and Public Health*, *17*(20), 7446. doi:10.3390/ijerph17207446 PMID:33066111

Sciascia, S., Mazzola, P., Astrachan, J. H., & Pieper, T. M. (2012). The role of family ownership in international entrepreneurship: Exploring nonlinear effects. *Small Business Economics*, *38*(1), 15–31. doi:10.100711187-010-9264-9

Sebrae. (2020). *O impacto da pandemia de coronavírus nos pequenos negócios*. Author.

Sebrae. (2021). *Resumo Setorial* (Vol. 2021). Retrieved from https://www.sebrae.com.br/sites/PortalSebrae/artigos/o-impacto-da-pandemia-de-coronavirus-nos-pequenos-negocios,192da538c1be1710VgnVCM1000004c00210aRCRD#

Segaro, E. (2010). Internationalization of family SMEs: The impact of ownership, governance, and top management team. *5th International Institute of Statistics and Management Engineering Symposium 2012: Data-Driven Management Science under Developing, IISMES 2012*, 29–32.

Segaro, E. L., Larimo, J., & Jones, M. V. (2014). Internationalisation of family small and medium sized enterprises: The role of stewardship orientation, family commitment culture and top management team. *International Business Review*, *23*(2), 381–395. doi:10.1016/j.ibusrev.2013.06.004

Setyawan, A. A. (2011). Global crisis and country's competitiveness: Lessons from Indonesia and Malaysia. *European Research Studies Journal*, *14*(3), 103–118. doi:10.35808/ersj/329

Setyowati, D. (2020). *Siasat Empat UMKM Bertahan di Tengah Pandemi Corona*. Available online: https:// katadata.co.id/berita/2020/04/20/siasat-empat-umkm-bertahan-di-tengah-pandemi-corona

Shafi, M., Liu, J., & Ren, W. (2020). Impact of COVID-19 pandemic on micro, small, and medium-sized Enterprises operating in Pakistan. *Research in Globalization*, *2*, 1-14. Available online: https://www.science direct.com/science/article/pii/S2590051X20300071?via%3Dihub

Shafi, M., Liu, J., & Ren, W. (2020). Impact of COVID-19 pandemic on micro, small, and medium-sized enterprises operating in Pakistan. *Research in Globalization*, *2*, 100018. doi:10.1016/j.resglo.2020.100018

Shah, S. N. (2016). *Historical GDP Accounts*. Economic History of Malaya. https://www.ehm.my/data/historical-gdp-accounts

Shakil, M. H., Munim, Z. H., Tasnia, M., & Sarowar, S. (2020). COVID-19 and the environment: A critical review and research agenda. *Science of the Total Environment*, 745. doi:https://doi.org/ 10.1016/ j.scitotenv.2020.141022

Shane, S., & Cable, D. (2002). *Network ties, reputation, and the financing of new ventures.* Retrieved from https://www.researchgate.net/profile/Daniel-Cable-2/publication/227447495_Network_Ties_Reputation_and_the_Financing_of_New_Ventures_Management_Science_Jg_48_3_S_364-381/links/00b495390a82e5ca78000000/Network-Ties-Reputation-and-the-Financing-of-New-Ventures-Management-Science-Jg-48-3-S-364-381.pdf

Shane, S., & Venkataraman, S. (2000). The promise of entrepreneurship as a field of research. *Academy of Management Review*, *25*(1), 217–226. https://doi.org/10.1007/978-3-540-48543-8_8

Shapero, A., & Sokol, L. (1982). The social dimensions of entrepreneurship. In C. A. Kent, D. L. Sexton, & K. H. Vesper (Eds.), *Encyclopedia of Entrepreneurship* (pp. 72–90). Prentice Hall.

Shapira, Z. (1995). *Risk taking: A managerial perspective*. Russell Sage Foundation.

Sharma, G. (2017). Pros and Cons of Different Sampling Techniques. *International Journal of Applied Research*, *3*(7), 749–752.

Sharma, P., Chrisman, J. J., & Chua, J. H. (1999). Defining the Family Business by Behavior. *Entrepreneurship Theory and Practice*, *23*(4), 19–39. doi:10.1177/104225879902300402

Sharma, V. M., & Erramilli, M. K. (2004). Resource-Based Explanation of Entry Mode Choice. *Journal of Marketing Theory and Practice*, *12*(1), 1–18. doi:10.1080/10696679.2004.11658509

Shin & Kim. (2015). Liquidity and credit risk before and after the global financial crisis: Evidence from the Korean corporate bond market. *Pacific-Basin Finance Journal*, *33*, 38-61.

Shleifer, A., & Vishny, R. W. (1997). A survey of corporate governance. *The Journal of Finance*, *52*(2), 737–783. doi:10.1111/j.1540-6261.1997.tb04820.x

Shook, C. L., Priem, R. L., & McGee, J. E. (2003). Venture creation and the enterprising individual: A review and synthesis. *Journal of Management*, *29*(3), 379–399. doi:10.1016/S0149-2063(03)00016-3

Shrivastava, P., & Mitroff, I. I. (1987). Strategic management of corporate crisis. *The Columbia Journal of World Business*, (Spring), 5–17.

Siddiquee, M. S. H., & Faruk, A. (2020). *COVID-19's Impact on Bangladesh Economy*. https://bigd.bracu.ac.bd/wp-content/uploads/2021/01/Working-Paper_COVID-19s-Impact-on-Bangladesh-Economy.pdf

Silverman, D. (2017). How was it for you? The interview society and the irresistible rise of the (poorly analyzed) interview. *Qualitative Research*, *17*(2), 144–158. doi:10.1177/1468794116668231

Sirmon, D. G., & Hitt, M. A. (2003). Managing Resources: Linking Unique Resources, Management, and Wealth Creation in Family Firms. *Entrepreneurship Theory and Practice*, *27*(4), 339–358. doi:10.1111/1540-8520.t01-1-00013

Small Business Majority. (2021). *Scientific Opinion Poll.* Small Business Majority. https://smallbusinessmajority.org/sites/default/files/research-reports/COVID-19-national-small-business-poll.pdf

Smallbone, D., North, D., & Kalantaridis, C. (1997). *Growth and Survival of Small Rural Manufacturing Firm.* Rural Research Report Number 32, Rural Development Commission, London and Salisbury.

Smallbone, D., Deakins, D., Battisti, M., & Kitching, J. (2012). Small business responses to a major economic downturn: Empirical perspectives from New Zealand and the United Kingdom. *International Small Business Journal*, *30*(7), 754–777.

SME Corporation Malaysia. (2020). *Guideline for SME definition.* https://smecorp.gov.my/images/garispanduan/2020/Guideline_SME_Definition_updated_Sept_2020.pdf

SMEDAN - NBS MSMEs Survey. (2013). *Small Medium Enterprises Development Agency and National Bureau of Statistics Collaborative Survey: Selected Findings.* https://www.smedan.gov.ng/images/PDF/2013-MSME-Survey-Summary-Report.pdf

SMERU. (2009). *Monitoring the socioeconomic impact of the 2008/2009 global financial crisis in Indonesia. Media Monitoring No.04/FS/2009. November.* SMERU Research Institute.

Snell, A. (2011). Developing talent intelligence to boost business performance. *Strategic HR Review*, *10*(2), 12–17. doi:10.1108/14754391111108301

Sonfield, M. C., & Lussier, R. N. (2000). Innovation, Risk and Entrepreneurial Strategy. *International Journal of Entrepreneurship and Innovation*, *1*(2), 92–93. doi:10.5367/000000000101298586

Souitaris, V., Zerbinatib, S., & Al-Lahamc, A. (2007). Do entrepreneurship programmes raise entrepreneurial intention of science and engineering students? The effect of learning, inspiration and resources. *Journal of Business Venturing*, *22*(4), 566–591. doi:10.1016/j.jbusvent.2006.05.002

Souza. (2016). *Empreendedorismo no Brasil. Global Entrepreneurship Monitor* (Vol. 21). doi:10.3916/c30-2008-01-013

Staniewski, M. W. (2016). The contribution of business experience and knowledge to successful entrepreneurship. *Journal of Business Research*, *69*(11), 5147–5152. https://doi.org/10.1016/j.jbusres.2016.04.095

Stock, R. M., & Zacharias, N. A. (2010). Patterns and performance outcomes of innovation orientation. *Journal of the Academy of Marketing Science*, *39*(6), 870–888.

Sulistyo, H., & Siyamtinah. (2016). Innovation capability of SMEs through entrepreneurship, marketing capability, relational capital and empowerment. *Asia Pacific Management Review*, *21*(4), 196–203. doi:10.1016/j.apmrv.2016.02.002

Sullivan, M. (2003). Retailers break new ground with open account trade programs. *AFP Exchange*, *23*(2), 30–33.

Sundari, L. S. (2020). *Dampak Pandemi Covid-19, Omzet UMKM di Kota Cimahi Turun 80 Persen.* Available online: https://www.galamedianews.com/?arsip=254042&judul=dampak-pandemi-covid-19-omzet-umkm-di-kota-cimahi-turun-80-persen

Suryahadi, A., Al Izzati, R., & Suryadarma, D. (2020). *The Impact of COVID-19 Outbreak on Poverty: An Estimation for Indonesia.* SMERU Working Paper. Jakarta: SMERU Research Institute.

Talke, K., Salomo, S., & Kock, A. (2011). Top Management Team Diversity and Strategic Innovation Orientation: The Relationship and Consequences for Innovativeness and Performance. *Journal of Product Innovation Management*, *28*(6), 819–832.

Tambunan, T. (1998). *Impact of East Asia currency crisis and economic development on Indonesia's SMEs and priorities for adjustment.* Paper prepared for the SME Resourcing Conference, ASEAN Chamber of Commerce And Industry, Jakarta.

Tambunan, T. (2020). *Dampak dari Covid-19 Terhadap UMKM*. Focus Group Discussion. Sigmaphi.

Tambunan, T. (2010a). The Indonesian experience with two big economic crises. *Modern Economy*, *1*, 156–167.

Tambunan, T. (2010b). *Global Economic Crisis and ASEAN Economy. Theory and Empirical Findings*. Lambert Academic Publishing.

Tambunan, T. (2011). The impact of the 2008-2009 global economic crisis on a developing country's economy: Studies from Indonesia. *Journal of Business and Economics*, *2*(3), 175–197.

Tambunan, T. (2019). The impact of the economic crisis on micro, small, and medium enterprises and their crisis mitigation measures in Southeast Asia with reference to Indonesia. *Asia & the Pacific Policy Studies*, *6*(1), 1–21.

Tambunan, T., & Busneti, I. (2016). The Indonesian experience with two big financial crisis and their impacts on micro, small and medium enterprises. *Asian Research Journal of Business Management*, *3*(4), 83–100.

Tanev, S. (2012). Global from the Start: The Characteristics of Born-Global Firms in the Technology Sector. *Technology Innovation Management Review*, *2*(3), 5–8. doi:10.22215/timreview/532

Taylor, S. J., Bogdan, R., & DeVault, M. L. (2016). *Introduction to qualitative research methods* (4th ed.). John Wiley & Sons Ltd.

TC Bilim Sanayi ve Teknoloji Bakanlığı. (2020). *KOBİ'ler ve girişimciler'in Türk ekonomisindeki yeri ve önemi*. https://anahtar.sanayi.gov.tr/tr/news/kobiler-ve-girisimcilerinturk-ekonomisindeki-yeri-ve-onemi/261

Tecson, G. (1999). Present status and prospects of supporting industries in the Philippines. In *Present status and prospects of supporting industries in ASEAN (I): Philippines—Indonesia*. Institute of Developing Economies. Japan External Trade Organization.

Tengeh, R. (2013). Advancing the case for the support and promotion of African immigrant- owned businesses in South Africa. *Mediterranean Journal of Social Sciences*, *4*(2), 347. doi:10.5901/mjss.2013.v4n2p347

The Daily Star. (2020, March 23). *Coronavirus outbreak: Govt orders closure of public, private offices from March 26 to April 4*. https://www.thedailystar.net/coronavirus-deadly-new-threat/news/govt-offices-closed-march-26-april-4-cabinet-secretary-1884730

The Daily Star. (2020, October 20). *Shopup raises $22.5 million Series A financing round*. https://www.thedailystar.net/online/news/shopup-raises-225-million-series-financing-round-1981209

The Organisation for Economic Co-operation and Development (OECD). (2020). Coronavirus (COVID-19): SME policy responses. *OECD Policy Responses to Coronavirus (COVID-19)*. Retrieved from https://www.oecd.org/coronavirus/policy-responses/coronavirus-covid-19-sme-policy-responses-04440101/

The Star. (2020a). Malaysia's online retail sales up 28. 9% in April. *The Star Malaysia*, 1–8. https://www.thestar.com.my/business/business-news/2020/06/11/malaysia039s-online-retail-sales-up-289--in-april

The Star. (2020b). Transport Minister: Container shortage issue to be discussed Monday. *The Star Malaysia*, 1–7. https://www.thestar.com.my/news/nation/2020/12/25/transport-minister-container-shortage-issue-to-be-discussed-monday-dec-28

The Star. (2021). A chance to tap into the global market. *The Star Malaysia*, 1–7. https://www.thestar.com.my/business/business-news/2021/04/14/a-chance-to-tap-into-the-global-market

The World Bank Group. (2019). *Financing Solutions For Micro, Small And Medium Enterprises In Bangladesh*. https://documents1.worldbank.org/curated/en/995331545025954781/Financing-Solutions-for-Micro-Small-and-Medium-Enterprises-in-Bangladesh.pdf

The World Bank Group. (2020). *Doing Business 2020. World Bank*. doi:https://doi.org/10.1596/978-1-4648-1440-2

The World Bank. (2020). *Beaten or broken? Informality and COVID-19*. The World Bank.

The World Bank. (2021). *Bangladesh Development Update*. doi:10.1596/26642

The World Bank. (2021). *ILOSTAT database: Unemployment, total (% of total labor force) (modeled ILO estimate) – Bangladesh*. https://data.worldbank.org/indicator/SL.UEM.TOTL.ZS?end=2020&locations=BD&start=1991&view=chart

Thomas, D. R. (2017). Feedback from research participants: Are member checks useful in qualitative research? *Qualitative Research in Psychology*, *14*(1), 23–41. doi:10.1080/14780887.2016.1219435

Thorgren, S., & Williams, T. A. (2020). Staying alive during an unfolding crisis: How SMEs ward off impending disaster. *Journal of Business Venturing Insights*, *14*(November), e00187. doi:10.1016/j.jbvi.2020.e00187

Thukral, E. (2021). COVID-19: Small and medium enterprises challenges and responses with creativity, innovation, and entrepreneurship. *Strategic Change*, *30*(2), 153–158. doi:10.1002/jsc.2399

Tranfield, D., & Denyer, D. (2009). Producing a systematic review. The Sage Handbook of Organizational Research Methods, 672–688.

Tranfield, D., Denyer, D., & Smart, P. (2003). Towards a Methodology for Developing Evidence-Informed Management Knowledge by Means of Systematic Review. *British Journal of Management*, *14*(3), 207–222. doi:10.1111/1467-8551.00375

Trisotto, F. (2021). *Mesmo com novo auxílio emergencial, renda total do brasileiro deve cair R$ 157 bilhões em 2021, diz estudo*. O Globo.

Tshwete, L. M. (2020). Strategies for the Growth and Survival of Small- and Medium-Sized Businesses. Walden Dissertations and Doctoral Studies Collection. Walden University.

Tsilika, T., Kakouris, A., Apostolopoulos, N., & Dermatis, Z. (2020). Entrepreneurial bricolage in the aftermath of a shock. Insights from Greek SMEs. *Journal of Small Business and Entrepreneurship*, *32*(6), 635–652. doi:10.1080/08276331.2020.1764733

Turner, S., & Endres, A. (2017). Strategies for Enhancing Small-Business Owners' Success Rates. *International Journal of Applied Management and Technology*, *16*(1), 34–49. doi:10.5590/IJAMT.2017.16.1.03

Uçkun, N. (2009). KOBİ'lerin finansal sorunlarına melek sermaye çözüm olabilir mi? *Muhasebe Finansman Dergisi*, *41*, 121–130.

UCL. (2021). *Small & Medium Size Enterprises (SMEs)*. https://www.ucl.ac.uk/procurement/suppliers/smes

UNCTAD. (2020a). *The Covid-19 shock to developing countries: Towards a "whatever it takes" programme for the two-thirds of the world's population being left behind*. Geneva: *United Nations Conference on Trade and Development*.

UNCTAD. (2020b). *Investment trends monitor: Impact of the coronavirus outbreak on global FDI*. Geneva: *United Nations Conference on Trade and Development*.

UNCTAD. (2021). *How COVID-19 triggered the digital and e-commerce turning point*. UNCTAD.

UNDP (2020). *A Preliminary Assessment of the Socio-economic Impact of Coronavirus (COVID -19) on Zimbabwe*. Policy Brief 001/2020.

UNDP. (2020a). *Assessment report on impact of COVID-19 pandemic on Chinese enterprises*. United Nations Development Programme.

UNDP. (2020b). *COVID-19: Looming crisis in developing countries threatens to devastate economies and ramp up inequality*. United Nations Development Programme.

UNICEF. (2009). *A Matter of Magnitude. The Impact of the Economic Crisis on Women and Children in South Asia.* Kathmandu: United Nations Children's Fund. Regional Office South Asia. Available online: https://www.unicef.org/infobycountry/files/amatterofmagnitude.pdf

US Small Business Administration. (2019). *Small business size standards*. https://www.sba.gov/document/support--table-size-standards

USP. (2013). *Vulnerability Mapping*. University of the South Pacific. https://www.usp.ac.fj/index.php?id=10045

Vaiman, V., Scullion, H., & Collings, D. (2012). Talent management decision-making. *Management Decision*, *50*(5), 925–941. doi:10.1108/00251741211227663

Van Stel, A., & Suddle, K. (2007). The Impact of New Firm Formation on Regional Development in the Netherlands. *Small Business Economics*, *30*(1), 31–47. doi:10.100711187-007-9054-1

Vaughn, P., & Turner, C. (2016). Decoding via coding: Analyzing qualitative text data through thematic coding and survey methodologies. *Journal of Library Administration*, *56*(1), 41–51. doi:10.1080/01930826.2015.1105035

Veciana, J. M., Aponte, M., & Urbano, D. (2005). University students' attitudes towards entrepreneurship: A two countries comparison. *The International Entrepreneurship and Management Journal*, *1*(2), 165–182. doi:10.100711365-005-1127-5

Verma, D. C., & Sarkar, R. (2018). Towards a better understanding of business models of social enterprise in an uncertain institutional environment. *Social Entrepreneurship and Sustainable Business Models*, 119-140.

Vig, S., & Agarwal, R. N. (2021). Repercussions of COVID-19 on small restaurant entrepreneurs: The Indian context. *Strategic Change*, *30*(2), 145–152. doi:10.1002/jsc.2398

Wallis, L. P. (2002). Managing your receivable in today's economy. *Strategic Finance*, *84*(2), 42–45.

Wang, Z., Huang, Y., Luo, J., & Feng, X. (2019). *Customer orientation and brand performance: A study of ROBAM.* China Branding.

Ward, T., & MacKenzie, J. (2020). *Research Report ESG in small and mid-sized quoted companies : Perceptions, Myths and Realities*. Quoted Companies Alliance.

Weaven, S., Quach, S., Thaichon, P., Frazer, L., Billot, K., & Grace, D. (2021a). Surviving an economic downturn: Dynamic capabilities of SMEs. *Journal of Business Research*, *128*(February), 109–123. https://doi.org/10.1016/j.jbusres.2021.02.009

Wedawatta, G., & Ingirige, B. (2012). Resilience and adaptation of small and medium-sized enterprises to flood risk. *Disaster Prevention and Management*, *21*(4), 474–488.

Weiner, B. (1961). *An attributional theory of motivation and emotion*. Springer-Verlag.

Wellner, L., & Pierce-Friedman, K. (2019). The Types of Case Studies in Research and Career-Based Endeavors. In Case Study Methodology in Higher Education (pp. 83-108). IGI Global. doi:10.4018/978-1-5225-9429-1.ch005

Wengel, ter J., & Rodriguez, E. (2006). SME export performance in Indonesia after the crisis. *Small Business Economics*, *26*, 25– 37.

Wennekers, A. R. M., & Thurik, A. R. (1999). Linking entrepreneurship and economic growth. *Small Business Economics, 13*(1), 27–55. doi:10.1023/A:1008063200484

Wenzel, M., Stanske, S., & Lieberman, M. (2020). *Strategic responses to crisis episodes.* Strategy Management Journal.

Westhead, P. (2008). International opportunity exploitation behaviour reported by "types" of firms relating to exporting experience. *Journal of Small Business and Enterprise Development, 15*(3), 431–456. doi:10.1108/14626000810892274

Westhead, P., Wright, M., & Ucbasaran, D. (2001). The internationalization of new and small firms: A resource-based view. *Journal of Business Venturing, 16*(4), 333–358. https://doi.org/10.1016/S0883-9026(99)00063-4

Westley, F. R., Tjornbo, O., Schultz, L., Olsson, P., Folke, C., Crona, B., & Bodin, O. (2013). A theory of transformative agency in linked social-ecological systems. *Ecology and Society, 18*(3), 27. doi:10.5751/ES-05072-180327

Whalen, P. S., & Akaka, M. A. (2015). A dynamic market conceptualization for entrepreneurial marketing: The co-creation of opportunities. *Journal of Strategic Marketing, 24*(1), 61–75.

Widarti, W., Desfitrina, D., & Zulfadhli, Z. (2020). Business process life cycle affects company financial performance: Micro, small, and medium business enterprises during the Covid-19 period. *International Journal of Economics and Financial Issues, 10*(5), 211–219. doi:10.32479/ijefi.10516

Wie, T. K. (2000). The impact of the economic crisis on Indonesia's manufacturing sector. *The Developing Economies, 38*(4), 420–453.

Wilmoth, D. (2021). The Effects of the COVID-19 Pandemic on Small Businesses. U.S. Small Business Administration. Office of Advocacy Brief Number 16.

Wiradi, G. (1998). *Rural Java in a time of crisis: With special reference to Curug village, Cirebon, West Java.* Paper presented at The Economic Crisis and Social Security in Indonesia, Berg-en-Dal, The Netherlands.

World Bank. (2009). *The Financial Crisis: Charting a Global Recovery.* Available online: https://www.worldbank.org/en/news/feature/2009/06/22/the-financial-crisis-charting-a-global-recovery

World Bank. (2019). *Small and Medium Enterprises (SMEs) Finance.* Retrieved May 20, 2021, from https://www.worldbank.org/en/topic/smefinance

World Bank. (2019). *Small and Medium Enterprises (SMEs) Finance: Improving SMEs' Access to Finance and Finding Innovative Solutions to Unlock Sources of Capital.* World Bank. https://www.worldbank.org/en/topic/smefinance

World Bank. (2020, June 8). *The Global Economic Outlook During the COVID-19 Pandemic: A Changed World.* Retrieved from: https://www.worldbank.org/en/news/feature/2020/06/08/the-global-economic-outlook-during-the-covid-19-pandemic-a-changed-world

World Health Organization. (2021). *Bangladesh COVID-19 Morbidity and Mortality Weekly Update (MMWU).* https://www.who.int/bangladesh/emergencies/coronavirus-disease-(covid-19)-update/

Wright, M., Westhead, P., & Ucbasaran, D. (2007). Internationalization of small and medium-sized enterprises (SMEs) and international entrepreneurship: A critique and policy implications. *Regional Studies, 41*(7), 1013–1030. doi:10.1080/00343400601120288

Wurjaningrum, F., & Hartami, B. (2020). The intervening effect of market orientation on entrepreneurial orientation, operations strategy, and business performance. *Proceedings of the 3rd Global Conference On Business, Management, and Entrepreneurship (GCBME 2018).*

Yadav, A., & Bansal, S. (2020). Viewing marketing through entrepreneurial mindset: A systematic review. *International Journal of Emerging Markets, 16*(2), 133–153.

Yang, X., Li, J., Stanley, L. J., Kellermanns, F. W., & Li, X. (2020). How family firm characteristics affect internationalization of Chinese family SMEs. *Asia Pacific Journal of Management, 37*(2), 417–448. doi:10.100710490-018-9579-7

Yin, R. K. (2017). *Case study research: Design and methods.* Sage Publications.

Zahra, S. A. (2003). International expansion of U.S. manufacturing family businesses: The effect of ownership and involvement. *Journal of Business Venturing, 18*(4), 495–512. doi:10.1016/S0883-9026(03)00057-0

Zahra, S. A. (2005). Entrepreneurial risk taking in family firms. *Family Business Review, 18*(1), 23–40. doi:10.1111/j.1741-6248.2005.00028.x

Zahra, S. A., Gedajlovic, E., Neubaum, D. O., & Shulman, J. M. (2009). A typology of social entrepreneurs: Motives, search processes and ethical challenges. *Journal of Business Venturing, 24*(5), 519–532. https://doi.org/10.1016/j.jbusvent.2008.04.007

Zapletalová, Š. (2017). International management of Czech family enterprises: Decisions on international entrepreneurial activities. *Central European Business Review, 6*(3), 51–61. doi:10.18267/j.cebr.186

Zautra, A. J., Hall, J. S., & Murray, K. E. (2010). *Resilience: A new definition of health for people and communities. Handbook of adult resilience.* Guilford.

Zerzri, M. (2017). *The threat of cyber terrorism and recommendations for countermeasures.* Center for Applied Policy Research. Retrieved from https://euagenda.eu/upload/publications/untitled-145478-ea.pdf

Zhang, J., & Duan, Y. (2010). Empirical study on the impact of market orientation and innovation orientation on new product performance of Chinese manufacturers. *Nankai Business Review International, 1*(2), 214–231.

Zhu, Y., Wittmann, X., & Peng, M. (2011). Institution-based barriers to innovation in SMEs in China. *Asia Pacific Journal of Management, 29*(4), 1131–1142. doi:10.100710490-011-9263-7

Zimbabwe Environmental Law Association (ZELA). (2020). State of Closed Large- and Small-Scale Mines and their Relationship with Artisanal Mining. Mining Sector Situational Report. Harare.

Zucchella, A., Palamara, G., & Denicolai, S. (2007). The drivers of the early internationalization of the firm. *Journal of World Business, 42*(3), 268–280. doi:10.1016/j.jwb.2007.04.008

About the Contributors

Simon Stephens is Senior Lecturer in Small Business Economics at the LYIT School of Business. His main teaching interests are in Applied Economics. His research explores issues and models in Entrepreneurship and Small Business Development. Simon has worked on numerous funded research projects (valued at over €1million). He is an award winning researcher and author. In 2011 he was awarded an Emerald Literati award for excellence. In 2018 Simon received a special recognition award from Lancaster University for publications from his post-doctorial research. Simon is Chair of the Entrepreneurship and Small Business track for the Irish Academy of Management annual conference.

* * *

Sabiha Abedin is a graduate student, currently pursuing her MBA degree from the Institute of Business Administration, Jahanginagar University. With immense interest in social inclusion and development and entrepreneurship, she aspires to facilitate learning through qualitative research.

Neeta Baporikar is currently Professor (Management) at Harold Pupkewitz Graduate School of Business (HP-GSB), Namibia University of Science and Technology, Namibia. Prior to this, she was Head-Scientific Research, with the Ministry of Higher Education CAS-Salalah, Sultanate of Oman, Professor (Strategic Management and Entrepreneurship) at IIIT Pune and BITS India. With more than a decade of experience in the industry, consultancy, and training, she made a lateral switch to research and academics in 1995. Prof Baporikar holds D.Sc. (Management Studies) USA, Ph.D. in Management, the University of Pune INDIA with MBA (Distinction) and Law (Hons.) degrees. Apart from this, she is an external reviewer, Oman Academic Accreditation Authority, Accredited Management Teacher, Qualified Trainer, FDP from EDII, Doctoral Guide, and Board Member of Academic and Advisory Committee in accredited B-Schools. She has to her credit many conferred doctorates, is a member of the international and editorial advisory board, reviewer for Emerald, IGI, Inderscience, etc, published numerous refereed papers, and authored books in the area of entrepreneurship, strategy, management, and higher education.

Andrea Brear is a postgraduate researcher that is currently studying for an International Business Masters degree at Ulster University. Andrea is a working professional in business management and aspires to be a university lecturer and research fellow in the near future. With aspirations to obtain a PhD, Andrea is currently studying part-time while working full-time and takes part in additional research outside of her degree for publishing. Andrea has a keen interest in business economics and entrepreneurship.

Rafael Luís Castro received his Bachelor's degree in Management from IPG, Guarda, and a Master's degree in Economics from the University of Aveiro, Portugal. He currently is a student in the Ph.D. of Marketing and Strategy at the University of Aveiro, University of Minho, and University of Beira Interior (Portugal). His research interests are internationalization, innovation, strategy management, competitiveness, and family businesses.

Joana Costa is Post-Doc -"lnnovation Persistence and National lnnovation Contexts.The Role of Open lnnovation" Faculty of Economics, University of Porto; PhD on Public Policy - Innovation Policy on the University of Aveiro. MPhil in Economics from the Faculty of Economics, University of Porto; a Post-Graduate in Industrial Management, from the ISEP – School of Engineering; a degree in Economics from the School of Economics and Management, University of Minho. She is an Assistant Professor in the University of Aveiro, at the Department of Economics, Management Industrial Engineering and Tourism. She lectures PhD, graduated and under graduated courses of Econometrics, Applied Econometrics, Economics of Innovation, Entrepreneurship and Innovation, Public Finance and Economic History. She is a member of the Governance, Competitiveness and Public Policy research unit (GOVCOPP), working on the research group on Competitiveness, Innovation and Sustainability. At present she is developing several works in Economics of Innovation, Entrepreneurship Dynamics, Regional Development, Social Responsibility and Public Policy.

Saptarshi Dhar is an Assistant Professor at the Institute of Business Administration (IBA-JU), Jahangirnagar University, Bangladesh. Prior to joining Jahangirnagar University, she served as a faculty member at United International University. Her research interests include entrepreneurship and small business development focusing on qualitative research. She is recognized for her work on entrepreneurs with disabilities in Bangladesh and for publishing research on entrepreneurship for persons with disabilities in national and international journals.

Marcelo Dionisio is a PhD student at Coppead/UFRJ (Rio de Janeiro, Brasil) and MBA from Institut Superieur de Gestion (Paris, France) with specializations at Pace University (New York, USA) and International Management University of Asian (Tokyo, Japan). 25 years of experience within multinational companies such as P&G and Japan Tobacco and for the last 10 years as entrepreneur in import & retail and as business consultant to foreign companies seeking oportunities in the Brazilian market.

Mufaro Dzingirai is a PhD candidate in Business Management at Midlands State University and a lecturer in the Department of Business Management, Midlands State University. He received his Master of Commerce in Strategic Management and Corporate Governance degree from Midlands State University in 2016. He was hired as a teacher by the Ministry of Education from 2014 to 2016. In 2013, he received the MSU Book Prize. His research interests include Higher Education, Strategy, Management, Finance, and Entrepreneurship.

Tahira Farzana obtained her MBA degree from Institute of Business Administration, Jahangirnagar University, Bangladesh. Currently, she is working as Assistant Professor at Institute of Business Administration, Jahangirnagar University, Bangladesh. She has experience of 10 years in market and social research. She has experience of working with the prominent research organizations of Bangladesh. Her major area of interest include Social Entrepreneurship, Entrepreneurship development for physically challenged people, Innovation and Marketing. She has affiliation with Physically Development Foundation (PDF) and Social Welfare Club of Institute of Business Administration, Jahangirnagar University, Bangladesh.

Meng Kui Hu, Chartered Banker, MBA, is a former senior banker with 26 years of banking experience in commercial and corporate banking. He is actively involved in various governmental agencies, providing his expertise in banking, financial technology, and best practices for the Small and Medium Enterprises (SMEs). He is presently a member of the United Nations ESCAP Sustainable Business Network (ESBN) and its task force member for the Digital Economy. He also serves as a member of the SME Expert Advisory Panel (SEAP) with SME Corp Malaysia; and the Examination Committee with the Asian Institute of Chartered Bankers (AICB). He earned his Master of Business Administration degree from the University of Strathclyde, UK, and has authored two books entitled "SME Challenges and Solutions" and "Transforming Family Businesses". He also writes regularly on financing and business for various publications. He is currently pursuing his Ph.D. candidacy with Universiti Sains Malaysia, Malaysia. He speaks English, Malay, Mandarin, and Cantonese.

Daisy Mui Hung Kee, PhD, MBA, is an associate professor at the School of Management, Universiti Sains Malaysia in Penang, Malaysia. Her areas of interest are in human resource management, organisational behaviour, work values, leadership, psychosocial safety climate, entrepreneurship, and small and medium enterprises. She earned her Master of Business Administration degree from the School of Management, Universiti Sains Malaysia, and her doctoral degree in business and management from the International Graduate School of Business of the University of South Australia. In 2006 she received the Merdeka Award from the Australia Malaysia Business Council of South Australia.

Theoneste Manishimwe is a research and teaching assistant at the American University of Nigeria. He is also the delegate of International MUN representing the Commonwealth of the Bahamas at the UNDP (United Nations Development Programme).

Engin Meric is a faculty at Trakya University. He has a bachelor's degree in Business Administration; MA with an emphasis on International Business Administration; and PhD with an emphasis on Business Administration. His general research interests focus on Financial Statements Analysis, Cost and Business Budgeting. Prior to his academic career, he worked as a management consultant (in the field of accounting and finance). He advised on budget and cost configurations in many SME-scale production and service enterprises. His research interests include but are not limited to cost and business budgeting in addition to Accounting Recording Systems, Cost and Feasibility, System Efficiency and Effectiveness, Investment Cost Optimization, etc. Finally, his publication studies on budget and cost applications are (especially related to SMEs) ongoing.

Rodgers Ndava holds a Master of Commerce in Strategic Management and Corporate Governance degree from Midlands State University (MSU) and a Bachelor of Commerce in Business Management (Honours) majoring in Finance from the same institution. He is a former Zimbabwe Revenue Authority (ZIMRA) employee hired on a seasonal basis. He is a keen scholar on Tax Compliance, Small Business Management, Entrepreneurship, Finance, and Strategic Management.

Lukman Raimi is an Assistant Professor of Entrepreneurship in the School of Business and Economics (SBE), Universiti Brunei Darussalam (UBD). Prior to joining the UBD, he was an Assistant Professor and the Chair of Entrepreneurship at the American University of Nigeria (AUN). Also, he was formerly the Coordinator of the Graduate Program in the School of Business & Entrepreneurship and the Director Centre for Entrepreneurship in AUN. He is an Entrepreneurship Educator trained at the Entrepreneurship Development Institute (EDI), Ahmedabad, India under the World Bank-Step B Project. He had specialized training in Enterprise Education for Employability (EEE) at the Pan-Atlantic University Nigeria under the British Council's sponsorship. He was an alumnus of the Cumberland Lodge Residential Mentoring (2014), Windsor, United Kingdom. He attended the 2019 Experiential Classroom XX organised for Entrepreneurship Educators at the University of Tampa, Tampa, Florida, United States. He had attended/delivered conferences/seminar papers in Turkey, Malaysia, Ghana, Togo, India, Belfast, Leicester, United States. His publications are listed in Scopus, Researchgate, Publons, and Google Scholar. He was honored with the Best Ph.D. Thesis Award for Faculty of Business and Law (2016), De Montfort University, Leicester UK. His paper titled "Corporate social responsibility, waqf system, and zakat system as a faith-based model for poverty reduction", was awarded Highly Commendable Academic Paper by World Journal of Entrepreneurship, Management and Sustainable Development, Emerald Group Publishing Limited, UK. His research interests include: Entrepreneurship: Social Entrepreneurship, Entrepreneurial/Digital Innovation, Medical Entrepreneurship, Development Economics, CSR & Sustainability, SDGs, and Family Business.

José G. Vargas-Hernández, M.B.A., Ph.D., Member of the National System of Researchers of Mexico and a research professor at University Center for Economic and Managerial Sciences, University of Guadalajara. Professor Vargas-Hernández has a Ph. D. in Public Administration and a Ph.D. in Organizational Economics. He has undertaken studies in Organisational Behaviour and has a Master of Business Administration, published four books and more than 200 papers in international journals and reviews (some translated to English, French, German, Portuguese, Farsi, Chinese, etc.) and more than 300 essays in national journals and reviews. He has obtained several international Awards and recognition.

Index

L

M

N

P

R

S

T

Z